200 YEARS OF

Identification and Price Guide

Dawn Herlocher

Antique Trader Books
Dubuque, Iowa

ISBN: 0-930625-29-3
Library of Congress Catalog Card Number: 95-83770

Manufactured in the United States of America

Published by
Antique Trader Books
Dubuque, Iowa

The author assumes full responsibility for facts and information contained in this book. Trademarks, trade names, and copyrights appearing herein are registered to their respective legal owners.

Front cover photographs: Top right, 15" Tete Bébé. Courtesy of Helen Brooke. Bottom left, Georgene's Raggedy Ann and Andy. Courtesy of Rusty Herlocher.

Back cover photograph: Yolando Bello's Picture Perfect Babies—Danielle, Emily, Sarah, Jason, Jennifer, Jessica, Amanda, Matthew, Michael, Heather, and Lisa.

This book is lovingly dedicated to my grandmothers:
Mamie and Janie, who let me believe as a little girl that
my dolls were full of mystery and enchantment.

Table of Contents

Table of Contents

Foreword

The gestation period of a child is nine months. The gestation period for antiques and collectibles books, even about dolls, is more often measured in years rather than months. This book is no exception.

Work first began on this book in the Spring of 1991. Beverly Marriner headed the research effort. The book was slated to be published as *Warman's Dolls*, a title in the Warman's Encyclopedia of Antiques and Collectibles series, by the Wallace-Homestead Book Company. You do not have to be a genius to see that the information that follows and its presentation is vastly different from a Warman's title format and that the book now resides with Antique Trader Books.

I firmly believe good books evolve. Most of the time the finished product is nearly identical to the concept initially proposed, with a few added refinements that tighten the presentation. Occasionally—and this is one of those instances—the evolution process is catastrophic. This book underwent four major reorganizations during its preparation. Frustration levels reached the barely tolerable, boiling, and breaking point more than once. Persistence counts, and perseverance pays. I never lost hope that this project would eventually evolve in such a way that it represents a major advance in the presentation of doll pricing information. My faith was justified.

If this project has a saint, it is Dawn Herlocher. My first contact with Dawn was as a participant in the Institute for the Study of Antiques and Collectibles' seminar programs that I taught. Dawn shared her love of dolls during seminar breaks. She invited me to visit her booth at the Atlantique City show. I did and was impressed.

Within a short period of time, Dawn became my informal doll advisor. When Beverly Marriner left the project, Dawn was the logical choice to succeed her. After reviewing existing work, a decision was made to start anew. I mention this because I want to make it clear that this book represents Dawn's work from its first page to its last.

While preparing this work, Dawn twice conducted two-day doll seminars for the Institute for the Study of Antiques and Collectibles. She maintained her show schedule, bought and sold dolls actively, and even found time to write a few articles for doll publications.

Dawn suffered and struggled through three of the four major reorganizations of this book. It is no easy task to ask someone to go back and start over again. Asking three times verges on mental cruelty. To Dawn's credit, she rolled up her sleeves each time and plowed ahead. I am proud of her and so is everyone at Rinker Enterprises, Inc. You will also be as you use and become familiar with this book.

What stands out the most in my mind about this book is detail—solid historical information, doll descriptions that do not sacrifice accuracy for brevity, and collecting tips and other information that provides guidance to the neophyte as well as the experienced doll collector. Compare the information in this book with information about the same group of dolls in other general doll price guides. You will see what I mean.

Another strength of this book is that it includes information on dolls from all time periods, including today. This is not an antique doll price guide; this is a price guide to dolls. The collecting of post-1945 dolls is the hottest portion of the mid-1990s dolls market. It more than deserves the attention Dawn has given it.

I mentioned earlier that Dawn is a saint. She is also a doll, one of my favorites. I look forward to working with her for years to come. She is a person whose frequent offers to help on other Rinker Enterprises, Inc., projects is welcome and worth accepting. I plan to call her shortly.

Harry L. Rinker, President
Rinker Enterprises, Inc.
Vera Cruz, PA

Acknowledgements

My life in the wonderful world of doll collecting has been remarkable. Over the years I have met the most fantastic people, many of whom helped me prepare this book.

My deepest appreciation goes to the hundreds of doll dealers, auction houses, and auctioneers across the country who supplied me with information. I especially want to thank: David Cobb, of Cobb's Doll Auction, for taking the time in the middle of preparing for one of his big doll auctions to find photographs of dolls desperately needed for this book; Sheri McMasters, of McMasters Worldwide Productions, for locating photographs during a time when she was not feeling well (what a sweetheart!); and Mrs. Charles Brooke, President of Dolls of Distinction, for always finding one more example of a doll I just had to use.

Thanks to the generous souls who loaned me dolls for study and/or photography. Their kindness was overwhelming. My special thanks to: Mr. and Mrs. Adam Condo, two of my dearest friends; Leah and Gene Patterson, who were never too busy to find a doll I needed from their beautiful collection; Carolyn Johnson; Joyce and Harry McKeague; and Helen Brooke, my best buddy. Helen crawled about in attics and basements to find the markings on dolls and read the end labels on doll boxes. In addition, she accompanied me on my dollin' trips where we experienced one exciting adventure after another. The stories we could tell about the places we've been and the things we did trying to locate a special doll!

Thanks to my good friends at Rinker Enterprises, Inc. These include Harry L. Rinker, who encouraged me to start this project, never lost faith, and celebrated its end. Also, Harry Junior, his talented son, who photographed many of the dolls that appear in this book; Ellen Schroy, who kept the project on course with the charts during her tenure at Rinker Enterprises; Dana Morykan, for the final restructuring and for her high level of professionalism; and Janice Bees, who was able to decipher my often questionable note, and who never once lost her cool.

My appreciation to Landmark Specialty Publications and Antique Trader Books for having faith in this project. Special thanks to my pal, Allan Miller, for his unending patience in managing this book through editing and production; Jaro Sebek for his talents in designing and laying-out the book; and Elizabeth Stephan for her accurate proof reading.

I put my wonderful family last in these acknowledgments, but it goes without saying that they are first in my heart. Jennifer, Maribeth, and Ty—my own living dolls—are three of the greatest kids in the world. I'm proud to be their mom!

Pat and Bill Tyson, my mother and father, taught me a love for antiques and instilled in me the belief that a person can do anything she sets her mind to. My sister Trina, her husband Billy, and their sons, Billy Grant and Jordan, offered encouragement and always, without fail, were able to make me laugh.

Finally, my husband and best friend, Rusty. I could not have written this book without his constant and unwavering support. Rusty's household skills broadened significantly while I did my research. He now knows how to run the vacuum, do the laundry, and wash the dishes. As for cooking—well, it may take another book or two before he masters that, but he is learning! Rusty encouraged me to keep writing when I was frustrated, and to walk away from it for awhile when I felt overwhelmed. He always knew the right words to say, which were usually simply "I love you."

—**Dawn**

Introduction

Welcome to our review of 200 years of dolls! I've been a doll collector all of my life. I have, for as long as I can remember, loved my genteel silent companions. They have provided a presence on which, as a child, I could project my fantasies, and as an adult develop an appreciation for the fine works of art that they are.

There is probably no rational explanation for the feelings collectors have for their dolls. Perhaps it's because they awaken memories and dreams, stirring our feelings of nostalgia, or the simple pleasure gained in admiring the beauty of these present-day reminders of a long vanished era.

The appeal of dolls seems to be immediate and universal, made obvious by the thousands of new enthusiasts who have excitedly embraced the world of doll collecting in recent years.

It is our hope that this book can help both the beginning and the more advanced collector enjoy doll collecting as an even more rewarding experience by avoiding bad investments. In addition to information for identifying and evaluating a wide variety of dolls, we will provide practical hints to help you recognize reproductions; identify the shortcomings of particular dolls; and heighten your awareness of superior and inferior examples of seemingly identical dolls, whether of early wood or contemporary vinyl.

No two dolls are ever exactly alike. A study of their various features indicate the factors that influence the value of a doll, including rarity, condition, quality of material and artistry; availability, originality, history of providence, and the ever-important visual appeal. All of these factors contribute to a doll's charisma.

To assist you further, we've included background information on social influences and technological improvements that have affected the doll-making industry over the years along with brief histories of the manufacturers and also pointed out the importance of condition. Please take the time to thoroughly inspect a doll. An antique bisque doll head should be checked not only on the outside, but also from the inside, for at times a repair or hairline crack will only be visible from the inside. Remember not to confuse maintenance with repairs. Reset eyes, restrung bodies, or patched kid seams are examples of necessary mainte-nance and are not repairs to a doll. Modern dolls should always be in perfect complete condition. Inspect the markings on a doll. You may find them on the back of the head, the torso, the bottom of a foot, or even on the derriere. Of course, many fine dolls will have no markings at all. Learn from every doll you see or handle, for there is almost as much fun in learning about a doll as there is in owning it. Visit doll shows and museums.

I encourage you to read and study as much as you can about dolls. The two volumes of Dorothy S., Elizabeth A., and Evelyn J. Coleman's *The Collector's Encyclopedia of Dolls* are an indispensible reference source. If you do not own a copy, visit a library that does.

Talk to other collectors. I have never met a doll collector that does not enjoy talking about their dolls. Consider joining a doll club. Clubs that are members of the United Federation of Doll Clubs (U.F.D.C.) "represent the highest standards of excellence for collectors...to create, stimulate and maintain interest in all matters pertaining to doll collecting." Write the U.F.D.C. at P.O. Box 14146, Parkville, MO 64152 to obtain the address of a club near you.

The format of this book is really quite simple. Dolls are arranged by manufacturer or type. Within each section, there are generalized sub-headings presented by material or style. These are further described by particular doll model, either by name, mold number, or a visual clue that identifies a particular doll.

There are several aspects of this book I'm sure you'll find to be not only extremely informative but also quite unique. We'll give you the detailed clues needed to identify a doll; in-depth descriptions of categories to establish classification; and we'll even share some "old doll secrets." However, we think you'll rank our new and distinctive approach to pricing—accomplished through easy-to-follow charts—among the most distinctive new features in this volume. I'm sure that you'll find them a quick and easy way to find and determine the value of a particular doll.

The astute collector and interim care-givers of dolls will use this book primarily for comparative purposes when assessing or assigning a value to their collection, wether building a new one, or researching an existing collection of a thousand dolls.

Collecting Tips

The following procedures are provided to inform and educate. Neither the author nor publisher accept liability or responsibility in respect to any type of loss or damage caused, or alleged to be caused, directly or indirectly, by the information or products contained in this book. We simply intend to share some old tricks and methods that have been used over the years.

Like real children, dolls require tender loving care. They need to be repaired, restored, handled, displayed, and stored properly. The following tips will help you develop skills to ensure that your dolls receive the loving treatment they deserve.

When dealing with dolls, the best approach is to be a minimalist. Do only the bare minimum to bring a doll to display level—retain, rather than destroy. Period features count heavily in a doll's value. Plan any repairs in a step-by-step process, evaluating as you go along.

Always approach the cleaning or maintenance of dolls with the greatest of care and respect. If you're not sure how to perform a certain procedure, ask an expert who knows. We have an obligation to future doll collectors to preserve the dolls in our care, and to maintain them in as good or better condition than they were when we received them.

CARE

Bisque, China, and Parian are all made of clay, feldspar, and flint. Differences between them are subtle. Parian is unglazed, untinted porcelain; china is a glazed porcelain; and bisque is unglazed porcelain with a flesh color.

The earliest bisque, china, and parian dolls were pressed into a mold by hand; later examples were poured.

Cleaning porcelain is fairly simple. The decorations have been fired-on, so it is highly unlikely that you would harm them by cleaning. Start with the least-abrasive technique—usually warm soapy water. If this is not sufficient, try a wet eraser. As a last resort, very, very gently clean with a low-abrasive cleaner such as Tilex or Soft Scrub. Use extreme caution as some cleansers contain bleaching agents that are devastating to antique clothing, wigs, or bodies. When displaying a bisque, china, or parian doll, avoid direct sunlight because ultra-violet rays are damaging.

If placed on a doll stand, assure that the doll is secure and that the stand is weighted sufficiently to support it.

Celluloid dolls are extremely perishable. They are easily broken and become quite brittle over time. Proper care and respect of a celluloid doll helps a perfect example remain in that condition. Heat is celluloid's worst enemy. Keep these dolls in a cool room with good ventilation, and never store celluloid in a sealed case—it can combust.

Cloth dolls have a special place in every doll collector's heart. Even a well-loved rag doll tugs at one's heartstrings. Vintage, and even the not-so-vintage cloth art dolls can be worth thousands of dollars and they deserve your best efforts to preserve them and prevent needless deterioration.

Clean fabric is a pre-requisite to preservation. Exposing a doll to any pollutants through storage or display weakens the fabric. Direct sunlight is an enemy of cloth dolls and should be avoided at all costs.

Inspect cloth dolls regularly for signs of insect activity. Insecticides designed especially for textiles are available under several brand names. When used according to the manufacturer's instructions, the results can be excellent.

If you decide to vacuum your doll, place a nylon screen over the fabric first to protect delicate fibers. Often, a thorough vacuuming is enough to restore a doll to display condition. Again, approach this procedure with appropriate caution. If a valuable or historically significant cloth doll is badly soiled, seek the advice of a professional who specializes in textile conservation.

Some stains on cloth dolls can be removed with an eraser—art gum, tapeten, and reinger-and-absorene appear to give the best results. Use this technique with careful, gentle application. Some stains, such as ink, may be removed with hair spray. It is essential to test the fabric first on an inconspicuous location to assure that no damage will occur. Apply the hair spray with a cloth, and wipe in a light rubbing motion with a clean white cloth.

Lenci once advertised that a Lenci doll could be cleaned by rubbing it with a piece of bread!

To preserve and display cloth dolls, it is best to keep them in protective cases and inspect them regularly. Moth crystals should be placed near your dolls. Many collectors recommend making a small cloth pouch, filling it with moth crystals, and placing it under the doll's hat or tying it around its waist beneath the clothing.

Composition and papier-mâché dolls, being made from pulp-based materials, require similar care. They are particularly susceptible to damage from temperature changes. Never store composition or papier-mâché dolls in a hot or cold attic, or in a damp basement.

Most collectors will accept some signs of aging on composition dolls—fine craze lines or crackled eyes, for example. Think long and hard before performing irreversible restorations which can compromise a doll's historical and practical value. Remember, a true restoration can later be undone. Several "temporary" cover-ups are acceptable.

There are several popular methods for cleaning composition. Test any method first on an inconspicuous area of the doll. Work quickly. Never leave any substance on the surface for any length of time. Pond's Cold Cream or Vaseline and a soft tissue are favorites of many collectors. Another option is paste window cleaner—not an ammonia type, but the old fashioned paste available at most hardware stores.

Wigs can be restyled after spraying with Johnson's & Johnson's No More Tangles, then carefully working out the tangles. Faded or worn-off facial features can be touched up with artist's colored pencils; when moistened they are quite easy to apply. Crackled eyes are best left alone.

Hard Plastic dolls are a favorite with collectors. Their sharp features and beautiful detailing are hard to resist.

Hard plastic is very resilient and can be cleaned with almost any soap detergent. Stubborn stains may be cleaned with cold cream or waterless hand cleaner. Avoid chlorine bleach and ammonia. Facial features may not be as durable, so approach painted surfaces with caution, checking paint stability before proceeding. Never use fingernail polish remover or lacquer thinner which may eat into the plastic.

Use Oxy-10 to remove stains that are not close to painted surfaces. Moisten a cotton ball and allow it to sit on the stain for several hours. You may need to repeat this process several times. After each cleaning, wash the doll with mild soap and rinse well.

When displaying or storing hard plastic dolls, avoid direct exposure to ultra-violet light. Though seemingly indestructible, hard plastic can slowly oxidize and change color. Direct heat may also cause warping.

Rubber dolls will deteriorate no matter what precautions are taken, but you may be able to delay the process. Any form of grease is harmful and accelerates deterioration. Always wear cotton gloves when handling a Magic Skin doll. I practice the old trick of rubbing corn starch on these dolls twice a year—once on my March birthday and once on my dad's September birthday. As with all dolls, maintain an even temperature and relative humidity.

Tin dolls often have chipped paint. When the metal becomes very cold, the paint lifts easily from the face. Store or display metal doll heads in an environment with a relatively constant temperature.

Vinyl dolls are probably the most lifelike in appearance and touch. Special care is needed to keep them looking good. Extreme room temperatures are harmful. Even quality vinyl dolls subjected to heaters or air conditioners can be damaged in just a few months. Direct sunlight can be deadly. Vinyl is also sensitive to fluorescent lighting; use indirect non-fluorescent lights. Finally, avoid tightly sealed show cases or glass domes, as condensation can form and damage vinyl dolls.

Wooden dolls have withstood the test of time quite well, as proven by the sheer number which have survived the years. Chipping paint is a major problem with wooden dolls. Humidity and mistreatment are the two main culprits. Keep wooden dolls in a dry atmosphere. Expanding and contracting associated with high humidity causes paint to chip. Knocks and bumps can also chip paint, so take care in moving or displaying wooden dolls.

Wax dolls tend to intimidate many collectors. They do require special care, but so do all types of dolls. Basic care and common sense will help preserve a wax doll in perfect condition. Of course, never place a wax doll in direct sunlight or near any heat source, such as a fireplace mantle.

A long-accepted practice for cleaning wax dolls is to start with the safest method and then gradually progress to more drastic measures until a suitable remedy is found. First, try a solution of cool water and Woolite. Saturate a cotton ball or Q-tip and wash the wax. If this is unsuccessful, try a dab

of cold cream on a Q-tip, followed by a rinse of the Woolite solution and then clean, cool water. As a last result, try denatured alcohol on a cotton ball, followed by a thorough rinsing. Never use turpentine to clean wax dolls. as it can soften the wax.

REPAIRS

Some long-time doll collectors recommend placing a drop of sewing machine oil in the crackled eyes of a composition doll. I neither recommend nor condemn this practice. Although it does seem to make the eyes appear more clear for a time, the downside is that the oil dries and leaves the eyes more deteriorated than they were before. It is always evident when eyes have been treated in this manner.

Green deposits found around Barbie pierced ears can be removed by covering the ears with a small piece of cotton soaked in Tarn-X silver cleaner. Wrap the head in saran wrap to keep the application moist. Check after two days—if the ears are still green, replace the saran wrap. If, the ears are still green after four days, repeat the procedure with fresh cotton balls. Once the green is gone, rub a paste of baking soda and water over the treated areas. After several days, flake off the dried baking soda and clean the area with warm, soapy water on a Q-tip. Tarn-X causes a chemical reaction that acts as a bleach; the baking soda neutralizes the reaction; and the warm, soapy water removes any residue. It is important to perform each step as described, and to inspect the doll periodically throughout the process.

Bubble Cut Barbies often have sticky or greasy faces. This is due to an ingredient being emitted by the vinyl. To alleviate the problem, carefully remove the head from the body and clean inside and out with a Q-tip soaked in alcohol. Dry thoroughly; fill the head cavity with baking soda; and replace it on the body. The baking soda will neutralize the chemicals and absorb the extracted grease.

SOME VERY OLD TIPS

Here are some old-fashioned tips suggested by doll collectors. They are neither recommended nor condemned and I have included them for your enjoyment only.

1. To remove mildew: soak in sour milk and salt, then lay in the sun. To remove milk therapy, follow with a warm soapy water wash and rinse.
2. To restore color to faded cloth: sponge with chloroform.
3. To soften old kid: saturate an old woolen rag with kerosene and rub in the kid.
4. To clean old ivory: scrub with Ivory soap; bleach in the sun for several days, re-applying the soapy solution often.
5. To remove tar: clean first with turpentine, then clean with Lux soap.
6. To remove paint: patient rubbing with chloroform.
7. To restore faded calico: wash in water with a teaspoon of sugar of lead; soak for fifteen minutes and launder.
8. Black taffeta is best washed in strong tea.

Dolls are a fascinating part of our culture and provide a look into our past. By scattering the seeds of doll collecting and furnishing basic information, I hope I've helped the reader build a collection that is enjoyable and profitable.

Price Adjustment Factors

Prices in this book are based on dolls in fine condition, appropriately dressed and with no damage. Unfortunately, dolls frequently have a number of faults.

What follows is a method by which you can take the prices listed in this book and adjust them to fit the doll you are examining. Admittedly, some of these adjustments do require you to make a judgment call. When analyzing a doll, it's always best to use your head, not your heart. That may sound easy, but it is difficult to do. Over-grading a doll and, hence, over paying for it, are major problems in doll collecting circles. Hopefully, the suggestions offered here will make you a wiser, more savvy buyer and/or seller.

BISQUE

Hairline in back, or under wig	- 50%
Crack or repair to bisque	- 70%
Very poor body (not normal wear)	- 20%
Replaced body	- 40%
Tinted or untinted ornamentation damage	- 30%
Original super-pristine condition and/or box	+ 100%

CHINA

Head cracked or repaired	- 75%
Cracked or repaired shoulder	- 50%
Worn or replaced body	- 40%
Exceptional, original doll	+ 50%

CLOTH

Face stained or faded	- 50%
Tears or large holes in face	- 80%
Mint or excellent condition	+ 200%

METAL

Lightly dented or lightly chipped head	- 50%
Badly dented or badly chipped head	- 80%

Bucherer Dolls are forgiven for some chips and damage. So desirable are these dolls that the adjustment would be only 20 - 30%, depending on severity and location.

COMPOSITION AND PAPIER-MÂCHÉ

Very light crazing	Acceptable
Heavy crazing or cracking	- 50%
Small splits at corners of eye and/or mouth	- 20%
Heavy chipping to face	- 75%
Face repainted	- 80%
Major cracks, splits, and peeling	- 30%
Redressed or undressed	- 35%
Mint and/or boxed	+ 100%

WAX

Minor cracks or minor warp to head	- 20%
Major cracks or major warp to head	- 80%
Softening of features	- 20%
Rewaxed	- 70%
All original with sharp features and good color	+ 200%

CELLULOID

Cracks	- 80%
Discolored	- 70%
Mint	+ 50%

WOOD

Light crazing or minute paint touch-up	Acceptable
Repainted head or heavy splits (depending on severity and location)	- 50% - 80%
Mint	+ 100%

PLASTIC

Crack or discoloration	- 70%
Hair combed	- 40%
Shelf dirt	- 30%
Redressed or missing accessories	- 50%
1950s, mint, boxed	+ 100%*
1960s, mint, boxed	+ 50%
1970s, mint, boxed	+ 30%
1980s, mint, boxed	+ 10%
1990s, mint, boxed	List Value

*Or more, depending on the desirability of the doll

Alexander Doll Company

14", early cloth.

The Alexander Doll Company was founded in 1923 by Beatrice Alexander Behrman and her sisters Rose Alexander Schrecking, Florence Alexander Rapport, and Jean Alexander Disick. The Alexander sisters, daughters of Maurice and Hannah Alexander—the owners and operators of the first doll hospital in the United States—had been raised to appreciate beauty along with a love of dolls. It was through the ambition and creativity of Beatrice that the company grew into the giant doll manufacturer it has become.

Originally sold in their father's shop, the first dolls were made of cloth and had flat faces. Molded faces with painted features soon replaced these earlier renditions.

In 1929, a high quality line of dolls appeared in the trade catalogs advertised as "Madame Alexander." The following year the Alexander sisters expanded this new line, now commonly known as "Madame Alexander Dolls."

Madame Alexander Dolls must be preserved in their original costumes, for herein lies the individuality of the doll. While over 6,000 different Madame Alexander personality dolls were introduced, a relatively small number of faces were developed. It is essential to have the original costume and/or wrist tag in order to identify the doll.

Alexander Doll Company's reputation for high quality has earned it the respect of doll lovers of all ages. The dolls are outfitted in exquisitely trimmed silks, velvets, satins, and other fine fabrics, with beautiful accessories completing the costume.

In 1988, the still active, 93-year-old Madame Alexander sold the company to Jeff Chodorow and Ira Smith, both attorneys and business men. The Alexander Doll Company changed ownership again in 1995 when it was acquired by The Kaizen Breakthrough Partnership, a private capital fund managed by Gefinor Acquisition Partners.

The Alexander Doll Company continues to produce quality dolls, albeit in larger quantities than in the past. Although Madame Alexander (Beatrice) has passed away, her endless reservoir of creativity provides the company with a vast supply of beautiful creations from which to draw in the future.

As with anything that is extremely popular, copies of Alexander Doll Company Dolls were produced. In the early years of hard plastic (late 1940s), a common factory was used by Alexander Doll Company, American Character Doll Company and Arranbee Doll Company. This factory produced the same body and limb molds, and very similar faces, for all three companies. Though not typical reproductions, they are very similar. No marked reproduction dolls, tags, or labels are known to exist.

When purchasing a Madame Alexander Doll, look carefully and critically at the condition. Check for a nice bright color on the face as well as even, unblotched coloring on the body. Pay particular attention to areas adorned with jewelry, as contact occasionally resulted in stains to the body. Determine if the hair retains its original set. Clothing should be original and in excellent condition. Check body and head seams for splitting, often a result of the dolls being strung too tightly. Cissy dolls tend to crack at the leg seams and below the ears. Lissy tends to crack around the ears.

CLOTH

Earliest cloth dolls had flat faces. From the early 1930s on, the faces were made of heavy felt suede pressed and molded, giving it a dimensional look. The features were hand painted with oil paints. Some early examples were done by Madame or one of her sisters. The features were very well done, showing that much time and artistic talent was involved. Most dolls had side-glancing eyes with white highlights. The inside corners of the eyes have small red dots.

The eyebrows are a single stroke, usually high on the face, giving a startled look. The closed mouth is small and somewhat heart shaped. There is a round "apple cheek" look to the blush. The mohair wigs are attached to a cloth base and either glued or pinned onto the head. The basic body was constructed of pink cotton or linen. The legs were "log" construction, having neither shape nor knee joints. The arms were slightly curved at the elbow. The hands were mitt-types at first, but later dolls show fingers stitched in. The head was socketed so as to turn. The clothes were made primarily of cotton with organdy one-piece undergarments. Clothes were pinned, never sewn onto the doll. Ranging in sizes from 10 to 30 inches. Early cloth dolls were not marked. Clothing tags had character names and "MADAME ALEXANDER/NEW YORK USA." Wrist tags were gold octagonal-shaped cardboard tags with the name of the doll on one side and "ALEXANDER DOLL COMPANY" on the other.

Examples of cloth dolls introduced include: Red Riding Hood, Tippit Toe, Pitty Pat, Grace Alice, Laughing Allegra, Edith With Golden Hair, Hiawatha, McGuffey Ann, and Dickens Characters.

And, Cherub Babies, Little Women, Susie Q, Bobbie Q, Little Shaver, Bell & Beau Brummel, Goldilocks, Alexander Rag Time, So-Lite, and Country Cousins.

Also, Cuddly, Evangeline, Priscilla, Tweedle-Dum, Tweedle-Dee, Doris Keane, Little Lord Fauntleroy, Baby Genius, Babbie, Blue Boy, Pinky, and others.

Modern cloth dolls made after 1960 include: Pechity Pam, Funny, Muffin, Pechity Pepper, Good Little Girl, and Carrot Top.

4", composition Tiny Betty Bride.

1935-1948:

Tiny Betty Face Doll: 7" and 8" one-piece, composition body and head; mohair wig; side-glancing painted eyes; very light peach color blush, painted very-red closed heart-shaped mouth; painted-on black shoes and white socks; right arm slightly bent. Either body or head is marked "MmE ALEXANDER or WENDY ANN." Clothing tag with character name and "MADAME ALEXANDER/NEW YORK USA." Octagonal gold cardboard wrist tag with name of doll on one side and "ALEXANDER DOLL CO." on other. More than 80 different personality dolls were introduced using this basic doll.

Examples of the Tiny Betty dolls introduced are: Bo Peep, Cinderella, Carmen, McGuffy Ana, Bride, Belgium, Pan American, Heidi, and Ding Dong Dell.

Little Betty Face Doll: 9" and 11" five-piece, all composition body jointed at neck, shoulder, and hip; found with either molded hair or wig; side-glancing painted eyes; very light pink color blush, painted closed bow-shaped mouth; barefoot, right arm slightly bent; marked "MmE. ALEXANDER NEW YORK" across back. Clothing tag with character name and "MADAME ALEXANDER/NEW YORK USA." Octagonal gold cardboard wrist tag with name on one side and "ALEXANDER DOLL CO. N.Y./USA" on other. More than 50 different personality dolls were produced using this basic doll.

Examples of the Little Betty Dolls introduced are: Hansel and Gretel, Virginia Dare, Dill Dally Sally, Bridesmaid, Swiss, Princess Elizabeth, Red Cross Nurse, Bo Peep, McGuffy Ann and Peasant.

Wendy Ann Face Doll: 11", 13", 18", and 21" five-piece, all composition body jointed at neck, shoulder, and hip; may have swivel waist; either molded hair or wig; either painted or sleep eyes; light pink color blush, closed mouth shows less of a smile; slightly round face. Marked "WENDY ANN" on back or "WENDY ANN/MmE. ALEXANDER" on head. Clothing tag with character name and "MADAME ALEXANDER/NEW YORK USA."

ALEXANDER CLOTH VALUE COMPARISONS:		
Size	Vintage Cloth	Modern Cloth
7"	300.00	
10"	350.00	
12"	400.00	
16"	500.00	75.00
18"	550.00	
20"	600.00	
24"	800.00	
30"	1,200.00	

COMPOSITION

Composition is a mixture of sawdust and glue. This mixture is put into heated two-piece molds allowing the doll to be molded and dried in one process. The dolls are then sanded and painted. Composition is very susceptible to damage from the environment, heat, dampness, cold, etc. It becomes increasingly more difficult to find composition dolls in mint condition. Some slight crazing is tolerated without effecting a doll's value. Badly crazed, cracked, or peeling dolls are valued much lower.

16", composition (Princess Elizabeth) McGuffey Ann.

Earlier dolls had either octagonal gold cardboard wrist tag with character name and "WENDY ANN/Mme ALEXANDER" on one side and "ALEXANDER DOLL CO. N.Y. USA" on other or a green foil clover-shaped tag with "WENDY ANN/ALEXANDER DOLL CO." and sometimes the character name. Wendy Ann dolls were released in more than 55 different characters. An extensive wardrobe could be purchased separately.

Examples of the Wendy Ann dolls introduced are: Queen Alexanderine, Carmen, W.A.V.E., Annie Laurie, Little Lord Fauntleroy, Mary Louise, Mother and Me, Dickens Character, Suellen Sally, Rosetta, Fairy Queen, Princess, and Little Women. Note: Add an additional $300.00 for Scarlett O'Hara (also spelled Scarlet) and Sonja Henie dolls.

Princess Elizabeth Face Doll: 13", 14", 15", 16", 17", 21", 24", and 27" five-piece, all composition body jointed at neck, shoulders, and hip; mohair or human hair wig; tin or glassene sleep eyes; open slightly smiling mouth with four insert upper teeth and felt tongue; very round face; marked "PRINCESS ELIZABETH/ALEXANDER DOLL CO." on head. Clothing tag with character name and "MADAME ALEXANDER NY/USA RIGHT RESERVE." Gold octagonal cardboard wrist tag character name and "ALEXANDER DOLL CO. NY." Some 13" and 16" closed-mouth Princess Elizabeth dolls resemble the Betty face. Princess Elizabeth was used for several different personality dolls.

Examples of the Princes Elizabeth introduced are: Snow White, Kate Greenaway, McGuffey Ann, Miss Victoria, Margaret Rose, Girl Scout, Flora McFlimsy, Cinderella and Princess Elizabeth. Note: Add an additional $100.00 for Flora McFlimsy with red hair and freckles.

Margaret Face Doll: 14", 18", and 21" all composition body jointed at neck, shoulder, and hip; mohair or human hair wig; single-stroke eyebrows lower on face giving shy look, oval sleep eyes, with real lashes and painted lower lashes; small turned up nose; wider, barely smiling mouth; marked "ALEXANDER" on head and across back. Clothing tag with character name and "Madame Alexander NY/USA;" green foil clover-shaped wrist tag with "ALEXANDER DOLL CO. N.Y. U.S.A." and occasionally the character name.

Examples of the Margaret dolls introduced are: Margaret O'Brien, Karen the Ballerina, Alice in Wonderland, and Hulda. Note: Add an additional $500.00 for Hulda doll.

Character Baby Face Doll: 11", 12", 15", 19", 21", 23", and 24" all composition, either five-piece baby body with bent legs and arms or cloth body with composition limbs; either molded and painted hair or fine mohair wig; sleep or painted eyes; molded open or closed painted mouth; clothing tag with baby's name and "MADAME ALEXANDER NEW YORK U.S.A." Gold octagonal-shaped wrist tag with baby's name and "ALEXANDER DOLL CO. NEW YORK USA" or green foil clover-shaped tag with "ALEXANDER DOLL CO. NEW YORK USA."

Examples of Character Babies introduced are: Princess Alexander, Precious, Little Genius, Cookie, McGuffey Ann, Slumbermate, Genius Baby, and Kitty Baby. Note: Add an additional $50.00 for Pinky Baby doll.

Occasionally, a personality was so popular that it merited its own face. Composition dolls which fall into this Individual Character category include:

Dionne Quintuplets: 7½", 10½", 14", 17", 19", and 23½", composition heads on either cloth body with composition limbs or composition toddler body; molded and painted hair or wig; marked on head "Dionne" and/or the individual name, or "Dionne Alex" or "Alexander" and possibly others. Accessories which could be purchased include: Ferris wheel, crib, bed, basket, swing, high chair, chair, and "Quintmobile." These usually had the quintuplet's name and their particular color: Annette, yellow; Cecile, green; Emeile, lavender; Marie, blue; and Yvonne, pink.

Dr. Dafoe: 14", Dionne Quintuplets doctor; cloth chubby body, composition limbs, swivel composition head and shoulder plate; gray mohair wig; blue painted eyes, painted upper lashes only; smiling face, chin dimple; unmarked doll, tagged "DR. DAFOE/MmE. ALEXANDER;" white jumpsuit and doctor's coat; octagonal gold cardboard Dr. Dafoe wrist tag. **1,400.00**

Minister: Dr. Dafoe body and face; clothing tag, wrist tag. **900.00**

Priest: Dr. Dafoe body and face; clothing tag, wrist tag. **1,100.00**

ALEXANDER COMPOSITION VALUE COMPARISONS:

Size	Betty*	Wendy Ann*	Princess Elizabeth*	Margaret*	Character Baby*	Jane Withers	Jeannie Walker	Sonja Henie	Dionne Quints
7"	300.00								
7½"	350.00								375.00
8"	375.00								
9"	350.00								
10"									475.00
11"	400.00	425.00			275.00				
13"		500.00	450.00			900.00			
14"		475.00		700.00			600.00		650.00
15"		500.00			350.00	1,000.00		800.00	700.00
16"			525.00						
17"			575.00			1,200.00			575.00
18"		650.00		900.00			800.00	1,000.00	
19"					425.00				850.00
20"						1,500.00			
21"		1,500.00	650.00	1,200.00	450.00			1,300.00	
23"					475.00				775.00
24"			750.00		525.00				
27"			900.00						

* The more famous characters and elaborately-costumed dolls will command higher prices.

Baby Jane: 16", named for child star Juanita Quigley; composition body jointed at neck, shoulders, and hips; brown human hair wig; brown sleep eyes, long painted upper and lower lashes; open smiling mouth, four teeth, felt tongue, chubby cheeks; marked "BABY JANE/ALEXANDER" on head; tagged "BABY JANE/MmE ALEXANDER" dress. **1,000.00**

Jane Withers: 13", 15", 17", and 20", child star of radio and films; composition body jointed at neck, shoulders, and hips, occasionally cloth body with composition limbs; mohair wig; sleep eyes, long painted upper and lower lashes; closed painted or open mouth with four teeth, felt tongue, smiling face; marked "JANE WITHERS/ALEX. DOLL CO.;" clothing tagged "JANE WITHERS/ALL RIGHTS RESERVED MADAME ALEXANDER," gold script pin with name.

Jeannie Walker: 14" and 18", composition jointed body, "able to sit in lady like fashion" as ads in early catalogs stated; wooden walking mechanism, worked by pulley and levers, first of kind in U.S.; oval-shaped face; human hair wig; sleep eyes; closed puckered mouth; marked "ALEXANDER DOLL CO./PAT NO 2171281" on body; tagged "JEANNIE WALKER/MADAME ALEXANDER NY USA."

Sonja Henie: 15", 18" and 21", named for three-time Olympic title winner and film star; composition body, may have swivel waist, less curved arms, jointed at neck, shoulder, and hips; blond mohair wig; sleep eyes, real eyelashes with dark eye shadow; face molded to appear fatter, dimples, open mouth with four teeth; marked "SONJA HENIE/MADAME ALEXANDER" (small Wendy Ann face dolls have closed mouth). The registration for Sonja Henie dolls reads "to be dressed in elaborate skating costumes in assorted styles, skates attached to high skate shoes." Clothing tag with "SONJA HENIE MmM ALEXANDER/ALL RIGHTS RESERVED N.Y. U.S.A.;" wrist tag with picture of Sonja Henie.

HARD PLASTIC

Hard Plastic was the miracle invention of the century for the doll industry. Developed during World War II, it could be washed, painted and molded, and it was the perfect weight for dolls. There was no need for new molds as the same ones designed for composition could now be used for hard plastic. Several Madame Alexander Dolls were made in both mediums, such as the Margaret O'Brien Doll. Hard plastic dolls shared another characteristic with composition in that a vast number of different personalities shared one doll face. The Wendy Ann/Wendy-kins Doll alone has assumed the identity of over 150 characters.

The mid-50s saw another major change in the doll world. New health regulations forbade the use of human hair wigs. Again, modern technology came through with saran—a fiber that could have a permanent set baked in, and nylon, which could be washed and set. Plastic was now also used for the eyes, thereby eliminating crackling problems. The clothing continued to be exceptionally beautiful, well-made creations. Tags on clothing showed the name of the doll and "MADAME ALEXANDER N.Y. U.S.A. ALL RIGHTS RESERVED." Wrist tag designs varied from green clovers and silver squares to gold metal medallions. Gold medallions were also used as necklaces to boast the Gold Medal for Fashion Award presented to Alexander Doll Company for the years 1951, 1952, and 1953.

Margaret (O'Brien) Face Doll: the bridge doll used for both composition and hard plastic. These 14", 18", and 22" dolls were hard plastic and jointed at the neck, shoulders, and hips; slightly bent arms; mohair, floss, human hair, saran, or nylon wig; single-stroke eyebrows lower on the face give a shy look, oval sleep eyes with real lashes and painted lower lashes; pert little nose; and a wider slightly smiling mouth. Marked "ALEXANDER" on head. Character name on clothing tag. This particular face was used for at least 55 different personalities, including a 23" black Cynthia.

Examples of the Margaret faced dolls introduced are: Alice in Wonderland, Snow White, Story Princess, Cinderella, Majorette, Peter Pan, Little Women, Prince Charming, Me and My Shadow—an 18" portrait doll with a 7½" matching miniature, which must have matching tags and labels—Renoir, Lady and Winston Churchill, Margot, and Karen the Ballerina, Little Men, Century of Fashion, Civil War, Hedy Lamar, Glamour Girls, and others. Note: Godey, Renoir, Victoria, Queen Elizabeth, and Me and My Shadow Series can easily command twice the values given.

Maggie Face Doll: 15", 18", and 23" all hard plastic, jointed at neck, shoulders, and hips; right arm slightly bent, left arm straighter; mohair, floss, human hair, saran or nylon wig; single-stroke eyebrows higher on face giving wide-awake look; pug nose; puckered, non-smiling closed mouth; overall effect is a younger, rounder face. Catalog ads stated "she walks when you lead her by the hand." After the mid-1950s, the phrase ". . . and moves her head from side to side" was added. Marked "ALEXANDER" on head. Name of character on clothing tag. This face used for at least 30 different personalities. In 1956, the Maggie face was used only for the Little Women series.

Examples of the Maggie faced dolls introduced are: Kathy, Garden Party, Picnic Day, Cherie, Alice in Wonderland, Beau Art Dolls, Little Men, Glamour Girls, Me and My Shadow, Betty, Maggie Teenager, Evening Gown, Victorian, and Century of Fashion. Note: Me and My Shadow Series, Century of Fashion, and Glamour Girls can easily command twice the values given.

Mary Ellen: 31", hard plastic walker; legs jointed at knees, arms jointed at elbows; rooted nylon hair; pretty oval-shaped face; single-stroke eyebrows lower on the face, smaller, more almond-shaped sleep eyes; pert nose; wider smiling mouth; pink blush lower on cheeks; overall effect is of an older child or teen. Marked "MME ALEXANDER " on head. Mary Ellen is relatively rare and quite beautiful. Her large size limits the market, resulting in a price lower than you might expect.

Wendy-Ann/Wendy/Wendy-Kins/Alexander-Kins and Billy (the boy): 7" to 8". Made continuously for the past 40 years. Molded and named for Madame Alexander's grandchildren, William and Wendy Ann. When the real Wendy Ann passed away in 1955, Ann was dropped from the doll's name. They all have chubby round faces with thin chins; single-stroke eyebrows, sleep eyes with molded upper lashes, and painted lower lashes; small, closed, unsmiling, almost pouty lower lips; and synthetic wigs. If marked at all it is "ALEX" across the back. Dolls made after 1976 will be marked "ALEXANDER."

In 1974, a new series was added called "United States." The tag contained a misspelled tag UNTIED STATES. Most were re-called. However, some did find their way to the general public. If one is found, it can add about $100.00 to the price of a doll in perfect condition.

Clothing tags will be printed in red, blue or red, "ALEXANDER-KINS," (Name of Doll), "BY MADAME ALEXANDER REG U.S. PAT. OFF. NY NY." A very few may be tagged with the (Name of Doll) "MADAME ALEXANDER/ALL RIGHTS RESERVED NEW YORK U.S.A." There are many prices quoted for Alexander-Kins, sometimes as high as several thousand dollars. But a realistic price today (as reflected in auction reports and major doll dealers across the country) is in the $300.00 to $700.00 price range. Of course location, rarity, and demand have an affect on this ever fluctuating market. Naturally there are exceptions, such as Baby Clown, Little Minister, Parlor Maid and Indian Girl, which were produced for only one year and therefore command a much higher price.

Madeline: 18", jointed at neck, shoulders, elbows, wrists, hips, and knees; vinyl head with an open/closed smiling mouth; nylon or saran wig; single-stroke eyebrows, sleep eyes; light dimples. Marked "ALEXANDER" on head.

	WENDY/ALEXANDER-KINS VALUE COMPARISONS:				
Date	Body Type	Body Color	Eyes	Mouth	Current Estimated Value
1953	Straight legs, non walker	Tannish color	Oval sleep eyes	Dark red	700.00
1954	Straight legs, walker	Tannish color, slightly shiny	Oval sleep eyes	Dark red	700.00
1955	Slightly bent legs, walker body	Tannish bisque look to shiny plastic	Oval sleep eyes	Red	675.00
1956	Jointed knees, walkers with turning heads	Pink color to plastic	Very oval sleep eyes	Dark pink	550.00
1974	Straight legs, jointed above knees	Very matte finish to plastic	Rounder eyes	Orange mouth, high blush	350.00

Penny/Barbara Jane: 29", 34", and 42" soft cloth body with vinyl stuffed head, legs, and straight arms; large hands with separate fingers; synthetic "Newtar" saran wig; single-stroke, very pale eyebrows lower on the face with sleep or painted eyes; turned up nose; wider, rather smiling mouth; longer chubby cheeks; features reveal a cute, happy face. It has been reported that this doll was made to appeal to boarding school and college girls. Dressed in assorted little girl and teen dresses and open-toe shoes. Marked "ALEXANDER" on the head. Penny is an awkward doll to display and, therefore, is not as desirable as other Alexanders.

Cissy Face Dolls (Winnie and Binnie Walker): 15", 18", 20/21", and 23/25". This most famous Alexander Doll Company Doll was first introduced in 1953 as Winnie Walker with full hard plastic arms on walker body. Re-released in 1954 as Binnie Walker. Cissy was introduced in 1955 using the Winnie and Binnie face with an adult figure, high heel feet, jointed elbows, and vinyl-over-hard-plastic arms on a walker body.

The Winnie and Binnie walkers were distinguishable by their hairstyle. Winnie had a glued-on wig with a feather cut combed in all directions. Binnie's hair is rooted to a vinyl skull cap and has a longer part and bangs. Both of these flat-footed walkers had identical faces. The faces of all dolls are a bit square shaped. The eyebrows are slightly raised, with oval-shaped eyes with real upper lashes and painted lower ones. Straight nose tapers at the bridge; closed, unsmiling mouth. A blush lower on the cheek gives a sculptured, almost debutante look. Both Winnie and Binnie are marked "ALEXANDER" on back of the head. Clothing tag reads, "CISSY, WINNIE, BINNIE," or one of the personalities using the Cissy face. Cissy, the most popular Alexander Company Doll ever made, was produced for nine years. In 1962, Cissy was used only for Queen.

Examples of other Cissy faced dolls introduced are: Flora McFlimsey, Agatha, Debutante Series, Mary Louise, Active Miss, *Lady Hamilton, Margot Ballerina, Skater's Waltz, and Princess. Note: Lady in Red, Godey Portrait or Ice Capades Series can easily command 3 to 4 times the values given.*

Along with these dolls, two other dolls were released using the Cissy body with different faces. Shari Lewis and Sleeping Beauty were both made in 21". (They also came in smaller sizes, but on different bodies.)

Shari Lewis: 21" hard plastic and vinyl body jointed at shoulders, elbows, hips, and knees; high heel feet; synthetic dark blond wig in original ponytail; heart-shaped face; feathered brows, blue sleep eyes, real upper lashes, painted lower lashes; very, very turned-up nose; pierced ears; closed, unsmiling full mouth; head marked "MmE 19©58 ALEXANDER" **900.00**

Sleeping Beauty: 21" hard plastic and vinyl body jointed at shoulders, elbows, hips, and knees; high heel feet; synthetic, very blond wig in original set; outstanding beautiful round-shaped face; lightly feathered and shaped brows, blue sleep eyes, real upper lashes, painted lower lashes; original satin gown trimmed with gold; gold tiara with rhinestone stars; gold brocade net floor-length cape; rhinestone necklace and ring; tagged "MADAME ALEXANDER PRESENTS WALT DISNEY'S AUTHENTIC SLEEPING BEAUTY;" head marked "ALEXANDER" **1,100.00**

Lissy Face Doll: 11" teenager dolls of hard plastic; medium high heeled feet; small bosom; jointed elbows, and knees. They have a much rounder face with large oval eyes with real upper lashes and painted lower lashes; very slight pug nose; blushed cheeky look; closed unsmiling and slightly puckered mouth. Referred to as "Sub-Deb" and as Cissy's "Saucy younger sister." The dolls were not marked. Clothing tag with Lissy or character name. About 40 different outfits were produced along with several different personality characters. Folded white booklet wrist tags.

Examples of the Lissy faced dolls introduced are: Ballerina, Bride, Bridesmaid, Little Men, Classic Group, and Cinderella. Note:

HARD PLASTIC VALUE COMPARISONS:

	Margaret*	Maggie*	Mary Ellen	Madeline*	Penny*	Cissy*	Lissy*	Elise*	Cissette*	Maggie Mix-Up
8"										650.00
10"									450.00	
11"							550.00			
14"	700.00									
15"		650.00				500.00				
16"								450.00		650.00
18"	900.00	800.00		500.00		550.00				
21"						650.00				
23"	1,500.00	900.00								
25"						900.00				
29"					500.00					
31"			700.00		600.00					
34"					700.00					

* The more famous characters and elaborately costumed dolls will command higher prices.

Southern Belle and McGuffey Ann can easily command twice the values given.

Elise Face Doll: 16" all hard plastic body with vinyl arms and jointed elbows, knees, and ankles; oval face; single-stroke brows lower on face; oval sleep eyes with real upper lashes, painted lower lashes; pierced ears; unsmiling, softer closed mouth. Marked "ALEXANDER" on head and "MmE ALEXANDER" on back. Paper book wrist tag. Clothing tag with "ELISE/MeM ALEXANDER" or character name and "MeM ALEXANDER." Over 40 different outfits were created for Elise, and most were sold separately.

Examples of the Elise faced dolls introduced are: Going Visiting, Bride, Lucy Bride, Bridesmaid, Scarlett O'Hara, Ball Gown, Queen, and Renoir. Another doll introduced using the Elise body but with her own face was Sleeping Beauty. (The 21" Sleeping Beauty used the Cissy body).

Sleeping Beauty: 16" hard plastic fully-jointed body; very blond synthetic wig in original set; strikingly beautiful round face; lightly feathered and shaped brows, blue sleep eyes with real upper lashes and painted lower ones; straighter nose; very full, wider, slightly smiling mouth; original satin gown trimmed in gold; gold tiara with rhinestone stars; gold brocade net floor length cape; rhinestone necklace and ring; tagged "MADAME ALEXANDER PRESENTS WALT DISNEY'S AUTHENTIC SLEEPING BEAUTY," head marked "ALEXANDER"................................**900.00**

Cissette Face Doll: 10" or 11" all hard plastic, jointed at neck, shoulders, hips, and knees; high heel feet. The hard plastic had a softer finish than other dolls of the time—they were advertised as having a "porcelain-like finish." Cissette has a somewhat heart-shaped face with broad forehead, full cheeks, tapering chin; single-stroke eyebrows painted higher on face, giving a wide-eyed look, oval sleep eyes with real upper lashes and painted lower lashes; most have pierced ears; small, pug, turned-up nose; fuller, very slightly smiling closed mouth. A great many outfits and personalities were created for Cissette. They were marked with a turquoise tag (except 1963 when they were blue) with "CISSETTE" or character name. Most dolls marked "MmM ALEXANDER" across back, some with no markings, booklet-type wrist tag.

Examples of Cissette faced dolls introduced are: Gainsborough, Ballerina, Barbary Coast, Gibson Girl, Liesl & Brigitta, Jenny Lind, Lady Hamilton, Klondike Kate, Margot, Tinker Bell, Portette, Southern Belle, Queen, Gold Rush, Fairy Princess, Godey, and Renoir. Note: Gold Rush and Klondike Kate can easily command 4 to 5 times the values given.

Maggie Mix-Up: 8" and 17". The 8" size has an all hard plastic body with jointed knees; the 17" size has the Elise body with vinyl arms jointed at elbows, knees, and ankles. Both sizes are easily identified by distinguishing characteristics of straight orangish-red hair, freckles, and sleep eyes. Marked "ALEX" on back and "Maggie" on tags. Paper booklet wrist tags.

VINYL

Vinyl is a tough, softer plastic that became the favorite for doll manufacturers. It can be dyed a natural skin color; has a more natural life-like feel; and is cheaper to produce than hard plastic. Vinyl came into its own in the late 1950s, and continues to be the makers' material of choice. For the sake of convenience, collectors tend to use vinyl as the bench mark for "modern" dolls.

Alexander Doll Company continues to use the same vinyl face for many different characters. Therefore, it is imperative to have the original clothing to accurately identify the doll. Most vinyl dolls have fully-jointed bodies and, in some cases, waists, elbows, knees, and ankles, along with shoulders and hips. Rooted synthetic hair replaces the wigs, and eyes are sleep-types with molded lashes. Some vinyl trademarks of 1957 were not actually made until 1958.

Kelly Face Doll: 12", 15", 17", and 22" ridged vinyl bodies and limbs with soft vinyl heads; fully jointed including the waist; square-shaped face; single-stroke brows lower on face, very big round eyes with molded lashes; small button nose; open/closed mouth with somewhat down-turned lip; rooted synthetic hair. Several characters produced using the Kelly face. Marked "MME ALEXANDER" in a circle, with 1958 underneath. (Same date used in 1958 and 1965). Booklet wrist tag. Note: Add an additional $200.00 for "Mary-Bel the Doll That Gets Well," in suitcase with sick child accessories.

Jacqueline Face Doll: 21", new face with jointed Cissy body; brown short-rooted hair combed to side; brown sleep eyes with thick lashes, eyeliner, and shaped brows; closed, smiling mouth, and soft blush on lower cheeks. In 1962, White House Press Secretary Pierre Salinger made a special request that the Alexander Doll Company not make reference to the First Lady, Jacqueline Kennedy, in advertising this doll. In 1962, the Jacqueline doll was dropped. She was re-introduced as the Portrait Series in 1965 and continues to be used. Marked "ALEXANDER 1961" on head (1961 is still on the head). Wrist tag was the booklet-type.

Caroline Baby Face Doll: 15" vinyl-head character baby; five-piece jointed hard plastic body; hair ribbon in very shiny, rooted blond hair parted on side; very big blue sleep eyes with lashes, soft single-stroke brows; open smiling mouth with dimple. Marked "ALEXANDER/1961" on head and "ALEX. 1959/13" on back. Booklet wrist tag.

Joanie Face Doll: 36" hard plastic jointed body; vinyl head with cute chubby character face; rooted saran hair; big, round flirty eyes with long curly lashes, single-stroke slanted eyebrows; closed, larger, smiling mouth. Marked "ALEXANDER/1959." Booklet wrist tag.

Mimi Face Doll: 30", rigid, hard plastic body jointed in twelve places; soft vinyl head and hands; more grown-up look with rooted hair in various styles from long curls to short bob cut; almond-shaped sleep eyes with molded lashes, single-stroke sweeping brows; smaller unsmiling closed mouth. Marked "ALEXANDER/1961" on head. Booklet wrist tag.

21", Coco. Photo courtesy of McMasters Doll Auctions.

Smarty Face Doll: 12" hard plastic, jointed toddler-type pigeon-toed body; vinyl, short rooted hair; oval sleep eyes with molded lashes, single-stroke brows; lightly blushed chubby cheeks; open/closed smiling mouth. Marked "ALEXANDER/1962" on head. Booklet wrist tag. Note: add an additional $200.00 for Katie (black version) and $100.00 for Brother (dressed as boy).

Janie Face Doll: 12" Smarty body with new chubby character face with rounder eyes, more pugged nose, and closed, smiling mouth; freckles found on some faces. Marked "ALEXANDER/1964" on head. Booklet wrist tag. Note: add an additional $100.00 for Lucinda, Rosy, or Suzy (identified by clothing label).

Melinda Face Doll: 16" and 22" hard plastic or vinyl body with swivel waist; almost white, rooted hair with full bangs; sweet character face; big, round, sleep eyes with lashes; open/closed smiling mouth with two teeth molded in top. Marked "ALEXANDER/1962" on head. Booklet wrist tag.

Brenda Starr: 12" eight-jointed hard plastic adult body; blond hair with one long lock on top; sleep eyes with long molded lashes, crescent-shaped brows higher up on forehead; closed, unsmiling mouth; also released as Yolanda. Brenda Starr was Alexander Doll Company's answer to Barbie, advertised as a "long stemmed American Beauty doll." Marked "ALEXANDER/1964" on head and "ALEXANDER" on back.

Coco: 21", fashioned after Paris designer Coco Chanel; portrait doll; plastic body jointed at waist, one-piece lower torso with bent right leg; vinyl arms and head; dramatic face with full cheeks, pointed chin; feathered brows, blue eye shadow and black liner over brown sleep eyes; shoulder length rooted blond hair. Every Coco carries a clear plastic wiglet box with extra hairpiece, rollers, comb, and hairpins. This was one of the finest creations of the Madame Alexander Doll Company. Patented in 1966 and never used again, she is one of the most desirable and hardest to find Alexander dolls. Marked "ALEXANDER/1966" on head.

First Lady Series: 14", Martha or Mary Ann face; six dolls, very good original condition; price for set.

First Series **700.00**	Fourth Series **600.00**
Second Series **600.00**	Fifth Series **600.00**
Third Series **500.00**	Sixth Series **600.00**

Peter Pan Series:

| Michael, 12" . . . . . .**300.00** | Tinker Bell, 10" . . . .**350.00** |
| Peter Pan, 14" . . . .**250.00** | Wendy, 14" . . . . . .**250.00** |

Sound of Music Series: all but the Kurt doll are available in two sizes.

Brigetta, 10" or 14" . . .**200.00**	Lisel, 10" or 11" **200.00**
Frederick, 8" or 11" . . .**200.00**	Louisa, 10" or 14" . . .**250.00**
Gretl, 8" or 11" **200.00**	Maria, 12" or 17" **250.00**
Kurt, 11" only **350.00**	Martha, 8" or 11" . . .**200.00**

VINYL VALUE COMPARISONS:

	Kelly	Jacqueline	Portrait	Caroline	Joanie	Mimi	Smarty	Janie	Melinda	Brenda Starr	Coco
12"	300.00						350.00	350.00		350.00	
14"											
15"	350.00			350.00							
16"									175.00		
17"	550.00										
21"		800.00	2,400.00								2,500.00
22"	575.00								200.00		
30"						500.00					
36"					400.00						

Henri Alexandre

Henri Alexandre, Paris, France, was named for its founder. The doll company was in existence for only a few years before being purchased by Tourrell Company which merged with Jules Steiner about 1891. Henri Alexandre is best known for designing and registering the line of Phenix Bébés, of which there were thirty models. Phenix Bébés were manufactured for many years, eventually by Jules Steiner. A beautiful closed-mouth doll, often referred to as an H.A. Bébé, was also produced. The company's many mergers account for the confusion which has occurred concerning the maker of the lovely Phenix Bébé and H.A. Bébé.

Closed Mouth H.A. Bébé: socket head; jointed wood-and-composition body; straight wrists; good wig; paperweight eyes; pierced ears; appropriately dressed; marked "H.A. Bébé."

Closed Mouth Phenix Bébé: socket head; jointed wood-and-composition body; straight wrists; good wig; paperweight eyes; pierced ears; appropriately dressed; marked "Phenix Bébé."

Open Mouth Phenix Bébé: socket head; jointed wood-and-composition body; good wig; paperweight eyes; appropriately dressed; marked "Phenix Bébé."

Henri Alexandre Phenix #90 Bébé with original waist ribbon.
Photo courtesy of Cobbs Doll Auction.

ALEXANDRE BÉBÉ VALUE COMPARISONS:

Size	Closed Mouth H.A. Bébé	Closed Mouth Phenix Bébé	Open Mouth Phenix B Bébé
10"		2,300.00	
12"	5,200.00	2,700.00	
14"	5,700.00	3,100.00	1,600.00
16"	6,000.00	3,500.00	1,800.00
17"	6,300.00	4,000.00	2,100.00
18"	6,800.00	4,500.00	2,300.00
20"	7,200.00	4,900.00	2,600.00
22"	7,500.00	5,200.00	2,700.00
23½"	8,000.00	5,600.00	2,800.00
25"	8,500.00	5,900.00	3,100.00

All-Bisque

Bisque, china, parian, and porcelain are all forms of ceramics derived from a clay-based material to which feldspar and flint have been added. This mixture is molded, fired, painted, and fired again. Quality ranges from the finest French porcelain with beautifully detailed decoration to coarse and crudely painted "stone bisque." Factors determining a doll's quality include the texture of the porcelain, the artistry applied in decorating the piece, and the presence or absence of a glaze.

Reproductions are found at almost every flea market and secondhand shop. When attempting to identify All-Bisque Dolls, look first for markings in the bisque. Most reproductions are marked only with a small paper label which is easily removed. Many older German and Japanese dolls are marked in the middle of the back, on the head, or at the crotch with a number or the country of origin. Early bisque dolls may have numbers incised on the limbs where they are joined to the body. If the arms or legs are separate, gently pull one away from the body. Does it look old? Arms on reproductions are usually attached at the joints with aluminum wire which frequently has been made to look old. Often, the aluminum will leave tell-tale signs of gray at the opening. While most French All-Bisque Dolls are unmarked, their superior quality makes it easy to differentiate an authentic example from a reproduction.

Prices listed are for dolls in good condition, unless otherwise noted. Normal wear, such as slight rubs or minute flakes at the joint openings, does not greatly affect the price. However, if areas are chipped, cracked, broken, or have been repaired, expect to pay much less. The value of a damaged All-Bisque Doll should directly reflect the degree of damage.

FRENCH

These little beauties are the most desirable of the All-Bisque Dolls, and, therefore, the most costly. Most French All-Bisque Dolls are not marked, making positive identification difficult. French dolls were made of an excellent quality of bisque which appears smooth and delicate. A "French Loop" or "Bell Top" is a molded loop found at the base of the neck. The loop enabled the head to be strung to the body. All French All-Bisque Dolls are jointed at the neck, shoulder, and hips. A few examples have additional joints at the elbows and/or knees. Limbs are jointed either with tiny wooden pegs, wire, or elastic. Joints were origi-

nally lined with kid. Although some French All-Bisque Dolls have painted eyes, most have glass eyes. Facial decoration is outstanding, with beautifully feathered brows, long eyelashes, and lips that are usually outlined in a darker red. The dolls are often found with cork pates at the crown opening. Most examples have slender legs and are either barefoot or have painted shoes and/or socks. Some dolls have wrestler-type legs which are very wide at the top and thin at the ankle.

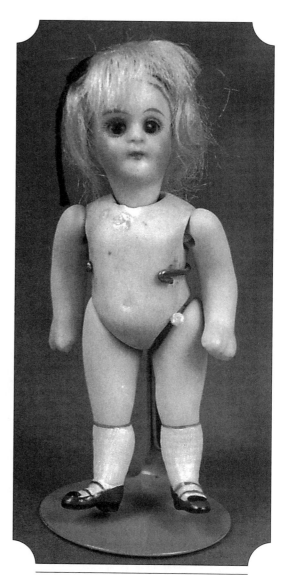

4" French-type, fully jointed, glass eyes. *Courtesy of Helen Brooke.*

FRENCH ALL-BISQUE VALUE COMPARISONS:

Size	Kid-lined jointed body, molded shoes, thin legs, glass eyes	Kid-lined body, extra joints at elbows, glass eyes	Kid-lined body, extra joints at elbows and knees, glass eyes	Kid-lined jointed body, wrestler legs, glass eyes	S. F. B. J., Unis, or later dolls	Painted eye
4"						650.00
5"	1,600.00	2,500.00		2,100.00	650.00	700.00
6"	2,400.00	2,900.00	3,800.00		700.00	800.00
7"	3,200.00	3,700.00	4,700.00	2,300.00	800.00	1,000.00
8"	4,500.00	4,800.00	5,800.00	2,400.00	900.00	1,100.00
9"	4,700.00	5,500.00	6,200.00	2,600.00	1,000.00	1,300.00
10"	4,900.00		6,500.00	2,800.00	1,100.00	1,500.00
11"	5,200.00	5,700.00	6,800.00	3,200.00		1,700.00
12"	6,500.00	7,000.00	8,500.00	3,500.00	1,200.00	2,000.00

Note: Add an additional $200.00 for molded bare feet.

GERMAN

German bisque quality ranges from outstanding to quite poor. These extremely popular dolls may be modeled as flappers, babies, comic characters, and brides and grooms.

Sizes range from less than one inch to well over a foot tall, with the most common being in the 4 to 8 inch size. Hair may be molded, or the doll may wear a wig; eyes are either painted or glass; and the mouth may be open or closed. Many dolls are found with the head and body as one piece. If the head is a swivel neck, it may be attached to the body with a small wooden neck plug, or the neck may be molded with holes on either side and strung with elastic.

Many will be marked on the back with "Germany" or a mold number. Several examples have been found with paper labels. Caution should be used when encountering a doll marked with a paper label. Japanese dolls were commonly marked in this manner.

Because of the many types of All-Bisque Dolls, categorization is staggering. Most All-Bisque Dolls fall into the groups shown below. Although there are many registered mold numbers from several factories, pricing is surprisingly close, with exceptions noted. Pay particular attention to detail when evaluating a doll, as condition and fineness of decoration are extremely important factors. In general, earlier dolls are the most desirable.

5" German, fully jointed, glass eyes. *Courtesy of Helen Brooke.*

4" German, jointed arms and legs, glass eyes. *Courtesy of Helen Brooke.*

GERMAN ALL-BISQUE VALUE COMPARISONS:

Size	Painted eyes, arms jointed, solid neck, hips either jointed or not*	Painted eyes, molded clothes	Glass eyes, stationary neck	Glass eyes, swivel neck	Extraordinary All-Bisque, glass eyes, fine decoration
1½"	75.00	60.00			
2"	85.00	60.00	250.00	275.00	
3"	125.00	100.00	300.00	325.00	
4"	175.00	150.00	325.00	400.00	
5"	225.00	175.00	350.00	500.00	1,500.00
6"	275.00	200.00	400.00	600.00	1,700.00
7"	300.00	250.00	450.00	800.00	1,900.00
7½"	325.00	275.00	500.00	900.00	2,400.00
8"	400.00	300.00	550.00	1,000.00	2,800.00
9"	450.00	360.00	750.00	1,200.00	3,200.00
10"	525.00	400.00	1,000.00	1,400.00	3,500.00
11"	600.00		1,200.00	1,600.00	3,700.00
12"	700.00		1,400.00	1,700.00	3,900.00

* Add an additional $50.00 - $100.00 for swivel neck.

IMMOBILES AND NODDERS

The most telling characteristic of these later dolls is their lack of artistry due to their cold-painted method of decoration. Cold painting is the absence of firing after the decoration is applied. It is not unusual to find pieces with the paint worn off. Some Nodders and Immobiles will be marked "Germany." Most are unmarked.

Young girls of the 1920s spent hours at the store scrutinizing these dolls in order to pick just the right one. Smaller dolls were called "Penny Dolls," while the larger dolls were prestigiously referred to as "Quarter Dolls." Quality was as important then as it is today. Quality of bisque ranged from good to very poor, and decoration from very cute to extremely crude. Examples listed are for average dolls.

3" German Immobile, Snow Flake. *Courtesy of Helen Brooke.*

Immobiles: no joints; molded and cold-painted features and clothing. Do not confuse Immobiles with German bisque figurines or Frozen Charlottes. Immobiles used an inferior quality bisque. The cold-painted decoration is brightly colored and poorly applied, resulting in a rather worn appearance to both facial features and clothing. Most immobiles are marked "Germany," although some are unmarked, or marked with a number.

Nodders: molded and painted features; solid one-piece bisque body joined at the neck by elastic knotted through hole at top of head; stringing enables doll's head to nod. Sometimes referred to by collectors as "Knotters." Nodders representing people have molded and painted clothes. Most animal Nodders have molded and painted fur. Animal nodders with molded clothes are uncommon and more costly.

3" German Nodder. *Courtesy of Helen Brooke.*

IMMOBILES VALUE COMPARISONS:

Size	Adult or Child	Comic/Personality Characters
2"	60.00	150.00
3"	85.00	160.00
5"	125.00	190.00
7"	165.00	225.00

NODDER VALUE COMPARISONS:

Size	Adult or Child	Comic Characters	Personalities	Animals	Dressed Animals
3"	75.00	125.00	235.00	150.00	250.00
4"	85.00	135.00	265.00	165.00	275.00
5"	100.00	150.00	285.00	185.00	300.00
6"	150.00	200.00	325.00	225.00	350.00

BABIES AND CHARACTERS

A few Character dolls stand out as being very desirable, usually because of the "character" portrayed rather than superior quality. While purest collectors assign value to quality of artistry, the popularity of these dolls cannot be disputed.

Baby Bo-Kaye: swivel neck; glass eyes; paper label on stomach.

Bonnie Baby: swivel neck; glass eyes; very distinctive character face; molded teeth; paper label on stomach.

Bye-Lo: typical Bye-Lo face; glass or painted eyes.

Didi, Mimi, Veve, Fefe: open/closed mouth; molded teeth; glass or painted eyes; paper label.

Hebee and Shebee: cute face; molded clothes and shoes with holes for ribbons.

Max (123) and Moritz (124): 5", very distinctive character with smiling face; marked "K★R."

Mibs, Baby Peggy, L. Amberg: some marked "1921," or with paper label.

Rag #890 (dog) and Tag #891 (cat): 5", jointed.

Sonny: swivel neck; round open/closed mouth; glass or painted eyes; bare feet; paper label.

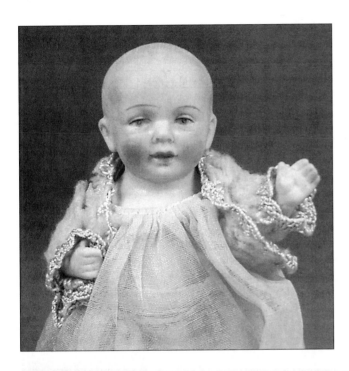

3¹/₂" German Bye-Lo, painted eyes. *Courtesy of Helen Brooke.*

4¹/₂" German character baby, jointed arms and legs, painted eyes. *Courtesy of Helen Brooke.*

ALL-BISQUE CHARACTER BABIES VALUE COMPARISONS:

Size	Baby Bo-Kaye	Bonnie Baby	Bye-Lo, Glass Eyes	Bye-Lo, Painted Eyes	Didi, Mimi, Veve, Fefe, Glass Eyes	Didi, Mimi, Veve, Fefe, Painted Eyes
4"						
5"	1,500.00	1,000.00	700.00	500.00	1,600.00	1,000.00
6"	1,900.00		900.00	600.00	1,700.00	1,100.00
7"		1300.00			1,900.00	1,200.00
8"	3,000.00	1,400.00	800.00			

ALL-BISQUE CHARACTER BABIES VALUE COMPARISONS:

Size	HeBee, SheBee	Max, Moritz	Mibs, Baby Peggy	Rag, Tag	Sonny, Glass Eyes	Sonny, Painted Eyes
4"	550.00		350.00			
5"	650.00	2,900.00	500.00	2,500.00		
6"	700.00				2,900.00	900.00
7"	900.00				3,400.00	1,200.00
9"	1,700.00					

FROZEN CHARLOTTE

All-Bisque Frozen Charlotte Dolls, made by various German firms, were called "Nacktfrosch," which means "Naked Baby." The names Charlotte and Charlie are reportedly derived from the popular 1860s ballad of "Young Charlotte."

Small Frozen Charlottes and Frozen Charlies were baked into birthday cakes as prizes for children. Larger 4 to 5 inch Frozen Charlottes and Frozen Charlies were placed in fine china cups to absorb the heat and prevent the cup from cracking. Divers searching for the Titanic wreckage knew they were in the right spot when they saw a Frozen Charlie looking up at them from the bottom of the sea.

In the 1970s, German-made reproductions of the 15" Frozen Charlie flooded the market. These well-made reproductions have

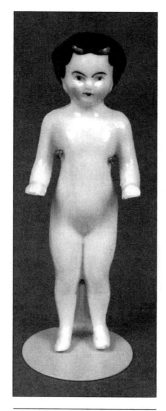

Frozen Charlotte. *Courtesy of Helen Brooke.*

no permanent markings. Some, but not all, of these reproductions have a hole between their legs large enough to insert a pencil. Another indication of age is a very clean slip. Most old bisque dolls have peppering, or tiny black specks, on the slip. If you are not sure of a doll's age, pass it by. A reproduction Frozen Charlotte would be a very costly purchase.

Frozen Charlotte and Frozen Charlie: glazed or unglazed finish; solid one-piece body, distinctive bent arms; straight legs separated to knees; molded and painted hair; delicate facial features; generally undressed and unmarked, but can be found with molded clothing, hats, and/or boots; occasionally marked with "Germany" or a mold number.

LATER EXAMPLES

Pink Bisque: jointed at shoulders and hips, mohair wigs, textured stockings, single-strap black shoes.

Painted Bisque: thin layer of flesh-colored paint applied over entire doll but not fired on. Note the difference between "cold painted," which has only particular parts painted and "painted bisque," which is an all-over coating.

There are many types of painted bisque dolls. Those listed below are small, All-Bisque Dolls jointed at the hips and shoulders with wire. They have mohair wigs or molded and painted hair and facial features, and painted-on socks and shoes. Most will be marked "Germany," either on the back or on the inside of the leg.

PINK BISQUE/PAINTED BISQUE VALUE COMPARISONS:

Size	Child/Adult, Glass Eyes	Child/Adult, Painted Eyes	Character Jointed at Neck	Painted Bisque
2"				35.00
3"	125.00	65.00	250.00	60.00
4"	150.00	100.00	300.00	
5"	175.00	125.00	350.00	100.00
6"	225.00	175.00	450.00	
7"	300.00	225.00	600.00	

FROZEN CHARLOTTE VALUE COMPARISONS:

Size	Charlotte or Charlie	Pink Tinted	Black Tinted	Molded Clothes or Boots	Unusual Hair
2"	65.00	225.00	150.00	250.00	325.00
3"	75.00	250.00	175.00	275.00	350.00
4"	125.00	300.00	200.00	325.00	375.00
5"	145.00	375.00	225.00	375.00	400.00
6"	185.00	400.00	250.00	400.00	425.00
7"	200.00	425.00	275.00	425.00	450.00
8"	250.00	450.00	300.00	450.00	475.00
9"	300.00	475.00	350.00	475.00	500.00
10"	350.00	500.00	400.00	500.00	550.00
11"	450.00	550.00	500.00	550.00	575.00
12"	500.00	600.00	550.00		
14"	550.00	650.00	650.00		
15"	650.00	750.00	750.00		

3¹/₂" and 3" Japan, cold painted, immobile. *Courtesy of Helen Brooke.*

JAPANESE

The various types of Japanese All-Bisque Dolls range in size from 1 to 8 inches. Most have molded and painted hair and facial features, and are either unjointed or jointed only at the shoulder. Rare examples have glass eyes, wigs, and/or additional joints. The more joints, the rarer the doll. Dolls may have molded and painted clothes, or no clothing.

Most Japanese All-Bisque Dolls are very poor in quality. The painted features are usually very crude. The bisque is often grainy—called "stone bisque" or "sugar bisque"—and seams are seldom cleaned. Occasionally, a very good quality Japanese All-Bisque can be found.

The most familiar doll is probably Betty Boop style, with bobbed, wavy, molded hair; big round eyes looking to the side; spiked eye lashes; and one-piece solid body and neck with shoulder joint. These dolls are often found wearing crepe paper dresses.

Another common Japanese All-Bisque is the "Candy Baby" premiums given away at the candy store with the purchase of candy. Thousands of Japanese All-Bisque Dolls were produced in the 1920s and 1930s. Many have survived. Look for better quality Japanese All-Bisque Dolls. They can be found. Most are marked "JAPAN" or "NIPPON" on the back. Many were originally marked with a paper label which is no longer present.

CHARACTER DOLLS

The quality of Japanese character dolls is generally superior to that of the standard All-Bisque Dolls. Many are decorated as skillfully as their German counterparts.

IMMOBILES

Bride and groom sets were once believed to be wedding cake decorations, but it is generally agreed now that this was not case.

Immobiles: no joints; molded and painted features and clothing.

JAPANESE IMMOBILES VALUE COMPARISONS:

Size	Child/Adult	Animal	Characters	Bride/Groom
3"	5.00	35.00	60.00	75.00
4"	10.00	45.00	65.00	
5"	15.00	55.00	70.00	75.00
6"	25.00	65.00	75.00	85.00

JAPANESE ALL-BISQUE VALUE COMPARISONS:

Size	Betty Boop	Character Baby	Kewpie-Type	Comic Character	Child or Adult	Two-Faced Dolls
2"		50.00				
3"			75.00	60.00		
3¹/₂"	30.00	75.00	95.00	65.00		
5"	35.00	85.00		70.00	65.00	200.00
5¹/₂"				95.00		
6"						225.00
7"	45.00					

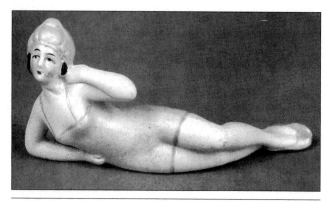

2¹/₂" Bathing Doll. *Courtesy of Helen Brooke.*

4" German Half Doll, beautifully detailed molding.

BATHING DOLLS

Bathing Dolls were made in both Germany and the United States. While All-Bisque Bathing Dolls are actually bisque figurines, they tend to be very popular with many doll collectors. Many of these beautiful little nymphs seem almost risqué.

Bathing Dolls range in size from a few inches to one foot. The 3 to 6 inch dolls are the most common. Bathing Dolls can be found sitting, reclining, or standing, and usually have very graceful arms and legs. Most have an Art Deco-style appearance. Facial features are usually painted, although a few examples have been found with a jointed head with tiny glass eyes. Bathing Dolls may be dressed in a bathing suit or draped in a toga. Some are delicately detailed nudes.

Bathing Dolls may be beautiful and graceful, or comical in appearance. An extremely lovely Bathing Doll could easily bring 2 or 3 times the price of the examples listed below. Look for chipped fingers and toes—a common fault of these delicate dolls.

Most Bathing Dolls are not marked. Rare examples may be found marked "Germany" or with a number.

BATHING DOLLS VALUE COMPARISONS:

Size	Fine, Delicate & Graceful	Standard Quality	Unusual Position 2 Dolls Molded as 1
3"	250.00	100.00	1,500.00
6"	450.00	150.00	
9"	600.00	200.00	1,900.00
12"	900.00		

Note: Add an additional $250.00 for glass eyes.

HALF DOLLS OR PIN CUSHION DOLLS

Half Dolls have been included in this edition because so many doll collectors are drawn to these All-Bisque and glazed-china ladies. The earliest examples were made in 1880, in Germany, by some of the most prestigious porcelain factories. Later examples were made in the United States. Extremely poor imitations were made in Japan.

Half Dolls are a classic example of the range of quality to be found in a single doll category. Even within the same factory, and using the same mold, one Half Doll can be exquisite while another is crudely executed. Craftsmanship varies from doll to doll. One may have an elaborate hair style, beautifully painted features, molded fancy clothing, and delicate hands extending gracefully from the body. Another may have splotchy paint, and heavy mitt-type hands molded to the body.

The most beautiful Half Dolls graced ladies' dressing tables at the turn-of-the-century. Half Dolls were used on pin cushions, powder boxes, music boxes, clothes brushes, jewelry boxes, and letter boxes. Some Half Dolls have a bottom half with legs only. Clever ladies of the time would attach the extending legs from the vessel.

Unmarked or marked with porcelain factory marked, "Germany," or "Japan."

HALF DOLLS VALUE COMPARISONS:

Size	Arms and Hands Attached	One arm Attached or Arms Extended, Hands Attached	Both Hands Extended	Detailed or Fancy Application
2"	25.00			
3"	35.00	175.00	400.00	
4"	55.00	200.00	425.00	600.00
5"	60.00	225.00	450.00	650.00
6"	65.00	275.00	500.00	700.00
8"	70.00	325.00	550.00	750.00
10"	75.00	400.00	650.00	850.00
12"	85.00	500.00	750.00	950.00

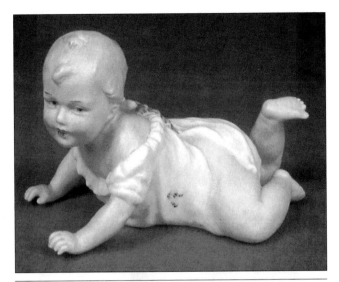

5" Heubach Piano Baby. *Courtesy of Helen Brooke.*

PIANO BABIES

What doll collector can resist the charm of these All-Bisque figurines? Unjointed babies in various positions, with deeply molded and painted hair; painted, often intaglio, eyes; character faces with painted, smiling, open-closed mouths; attired in molded and painted clothes. It is understandable that most Victorian homes had one—or better yet a pair—of Piano Babies resting on the piano scarf. Several of the better German porcelain factories such as Kestner, Limbach, Dressel, and Gebrüder Heubach produced superior quality Piano Babies around 1880. Do examine Piano Babies carefully as lesser-quality examples do exist.

Buyer Beware! Reproduction Piano Babies are everywhere! With some practice, reproductions are easy to spot. Authentic Piano Babies are often, but not always, marked with the name or symbol of the porcelain factory where they were made. Reproductions have no factory markings, but many have a red number painted on the bottom. However, red numbers alone are not a sure sign of a reproduction as some antique Piano Babies are also marked in this way. Many reproductions have a large hole (about the diameter of a pencil) in the bottom. Old Piano Babies may also have a hole, but it is usually much smaller. Subtle but distinct differences can also be found in flesh tone. Antique Piano Babies have a human flesh color, while the arms and legs of reproductions often exhibit a chalky pallor.

2" Snow Baby.

SNOW BABIES

Although Snow Babies were produced as early as the 1880s, they did not reach their peak of popularity until after the turn-of-the-century. This surge in popularity is due to the birth of Marie Ahnighito Peary, daughter of Admiral Peary. Marie was affectionately called a "Snow Baby" by the Eskimos with whom she lived. In 1901, Mrs. Peary wrote a book showing a picture of her daughter wearing a white snow suit and referred to her as a "Snow Baby." Suddenly these German-made figurines were in demand.

Snow Babies are usually small All-Bisque figurines, with no joints, covered with tiny bits of ground porcelain which resembles snow. Despite having originally been produced as simple Christmas novelties or party favors, Snow Baby faces have lifelike detail with excellent coloring.

Hertwig & Company of Thüringia, Germany, is believed to have made the first Snow Baby. Other German manufacturers soon followed suit. Groups were made, as were jointed figures.

As with the other All-Bisque Dolls, value is dependent upon detail and workmanship.

Reproductions of the German Snow Babies exist in two distinct forms. Japanese industry, the great imitators of the 1940s and 1950s, produced Snow Babies of inferior quality. These pieces were marked only with a paper label, which is usually removed. These Japanese Snow Babies are now collectible in their own right, but do not command the higher price of the fine German Snow Babies. Common sense and careful study will enable the buyer to recognize differences between German and Japanese examples. German manufacturers produced superior Snow Babies. The faces of German Snow Babies, and the variety of activities in which they are engaged, are extremely appealing.

Size	Excellent	Unusual	Standard
4"	400.00		175.00
7"	650.00	1,000.00	300.00
9"	750.00	1,200.00	325.00
11"	900.00	1,400.00	400.00
16"	1,400.00	1,900.00	

PIANO BABIES VALUE COMPARISONS:

A more recent reproduction has been imported for Department 56®. These fine quality Snow Babies are posed well and have a delightful look to them. They are easily identified by their name marked on the bottom. Ironically, unmarked copies have been made of these contemporary figurines, with no attempt being made to make them look old. A casual glance is sufficient to distinguish these Snow Babies from the earlier German examples.

SNOW BABIES VALUE COMPARISONS:

Size	Japanese	German, Standing, Lying, or Sitting on a Sled	German, Shoulder Head Cloth Body	German, Tumbling or on a Sled	German, with Animals	German, Snow Man, Santa, or Other
1½"	45.00	75.00		125.00	150.00	
2"	95.00	150.00		175.00	250.00	
3"	100.00	200.00		225.00	350.00	375.00
4"	110.00	225.00	200.00	250.00		
9"	150.00	300.00	275.00	350.00		500.00

Allied Imported

Child: one-piece vinyl body; painted side-glancing eyes; molded hair with top knot, appropriately with ribbon; typically marked "Allied Grand Doll Mfg. Inc., 1958" and "A."

Teen: all hard plastic, adult body, jointed at neck, shoulders, elbows, hips, knees, and ankles; ball rotation above elbows and at waist; vinyl head; rooted hair; sleep eyes; heavy make-up look; long lashes; typically marked "KT" and "Made by Allied Doll Co."

Bride: heavy vinyl body with high heel feet; rooted hair; sleep eyes, blue eye shadow; very red lips; pierced ears with pearl earrings; bridal gown with lace overlay; typically marked "AE."

29" teen doll. *Courtesy of Maribeth Herlocher.*

Allied Imported, circa 1950s, was an eastern company which manufactured mainly larger-sized vinyl and hard plastic high fashion dolls. These mass produced dolls were sold in bulk to smaller companies which in turn marketed them under several different names. These dolls are referred to as "knock-offs." Due to their affordability and impressive size, several of the dolls were extremely popular, particularly the bride doll.

ALLIED IMPORTED VALUE COMPARISONS:

Size	Child	Teen	Bride
10"	25.00		
15"	35.00	75.00	100.00
21"	50.00	100.00	125.00
24"		125.00	150.00
28"		150.00	175.00

Alt, Beck & Gottschalck

Alt, Beck & Gottschalck was located in Nauendorf, near Ohrdruf, Thüringia, Germany, from 1854 until 1930. Along with the traditional bisque child and character babies, A.B.G., as it is commonly known, is credited by most doll historians with producing a series of beautifully detailed glazed and unglazed shoulder heads. More than 50 mold numbers, all between 639 and 1288, have been identified. While it is assumed these fine quality dolls were made by A.B.G., there are other possible manufacturers, such as Kestner and Simon & Halbig. Notably, the #639 mold has a very "Kestner" look to it, as do several others. Many of these mold numbers correspond exactly to gaps in the sequence of known registered mold numbers of Simon & Halbig.

Reproductions are numerous, for there are molds available to today's doll maker for almost every doll credited to Alt, Beck & Gottschalck. The majority of these reproduction dolls are made for the pleasure or profit of a legitimate doll artist. However, an occasional fake A.B.G. Doll will surface. Check markings carefully. Lightly run your fingers over the cheek or shoulder of the doll. Old bisque will have a slightly rough feel. The new bisque of a reproduction will feel satiny smooth.

Prices listed are for dolls with no damage. Normal wear, slight damage, or well-made repairs to the body do not greatly affect price. Slight flakes from a delicate ruffle or petal of a flower would detract from the value in direct relation to the degree of damage. If the bisque is cracked or repaired, or if significant damage to the trim exists, expect to pay less than half the amount listed. It is perfectly acceptable to show a missing or repaired finger, or a patch to the body.

Bisque Shoulder Head: kid or cloth body; cloth, kid, or bisque limbs; some with wig, most with molded hair; some with bonnet, hat, scarf, or other molded ornamentation; most with painted eyes, occasionally glass eyes; many with pierced ears; most with closed mouth, several (usually those with ½ after the mold number) with open mouth; short neck with shoulder plate extending to the shoulders of body; few with socket head and separate shoulder plate (in these cases the mold number is found on both the rim of the head and the lower edge of the plate); appropriately dressed. Typically marked "639," "698," "772," "870," "882," "890," "894," "898," "911," "916," "974," "978," "980," "990," "996," "998," "1000," "1002," "1028," "1044," "1054," "1056," "1062," "1064," "1123," "1127," "1142," "1154," "1214," "1218," "1222," "1226," "1234," "1235," "1254," or "1288," followed by "XX" (the first X slightly higher than the second), or #, or No., followed by size number. May also be marked "Germany."

27" 1362 Sweet Nell.

China Shoulder Head: kid or cloth body; cloth, kid, or china limbs; molded black or blond hair; many with molded bonnet, scarf, or other headwear; most with painted eyes; but at least one china head (mold 1008) has been found with glass eyes; many with pierced ears; closed mouth, short neck; shoulder plate usually extends over tops of arms; appropriately dressed. Typically marked "784," "880," "882," "1000," "1008," "1028," "1030," "1046," "1056," "1112," "1142," "1210," or "1214," followed by "XX" (the first X slightly higher than the second), or # or No., followed by size number.

22" bisque
shoulder head.

CHILD DOLL AND CHARACTER BABY

Closed Mouth: bisque socket head; composition-and-wood ball-joint body; good wig; glass eyes usually sleep type; appropriately dressed. Typically marked "630," "911," "938," "989," and possibly others.

Open Mouth: bisque socket head; composition-and-wood ball-joint body; good wig; glass eyes usually sleep type; appropriately dressed. Typically marked "630," "1326," "1357," "1358," "1359," "1361," "1362," or "1367."

Baby: bisque socket head; five-piece bent-limb baby body; good wig; glass eyes; open mouth with teeth and tongue; appropriately dressed. Typically marked "1322," "1352," or "1361."

SHOULDER HEAD VALUE COMPARISONS:

Size	Molded Hair, Painted Eye, Closed Mouth	Molded Hair, Glass Eyes, Closed Mouth	Molded Elaborate Hair, Closed Mouth*	Molded Cap, Hat, Or Scarf, Closed Mouth*	Wearing Wig, Glass Eyes, Closed Mouth	1/2 Mold Number, Open Mouth	China Shoulder Head**
12"	375.00	550.00	900.00	750.00	700.00	500.00	350.00
14"	400.00	600.00	1,000.00	800.00	800.00	550.00	375.00
16"	500.00	700.00	1,200.00	900.00	900.00	600.00	425.00
18"	550.00	800.00	1,400.00	1,100.00	1,000.00	700.00	500.00
22"	600.00	1,100.00	1,500.00	1,300.00	1,200.00	800.00	600.00
24"	750.00	1,300.00	1,700.00	1,500.00	1,500.00	1,000.00	650.00
27"	900.00	1,500.00	1,900.00	1,700.00	1,700.00	1,200.00	700.00
29"	1,000.00	1,700.00	2,400.00	2,000.00	2,000.00	1,500.00	750.00

* Add an additional $100.00 for pierced ears
** Add an additional $300.00 for glass eyes

CHILD AND CHARACTER BABIES VALUE COMPARISONS:

Size	Closed Mouth 911/630/1322	Closed Mouth 938	Closed Mouth 989	Open Mouth, Typical Dolly-face (1361, 1362, 1367)	Open Mouth, Unique Face (630, 1357, 1358, 1359)	Character Baby (1322, 1352, 1361)*
10"						500.00
12"	2,000.00	3,000.00				550.00
14"	2,200.00	3,200.00		500.00	1,200.00	600.00
16"	2,500.00	3,500.00	3,800.00		1,500.00	
18"	2,800.00	3,800.00	4,000.00	600.00	1,800.00	700.00
20"	3,000.00	4,000.00	4,200.00	700.00	2,000.00	800.00
22"	3,200.00	4,200.00	4,500.00			1,000.00
24"	3,500.00	4,500.00	5,000.00	900.00		1,200.00
26"	4,000.00	5,000.00				
30"				1,300.00		1,700.00
36"				2,500.00		

* Add an additional $100.00 for flirty eyes, and $300.00 for toddler body

Louis Amberg & Son

Louis Amberg & Son was located in Cincinnati, Ohio, in 1878, and in New York City from 1893 until 1930. Louis Amberg was an importer and later a manufacturer of both bisque and composition dolls. In 1907, Louis' son, Joshua, joined the firm and it became Louis Amberg & Son. In 1909, Louis Amberg was listed as the artist and owner of "Lucky Bill," the first known American copyrighted doll head. By 1928, Louis Amberg advertised over six hundred style numbers available (including some imported from Germany and France). Louis Amberg & Son was sold to E.I. Horsman in 1930.

Molds for several different Amberg Dolls are still available. The intent is not to forge reproductions, but for the legitimate doll maker of today to make "reproduction" dolls for pleasure or profit. Although these dolls are usually dated and signed by the artist, bear in mind two things: First, the doll world has its share of unscrupulous individuals who are not above deliberately omitting the date and signature. Second, assume the responsibility of thoroughly inspecting each doll you may be interested in purchasing. Remember, if a deal sounds too good to be true, it probably is. Look carefully at the doll. Does it look seventy-five years old? Dolls made for and by Amberg were well-made, reasonably priced dolls. While the workmanship was good, the dolls were not intended to be works of art.

Prices listed are for dolls in good condition. Normal aging or slight body wear does not greatly affect value. Damaged or repaired dolls would be valued at less than half the amounts given.

18" bisque Baby Peggy. *Photo courtesy of McMasters Doll Auction.*

BISQUE

Baby Peggy: jointed, two body types: composition-and-wood or kid; happy or sad expression; head made by German manufacturer Armand Marseille; brown mohair wig with bobbed style; glass eyes with real lashes; closed mouth with smiling or serious expression; appropriately dressed. Marked "19 c 24/LA & S/Germany/-50-/ (style number)." A socket head on a jointed body with a smile would be marked "973." A socket head on a jointed body with a sad expression would be marked "972." A shoulder head on a kid body with a smile would be marked "983." A shoulder head on a kid body with a sad expression would be marked "982." These 1924 character dolls are somewhat hard to find, but well worth the search for the lucky collector who locates one.

Fulper: socket head, jointed composition-and-wood body; good wig; glass sleep eyes with thick upper and lower eyelashes; open mouth with two upper teeth showing; appropriately dressed. Marked "Amberg Dolls the World Standard Fulper Made in USA." The quality of the Fulper dolls is far below that of their German counterparts. The bisque is often grainy and the painting splotchy, with thick and heavy facial features.

Newborn Baby: designed by Jeno Juszko for Amberg to represent a two day old infant; solid dome with flange neck on cloth body; lightly spray-painted hair; flat broad nose, sunken chin, full cheeks, small flat ears, and closed mouth; appropriately dressed. Made by at least three German factories, including Armand Marseille (one can see the resemblance to Dream Baby), Recknagel, and Herm Steiner. Typically marked "L.A.& S 1914/No.G45520."

Vanta Baby: German made character baby; flange neck on cloth body with bent composition limbs; lightly spray-painted hair; glass sleep eyes with real lashes; open mouth with two teeth; slight orangish flesh tone, originally dressed in Vanta Baby undergarments and with rattle, Baby's Record Book, and a gift card. Marked "Vanta Baby/LA & S 3/0 D.R.G.M. Germany."

COMPOSITION

Babies: all composition, bent-limb baby body; molded and painted hair; painted eyes; closed mouth; "Bisc Finish," appropriately dressed. Typically marked "L.A.S. c/414/1911." Amberg advertised its dolls as being superior to other dolls. Slogan included "American Dolls for Americans" and "The American Standard."

Baby Peggy: shoulder head, cloth body, composition limbs; most with molded and painted brown hair in bobbed style, occasionally with mohair wig; painted eyes; open/closed mouth with slight hint of teeth showing; appropriately dressed. Although this doll is named Baby Peggy, her appearance more closely resembles a child than a baby.

Charlie Chaplin: portrait head, cloth body, composition hands; dark molded and painted hair; painted eyes looking to side; closed mouth below molded and painted mustache; cloth label sewn inside jacket reads "Charlie Chaplin Doll/Worlds Greatest Comedian/Made Exclusively by Louis Amberg & Son N.Y./By Special Arrangement with Essanay Film Co."

Lucky Bill: composition, boy's character face, teddy bear-type body. This rare doll seldom surfaces. When it does, its desirability is due more to its historical significance than artistic value.

Mibs: shoulder head, cloth body, composition limbs, slightly bowed legs; molded and painted strawberry blond hair with wave falling down center of forehead; perplexed expression with detailed painted blue eyes looking down, thick lashes, slightly feathered brows; closed mouth; appropriately dressed. Some marked "L. A. & S. 1921/Germany." Many unmarked. Original school girl dress tag reads "Amber Dolls/Please Love Me/I'm Mibs." Wrist tags read "Amberg Dolls/Please Love Me/I'm Mibs" or "Please Love Me/I'm Mibs."

12" composition character baby.

Sis Hopkins: first made with shoulder head, later with socket head on composition shoulder plate; white cloth body with composition arms or pink sateen body with pink sateen arms; character face of laughing child; molded hair with pigtails or wig with two braids; painted eyes looking to side; open/closed mouth either grinning with top and bottom teeth showing, or molded with tongue sticking out; appropriately dressed. Marked "SIS HOPKINS."

Sunny Orange Blossom: shoulder head, cloth mama body, composition limbs; molded and painted bonnet resembling an orange with holes for ribbon to tie under chin; painted eyes; closed mouth; originally dressed in orange organdy dress with ribbon across front which reads "Sunny Orange Blossom" and molded and painted socks and shoes. Marked "L. A. & S./1924."

Vanta Baby: shoulder head, cloth body with crier, composition bent limbs; molded and painted hair; tin

Size	Baby Peggy Kid Body	Baby Peggy Composition Body	Fulper Doll	Newborn Baby	Vanta
8"				400.00	
10"				450.00	
12"				550.00	
14"			350.00	700.00	
17"				900.00	
18"	2,400.00	2,800.00			1,000.00
20"	2,600.00	3,000.00	400.00		1,200.00
22"	2,800.00	3,200.00			1,400.00
24"	3,200.00	3,500.00	450.00		1,500.00

AMBERG BISQUE DOLL VALUE COMPARISONS:

AMBERG COMPOSITION VALUE COMPARISONS:

Size	Baby	Baby Peggy	Charlie Chaplin	Lucky Bill	Mibs	Sis Hopkins	Sunny Orange Blossom	Vanta Baby	Victory	Jointed Waist
8"										250.00
10"				700.00						
12"	250.00									
14"	300.00		600.00	400.00		500.00	350.00	350.00		550.00
16"					1200.00	600.00			300.00	
18"								375.00		
20"	400.00	850.00	800.00			900.00		400.00	275.00	
22"	500.00									
24"								450.00	450.00	
25"								600.00		

sleep eyes or painted eyes; open mouth with two teeth; dressed in Vanta baby undergarments. All dolls originally came with celluloid baby rattle, gift card, and a Dolly Record Book. Marked "Vanta Baby" or "Vanta Baby/Trade Mark Reg./An Amberg Doll."

Victory Doll: socket head, ball-jointed wood-and-composition body; good wig; glass sleep eyes; open mouth with teeth showing; appropriately dressed. Marked "Amberg Victory Doll." Very similar in appearance to German dolly-face dolls.

Waist Jointed: all composition, one-piece upper body and head on separate lower body, straight arms and legs, extra joint at waist. This extra joint was a popular feature with many Amberg dolls such as Tiny Tots, Edwine, IT, Sue, and Peter Pan. The waist joint was constructed with a rounded ball in the lower half of the body and a socket in the upper waist, thus allowing the doll to be posed in various positions.

FELT

Louis Amberg responded to the public's desire for Lenci-style dolls, producing various sizes and at least fourteen different styles. The dolls were jointed at the neck, shoulders, and hips. They had washable faces and were nicely dressed with bonnets or hats and single-strap shoes. When Horsman bought Louis Amberg & Son in 1930, the Amfelt doll was the only doll excluded from the sale. Instead, it was purchased by Paul Cohen Co. with the trade name "Art Felt Dolls."

AMFELT VALUE COMPARISONS:

Size	
16"	500.00
18"	700.00
24"	800.00

American Character

The American Character Doll Company was located in New York City from 1919 until 1968. All American Character Dolls are collectible, not only because the company no longer exists, but because each and every doll was well designed and produced.

American Character was also known as The American Doll and Toy Corporation. Early in the company's history sixteen styles of composition dolls were made with the trade name Aceedeecee (A C D C for American Character Doll Co.).

The first dolls marketed by American Character were composition bent-limb babies with cloth bodies. By 1923 the trade name Petite was adopted for these Mama dolls. Due to the company's success, a larger factory was needed and in 1926 the American Character Doll Company moved to Brooklyn. In 1928, it received exclusive permission from Campbell Soups to make Campbell Kids.

When considering an American Character Doll, look for originality in addition to condition. Although these dolls were extremely well made, they were toys, and led a perilous life. Also, smaller size Betsy McCall Dolls were very susceptible to splitting at the knees.

COMPOSITION

Campbell Kids: all composition, character face; slightly bent arms, straight legs slightly pigeon-toed; short molded and painted hair; painted round side-glancing eyes; pug nose; smiling closed mouth; full cheeks; originally dressed in outfits resembling those in Campbell Soup advertisements. A similar doll named Puggy was the man of the Campbell Kid family. He had a frowning face, shorter hair, and smaller eyes. Marked "A/Petite/Doll." Campbell Kids are similar to the Dolly Dingle design copyrighted by Grace G. Drayton for the Averill Manufacturing Company

Character Babies: Petite Babies, and Mama Dolls; composition head, cloth body, bent limbs; molded and painted hair or wearing wig; sleep eyes; open or closed mouth; appropriately dressed. Typically marked "Petite American Character;" "Amer. Char. Doll Co.;" "AC;" or "Wonder Baby."

Tots: composition shoulder head or socket head with composition shoulder plate, cloth or composition body, arms slightly bent (straighter than Babies), thinner legs, good wig; tin sleep eyes (a few have been found with glassine eyes); real lashes; mouths are open or open/closed with teeth; many with dimples; appropriately dressed. Typically marked "Petite Am. Char."

Child: composition socket head, shoulder plate, and limbs, cloth body; molded and painted bobbed hair; painted eyes or good wig and glassene sleep eyes; appropriately dressed. Typically marked "Amer. Char.," "Petite Sally;" or "Sally" below a horseshoe with an embossed doll standing in center. American Character's response to the public's demand for the Patsy doll in 1930.

VINYL AND HARD PLASTICS

American Character vinyl and hard plastics dolls are as varied as their composition predecessors. The babies that dominated the 1930s and 1940s were slowly being replaced by lady dolls. However, as long as little girls enjoy playing mommy, there will be character babies. The doll industry experienced another wave of interest for character babies during the 1950s. American Character was there to meet the demand.

Betsy McCall: hard plastic, vinyl, or combination of both; socket head; rooted hair; sleep eyes with lashes; closed mouth, slightly smiling expression; appropriately dressed. Typically marked "McCall Corp" in a circle, "McCall 1958," or unmarked. Betsy had a 39" brother with molded hair. Production began in 1957. Betsy McCall was first produced by Ideal in 1952. The 7½" is a favorite with doll collectors everywhere. Over time Betsy grew not only in fame, but in size. The tallest Betsy was introduced in 1959 with an impressive height of 36".

20" composition Mama Baby.

American Character lived up to its name when in 1955 they began production of some truly wonderful characters. A sampling of these dolls are listed below. Consider size and condition when purchasing a doll.

Ben Cartwright: solid vinyl, fully jointed; molded hair; painted features; molded clothes. Marked "C/American Character."

Cricket: plastic, vinyl teenage body, bendable limbs; hair grows when stomach button is pushed, shortens when metal key is inserted and turned in back; painted eyes; closed mouth. Marked "American Character."

Freckles: small two-faced girl changes expression when left arm is moved up (happy) and down (sad); rooted hair; painted eyes; mouth either open/closed smiling or closed sad expression; freckles painted across nose. Marked "Amer. Char. Inc./1966."

AMERICAN CHARACTER COMPOSITION VALUE COMPARISONS:					
Size	Campbell Kid	Puggy	Character Babies, Petite Baby, Mama	Tots	Child
12"	400.00	650.00			
14"			250.00		300.00
16"			275.00	300.00	350.00
18"			300.00		
20"			325.00	325.00	425.00
22"			350.00		
24"			425.00	350.00	500.00
28"			550.00		

AMERICAN CHARACTER VINYL AND HARD PLASTICS VALUE COMPARISONS:

Size	Betsy McCall/ Sandy	Ben Cartwright	Cricket	Freckles	Eloise	Hedda Get Betta	Whimsies	Ricky Jr.	Sweet Sue/ Toni	Tiny Tears	Toodles
7½"	225.00	75.00									
8"										100.00	
10"			65.00								
10½"									250.00		
13"										175.00	
14"	300.00		95.00	45.00				75.00	300.00		200.00
16"					300.00			150.00			
17"										250.00	
18"									350.00		
20"	400.00			75.00				250.00	375.00		
21"											225.00
22"	450.00			75.00	500.00	175.00	200.00		400.00	350.00	
23"											250.00
24"									450.00		
25"											300.00
30"	500.00										350.00
31"									550.00		
36"	650.00										
39"	800.00										

Eloise: all cloth; yellow yarn hair; painted almond-shaped eyes; darling character molded face; tiny nose; closed smiling mouth; appropriately dressed.

Hedda Get Betta: all vinyl; hard plastic bonnet; three-sided vinyl head; knob on top of bonnet rotates molded faces (one awake and smiling, one asleep with half a grin, other sick); appropriately dressed. Marked "American Doll and Toy Corp. 1961" on head and "Whimsie/Amer. Doll and Toy Corp. 1960" on back. Hedda Get Betta is one of the few dolls issued with two dates.

Whimsies: one-piece vinyl body; face with elf-like quality; rooted blond curly hair with braids; very large eyes; full smiling closed mouth; appropriately dressed. Marked "Whimsies/1960/American Doll & Toy."

Little Ricky Jr.: vinyl socket head, one-piece stuffed vinyl body; molded and painted hair; blue plastic sleep eyes; open nurser mouth; appropriately dressed. Marked "Amer. Char. Doll." The introduction of the Little Ricky Jr. doll, inspired by the "I Love Lucy Show," was as eagerly anticipated in 1956 as Ricky Jr.'s birth.

Sweet Sue and Toni: hard plastic socket head on plastic and vinyl or all hard plastic body; arms slightly bent, well manicured hands, occassionally with painted nails; jointed shoulders and hips, various combination of jointed elbows, waist, knees, and ankles; wig or rooted hair; sleep eyes with real lashes; closed mouth; Toni version with high heel feet and pierced ears. Also made as a walker, Sweet Sue's head turned when her legs walked. Sweet Sue and Toni costumes are some of the loveliest ever made — gowns of chiffon, silk, or satin trimmed with lace, ruffle, and/or rhinestones. Typically marked "Amer. Char. Doll," "American Character Doll," "Amer Char," "A.C.," or unmarked. Introduced in 1953, Sweet Sue and Toni were popular bride dolls. They were usually owned by older girls and/or used as bed dolls. Because of this, they are often found in excellent condition. A boy version, called "Groom," had a lamb's wool wig and was dressed in a tuxedo. Add an additional $100.00 to the prices listed for a Bride or Groom Doll.

Tiny Tears: all vinyl body jointed at neck, shoulders, and hips; rooted or molded and painted hair; sleep eyes with lashes; nicely molded fingers and toes; open nurser mouth; tiny holes at corners of eyes for tear ducts; appropriately dressed. Typically marked "American Character Doll/Pat." Tiny Tears was a special baby and many a little girl's favorite. She cried real tears, drank from a bottle, and wet her diaper. She was also equipped with her own tub and monogrammed towel for bathing, a high chair, and stroller

Toodles: chubby bent-limb baby body, many with "rolling joint" at elbows and knees; rooted or molded hair; sleep eyes; open nurser mouth, older toddler version with molded teeth and open smiling mouth; appropriately dressed. Typically marked "AM," "Amer-9," "American Char.," or unmarked. Some rare early dolls marked "Toodles." Mark is sometimes obscured by the holes on rooted hair dolls. A 1953 advertisement states that the popular baby "...Toodles can kneel, sit, play with her toes and fingers, and assume 1000 different positions."

Max Oscar Arnold

11", MOA 200/Welsch child doll. *Courtesy of Helen Brooke.*

This company was located in Neustadt, Germany, from 1878 to 1930. Although Max Oscar Arnold made and distributed all types of dolls, the company is most noted for its patented mechanical dolls. These mechanical dolls included walking dolls, talking dolls, and even a bathing doll. The first mechanical doll patented by Arnold in 1904 moved on wheels, said "Mama" and "Papa," turned its head from side to side, and swung its arms forward and backwards.

Soon Arnold became interested in phonograph dolls. These dolls had bodies that separated above the hips so that a phonograph could be put inside. A metal front amplified the sound.

Arnold obtained many patents for talking dolls. "Arnoldia" was the trade name for a 1906 doll which talked and sang. Patented in both Germany and France, Arnoldia could count, do arithmetic, pray, and talk and sing in three languages—English, German, and French. Advertising boasted that children could learn their lessons and foreign languages with only Arnoldia as teacher. Fifty-one English records, twenty-eight German, and twenty French were available. Strange titles of some of these records include The Dead Doll, Dolly's Funeral, Mr. Nobody, Bald-headed Billy, My One Legged Doll, The Groo Groo Man, The Gobles 'uns and The Little Girl, Seein' Things at Night, A Terrible Tale, and There's Another Picture In My Mama's Frame. If nothing else, Arnoldia was certainly a morbid doll.

When considering an M.O. Arnold Doll, check condition carefully. The prices listed are for dolls with no damage to the bisque. Normal wear, slight damage or well-done repairs to the body do not greatly affect the value. If the bisque is damaged or repaired, expect to pay less than half the amounts listed. It is perfectly acceptable to show a missing or repaired finger, joint, or patched kid.

Dolly-Face: bisque socket head, jointed composition-and-wood body or shoulder head on kid body; good wig; glass eyes, painted lashes, feathered brows; open mouth with upper teeth; appropriately dressed. Typically marked "MOA" within star; helmeted man inscribing block with "MOA;" or "MOA" with sunburst and eagle.

Arnoldia: bisque socket head, jointed composition-and-wood body, phonograph in body; mohair wig; sleep eyes, painted upper and lower lashes, feathered brows; open mouth with upper teeth; appropriately dressed. Typically marked "Arnoldia 54/14." Arnoldia stood an impressive 30" high and came elaborately dressed with matching socks, shoes, and hat. Later examples of this doll can be found in composition.

	MAX OSCAR ARNOLD VALUE COMPARISONS:		
Size	Bisque Socket Head, Composition Body, Open Mouth	Shoulder Head, Kid Body, Open Mouth	Arnoldia Phonograph Doll
15"	475.00	400.00	
17"	500.00		
18"	525.00	425.00	
22"	600.00	475.00	
24"	675.00	500.00	
28"	850.00	525.00	
30"	950.00		3,200.00

Arranbee Doll Company

The Arranbee Doll Company was founded in New York in 1922 and operated until 1959. In its early years the company imported dolls, doll heads, doll parts, and doll hospital supplies. Arranbee originally assembled imported doll parts but later manufactured its own doll heads. Miss Ruby Hopf, Georgene Averill's sister, was Arranbee's principal designer. As with so many of the earlier American doll companies, Arranbee was absorbed by another larger company. Vogue bought out Arranbee in 1959 but continued to use the "R & B" marking until early in 1961. Arranbee Dolls are highly collectible, mainly due to the dolls' high quality.

BISQUE

My Dream Baby: flange neck on cloth body or socket head on composition bent-limb baby body, solid dome head; lightly spray-painted hair; small glass sleep eyes; open mouth (mold 351) or closed mouth (mold 341); appropriately dressed. Made by German manufacturer Armand Marseille. Typically marked "AM Germany/341/3/1/2K; Germany/Arranbee" or "AM 351/4 Germany Arranbee." Socket heads typically marked with "K" in addition to mold and size numbers.

Child Doll: typically marked "Simon & Halbig/Arranbee./Patent/Germany."

Although child dolls are harder to find than the My Dream Babies, you will occasionally find a lovely German bisque child doll made for and imported by Arrranbee. Quality is important, as is the company of manufacture. The quality of each doll head produced by a particular company will be similar. For instance, a bisque socket head made by Simon and Halbig, whether imported for Arranbee or used on a Simon and Halbig Doll, will have a comparable value. Refer to the manufacturing company for further information.

Look for nicely dressed and decorated dolls with good color and in good condition. Prices given are for dolls with no damage. Normal wear, slight damage, or well-done repairs to the body do not greatly affect value. When the bisque is damaged or repaired, expect to pay less than half the amount listed.

19" composition Little Angel. *Courtesy of Marilyn Merry.*

	My Dream Baby Comparisons:				
Size	Mold 351, Open Mouth, Cloth Body	Mold 341-K, Open Mouth, Composition Body	Mold 341, Closed Mouth, Cloth Book Body	Mold 351-K, Closed Mouth, Composition Body	Child, Composition Body
9"	275.00	325.00	350.00	375.00	
12"	400.00	450.00	475.00	500.00	
15"	600.00	675.00	700.00	775.00	
18"	700.00	775.00	800.00	875.00	800.00
20"	800.00	875.00	900.00	1,000.00	850.00
24"	900.00	975.00	1,000.00	1,200.00	1,000.00

Size	Nursery Rhyme	Mama Dolls	Child Dolls	Kewty	Littlest Angel	Nanette Family
7"		175.00				
9"	250.00					
10"	200.00				100.00	
12"			250.00			
14"		250.00	300.00	275.00		300.00
16"		300.00		350.00		
17"			350.00			350.00
18"		350.00				
21"		375.00	450.00			400.00
23"						450.00

ARANBEE COMPOSITION AND HARD PLASTIC DOLLS VALUE COMPARISONS:

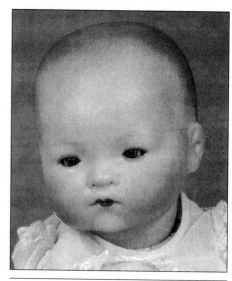

15" bisque Dream Baby.

COMPOSITION

Composition Arranbee Dolls are generally quite lovely and were so well made that they have survived in better condition than other dolls from the same period. In order to avoid confusion, collectors should be aware that many Arranbee composition dolls were purchased from Ideal.

CHARACTER DOLLS

Nursery Rhyme: all composition, jointed neck, shoulders and hips; molded and painted hair; painted eyes; closed mouth; dressed in costume of character it represents. Marked "R & B Doll Co." or "R & B." Nursery Rhyme Dolls were very popular during the 1930s. The doll's character and nursery rhyme is printed on its elaborate suitcase-style box.

Mama or Character Baby: socket head or shoulder plate, cloth or composition body; molded and painted hair; painted or tin sleep eyes; closed or open mouth; appropriately dressed. Typically marked "R & B," "Arranbee," or "Little Angel R & B."

Child Dolls: styled as older child or teenager; all composition, jointed at neck, shoulders, and hips; molded and painted hair; painted eyes; and closed mouth (later dolls manufactured with wigs, sleep eyes with real lashes, and applied eye shadow); appropriately dressed. Typically marked "Nancy/Arranbee/Dolls," "R & B," or "Debuteen." Examples of child dolls include Nancy, Nancy Lee, Debu-Teen, Girls From The Southern Series, Nancy Jean, and Princess Betty Rose. All these lovely young ladies have beautiful faces and are made from the highest quality composition.

Kewty: all composition, jointed at neck, shoulders and hips; molded hair with deep side part and hair swirled across forehead; sleep eyes; open or open/closed mouth; appropriately dressed. Marked "Kewty." Due to similarities in hair style to the Nancy Doll, it is generally accepted that Kewty is an Arranbee product. However, some believe Kewty is actually a carnival doll produced by the small Pennsylvania factory of Domec.

HARD PLASTIC

Arranbee's most popular all hard plastic dolls are Nanette and Nancy Lee, cousins to the composition Nancy Lee and Debu-Teen. Production of hard plastic dolls began in the 1940s. Although similar to composition in appearance, the thinner consistency of hard plastic allows a sharpness of detail that could not be achieved with composition. Also, hard plastic is not prone to crazing, as is composition. These are two reasons why hard plastic doll values have been increasing in recent years. The beauty and durability of hard plastic dolls make them very desirable to collectors.

Most Arranbee hard plastic dolls are marked "R & B," although some are marked with the mold number "210 Pat/Pen." or simply "Made in USA."

Littlest Angel: hard plastic body with chubby bent arms, short stocky legs with joints at hips and knees; synthetic wig; sleep eyes with molded (occasionally real) lashes; closed mouth; head moves from side to side when legs are made to walk; appropriately dressed.

Nanette and Nancy Lee: hard plastic, jointed neck, shoulders and hips, long thin legs; synthetic wig; sleep plastic eyes with lashes; molded (occasionally real) lashes; closed smiling mouth; appropriately dressed. Nanette and Nancy Lee are teenage-style dolls. They are also known as Angeline, Dream Bride, Taffy (wearing a caracul wig), Prom Queen, and Francine.

RUBBER

Arranbee made a few rubber-type dolls in the late 1940s. Collectors often refer to this type of doll as "Magic Skin," perhaps because it can vanish right before your eyes. When considering the purchase of a Magic Skin doll, remember that the rubber will get sticky and rot away. The process may be slowed by regularly rubbing corn starch on the doll. Eventually, however, age will triumph and the doll will deteriorate. A rubber doll is only a temporary addition to your collection.

VINYL

Arranbee began producing vinyl dolls around 1950. Babies, toddlers, children, and teens were made. Arranbee Dolls were made of heavy vinyl, with high quality clothing similar to that found on the earlier dolls. Wise collectors can purchase a vinyl doll at a reasonable price. Remember, well-made vinyl dolls are the collectible of tomorrow.

Little Dear: socket-head baby, stuffed vinyl body, bent chubby baby-type arms and legs; rooted synthetic hair; sleep eyes with molded lashes; open/closed mouth, marked "R & B."

Nancy Lee, socket head, older child, stuffed vinyl body, straight arms and legs; saran wig; sleep eyes, molded lashes, distinctive eyebrows shaped like an "S" on its side; closed mouth, appropriately dressed; marked "Arranbee."

Susan: socket head, older child, stuffed vinyl body, straight arms, toddler legs; synthetic wig; sleep eyes with molded lashes; closed mouth, molded lips slightly parted; appropriately dressed; marked "Arranbee."

Angel Baby: socket head, stuffed vinyl baby body; curly rooted synthetic hair; sleep eyes; open drink and wet mouth; socks, appropriately dressed; marked "R & B."

My Angel Walking Doll: socket head, hard polyethylene vinyl body; rooted straight hair; sleep eyes with molded lashes; smiling rosebud mouth; appropriately dressed. Marked "Arranbee."

ARRANBEE VINYL DOLL VALUE COMPARISONS:

Size	Little Dear	Nancy Lee	Susan	Angel Baby	My Angel
8"	25.00				
12"	35.00				
14"		250.00	75.00		
16"			100.00		
18"		300.00			
20"				60.00	200.00
24"				75.00	
36"					400.00

Arrow Novelty Company

The Arrow Novelty Company, founded in New York City in 1920, is best known for its Skookum Indian Dolls. Designed by Mary McAboy of Montana, the first doll heads were made of dried apples. Due to the short life of apples, the heads were later made of composition. Indian blankets were wrapped around wooden frames, leaving very little of the bodies to be seen. The dolls' costumes were made to represent various tribes, with sizes ranging from a few inches to several feet. Most are marked with a paper label on the foot which reads "Skookum Bully Good Indian."

Because Skookum Dolls were produced for the souvenir trade rather than as playthings, most Skookum Dolls are found in good condition. Look for nicely painted dolls with good color and no crazing.

Composition: composition head; wrapped legs.

Hard Plastic: hard plastic head; later production.

SKOOKUM INDIAN VALUE COMPARISONS:

Size	Composition	Hard Plastic
8"	75.00	35.00
18"	275.00	150.00
20"	300.00	
36"	600.00	

12" Skookum Indian Brave. *Courtesy of Bill Tyson.*

Artist Dolls

These contemporary dolls are individually handcrafted, designed and produced as objects of art. Artist Dolls therefore, should be viewed as works of art, not as toys of long ago which have survived the test of time. Material, workmanship, subject matter, and visual or decorative appeal are all factors that can make an Artist Doll a wise investment.

When purchasing an Artist Doll check condition carefully. This type of doll must be in mint condition in order to achieve the values shown. Because of the high investment potential and speculative nature of these dolls, few are purchased for children as play dolls. There is little forgiveness for dolls that are not in mint condition.

Adams, Christine: 18", Tiny Tots, 1981; handmade, painted oilcloth head, mohair wig, cloth body and limbs with stitched fingers; contemporarily dressed; paper label "Christine Adams Tiny Tots Handmade Dolls." . . .**150.00**

Blakely, Halle: 18", Court Lady, 1953; bisque shoulder plate, arms, and legs, beautifully molded hands, cloth body; painted long curls; expressive eyes; smiling closed mouth; earrings; beauty mark; elaborate gown with trim and beading decoration; feathers in hair. **1,500.00**

Brouse, Mary: 11", Hanna, 1989; bisque shoulder head and limbs, cloth body; nicely molded long blond hair with bangs; delicately painted blue eyes with highlights; closed mouth; layers and layers of well-made cotton undergarments, dress, and pinafore; marked "MKB" on back shoulder plate. **150.00**

Bruns, Nancy: 21", Rebecca, 1986; carved wood head, cloth body with wire armature; curly long wig; carved and painted eyes; painted freckles; open/closed mouth with upper and lower teeth; two-piece cotton jumper and blouse; bare feet with stitched toes; certificate marked "Burnswood Dolls 8/100." **500.00**

Burnell, Patricia: 16", Scotsman; clay composition shoulder head, hands, and legs, cloth body with wire armature; red fur wig and mustache; painted eyes; closed mouth; traditional Scottish dress of plaids and wool tam. **700.00**

Clear, Emma: 19", Martha and George Washington, 1940; bisque shoulder head and limbs, cloth body; molded and painted hair; insert glass eyes; closed mouth; Martha with molded cap, dressed in period clothing; marked "Clear," price for pair. **900.00**

Fisher, Ruth E.: 10", Grand-Daughter, 1939; bisque, one-piece head and body, jointed at shoulder and hips; black short wig; brown glass eyes; painted Oriental features; closed mouth; molded socks and shoes; sleeveless dress; marked "REF." **250.00**

Martha and George Washington by Emma Clear.
Courtesy of Billie Nelson Tyrrell.

Head, Maggie: 14", Caldonia, 1966; black bisque shoulder head, arms, and legs; very expressive older Black lady-type face; white wool wig; glass insert eyes; painted closed mouth; simple cotton dress; marked "Maggie Head-Caldonia 1966." **900.00**

Motter, Jennifer Berry: 18", Mable, 1987; all cloth, face treated to simulate old oilcloth, face has a three-dimensional look; painted and shaded hair shows curls and parts; beautifully painted eyes with great detail; closed mouth; stitched hands; dressed in several layers of vintage fabrics and hat; signed on torso "Jennifer Berry Motter" and date. **350.00**

Parker, Ann: (British), 8", Alice In Wonderland, 1982; sculptured resin, translucent look of finest porcelain; blond mohair wig; delicately painted eyes and closed mouth; classic Sir John Tenniel-style outfit; walnut stand; marked "Alice" on wrist tag, "English Costume Doll by Ann Parker." **300.00**

Redmond, Kathy: 16", Catherine de Medici; bisque shoulder head, hands, and legs; elaborate plate; molded short hair; gold fired porcelain collar and snood in hair; molded and painted eyes; closed mouth; dressed in court gown with beading and gold lamé. **700.00**

Sorensen, Lewis: 26", Mother Goose, 1972; wax socket head and hands; head covered with cap; human hair eyebrows; glass blue eyes; open/closed mouth with molded teeth; beautifully detailed character face; realistic hands molded to hold staff; marked with label inside skirt. **1,600.00**

Thompson, Martha: 20", Princess Margaret Rose, 1956; bisque shoulder head and arms, cloth body; molded and painted hair; painted eyes; closed mouth; pierced ears; molded necklace; print gown with velvet sash; marked "1956." **2,400.00**

Wallace, Shelia: Sir Walter Raleigh; wax shoulder head and hands, cloth body, composition legs; brown wig and beard (some hairs inserted into wax for realistic appearance, also on backs of hands); painted eyes; closed mouth; historically correct court costume with cape and hat; wearing rings; original stand. . . . **2,500.00**

Webster, Mary Hortence: assisted by Loredo Taft; 28", Flapper Doll, 1925; composition shoulder head, cloth body, long thin arms and legs; black wig with bangs; large nicely painted eyes; closed mouth; off-the-shoulder long gown; pearl necklace. **300.00**

Wick, Faith: 14", Bertha Bag Lady, 1983; porcelain shoulder head and hands, cloth body; gray mohair wig; painted eyes; closed frowning mouth; bag lady dress, coat, and hat; carrying three bags; marked "Faith Wick" and certificate. **400.00**

Wilson, Lita: 15", Liz Taylor, mid 1970s; bisque shoulder head, cloth body, bisque arms and legs, molded ring on left hand; black wig; beautifully detailed and painted blue and violet eyes; closed mouth; white dress with gold trim; gold band in hair; marked "Petite Portrait" on front, "Liz Taylor L.W." on back. **700.00**

Wright, John: 17", Farmer, 1959; pressed felt head and body, disc joints at shoulder and hips; mohair wig and beard; painted eyes; character face with molded and stitched mouth, applied ears; tan pants, plaid skirt, felt hat; holding pitch fork; high laced boots; unmarked. **1,700.00**

Zeller, Fawn: 15", Miami Miss, 1961; made from artist original kit, bisque shoulder head, arms, and legs, cloth body; molded and painted hair and features; dressed with underwear; marked "Fawn Zeller UFDC 1961" **300.00**

25" Mother Goose (wax) *by Lewis Sorensen.*

OTHER ARTISTS

Adair-Kertzman, Linda: magical little fairies. **400.00**

Aprile, Paulette: one-of-a-kind and limited edition. **3,000.00**

Bello, Yolanda: children. **1,700.00**

Brahms, Abigail: one-of-a-kind and limited edition. **5,000.00**

Cameron, Beth: Santas. **1,200.00**

Campbell, Astry: porcelains. **1,200.00**

Crees, Paul: wax ladies. **1,800.00**

Deval, Brigette: one-of-a-kind. **5,000.00**

Koerling, Cyndy: Native American babies. **600.00**

McClure, Cindy: limited edition child. **900.00**

Nelson, Bill: 18" to 21", molded character faces on wire armature, cloth bodies. **4,000.00**

Roche, Lynn and Michael: porcelains. **1,700.00**

Smith, Sherman: carved wood. **300.00**

Soniat, Mary: realistic people. **2,400.00**

Thompson, Pat: cultured glass medium. **2,500.00**

Trobe, Carol: feeling children. **1,500.00**

Wright, Phyllis: sweet child dolls with wigs and painted eyes. **400.00**

Automata

Automata are French, German or American-made mechanical dolls. Although references to automated dolls can be found dating as early as the mid-17th century, automata's peak popularity scanned the years from 1860 to 1900.

There are several types of Automata: Automatons; Animated platform dolls; Autoperipatetikos; Bellows-Type; Marottes; Pull Toys; Phonograph Dolls; and Walking/talking/kicking/kiss-throwing Dolls. The most popular and actively sought examples are the lavishly costumed French Automatons which perform elegant activities.

Keys to evaluating Automata are originality, clothing condition, and visual appeal of the doll's face, and the intricacy of its movement. Generally, value increases in direct relation to the doll's complexity. The more intricate the movements and the greater their number, the more valuable the doll. Working condition is extremely important. Animated repairs can be very costly, and sometimes impossible, to make.

Lady holding bird cage. *Courtesy of Helen Brooke.*

AUTOMATON

Automatons are charming, musical mechanical dolls. The music box consists of revolving cylinder with a series of small pins which strike a metal comb. The music box and/or clockwork mechanism is hidden in a velvet-covered platform base. When wound, the music plays and the doll performs a series of movements. Most Automatons were intended for the entertainment of adults rather than children. Well-known manufacturers of Automatons include Rousselot, Phalibois, Vichy, Fleischmann and Blodel, Lambert, Roullet, and Decamps. Marks may be found on keys or on the insides of the housings. Doll heads were supplied by various doll manufacturers and will be marked accordingly.

Black Banjo Player: 12", bisque head and arms, composition body; brown eyes; human hair wig; open mouth; velvet covered music box; hands move as if playing the banjo, head moves from side to side **4,800.00**

Lady with Bird: 17", bisque head, wire frame body in sitting position, composition hands and feet; human hair wig; blue paperweight eyes; open mouth; silk dress; wooden music box with drawer which operates mechanism; lady holds bird cage in her hand, when music plays the bird spins while doll's head moves from side to side, other hand shakes a finger at a composition cat sitting at her feet **4,600.00**

Lady at her Toilette: 21", bisque head, composition body, bisque hands; human hair wig; glass eyes; open mouth; satin dressing coat; sitting at dressing table with mirror and several covered boxes, lady holds powder puff in hand, when music plays doll powders her face **4,200.00**

Clown Mandolin Player: 23", papier-mâché head, wire frame body, detailed papier-mâché hands and feet; molded and painted clown facial features; multicolored mohair wig; open mouth with tongue; wearing paisley outfit adorned with sequins and lace; sitting on stool, holding painted wooden mandolin with metal strings; music plays; clown's head moves from side to side, tongue moves in and out; left leg crosses over right, foot taps, one hand plucks strings, other hand moves up and down on the mandolin **7,000.00**

ANIMATED PLATFORM DOLLS

Animated Platform Dolls often originate in Germany and greatly resemble Automatons. The spring clockwork mechanism on an automata is replaced with a crank movement, causing the figure to move only while the crank is turning. Animated Platform Dolls are less costly than Automatons, with visual appeal accounting for more of their value than complexity (or the lack thereof) of their stiff and awkward movements.

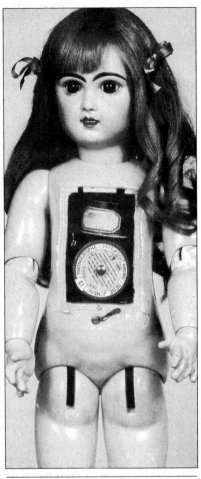

Lady with a Dancing Doll.

Clown Cymbal Player.

Phonographe Jumeau. *Photo courtesy of McMasters Doll Auction.*

Lady Playing Piano: 12", bisque head, wire frame body; papier-mâché hands; human hair wig; blown glass eyes; open mouth; sitting at wooden piano, wearing satin dress, lady's hands move over piano keys **2,500.00**

Dancing Couple: 15", two bisque headed dolls, composition bodies; painted shoes; mohair wigs in fancy court style; painted eyes; closed mouth; wearing satin formal dress; dancing **2,700.00**

AUTOPERIPATETIKOS

Autoperipatetikos were made in France, Germany, and America. They were made to represent children, ladies, and occasionally gentlemen complete with mustache and goatee. The head and arms were attached to a walking body by means of a clockwork mechanism which caused the feet, usually made of pressed metal, to move back and forth. Most autoperipatetikos are about 10" high and marked "Patented July 15th 1862 also in England."

Lady: 10", pressed cloth head, cardboard body, leather arms; painted features; molded and painted hair **1,300.00**

Lady: 10", china head, cardboard body, china arms; painted features; molded and painted hair . . . **1,900.00**

BELLOWS-TYPES/CYMBALERS

Bellows-type dolls: also known as cymbalers, contain pressure/bellow mechanisms housed in their bodies. When the body is compressed the arms come together. Heads are most often bisque and usually resemble a baby or a clown.

Pat-a-Cake Doll: 10", bisque head, composition bent-limb baby body; wooden mitt-type hands; painted eyes; closed mouth; hands clap when tummy is pressed. Head marked "Heubach." **600.00**

Cymbaler Clown: 12", bisque head, wire frame body; wooden mitt-type hands holding tin cymbals; molded and painted clown features; molded cap; cymbals clash when tummy is pressed. Head marked "11/9." . . . **600.00**

MAROTTES

Marottes from France and Germany fall somewhere between a doll and an Automata. By definition, a Marotte is a doll's head on a stick. Most Marottes are lavishly dressed bisque dolls which sit atop music boxes housed in drums perched atop sticks. When the stick is waved, the musical movement is activated, creating a beautiful effect. Marottes are also made of papier-mâché molded and painted to represent a variety of characters from clowns to animals.

Bisque Head, 12", mohair wig in tight curls; blue paperweight eyes; open mouth with teeth; wearing peach satin costume with lace overlay; matching cap; ivory handle allows music box to be swung around. Marked "3200." **900.00**

Papier-mâché Clown, 12", molded and painted features and hair; wearing fringed costume with tiny bells hanging from ribbons attached to neck; wooden handle allows music box to be swung around. **500.00**

PULL TOYS

Pull Toys are usually German in origin. These entertaining toys have several small bisque dolls mounted on a wheeled wooden platform. The dolls may be stationary or simple movements may be incorporated into the toy's design. Condition of the dolls and the toy's overall appeal are important factors in determining a pull toy's value.

Reproduction Pull Toys do exist. Markings on the dolls can help in determining authenticity, although some antique Pull Toys have no markings. The wooden platforms of reproductions are much smoother with a more finished look. The wheels are poured and molded cast-cold metal. Also, reproductions tend to be made on a larger scale. Most older Pull Toys are more petite, usually less than 12" long.

Band: 9", five dolls with bisque heads, composition hands, mohair wigs; glass eyes; and open mouths. Four dolls are in seats holding small wooden musical instruments, conductor doll standing and holding a baton while leading the band; conductor's hand moves up and down when toy is pulled **1,500.00**

Lady with Child: 12", lady with bisque head, composition body; mohair wig; glass eyes; and open mouth. Five inch child with mohair wig; painted eyes; and closed mouth **900.00**

PHONOGRAPH DOLLS

In 1887 Thomas A. Edison invented and patented a "phonographic" doll. The first Phonograph Doll bore little resemblance to his later and better-known dolls. The first dolls had arms and head attached to tube-shaped bodies. This crude ancestor opened the door for the more sophisticated Phonograph Dolls which followed. Finding an antique Phonograph Doll is truly a rare treat. Be sure that the mechanical parts are in working condition and that the doll itself is not damaged.

Edison Phonograph Doll: metal torso containing talking mechanism, wooden jointed arms and, legs bisque head made in Germany. Records from the Edison Phonographic Toy Company indicate that there were two manufacturers of bisque heads for these dolls, although the only known examples are from Simon and Halbig.

Bébé Phonographe by Jumeau: ball-jointed composition body; beautiful paperweight eyes; open mouth with molded teeth. The cylinders were made of white wax and were made to talk and sing in French, English, and Spanish.

Max Oscar Arnold: jointed composition body. The body separated above the hips with a phonograph placed inside. The bodies were later improved with a metal front for the speaker.

Primadonna made by Giebeler-Falk: aluminum head and body; human hair wig. The crown of the head was hinged and lifted forward. The horn and turntable were in the head and the mechanism was in the body. The doll would sing or talk when a record was placed in the head.

Dolly Record by Madame Hendren/Averill: composition head; metal eyes; phonograph housed in cloth body. At about this time the Mae Starr Phonograph Doll appeared on the market and Effanbee began putting phonographic devices in some of its larger Lovem dolls.

Charmin Chatty by Mattel: later Phonograph Doll familiar to most doll collectors. Finding one in working condition is becoming difficult. Phonograph Dolls did not live up to the expectations of the doll manufacturers.

WALKING AND TALKING DOLLS

Walking and Talking Dolls are often found with chain mechanisms. Others have wire arrangements connecting the arms and feet, a technique first used by Schoenhut wooden dolls. The talking device in early Talking Dolls consists of a bellows in the body which was activated by pulling strings, exerting pressure, or moving some part of the body. After the body was cut in two the bellows were placed inside and then the body was put together again with strips of kid. Different sounds could be produced with different tubes and objects placed in the bellows. The reeds-and-bellows type mechanism made Mama dolls of the 1920s very popular. Regardless of the type of talking device used, a simple "Mama" or "Papa" was all that was achieved.

Girl Pulling Cart: 14", bisque head, composition body; mohair wig; glass eyes; open mouth; key wound walks. Original mechanism pulls cart; pull-strings produce mama sound **2,200.00**

PHONOGRAPH DOLLS VALUE COMPARISONS:							
Size	Edison	Juneau	M.O. Arnold	Primadonna	Dolly Record	Mae Starr	Charmin Chatty
25"	3,700.00	14,000.00	3,000.00	1,900.00	750.00	750.00	200.00

Walking, Kiss Throwing, Talking, Flirting Doll: 22", bisque head, composition body, pin joints at hips, human hair wig; slight movement causes glass flirty eyes to move from side to side, real lashes; pierced ears; head turns and doll throws kiss when walking; pull-string at side controls mama/papa talking box **2,200.00**

Walking Doll: 24", celluloid head, metal body, metal legs, celluloid arms; molded and painted hair; painted eyes, closed mouth; key-wind spring on side causes doll to walk **250.00**

WALKING, KICKING, CRYING, AND TALKING DOLLS

First patented in September 1855 by Jules Steiner, Walking, Kicking, Crying, and Talking Dolls were modified several times over the following twenty years. The key-wind body houses the flywheel regulator and clockwork mechanisms. Most of these mechanical Steiner Dolls have no visible markings, although a few have been reported marked "1," "2," or "3." Look for a doll in good working order with undamaged bisque. The bodies will undoubtedly show wear. Normal wear is to be expected and does not affect value.

Bébé: 20", bisque head, composition torso, one-piece arms and lower legs, jointed together with leather strips; mohair wig; small paperweight eyes; open mouth with upper and lower teeth; pierced ears; doll moves head, cries, and kicks legs when wound **3,400.00**

SWIMMING DOLL

Another type of Automata is the Swimming Doll, also known as Ondine. These hard-to-find dolls were once advertised as "Parisian Mechanician for Adult Amusement." They were made with either a bisque or celluloid head and had a cork body with jointed wooden arms and legs which simulated swimming when wound by a key. Despite the rarity of these dolls, they do not command as high a price as the previous types, possibly due the difficulty in displaying them.

Swimming Doll: 12", bisque head, cork body, wooden arms and legs; mohair wig; glass eyes; open mouth; pierced ears; when doll is wound its arms and legs move in a swimming motion **1,900.00**

Averill Manufacturing Company

verill Manufacturing Company was located in New York, NY, from 1913 until 1965 when operations ceased and assets were liquidated. The company was headed by the husband and wife team of Georgene and James Paul Averill. Georgene's brother, Rudolph A. Hopf, served as president. The variety of dolls produced by Averill Manufacturing Company was vast and bridged the gap from bisque to vinyl.

Georgene and James Paul Averill branched out in 1923 and formed the Madame Georgene Inc. Doll Company, with James Paul as president. They later went on to form Georgene Novelties, Inc.

In addition to promoting her own line of dolls, Georgene Averill also did design work for Borgfeldt, her most popular doll being the Bonnie Baby, and served as Superintendent of Borgfeldt's Toy Department.

Another area of confusion to new doll collectors concerns the Madame Hendren line of dolls. Madame Hendren is a trademark used by Averill Manufacturing Company.

See also All-Bisque, Automaton, and Raggedy Ann & Andy.

15" Bisque Bonnie Baby. *Photo courtesy of McMasters Doll Auction.*

COMPOSITION

Mama Doll: composition head, cloth body, composition limbs; painted tin sleep eyes; closed or open/closed mouth with molded and painted teeth; molded and painted hair or good wig; appropriately dressed. Typically marked "Genuine Madame Hendren Doll 1717 Made in USA."

Bobby and Dolly Dolls: composition head and limbs, cloth body; molded and painted hair, round painted side-glancing eyes; round pug nose; closed smiling single-line painted mouth; appropriately dressed. Typically marked "G. G. Drayton." Neither the Averill nor Hendren names appear on this doll.

Whistling Dolls (Cowboy, Dutch Boy, Indian, Nell, Sailor, Dan, Dolly Dingle, and Rufus): composition head, cloth body; molded and painted hair with rows of curls in back; painted side-glancing eyes; puckered mouth with hole for whistling; cloth covered spring legs are part of whistling mechanism, whistling sound is made when feet are pushed; appropriately dressed. Marked "USA" or unmarked. Cardboard identification tag "I whistle when you dance me on one foot/and then the other/Patented Feb. 2, 1926, A Genuine Madame Hendren Doll."

Body Twist (Dimmie and Jimmie): all composition, jointed neck, shoulders, and hips, large ball joint at waist; molded and painted hair; painted eyes with large pupils and eye shadow; appropriately dressed. Advertised as being "pleasingly plump, and able to stand and pose a thousand ways." Unmarked. Wrist tag reads "Dimmie/Jimmie, Another Madame Hendren Doll/Made in USA" or "Jimmie/Dimmie's Boy Friend/Another Madame Hendren Doll/Made in USA."

Val-encia: composition shoulder head and limbs, slim body with voice box, low center of gravity allows doll to walk; composition face flocked to resemble felt and imitate Lenci Dolls; mohair wig; big painted eyes surrounded by dark eye shadow; dressed in felt or combinations felt and organdy. "Genuine/Madame Hendren/Doll/1714 Made in U.S.A." stamped on cloth body.

Harriet Flanders: all composition, jointed at neck, shoulders, and hips; molded tufts of hair, painted eyes with three eyelashes above each eye; open mouth with painted tongue; appropriately dressed. Marked "Harriet Flanders/1937."

CELLULOID

Sunny Boy and Sunny Girl: celluloid head, composition arms and legs, slender cloth body; molded hair; glass eyes. Marked with a turtle and a sun burst with "Sunny Girl." Original wrist tag reads "Sunny/Girl/the doll with the/beautiful bright eyes, Averill Manufacturing Co. USA."

Averill Celluloid Value Comparisons:	
Size	**Sunny Boy and Sunny Girl**
14"	400.00
17"	425.00
19"	450.00
22"	550.00

CLOTH

Grace G. Drayton: cloth doll; painted flat face; large round side-glancing eyes; pug nose; single line smiling mouth; movable limbs; separate clothing. Drayton dolls copyrighted by Averill include Dolly Dingle, Chocolate Drop, Happy Cryer, Sis, Baby Bunny, Mah-Jongg Kid, Kitty Puss, and Susie Bear. Marked "Dolly Dingle/Copyright By/G. G. Drayton."

Maud Tousey Fangel: sweet and charming printed cloth doll; flat printed face; very big eyes with long lashes; little nose; closed smiling mouth; printed material clothing and flesh colored body; painted on hair; some with yarn braids attached under hat marked "MTF" at seam on side of head. Occasionally unmarked, possibly

5" Madame Hendren composition Indian. *Courtesy of Helen Brooke.*

Averill Composition Value Comparisons:						
Size	**Mama Baby**	**Bobby Dolly**	**Whistling Doll**	**Body Twist**	**Val-encia**	**Harriet Flanders**
10"	175.00					
12"						250.00
14"		600.00	350.00	500.00		
15"	350.00				500.00	
16"		450.00				350.00
17"	400.00					
22"	550.00					
24"	600.00					

AVERILL CLOTH VALUE COMPARISONS:

Size	Grace Drayton*	Maud T. Fangel	Character Sateen	International Series	Comic Characters	Characters
11"	600.00					
12"		600.00	400.00	200.00	1,500.00	
14"		700.00			1,500.00	
15"				250.00		
16"	800.00	800.00	550.00			
18"		900.00				
21"						700.00
22"		1,200.00	700.00			
24"				350.00		

* Add an additional $100.00 for Chocolate Drop (Black cloth doll).

18" Maud Tousey Fangel doll.
Photo courtesy of McMasters Doll Auction.

due to mark being sewn into seam. Original paper tag pinned to front of dress reads "Soft Baby Doll/Created Exclusively for us by/Maud Tousey Fangel/America's Foremost Baby Painted/Georgene Novelties, Inc. New York, N.Y." An article in a 1936 edition of *Toys and Novelties* reads as follows: "Snooks and Sweets are new creations in novelty dolls. These dolls are accurate reproductions from the works of the celebrated artist Maud Tousey Fangel, whose drawings have appeared as cover designs on many important magazines of wide circulation. (Her work is in demand by national advertisers.) These dolls are soft and cuddly, distinctly baby-type, washable and waterproof. Anyone familiar with the work of Maud Tousey Fangel knows the lovable expressions and natural baby charm she puts into her creations. It is the irresistible appeal which the manufacturers have captured and reproduced with such convincing accuracy. The dolls are copied from pastel drawings preserving all the color value of the originals. The Maud Tousey Fangel Dolls are made in two faces and in four sizes. The brunette is Snooks and the blonde is Sweets."

Child or Baby Doll: mask face; cloth body; yarn hair; painted features; some with attached real eyelashes; appropriately dressed. Unmarked. Bridesmaid, Ring bearer, Flower Girl, Mary Had a Little Lamb, Girl Scout, Brownie, and international dolls are less valuable than the sateen character dolls. One clue to identifying an Averill cloth doll is that the body is hand-sewn with an overcast stitch.

Comic Character: charming cloth doll; swivel head; mask face; yarn hair; painted eyes; applied ears; closed mouth; dressed in cotton, felt, knit, or a combinations of the three. Unmarked. Original label includes name of the character and "Georgene Novelties, Inc. New York City, Exclusive Licensed Manufacturers Made in U.S.A." These dolls are easily identified because of their striking resemblance to the character they portray. Comic characters include Alvin, Little Lulu, Nancy, Sluggo, and Tubby Tom. Check carefully for damage. Mask faces are

vulnerable to dents. The doll must be in mint condition to command its highest price.

Character Doll: popular in the mid-1930s; all cloth; shaped face and body; painted features. Unmarked. Attached paper tag reads "Georgene Averill." Nurse Jane and Uncle Wiggily are among the most collectible examples.

Bonnie Babe: resembles one year-old baby; bisque head, most with cloth body and composition limbs, some with composition bent-limb baby body; molded and painted hair; sleep eyes; open smiling slightly crooked mouth with two lower teeth; appropriately dressed. Marked "Copr. By/Georgene Averill/Germany/1005-3653/1386" (or "1402") on the back of the head. Small sizes of the Bonnie Babe may be found in all-bisque although some Bonnie Babes had a celluloid head. Bisque heads were produced in Germany by Alt, Beck & Gottschalk or Kestner. American K & K body. Distributed by George Borgfeldt. Georgene registered a U.S. trademark of Bonnie Babe in 1926 and quickly transferred it to G. Borgfeldt. A renewal of U.S. trademarks indicates that Bonnie Babes were still being produced in 1946.

BONNIE BABE VALUE COMPARISONS:

Size	Bisque Head, Cloth body	Bisque Head, Composition body	Celluloid Head
12"	1,300.00	1,900.00	400.00
14"	1,500.00	2,200.00	500.00
16"	1,800.00	2,700.00	800.00
18"	2,000.00	3,000.00	850.00
20"	2,100.00	3,200.00	875.00
22"	2,200.00	3,000.00	900.00
24"	2,400.00	3,600.00	1,000.00

Babyland Rag

Babyland Rag is the trade name of various types of cloth dolls produced and/or distributed by Horsman. The earliest Babyland Rag Dolls had simple hand-painted features with little detail—single-stroke brows, nice eyes, pug nose, and slightly smiling bow-type mouth. Later dolls had lithographed faces.

Look for dolls with nice coloring and little or no fading. Slight wear and signs of aging such as a settled body do not greatly affect prices. If a doll is stained, torn, badly mended, or faded, expect to pay less than half the value listed.

OIL-PAINTED FACE

Painted Babyland Rag: painted cloth; mitt-type hands; mohair sewn on front of head; flat face with painted features; removable appropriate clothing. Marked "Genuine Babyland Trade Mark" or unmarked. Black versions of Painted Babyland Rag dolls were also produced, as was a Topsy-Turvy model with one white face and one Black face.

LITHOGRAPH BABYLAND RAG DOLL

Printed Babyland Rag: cloth doll; printed life-like features and hair; removable appropriate clothing. Unmarked. Black versions of Printed Babyland Rag Dolls were also produced, as was a Topsy-Turvy model with one white face and one Black face.

Martha Chase Doll holding Black-painted Babyland Rag Doll. *Photo courtesy of McMasters Doll Auction.*

	BABYLAND RAG VALUE COMPARISONS:					
Size	Oil-Painted Face	Black Oil-Painted Face	Topsy-Turvy Oil Painted	Lithograph	Lithograph Black	Lithograph Topsy Turvy
13"	900.00					
15"	1,000.00	1,100.00	1,000.00	600.00	750.00	600.00
17"		1,200.00				
18"			1,200.00	700.00		
22"	1,400.00	1,500.00		800.00	950.00	800.00
26"		1,800.00				
28"	2,000.00	2,200.00		900.00		

Bähr & Pröschild

Bähr & Pröschild was a porcelain factory in Ohrdruf, Germany, which was founded in 1871 and continued operating until 1910. The company's first doll mold was registered in 1888. The original owners were George Baehr and August Proeschild, who changed the spelling of their names in order to facilitate correspondence with American customers. Some of the loveliest German dolls were by made by Bähr & Pröschild.

Dating a Bähr & Pröschild Doll is relatively easy. The first Bähr & Pröschild Dolls were marked with only a mold number. In 1888 "dep" was added. Around 1895 the initials B & P were added. In 1900 a crossed swords symbol was added. Finally, in 1919 when Bruno Schmidt purchased the business, Bähr & Pröschild adopted the heart as a trademark and incorporated it into its markings.

Mold numbers registered by Bähr & Pröschild include 201, 204, 207, 209, 212, 213, 217, 219, 220, 224, 225, 226, 227, 230, 239, 244, 245, 247, 248, 251, 252, 253, 259, 260, 261, 263, 264, 265, 269, 270, 273, 275, 277, 278, 281, 283, 285, 287, 289, 292, 297, 300, 302, 305, 306, 309, 313, 320, 321, 233, 323, 324, 325, 330, 340, 342, 343, 348, 350, 374, 375, 376, 378, 379, 380, 381, 389, 390, 393, 394, 424, 425, 441, 482, 499, 500, 520, 525, 526, 529, 531, 535, 536, 537, 539, 541, 546, 549, 554, 557, 568, 571, 581, 584, 585, 600, 604, 619, 624, 640, 641, 643, 644, 645, 646, 678, 707, and 799.

Molds 529, 534, 536, 537, and 539 were among the molds made for Bruno Schmidt and will have a 2000 series number, i.e., 537/2033. The three-digit number is the Bähr & Pröschild number, the four-digit number is the registered Bruno Schmidt number. The name Buporit was registered for celluloid.

Some Bähr & Pröschild mold numbers identify specific dolls. For example, 217 is a Black doll, 220 is Oriental, and 678 is a closed mouth Googly. Other mold numbers are not so definitive. The same number may be found on a doll with either an open or closed mouth or an open head or Belton-style dome head with holes. Descriptions and classifications are listed as pricing comparisons. Check for damage or repairs, remembering that normal body aging is to be

Oriental Girl 220. *Photo courtesy of McMasters Doll Auction.*

	BÄHR & PRÖSCHILD VALUE COMPARISONS:					
Size	Closed Mouth, Belton-Type, Composition Body	Closed Mouth, Socket Head, Composition Body	Closed Mouth, Shoulder Head, Kid Body	Open Mouth, Dolly-Face, Composition Body	Open Mouth, Dolly-Face, Kid Body	Character Baby, Bent-Limb Body*
10"	1,700.00			600.00	350.00	550.00
12"	2,000.00	1,100.00	1,000.00	700.00		600.00
14"			1,400.00			700.00
16"		1,700.00			700.00	800.00
18"	3,000.00			1,000.00		900.00
20"	3,500.00	2,200.00	1,900.00	1,100.00	750.00	1,000.00
22"				1,300.00	800.00	1,200.00
24"	4,200.00	2,800.00	2,300.00	1,500.00		1,400.00

* Add an additional $300.00 for toddler.

expected and does not greatly affect the value of the doll. If the bisque is damaged or repaired, expect to pay about half the value listed.

Belton-Type Doll: solid dome or solid flat top usually with two or three holes; French jointed composition-and-wood body; good wig; nice paperweight eyes; pierced ears; closed mouths; appropriately dressed. Mold numbers typically in the 200 series.

Closed Mouth Child Doll: bisque shoulder head on kid body or socket head on jointed straight wrist body; good wig; glass eyes; pierced ears; closed mouth; appropriately dressed. The same mold numbers were used on both open and closed mouth dolls. Mold numbers typically in the 200 and 300 series. Closed mouth dolls command a higher price.

Open Mouth Child Dolly-Faced Doll: socket head and jointed body or shoulder head on kid body; generally with nice even coloring and soft blush; good wig; blown glass eyes; pierced ears; open mouth; appropriately dressed. Mold numbers typically in the 200 and 300 series.

Character Babies: socket head, bent-limb baby body; solid dome or wearing wig; sleep eyes; open mouth; appropriately dressed. Typically mold numbers 585, 587, 604, 619, 620, 624, and 678.

Character Baby 585.

Barbie® *& Friends*

The Barbie era began in 1958, when Ruth Handler, wife of the co-founder of Mattel, decided that a fashion doll with an expansive wardrobe would be a wonderful idea. Her intuition could not have been more correct. Mattel's Barbie has been so successful that there is now a third generation of children playing with Barbie and her friends.

Barbie has changed with the times. There have been at least two instances in which Mattel has instigated a trade-in program. The first was in May of 1967. A new Twist 'N Turn Barbie could be had in exchange for $1.50 and a used Barbie doll in any condition. Over 1.4 million Barbies were traded that month. The second trade-in program was for Living Skipper in 1970. This also proved to be very well received.

Barbies can twist, walk, dance, wink, kiss, grab things, hunch their shoulders, and talk. Barbie's "A" list of friends is endless, as are their costumes.

Recently Mattel released a talking Barbie programmed to say four different phrases which had been randomly selected from a total of 270 recorded by Mattel. Of the 350,000 dolls produced, an estimated 3,500 uttered the controversial line "Math class is tough." This seemingly innocuous phrase proved to be offensive to many people who claimed it reinforced the dangerous stereotype that girls do not do well in math. The phrase was dropped from future production and Mattel offered to exchange any of the "offensive" dolls already purchased. For Barbie collectors this was a dream come true. The limited production run coupled with the number of dolls returned to Mattel meant Teen Talk Barbie would be a fairly rare find. Additionally, there was nothing on the box to indicate which Teen Talk Barbie spoke the offensive phrase. One had to buy the doll, insert batteries, and try it out. What a time Barbie collectors had trying to acquire a "politically incorrect" Barbie. The original price of Teen Talk Barbie was under $20. Today, collectors will happily pay $300.00 to add this Barbie to their collections.

When examining a Barbie doll, check condition carefully. Any doll in less than very good condition will quickly drop in value. Vinyl fading and spotting is acceptable to collectors as it is a normal aging process and therefore does not greatly affect value. A damaged Barbie, or one which is missing accessories should be valued at less than half the prices listed.

21 years of Barbie. Early Barbie in black and white swimsuit (center). Beauty Secrets Barbie (sitting on top). Sun Lovin' Malibu Barbie (front); *Front row, left to right:* Kissing Barbie, Pretty Changes Barbie, Black Barbie, Hispanic Barbie, Super Star Barbie, Ballerina Barbie. *Back row:* Miss Barbie, Gold Medal Barbie, Busy Barbie, Malibu Barbie, Fashion Queen Barbie, Talking Barbie, Fashion Barbie, Barbie's Sweet 16, Barbie with bendable legs, Twist 'N Turn Barbie, Living Barbie, Quick Curl Barbie.

Barbie #1: 1959, vinyl, heavy solid body most likely faded to a very pale or whitish color, vinyl usually has an aroma of crayons, chocolate, or wax; soft silky floss blond or brunette hair styled in ponytail with curly bangs; highly arched (upside down V-shaped) eyebrows, painted black and white eyes with heavy black eyeliner and a thin line of blue on the eye lid; bright red lips and nail color may be faded to orange-red; holes in balls of feet with copper tubes running up into legs to accommodate prongs of posing stand; wearing one-piece black and white striped swimsuit, gold hoop earrings, and black high heel plastic shoes with holes in soles which correspond to holes in feet. Number One Barbies are typically marked "Japan" on the arch of the foot and marked on the hip:

Barbie T. M.
Pats. Pend.
© MCMLVIII
by
Mattel Inc.

The #1 doll stand is a round black plastic base with two prongs and a cross bar underneath for support. It is marked "Barbie T.M." The fashion booklet has Barbie's profile on the cover and is marked "Barbie T.M." The box is marked "Barbie T.M." and "850."

Barbie #2: made for three months in 1959-1960, identical in appearance to Barbie #1, but without holes in the feet and most have pearl stud earrings. The Barbie #2 stand is a round black plastic base with a "T" wire support placed one inch from the edge of the stand. The wire was designed to fit under Barbie's arms. Barbie #2 is typically marked the same as #1. Most fashion booklets and boxes were also marked the same, although a few #2 Barbies have been found with the "Barbie ®" mark.

Barbie #3: 1960, same heavy solid body usually faded to a very pale or whitish color with same familiar "waxy" smell; blond or brunette soft floss hair styled in ponytail with curly bangs; rounded and tapered eyebrows, blue eyes, most with dark brown eyeliner, some with blue eyeliner on upper eye lid; bright red lips and nails which may have faded to orange-red; most #3 Barbies do not have holes in their feet, although a few transitional models were made; wearing one-piece black and white striped swimsuit, pearl earrings, black plastic high heel shoes. Typically marked in the same manner as #1 and #2 Barbies. The major differences between Barbies #1 and #2 and the 1960 Barbie #3 are the eyebrows and eyes. Mattel felt that the earlier Barbies were too Asian in appearance, so the eyebrows were softened and given a more rounded and tapered look without the arch. Another distinction is the addition of eye color. Barbie #3 was the first to have real eye color.

Barbie #4: 1960, vinyl, heavy solid body retains its nice flesh tone color; same hair and hair style; softly rounded and tapered eyebrows, blue eyes with blue eyeliner on lids; original bathing suit, earrings, and shoes. The vinyl used for Barbie #4 has a tendency to turn green at the earring holes. The stand is a round

black plastic base hollowed out underneath and with the "T" wire support stand placed 1/4" from the edge of the stand. Marked "Barbie ®" fashion booklet and box. There may be some overlap in stands supplied with Barbie #3 and #4 but value is unaffected. Barbie #4 is typically marked in the same manner as #1, #2, and #3.

Barbie #5: 1961, first hollow body doll, much lighter in weight than the earlier Barbies; blond, brunette, or red saran hair styled in same ponytail and curly bangs, hair texture is sturdier and firmer than floss; longer eyebrows, smaller pupils show more blue eye color, blue eyeliner; most with red lips, some with a more delicate lip and nail color; original swimsuit, earrings, and shoes. Black wire stand with square base. Fashion booklet and box marked "Barbie ®." Gold colored wrist tag with "Barbie" written in script across front. First box to offer red hair. Barbie #5 is typically marked in the same manner as #1, #2, #3, and #4.

Barbie #6: 1962-67, hollow body; transitional style ponytail; lip and nail colors include pink, coral, and peach (which often fades to yellow or white); earlier Barbie #6 with dark royal blue eye color, models produced from 1963 on with aqua blue eye color; blond, brunette, red, ash blond, or platinum hair colors; one-piece red swimsuit. Typically marked on hip:

Barbie T. M.	_or_	MIDGE	_or_	1958	_or_	1960
Pats. Pend.		©1962		Mattel Inc.		By
©MCMLVIII		BARBIE®		US Patented		Mattel Inc.
by		1958		US Pat. Pend.		Hawthorne
Mattel		by				Calif, USA
Inc.		Mattel, Inc.				

Bubble Cut Barbie: 1962-67, hollow body; sturdier, firmer saran hair styled in full bubble cut, brunette, light brown, blond, or red hair; various lip and nail colors often faded to yellow or white; one-piece red swimsuit and red plastic high heels. Typically marked:

Barbie T. M.	MIDGE
Pats. Pend.	©1962
© MCMLVIII	BARBIE ®
by	1958
Mattel	by
Inc.	Mattel, Inc.

Boxed outfits with dolls. All sets in mint condition in original boxes or packages.

See Doll Care for helpful tips concerning Barbie problems.

Barbie #	Doll Only, Very Good Condition	Doll Only, Good Condition	Doll Only, Poor Condition	Stand
#1	3,000.00	2,200.00	900.00	350.00
#2	3,000.00	2,000.00	700.00	300.00
#3	900.00	500.00	100.00	150.00
#4	500.00	200.00	50.00	75.00
#5	400.00	175.00	40.00	45.00
#6	200.00	100.00	10.00	45.00
Bubble Cut	250.00	150.00	25.00	

Date	Name	Description	MINT
1959	Barbie #1	Vinyl, heavy solid body; soft silky floss or saran hair, blond or brunette, ponytail with curly bangs; very arched eyebrows, painted black and white eyes, heavy eyeliner; bright red lips and nails; holes in feet, one-piece black and white swimsuit	$4,200.00
1959-60	Barbie #2	Same as Barbie #1; no holes in feet; pearl stud earrings; change to stand	4,000.00
1960	Barbie #3	Vinyl, heavy solid body; blond or brunette ponytail, curly bangs; changes to eyebrows	1,100.00
1960	Barbie #4	Vinyl, heavy solid body; same hair and style; blue eyes; same swimsuit, earrings, OR shoes, slight change to stand	900.00
1961	Barbie #5	Hollow body; sturdier saran hair in ponytail and curly bangs, blond, brunette, and red head; original swimsuit	700.00
1962-67	Barbie #6	Hollow body; dark royal blue eyes until 1963, then more aqua blue; blond, brunette, red head, ash blond, OR platinum hair	400.00
1962-67	Bubble Cut Barbie	Hollow body; sturdier saran, bubble-cut style brunette, light brown, blond, red; lip and nail colors vary; one-piece red swimsuit, red shoes	400.00
1963	Fashion Queen	Egyptian-style gold and white swimsuit and head covering; 3 interchangeable wigs and wig stand	600.00
1964	Miss Barbie (Sleep Eye Barbie)	Open/close eyes; 3 interchangeable wigs; lawn swing, swimming cap, pink swimsuit	1,200.00
1964	Swirl Ponytail Barbie	Rooted hair, long sweeping bang crosses forehead; one-piece red swimsuit	700.00
1965	Bendable Leg Barbie, center part	4 different hairstyles; swimsuit with striped top, teal green bottom	2,500.00
1965	Bendable Leg Barbie, Doris Day-style side part	Specially rooted; swimsuit with striped top, teal green bottom	6,000.00
1965	Color Magic	Blond hair changes to scarlet red; swimsuit changes color	1,700.00
1965	Color Magic	Midnight Black hair changes to ruby red; swimsuit changes color (hair fails to return to black)	2,000.00
1966	Twist 'N Turn "TNT"	Real rooted eyelashes	500.00
1968	Talking Barbie, Spanish Barbie	Ponytail to one side; pull-string at back	350.00
1969	Talking Truly Scrumptious	Pink gown; pull-string from back (from the movie, *Chitty Chitty Bang Bang*)	800.00
1969	Non-talking Truly Scrumptious	Pink gown; pull-string from back	1,000.00
1970	Living Barbie	Jointed wrists, bendable elbows and ankles	400.00
1971	Malibu Barbie	Tanned tone vinyl	45.00*
1971	Live Action Barbie	Battery operated stage moves Barbie in a dancing motion	250.00
1971	Growing Pretty Hair Barbie	Pink dress; hair piece, hair ornaments	400.00
1971	Hair Happening Barbie (Limited Edition offered exclusively through Sears.)	Red haired Twist 'N Turn, several hair pieces to add; wearing pink skirt, white blouse	1,000.00
1972	Walk Lively Barbie	Red jumpsuit; Miss America; battery operated walker stand	200.00
1972	Busy Barbie with Holding Hands	Hands open and close to hold things, 5 accessories for holding	400.00
1972	Ward's Anniversary Barbie	Montgomery Ward exclusive; copy of Barbie #5 or 6; surprised look, brows high on forehead	600.00
1973	Quick Curl Barbie	. . . .	85.00
1974	Sun Valley Barbie	Mint on card, no box	200.00
1975	Gold Medal Sports Barbie	. . . .	125.00
1976	Beautiful Bride Barbie	. . . .	250.00

Date	Name	Description	MINT
1976	Ballerina Barbie	. . . .	$45.00
1976	Super Star Barbie	. . . .	200.00
1980s	International Barbie	Eskimo	200.00
		German	100.00
		Hawaiian	75.00
		India	175.00
		Italian	250.00
		Japanese	125.00
		Parisian	175.00
		Scottish	200.00
1986	Blue Rhapsody	Porcelain, limited to 6,000	900.00
	Bride	Porcelain	600.00
	Gay Parisian	Porcelain	250.00
	Benefit Performance	Porcelain	500.00
	Solo in Spotlight	Porcelain	250.00
	Plantation Belle	Porcelain	350.00
1988	Happy Holiday	Red gown	700.00
		White gown	300.00
1990	Bob Mackie Line	Gold	800.00
1991		Platinum	650.00
		Starlight Splendor	700.00
1992		Empress Bride	700.00
		Neptune Fantasy	750.00
1993		Masquerade Ball	600.00
1994		Queen of Hearts	300.00
1992	Classique Line	Benefit Ball Barbie, Carol Spencer	300.00
		Opening Night, Janet Goldblatt	300.00
1994	Special Edition	Bloomingdales	250.00
		Hallmark	250.00
		Golden Jubilee	1,600.00

* There were no boxes made for these dolls

GIFT SETS

Boxed outfits with dolls. All sets in mint condition in original boxes or packages.

Date	Name	Doll	Value
1962	Mix and Match Set	Barbie	$1,500.00
1963	Sparkling Pink Gift Set	Barbie	1,200.00
1964	Party Time Gift Set	Skipper	500.00
1964	Round The Clock Gift Set	Barbie	1,400.00
1964	Wedding Party Gift	Barbie in Bride's Dream Ken in tuxedo Midge in Orange Blossom Skipper as Flower Girl	3,200.00
1967	Cut 'N Button	Skooter	500.00
	On Parade Gift Set	Barbie, Ken, and Midge	2,100.00

OTHER ACCESSORIES

Barbie's life has been filled with accessories of all kinds. Here is a sampling of current accessory prices:

Barbie's Fashion Shop $4,000.00

Barbie & Ken Little Theatre 3,500.00

Barbie & Skipper School 1,700.00

Skipper Dream Room 700.00

Barbie's Dream Kitchen and Dinette 2,800.00

Barbie's Music Box Piano and Bench 2,500.00

Barbie's Lawn Swing and Planter 200.00

Barbie's Sports Car 250.00

BARBIE'S FRIENDS AND FAMILY

Date	Name	Description	Mint in Box	Date	Name	Description	Mint in Box
1961	Ken	Boyfriend, #1, flocked hair $300.00		1967	Francie	Cousin, Black $1,400.00	
		Bendable leg 400.00		1968	Christie	Barbie's Black friend $175.00*	
1963	Midge	Best friend 400.00				Talking 250.00	
		Bendable Leg 600.00				Twist 'N Turn 225.00	
1964	Allan	Ken's friend, Midge's boyfriend 400.00		1968	Stacey	Barbie's British Friend, long hair 250.00	
		Bendable Leg 600.00				Short hair 400.00	
1964	Skipper	Barbie's Little Sister 400.00				Twist 'N Turn 350.00	
1965	Ricky	Skipper's friend 200.00		1969	P.J.	Barbie's friend 200.00*	
1965	Skooter	Skipper's friend 200.00				Twist 'N Turn 275.00	
		Bendable Leg 300.00		1970	Brad	Ken's friend, Christie's boyfriend, black **100.00***	
1966	Francie	Cousin, white 400.00		1971	Fluff	Skipper's friend 125.00*	
		Cousin, white, no bangs 1,200.00		1972	Tiff	Skipper's friend, Pose 'N Play 250.00	
1966	Tutti	Baby Twin, Bendable vinyl body 200.00		1972	Steffie	Barbie's friend 250.00	
1966	Tutti	Packaged set, Me & My Dog 450.00				Walk Lively 200.00	
1966	Todd	Baby Twin, Bendable vinyl body 200.00		1973	Kelley	Barbie's friend, Yellowstone 225.00	
1966	Todd	Packaged set, Sundae Treat 500.00				Quick Curl 100.00	
1967	Casey	Francie's friend, clear plastic stand . .300.00		1974	Cara	Friend, black 50.00*	
		Twist 'N Turn 250.00				Ballerina 50.00	
1967	Chris	Tutti & Todd's friend 150.00*		1975	Curtis	Cara's boyfriend, black 75.00	
				1975	Casey	Francie's friend, packed in plastic 65.00*	

* There were no boxes made for these dolls

BARBIE'S OUTFITS

Barbie outfits must be complete and in excellent condition. Values shown are for outfits mint in the original package (MIP). Very good complete condition unpackaged outfits would be valued at half of the MIP prices. Incomplete outfits or those in played-with condition are valued at one-quarter the MIP prices.

Name	Description	Packaged Value
Easter Parade	Tight black dress, multicolored donut print; black coat, hat, bag, and shoes $2,400.00
Gay Parisian	Blue bubble dress; fur cape; gold bag; blue shoes 1,900.00
Roman Holiday	Straight dress, gray skirt, striped top; matching red and white striped coat; red hat, shoes, and bag 2,200.00
Solo in the Spotlight	Very tight black sparkly dress, net kick flounce; long black gloves; long scarf, black shoes; plastic microphone 750.00
Enchanted Evening	Beautiful long pink gown with long attached train; long white opera-length gloves; fluff shoulder cap; matching shoes 350.00
Plantation Belle	Pink dotted Swiss dress with lace inserts, fitted to waist, full skirt, pink net wide brim hat; straw bag; short white gloves; pink shoes 350.00
Picnic Set	Red and white checked blouse, blue jean pedal pushers; straw hat and bag; fishing line and plastic fish . . .350.00
Busy Gal	Red suit, red and white striped blouse; glasses; hat; portfolio; red shoes .400.00
Commuter Set	Dark two-piece suit with white blouse and pearls; large red flowered hat; shoes, hat box; and extra blouse 750.00
Wedding Day Set	Wedding gown with layers of lace; head piece with net veil; holding flowers; white shoes; white gloves 450.00
Sophisticated Lady	Pink gown, deep pink long coat; head piece; matching shoes; long white gloves 350.00
Midnight Blue	Gown with sleeveless blue long coat with white fur collar; long white gloves; gold evening bag and shoes 700.00
Reception Line	Pretty blue dress, fitted to waist with lace over skirt; blue pillbox-style hat; white long gloves; white shoes 450.00
Here Comes The Bride	Long straight gown, somewhat fitted, lace overlay; very long veil; white gloves, flowers, and shoes 800.00
Golden Glory	Gold gown with matching coat with mink collar; white gloves, evening bag, and shoes 450.00

Name	Description	Packaged Value
Nighty Negligee	Pink nightie and chiffon robe; pink felt dog; slippers	$150.00
Sheath Sensation	Red sheath dress, square neck; white straw hat; short white gloves and shoes	175.00
Fun at the Fair	Red skirt, print blouse; matching scarf with red shoes; and cotton candy on a wooden stick	300.00
Riding in the Park	Tan riding pants, plaid jacket, white shirt; riding hat; high boots; riding crop	500.00
Stormy Weather	Yellow belted rain coat; rain hat; umbrella and high boots	125.00
Sporting Casuals	Blue slacks, knit sweater with cowl neck; blue shoes	175.00
Saturday Matinee	Stylish suit with matching hat, fur trim; tan gloves; shoes; bag	900.00
Gold N' Glamour	Gold two-piece suit with scarf and matching hat, all with fur trim; tan gloves and shoes	900.00
Japan Outfit	Red kimono; fan; head ornament; musical instrument; sandals	850.00
Miss Astronaut	Silver space suit; head gear; American flag	900.00

E. Barrois

24" Fashion Lady. *Photo courtesy of McMasters Doll Auction.*

E. Barrois, located in Paris, France, from 1844-1877, was one of the earliest manufacturers of porcelain-head dolls in France. The bisque-head dolls tend to be quite pale, with delicate blush and eyebrow decorations. Mouths are small with just a hint of a smile. Eyes may be either glass or painted. If painted, the lashes are very long. China heads have painted eyes and hair. The pressed method was used in making E. Barrois doll heads. Most have a shoulder head, although a few socket heads on bisque shoulder plates can be found. Lady bodies are made of kid, although some examples have cloth bodies. Hands are either kid with stitched fingers or wooden upper arms with bisque hands, a rarer version. Sizes range from 9 inches to 23 inches with the sizing codes of 3/0 to 7. Dolls should be appropriately dressed. Typical markings include "E (size number) B;" "E (size number) Depose B," and "EB."

Examine dolls carefully before buying. Prices listed are for dolls with no damage to the bisque. Normal wear, slight damage or well-done repairs to the body do not greatly affect the price. If the bisque is damaged or repaired expect to pay less than half the amount listed. It is perfectly acceptable to show a repaired finger, joint, or seam to the body.

E. BARROIS VALUE COMPARISONS:

Size	Painted Eyes	Glass Eyes	Jointed Wood Body	Black Lady
9"	2,000.00	2,500.00	2,800.00	
11"	2,500.00	2,800.00	3,100.00	
13"	3,000.00	3,300.00	3,600.00	
15"	3,200.00	3,500.00	3,900.00	
17"	3,400.00	3,800.00	4,200.00	
19"	3,700.00	4,200.00	4,700.00	35,000.00
21"	4,000.00	4,500.00	4,900.00	
24"	4,400.00	4,900.00	5,400.00	

Beecher Baby

Beecher Baby Dolls were produced in Elmira, NY between 1893-1910 by Julia Jones (Mrs. Thomas) Beecher. She was the granddaughter of Noah Webster, the sister-in-law of Henry Ward Beecher and Harrier Beecher Stowe, and the wife of a Congregational Church pastor. Mrs. Beecher's first doll was made for her niece Daisy Day. These charming dolls were made of pink or black cotton or silk with needle sculptured, painted features. The bodies were hand stuffed and the hair was looped wool yarn. Beecher Babies are unmarked. Devoted ladies of the Church's Sewing Circle made the dolls, with all proceeds used for missionary work, which explains why these dolls are often referred to as Missionary Ragbabies.

When considering a Beecher Baby for your collection, consider yourself lucky just to find one! Their irresistible charm accounts in part for their scarcity and usually well-loved condition.

23" Beecher Baby. *Photo courtesy of McMasters Doll Auction.*

BEECHER BABY VALUE COMPARISONS:

Size	Caucasian Extra Clean Condition	Caucasian Good Condition	Caucasian Fair Condition	Black Extra Clean Condition	Black Good Condition	Black Fair Condition
15" h	4,500.00	3,000.00	2,000.00	5,000.00	3,500.00	2,500.00
21" h	7,500.00	6,000.00	5,000.00	8,500.00	7,000.00	5,500.00

Belton-Type

Although Belton-Type Dolls are generally accepted as French, these beautiful bisque dolls were probably manufactured in Germany after 1870. A distinguishing characteristic of a Belton is its uncut pate section with one, two, or three small holes. The top of the head may be concave, flat, or convex. Over the years almost every manufacturer of dolls has been suggested as a possible source for this type of doll. To date, no firm evidence has surfaced confirming any one company. Other common factors include a good wig, closed mouth, good quality paperweight eyes with long painted lashes, and pierced ears. Bodies are usually jointed composition with straight wrists, small hands, and long wooden stick-type upper legs. Some examples have a shoulder head on a

BELTON-TYPE VALUE COMPARISONS:

Size	Very Good Quality	Standard Quality
9"	2,000.00	1,400.00
12"	2,400.00	1,600.00
14"	2,800.00	1,800.00
16"	3,100.00	2,000.00
18"	3,500.00	2,400.00
20"	3,700.00	2,600.00
22"	4,000.00	3,000.00
24"	4,500.00	3,500.00

kid body with fine quality bisque hands. Dolls should be appropriately dressed. Most Belton-Type heads are unmarked or marked with only a size or mold number.

There are variations in the faces and the quality of the bisque and decoration. Evaluate dolls carefully. Check the feathering of the eyebrows — they should be painted as several single strokes. Eyes should be paperweight. The bisque should have a pale rather than ruddy complexion. Prices listed are for dolls with undamaged bisque. Slight damage and well-done repairs to the body do not greatly affect price. If bisque is damaged or repaired, expect to pay less than half the amount listed. It is perfectly acceptable to show a missing or repaired finger or joint.

Belton-Type Dolls range in size from 9 inches to 24 inches. Size number markings correspond roughly to the following: 1 = 9", 3 = 12", 6 = 14", 8 = 16", and 12 = 24".

18" Belton-Type.

C.M. Bergmann

24" C. M. Berman "1916." *Courtesy of Rachael Bowser Herlocher.*

As a young man, C.M. Bergmann lived and worked in America both as a miner and a cowboy. Upon his return to Waltershausen, Germany in 1877, he spent eleven years learning the doll-making business. Bergmann launched his own company in 1888 with just two employees. He specialized in ball-jointed composition bodies with bisque heads from the factories of Armand Marseilles, Simon & Halbig, Alt Beck & Gottshalck, and perhaps other German companies. Bergmann's dolls were distributed in the United States by Louis Wolf, who registered several Bergmann trademarks. Among them were Cinderella Baby, Baby Belle, and Columbia. C.M. Bergmann entered into bankruptcy in 1931.

Prices listed are for dolls with no damage. Slight damage and well-done repairs to the body do not greatly affect price. If the bisque is damaged or repaired, expect to pay less than half the amount listed. It is perfectly acceptable to show a missing or repaired finger or joint to the body.

Standard Quality: by Armand Marseilles or other unknown manufacturers; composition body; good wig; glass eyes, open mouth; appropriately dressed. Typically marked "C.M. Bergmann Waltershausen Germany 1916," "A.M. Columbia." These dolls are a bit more modestly priced than their Simon & Halbig counterparts.

Better quality: C.M. Bergmann dolls by Simon & Halbig and others; jointed composition body; good wig; open mouth; appropriately dressed. Some dolls have pierced ears, and eyebrows are painted and molded, a characteristic often found in heads by Simon & Halbig. Typically marked "C. M. B. Simon & Halbig;" "Eleonore."

Character Babies: five-piece bent-limb baby body; good wig; glass eyes; open mouth; appropriately dressed. Typically marked "A. M. C. M. B."

612: made by Simon & Halbig for C. M. Bergmann; open or open/closed mouth; appropriately dressed. Typically marked "Simon & Halbig/612/C.M. Bergmann."

C. M. BERGMANN VALUE COMPARISONS:

Size	Shoulder Head on Kid Body	Standard Quality A.M., or Others, Socket head, Jointed Body	Better Quality Simon & Halbig, Socket head, Jointed Body	Marked Eleonore	Standard Character Baby	S.H. 612 Character Baby
10"	350.00	450.00	550.00			
12"	375.00	475.00	575.00			
14"	400.00	500.00	600.00		500.00	2,000.00
16"	425.00	525.00	625.00			
18"	450.00	550.00	650.00			
20"	475.00	575.00	675.00	950.00	700.00	2,600.00
22"	500.00	600.00	700.00	1,000.00		
24"	550.00	650.00	800.00	1,100.00		
26"		750.00	900.00	1,200.00		
28"		850.00	1,000.00	1,300.00		
30"		1,000.00	1,250.00	1,600.00		
32"		1,200.00	1,450.00			
34"		1,600.00	1,850.00			
36"		2,000.00	2,300.00			
38"		2,400.00	2,700.00			
40"		2,600.00	3,000.00			
42"		3,000.00	3,500.00			

Bing Brothers

ing Brothers, later known as Bing Werke and Bing Wolf Corp., was a large corporation operating from 1882 until 1932. In addition to its home office in Nuremberg, Bing had headquarters all over the world, with John Bing being the American representative. In 1920, Bing Werke was a large conglomerate consisting of thirty-one subsidiary companies including Bing, Kämmer and Reinhardt, Max Oscar Arnold, Welsch & Co., and Louis Wolf. Bing Corp. was the only toy factory in Nüremberg that was not closed during World War I. The company went bankrupt in 1932.

Art Doll (resembles Käthe Kruse doll): painted mask face; cloth body; mitt hands with stitched fingers and separate thumb; painted hair; molded and painted features in the "Käthe Kruse style;" appropriately dressed. Typically marked "Bing."

Felt Doll (resembles Lenci doll): pressed face; felt wool body; mohair wig; painted side-glancing eyes; molded and painted features in the "Lenci style." Marked "Bing."

6½" and 10½" Bing Art Dolls. *Photo courtesy of McMasters Doll Auction.*

BING CLOTH DOLL VALUE COMPARISONS:

Size	Art Doll	Felt Doll
10"	700.00	350.00
15"	1,000.00	500.00

George Borgfeldt & Co.

George Borgfeldt & Co., located in New York City from 1881 through the 1950s, was an international importing company, not a doll manufacturer. Borgfeldt was responsible for importing thousands of dolls into America. The Germans described Borgfeldt as a "Verlegers" meaning assembler. Many famous designers were employed by Borgfeldt as were various companies who made the heads or complete dolls. Many of the dolls will be found with a "GB" mark on them, many will not.

Before World War I, Borgfeldt had exclusive American and Canadian rights to many dolls, including Kestner, Kämmer & Reinhardt, Handwerck, Steiff, Käthe Kruse, and Buschow & Beck. George Borgfeldt & Co. did not ignore American-made dolls. Some of the companies which distributed through Borgfeldt were Aetna Doll Co., K & K Toy, Dreamland Doll, Cameo Doll Co., and Bergfeld & Son. Borgfeldt was responsible for commissioning two of the most successful dolls ever made — Rose O'Neill's Kewpie and Grace Putnam's Bye-Lo.

Trademarks registered by Borgfeldt are Alma, Bonnie Baby, Lilly, Skookum, Celebrate, Uwanta, Juno, Florodora, Kidlyne, My Playmate, My Dearie, Pansy Doll, Little Bright Eyes, My Girlie, Happifat, Cubist, Peero, Butterfly, Prize Baby, September Morn Doll, Mamma's Angel Child, Bettijak, Nobbikid, Rastus, Skating Charlotte, Preshus, Em-Boss-O, Hollikid, Come-A-Long, Bye-Lo Baby, Mimi, Daisy Doll, Rosemarie, Felix, Bringing Up Father, Whatsmatter, Ko-Ko, Little Annie Roonie, Jackie Coogan, Buttercup, Featherweight, Rolly-I-Tot, Bonton, Jolly Jester, Rag & Tag, Fly-Lo, Gladdie, Mignonne, Nifty, Rosy Posy, Sugar Plum, Just Me, Babykins, Mary Ann, and Mary Jane.

Prices listed are for dolls with no damage. Normal wear, slight damage and well-done repairs to the body do not greatly affect the price. If the head is damaged or repaired, expect to pay less than half the amount listed. It is perfectly acceptable to show a missing or repaired finger or joint to the body.

See also All-Bisque, Averill, Googly-Eyed Dolls, Kewpie, and Cameo Dolls.

BISQUE

Shoulder Head Dolly-Face Doll: kid, cloth, or imitation kid body; good wig; glass eyes; open mouth; appropriately dressed. Typically marked "G. B." or "Germany." Imported by the thousands by George Borgfeldt Co.

Socket Head: jointed composition body; good wig; glass eyes; open mouth; good molding, nicely painted or haphazardly applied features; appropriately dressed. Typically marked "My Dearie," "Pansy," "My Girl," or "G. B." Judge quality carefully.

21" Gladdie.

BORGFELDT BISQUE VALUE COMPARISONS:

Size	Dolly-Face, Shoulder Head	Stand Quality, Dolly-Face, Socket Head	Better Quality, Dolly-Face, Socket Head	Character Baby	Bye-Lo Cloth Body	Bye-Lo Composition Body	Fly-Lo	Baby Bo-Kaye	Gladdie Bisque	Gladdie Biscaloid
12"	200.00	400.00	450.00	400.00	550.00		4,200.00	1,800.00		
14"		450.00	475.00	575.00	1,000.00	1,400.00	4,800.00			
16"	250.00	500.00	600.00		1,400.00	1,800.00	5,500.00			
18"	350.00	550.00	700.00	700.00	1,800.00	2,400.00		3,000.00	4,500.00	1,200.00
20"	400.00	600.00	800.00		2,200.00			3,500.00	5,500.00	1,400.00
22"	425.00	650.00	900.00	800.00						
24"	450.00	700.00	1,000.00	900.00					6,800.00	2,400.00
26"		800.00	1,200.00							
30"		1,000.00	1,400.00							
32"		1,100.00	1,600.00							
34"		1,400.00	1,900.00							
36"		1,900.00	2,400.00							

Character Baby: composition bent-limb baby body; good wig; glass eyes; open mouth; appropriately dressed. Typically marked "251," "326," "327," "329," or "G B."

Bye-Lo Baby: (often called Million Dollar Baby), designed by Grace Storey Putnam with Borgfeldt as sole distributor. Bisque Bye-Lo dolls were made by Alt, Beck & Gottschalck, Kestner, Kling, and Hertel, and Schwab & Co. Composition Bye-Lo dolls were made by the Cameo Doll Company. Most with specially designed cloth "frog" body with celluloid hands, some with five-piece bent-limb baby body; solid dome; painted hair; tiny glass eyes; closed mouth; appropriately dressed. Typically marked "1923 Grace S. Putnam/Made in Germany" or "1369 Grace S. Putnam." Also available in a Black version, with the same value as the white Bye-Lo.

Fly-Lo (also called Baby Aero): designed by Grace S. Putnam, flange-type neck, cloth body; molded and painted hair; glass sleep eyes; closed slightly smiling mouth; non-removable satin suit with wings, wire is attached from wing to doll's wrist. Typically marked "Grace S. Putnam Germany 1418/#."

Baby Bo-Kaye: designed especially for George Borgfeldt by Joseph Kallus; bisque baby head made in Germany by Alt, Beck & Gottschalck; sweet, wistful, almost pouting expression; cloth body; composition limbs; molded and painted hair; glass oval sleep eyes;

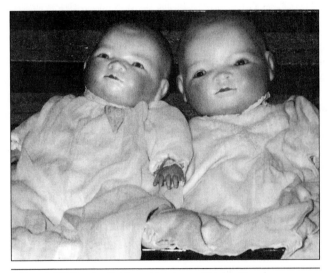

16" and 20" Bye-Lo Babies. *Courtesy of Helen Brooke.*

open/closed full mouth with two lower teeth; appropriately dressed. Typically marked "Copr. by J. L. Kallus, Germany 1394. "Supposedly, after Kallus designed this doll, he went to the office of Fred Kolb (President of George Borgfeldt) with the sculpted head. The two men were pondering over names when the secretary entered with a bouquet of flowers. The problem was solved."Bo-Kaye" was the perfect name for Bo (Borgfeldt) and Kaye (Kallus).

Gladdie: created and designed by Helen W. Jensen in 1929, most with biscaloid (imitation bisque composition) flange head, some with bisque head with cloth body; and composition limbs; deeply molded and painted hair; glass eyes; open/closed laughing mouth with molded upper teeth; appropriately dressed. Typically marked "1410 Germany" or "Gladdie Copyriht by Helen W. Jensen/Germany." The word "copyright" is misspelled as "copyriht" on many markings.

COMPOSITION VALUE COMPARISONS:

Size	Characters	Bye-Lo	Fly-Lo	Baby Bo-Kaye
10"		350.00		
12"	300.00	400.00	800.00	500.00
14"	350.00	450.00	1,200.00	600.00
17"	375.00	700.00		
20"	400.00			

COMPOSITION

Many composition dolls were also distributed by George Borgfeldt, both German and American made. Examples include Mamma's Angel Child, Hollikid, Com-A-Long, Daisy Bye-Lo, Fly-Lo, and Baby Bo-Kaye. Most have cloth bodies, with varying characteristics. Typically marked "My Playmate," "Borgfeldt," or with identical markings as the bisque dolls.

TIN

At least one metal head was imported by George Borgfeldt from Germany. This doll is known as Juno and was designed by Karl Standfuss.

Juno: 12", tin shoulder head, cloth body with cloth stitched fingers; molded and painted hair; painted eyes; closed mouth; appropriately dressed. Marked "Juno" in an oval **115.00**

Boudoir Dolls

20" "Smoker" Boudoir Doll. *Courtesy of Helen Brooke.*

Boudoir Dolls, also known as Flapper or Sofa dolls, acquired their name because of their use as decorations on beds and divans. They were made in France, Italy, and the United States from 1915 through the 1930s. Paris doll artists developed boudoir dolls into an art form.

Boudoir Dolls were never intended as children's toys. Most had cloth bodies, exaggerated long limbs, heads made of various materials such as cloth, composition, wax, china, or suede, and mohair or silk floss hair. Features were usually painted. Costumes were very fashionable, often consisting of silk pantsuits, ruffled gowns, patriotic attire, or theatrical costumes. Most shoes had a very high heel. Some dolls even had a cigarette dangling from their mouths. A few celebrities who were represented as Boudoir Dolls were Marlene Dietrich in a satin pantsuit, Joan Crawford in a ruffled gown, and Josephine Baker.

Clothing is an important factor in determining the value of a Boudoir Doll. If the original clothing is missing, the value would be less than half the amount listed. Most Boudoir dolls are unmarked.

	BOUDOIR DOLL VALUE COMPARISONS:				
Size	Extraordinary Quality, 1920s Art Deco or Elaborately Costumed	Standard Quality, 1930s, Mohair or Floss wigs	Lesser Quality Composition, 1940s, Heavy Painting	Lenci	Wax
14"	300.00	150.00	75.00		
18"	325.00	175.00	90.00		
20"	350.00	200.00	100.00		600.00
26"	400.00	225.00	120.00	2,400.00	800.00
30"	500.00	250.00	130.00	2,600.00	1,000.00
36"	700.00	300.00	150.00	3,000.00	1,500.00

Jne Bru & Cie

Jne Bru & Cie, commonly known as Bru, is one of the most famous bisque doll manufacturers known to collectors. The company was located at Paris and Montreuil-sous-Bois, France, from 1866 to 1899.

There is no doubt that the delicately molded, limpid-eyed bébés produced by Bru during the last quarter of the 19th century are among the most treasured prizes of the doll world. An 1872 catalog provides the following information: "Without clothes a number 4 doll will cost $1.20 to $2.10. If this doll was dressed in wool and had a kid body it cost $4.40 and with a wooden body it was $4.60. But if a number 4 doll was dressed in silk it cost $6.00 to $100.00 depending on the outfit." Imagine a doll in 1872 costing $100.00!

After 1899, S.F.B.J. (Society Française de Fabrication de Bébé & Jouets), of which Bru was a charter member, made Bru Dolls and Bébés.

There are three basic types of Bru Dolls: The Fashion Lady; The Bébé on a kid body with beautifully molded shoulder plate and hands; and the Bru Doll on a wood-and-composition body. Prices listed are for dolls with no damage to the bisque. Normal wear and slight damage or well-done repairs to the body do not greatly affect price. When the bisque is damaged or repaired, expect to pay about half the amount listed.

Reproduction Note: Beware of reproductions! Reproductions can be very convincing. In 1989 a reproduction of a Black Bru Jne won a national doll competition in which it was entered. This doll fooled several experts. A few tips to help distinguish an authentic Bru from a reproduction are:

22" Open Mouth Bru Jne R. *Photo courtesy of McMasters Doll Auction.*

	Reproduction	Authentic
Head Mark:	Bru Jne	Bru Jne (plus size #)
Body:	Hand sewn	Machine sewn
Stuffed:	Sawdust	Stuffed: Ground cork & grass
Elbows:	Bisque arms put directly into kid	Hinged joint
Cutting of leather:	Scalloped	Scalloped with pinking
Arms:	Hang straight	Graceful curve
Head:	Pouring rim cut off	Pressed
Ear Piercing:	Into the head	Through the lobe

There are more reproductions of Bru Jne Dolls than most other doll types. Genuine copies made by doll makers will have the artist's name, and usually the date, marked in order to prevent mis-identification.

FASHION LADY

Poupeé de Modes (Fashion Ladies): bisque swivel head, shoulder plate; gusseted kid lady body with pinking around top of leather; human, mohair, or skin wig; most with paperweight eyes, some with painted eyes; pierced ears; most with small, closed, smiling mouth; appropriately dressed. Shoulder plate occasionally marked "B. Jne & Cie." Bru Fashion dolls are marked on the head with an incised number or letter. In 1869, a patent was obtained by Bru for a wooden body with joints at the waist and ankles in addition to the usual shoulder, elbow, hip, and knee joints.

BÉBÉ BRU

Brevete Bébé: bisque socket head, kid-lined bisque shoulder plate; kid body pulled high on shoulder plate and straight cut (leather pinked where cut); bisque

19" Bru Jne R. Photo courtesy of McMasters Doll Auction.

Jne Bébé: bisque socket head, kid-lined deep shoulder plate with molded breasts; kid body with scalloped edge at shoulder plate; bisque lower arms with graceful hands, kid-over-wood upper arms, hinged elbows; wooden lower legs; good wig; cork pate; paperweight eyes with dark eyeliner and long lashes; pierced ears; closed mouth; appropriately dressed. Marked "Bru Jne. 9," and label on body reads "Bébé Bru" and "BTE SGDG." Add an additional $700.00 for a wooden jointed body, provided the markings are not that of a Bru Jne R. If there is an "R" in the marking, a wooden body is appropriate.

Bru Jne R Bébé: wood-and-composition jointed body; good wig; paperweight eyes; pierced ears; open or closed mouth (closed mouth version more costly); quality of bisque ranges from beautiful with fine decoration to less attractive standard quality, which greatly affects the pricing. Appropriately dressed. Typically marked "Bru Jne R# (number)," and may have a stamp on the body.

Bébé Teteur (Bru Nursing Bébé): bisque socket head, kid-lined bisque shoulder plate; kid body with bisque lower arms, kid-covered metal upper arms and legs, and carved wood lower legs or jointed wood-and-composition body; skin wig; paperweight eyes; mouth opened into an "O" with hole for nipple. Mechanism in head sucks liquid as key is turned; appropriately dressed. Typically marked "Bru June N 3 T."

lower arms; skin wig with cork pate; paperweight eyes with shading on upper lid, long lashes painted on upper and lower lids, lightly feathered brows; pierced ears; closed mouth with white space between lips; full cheeks; appropriately dressed. Typically marked "#" on head and sticker on body "Bébé Brevete SGDG Paris."

Circle Dot: bisque socket head, kid-lined bisque deep shoulder plate with molded breasts; kid gusseted body with bisque lower arms with no joints at the elbows; fine mohair wig; cork pate; paperweight eyes with eyeliner, heavier feathered brows; pierced ears; closed mouth with slightly parted lips and a suggestion of molded and painted teeth; plump cheeks; appropriately dressed. Marked with a dot within a circle.

BRU VALUE GUIDE:

Size	Poupeé de Mode with number*	Poupeé de Mode with letter*	Brevte Bébé	Circle Dot Bébé	Bru Jne Bébé	Early Nursing Bru Exceptional	Later Nursing Bru Standard	Closed Mouth Bru Jne R Exceptional	Closed Mouth Bru Jne R Standard	Open Mouth Bru Jne R
11"	2,800.00	3,000.00	12,000.00	11,000.00	11,500.00			6,000.00	5,200.00	2,500.00
12"	3,000.00	3,200.00	13,000.00	13,000.00	14,000.00					
13"			14,000.00	14,000.00	14,500.00	9,000.00	6,000.00			
14"	3,000.00	3,600.00	15,000.00	15,000.00	15,500.00			6,500.00	5,900.00	3,600.00
16"	4,000.00	4,200.00	17,000.00	18,000.00	18,500.00	10,000.00	7,000.00	7,300.00	6,400.00	4,500.00
17"		5,200.00	18,000.00	19,000.00	19,500.00					
18"	4,800.00		19,000.00	20,000.00	21,000.00					
19"	5,200.00	5,900.00	21,000.00	22,000.00	22,500.00					
20"	5,800.00	6,500.00	22,000.00	23,000.00	24,000.00					
22"	6,200.00	6,800.00	24,000.00	25,000.00	26,000.00			8,500.00	7,000.00	5,700.00
24"			26,000.00	27,000.00	28,000.00			9,500.00	8,000.00	
25"	6,800.00	7,500.00	27,000.00	28,000.00	29,000.00					
26"		28,000.00	28,000.00	30,000.00						6,500.00
28"	7,600.00	8000.00	29,000.00	33,000.00	35,000.00			12,500.00	9,500.00	
30"			32,000.00	35,000.00	35,500.00					
33"										
35"			34,000.00							

* Add an additional 2,000.00 for jointed wooden body.

Albert Brückner

New York City and Jersey City, New Jersey, were the homes for this doll manufacturer from 1901 until 1930. Doll maker Albert Brückner was joined in his business by his sons several years before his death, resulting in the name "Albert Brückner's Sons." Albert's 1926 obituary provided the following information: "In 1901, while watching one of his friends working through the tedious process of tuffing and shaping the faces then used on rag dolls, he conceived the idea of giving form and expression to the faces by stamping out or embossing the features into a mask. His knowledge of lithographing and printing trades enabled him to perfect his idea and he obtained a patent for it in July 1901. His earlier days had been spent with the Gray Lithographing Co. In 1901 he proceeded with the manufacture of doll faces and within a few months had a small factory established for the manufacture of a full line of rag dolls. He held several patents pertaining to the manufacture of dolls and at the time of his death he was treasurer of the Up-To-Date Manufacturing Co., manufacturers of cry voices for dolls. . . . He had a 'Museum' which contained samples of the various dolls produced from 1901-26, showing their changing dress styles."

Several of Brückner's rag dolls were released through Horsman and sold as part of Horsman's Babyland Rag Doll series. Look for dolls with good color and little or no fading. These dolls are particularly prone to rubs. Avoid paying top prices for dolls that are torn or badly mended.

Mask-type Cloth Doll: painted hair and facial features; appropriately dressed. Typically marked "Pat'd July 9th 1901."

Topsy-Turvy Doll: two dolls in one, mask-type faces, one head with white face, other with black, white doll with blond hair and blue eyes and wearing dress and bonnet; Black doll with black mohair wig; painted large eyes with white highlights; laughing mouth with two rows of teeth; and wearing red dress and kerchief. When correctly positioned, the skirt of one doll completely covers the unused doll.

Brückner Cloth doll. *Photo courtesy of Cobbs Doll Auction*

BRÜCKNER VALUE COMPARISONS:			
Size	White Cloth	Black Cloth	Topsy-Turvy
12"	350.00	400.00	600.00
14"	400.00	450.00	700.00

A. Bucherer

Bucherer, Amriswil, Switzerland, 1921-1930, made numerous styles of dolls with a patented metal ball-jointed body. Advertised as having changeable heads, the dolls represented comic characters and celebrities as well as everyday civilians such as chauffeurs, policemen, and firemen. Many were dressed in regional costumes with outfits sewn directly onto the doll.

These cabinet sized dolls are popular with collectors today and command impressive prices. Comic characters are generally valued higher than common examples. Prices listed are for dolls with no damage. Because clothing is sewn on the body it is sometimes difficult to inspect the doll. Always ask for assistance before removing clothing.

Dolls range in size from 6½ to 7½ inches tall and have composition head, hands, and feet; metal-jointed body; painted hair and features; and are appropriately dressed. They are marked with a stamp on the front of the torso which reads "Made in Switzerland Patents Applied For."

A. Bucherer Character. *Courtesy of Helen Brooke*

BUCHERER VALUE COMPARISONS:				
Size	Regional Costumes	Civilian-type	Characters and Animals	Comic Characters
6½" to 7½"	250.00	325.00	350.00	450.00

Cabbage Patch® Dolls

Newborn Cabbage Patch.

Cabbage Patch dolls were delivered at the Babyland Hospital in Cleveland, Georgia, first by Coleco Industries and later by Hasbro Toys. Their creation evoked a frenzied level of demand unrivaled by any other doll. They are extremely popular as both play dolls and collectibles.

The Cabbage Patch fantasy was created in 1977 in the mountains of Georgia. The first Cabbage Patch dolls were known as "Little People." These original creations of Xavier Roberts were hand-stitched sculptured dolls. They were so popular at craft shows that Roberts borrowed $400.00 on a Visa Card and started the Babyland Hospital, with local women helping to stitch the faces. Roberts visited yard sales to obtain clothing for his creations. The first Little People were not signed. Right from the start, Roberts' dolls had to be adopted rather than bought. In exchange for a signature and adoption fee, the new "parent" received a baby and birth certificate. To quote Roberts, "from the very beginning, the whole concept was for the babies to be different." These original Little People were so popular that Roberts licensed many adoption centers to make babies available for adoption. More than 500,000 of the Little People were adopted.

In 1982, Coleco was granted a license to mass produce the babies. Renaming them Cabbage Patch Kids, they were a smaller version of the original Little People. World-wide, 57 million Cabbage Patch Kids were adopted. Despite the tremendous popularity of Cabbage Patch Kids, Coleco closed its doors in 1989. That same year, Hasbro was licensed to mass produce Cabbage Patch Kids.

Every year there is a Cabbage Patch Convention in Cleveland, Georgia. At the 1993 Convention, over 5,000 people celebrated the adoption of more than 73 million Kids during the past fifteen years.

Values given are reported estimated values from collectors and devotees of Cabbage Patch Kids and Little People. Remember that the Birth Certificate, Adoption Papers, and Name Tags are important components. Use the Current Estimated Value as a tool to help you determine values. The secondary market for contemporary dolls is extremely volatile. All values given are for dolls in mint condition.

CABBAGE PATCH VALUE COMPARISONS:

Year	Edition	Birth Mark	Estimated Number Issued	Current Estimated Value
1978	Helen Blue	Signed	1,000	2,400.00
1978	"A" blue papers	Signed	1,000	1,700.00
1978	"B" red papers	Signed	1,000	1,400.00
1979	"C" burgundy papers	Signed	5,000	1,000.00
1979	"D" purple papers	Signed	10,000	900.00
1979	"X" Christmas, Limited Edition	Signed	1,000	1,400.00
1979	"E" bronze papers	Signed	15,000	800.00
1980	"SP" Preemie	Signed	5,000	700.00
1980	Christmas Set, Nicholas, Noel	Signed	2,500	600.00
1980	Grand Edition	Signed	1,000	900.00
1981	"U" Unsigned	Stamped	73,000	250.00
1981	New Ears Edition	Stamped	15,000	200.00
1981	"PR" II Preemie	Stamped	10,000	150.00
1981	Standing Edition	Stamped	5,000	250.00
1982	"PE" New Ears, Preemie	Stamped	5,000	275.00
1982	"U" Unsigned	Stamped	21,000	150.00
1982	Christmas Set, Christy, Nicole, Baby Rudy Cabbage Patch Kids Editions	Stamped	1,000	1,000.00
1982	Cabbage Patch Kids 10 Character Kids Set	Stamped	2,500	1,200.00 each 12,500.00 set
1983	Cleveland Green	Stamped	2,000	400.00
1983	"KP" dark green	Stamped	2,000	600.00
1983	"KPR" red	Stamped	2,000	600.00
1983	"KPB" burgundy	Stamped	10,000	250.00
1983	Oriental	Stamped	1,000	900.00
1983	Indian	Stamped	1,000	900.00
1983	Hispanic	Stamped	1,000	800.00
1983	Powder Scent	Stamped	Mass	125.00
1983	Bald Babies	Stamped	Mass	125.00
1983	Baby with pacifier	Stamped	Mass	200.00
1983	White, with freckles	Stamped	Mass	100.00
1983	Black, with freckles	Stamped	Mass	200.00
1983	Red fuzzy haired boy	Stamped	Mass	200.00
1984	"KPP" purple	Stamped	20,000	300.00
1984	"KPG" bronze	Stamped	30,000	150.00
1984	"KPF" turquoise	Stamped	30,000	150.00
1984	"KPG" coral	Stamped	35,000	150.00
1984	Single tooth	Stamped	Mass	175.00
1984	Popcorn hairdo	Stamped	Mass	200.00
1984	Gray eyed Kid	Stamped	Mass	175.00
1984	Champagne, Maderia, Andre	Signed	1,000	1,000.00
1984	Sweetheart, Candi, Beau	Stamped	750	450.00
1984	Bavarian Set	Stamped	1,000	1,750.00
1984	World Class Set	Stamped	2,500	900.00
1984	Daddy's Darlin's, Pun'kin, Tootsie, Princess, Kitten	Stamped	500	700.00
1984	Christmas, Carole, Chris	Stamped	1,000	200.00

CABBAGE PATCH VALUE COMPARISONS:

Year	Edition	Birth Mark	Estimated Number Issued	Current Estimated Value
1984	Green signature	Stamped	Mass	100.00
1985	Blue Signature	Stamped	Mass	85.00
1985	Christmas, Sandy, Claude	Stamped	2,500	200.00
1985	Emerald	Stamped	35,000	125.00
1985	Four Seasons, Crystal, Morton, Sunny, Autumn	Stamped	2,000	150.00
1985	Gold	Stamped	50,000	100.00
1985	Iris	Stamped	N/A	250.00
1985	Irish	Stamped	4,000	175.00
1985	Ivory	Stamped	45,000	100.00
1985	Preemie Show Baby	Stamped	15,000	150.00
1985	Preemie Twins, set	Signed	3,000	600.00
1985	Rose	Stamped	40,000	100.00
1985	Sapphire	Stamped	35,000	100.00
1986	Amethyst	Screened	10,000	100.00
1986	Christmas, Hillary, Nigel	Monogram	2,000	250.00
1986	Corporate Kids	Signed	2,000	600.00
1986	Georgia	Monogram	4,000	200.00
1986	Identical Twins, set	Stamped	5,000	200.00
1986	Mark Twain, Tom Sawyer, Huck Finn, Becky Thatcher	Monogram	2,500	400.00
1987	Baby Otis	Monogram	2,000	350.00
1987	Big Top Clown, Baby Cakes	Monogram	2,000	350.00
1987	Christmas, Katrina, Misha	Monogram	2,000	350.00
1987	Iddy Buds	Monogram	750	500.00
1987	Polynesian, Lokelina, Ohana	Monogram	1,000	400.00
1987	Sleeping Beauty, Prince Charming	Monogram	1,250	350.00
1987	Topaz	Screened	5,000	150.00
1988	Aquamarine	Screened	5,000	100.00
1988	Christmas, Kelly, Kane	Monogram	1,000	300.00
1988	Nursery Edition, Baby Marilyn Suzann, Baby Tyler Bo, Baby Dorothy Jane, Baby Sybil Sadie	Monogram	2,000	150.00
1989	Amber	Screened	3,000	135.00
1989	Christmas Joy	Monogram	500	400.00
1989	Fourth of July	Signed	3,000	175.00
1989	Lapis	Screened	2,000	150.00
1989	Mother's Day	Signed	5,000	150.00
1989	Ruby	Screened	1,325.00	100.00

There are over 25 different faces, many hairstyles, and a wide array of outfits. It would be impossible to list them all, but these examples should prove helpful. Most of the Cabbage Patch Kids not listed fall in the $75.00 to $100.00 range for dolls made before 1989. Assume a retail value for later dolls.

Vinyl heads are often marked:

Copy R 1978 Σ 1982
ORIGINAL APPALACHIAN ART WORKS INC.
MANUFACTURED BY COLECO IND. INC.
MADE IN HONG KONG

3

Cameo Doll Company

Mint Scootles with original box.

The Cameo Doll Company operated in Port Allegheny, PA, from 1922 until 1970. Joseph Kallus, the founder and president, gained notoriety through his work with Rose O'Neill in the modeling of dolls she created, especially the Kewpies. Cameo Doll Company became the sole manufacturer of composition Kewpies in the United States. They were distributed by George Borgfeldt & Company along with other dolls by Cameo such as Bye-Lo, Baby Bo-Kaye, and Little Annie Roonie.

The entire Cameo Doll Company, including equipment, was acquired by the Strombecker Corporation of Chicago in 1970.

Doll collectors are becoming more and more interested in dolls produced between World War I and World War II. The dolls of Cameo and Joseph Kallus are among the most avidly sought by collectors. While perhaps not having the appeal of the European bisque dolls, they have their own charm and, in terms of both artistry and construction, they are among the finest quality American dolls made in the 20th century.

It is not unusual for an early Cameo Doll to have no markings, or have only a paper wrist tag. Later Cameo Dolls were marked and, after 1970, the markings include "S71."

Prices listed are for dolls with no damage. Avoid restored and/or repainted composition dolls as the integrity of the doll is lost along with at least half its value.

See also Kewpie, Borgfeldt.

COMPOSITION

Scootles: all composition, jointed at neck, shoulders, and hips; deeply molded wavy hair; painted side-glancing eyes; closed smiling watermelon mouth; wearing original cotton romper.

Dog: dog head on wooden fully-jointed body. Marked paper label "Des & Copyright by J. L. Kallus."

Pete the Pup: segmented wood body, ball hands, large feet; large side-glancing eyes; round nose; wide smiling mouth. Marked "Pete the Pup" on chest, "Cameo" on foot.

Joy/Pinkie: segmented body, composition hands; molded and painted hair; side-glancing eyes; tiny pug nose; closed smiling mouth; wearing original sun dress.

Margie: separate neck piece attached by hook to eighteen-piece wood segmented body; painted hair and head band; side-glancing eyes, upper lashes, no lower lashes; painted, open, smiling mouth with four teeth; wearing original rayon shirt and lawn skirt.

CAMEO COMPOSITION VALUE COMPARISONS:

Size	Scootles	Black Scootles	Dog	Pete the Pup	Joy & Pinkie	Margie Marcie	Betty Boop	Giggles	Sissy	Little Annie Rooney	R.C.A. Radiotrons Pop-Eye/Crownie	Bandmaster	Baby Blossom
8"	450.00		600.00	400.00									
10"	500.00	750.00	700.00	450.00	350.00	300.00							
12"	600.00	900.00					700.00	800.00	250.00				
13"	700.00	1,200.00											
15"	850.00				450.00			1,000.00		900.00			
16"	900.00										900.00		
18"											1,000.00	700.00	
20"													1,200.00

Betty Boop: segmented body, composition hands, upper torso, and skirt; molded and painted black hair; side-glancing eyes; molded and painted red swimming suit. Marked "Betty Boop/Des & Copyright by Fleischer/Studios."

Giggles: starfish hands; painted hair with bun in back and bangs in front; side-glancing eyes; closed smiling mouth; wearing original romper. Wrist tag reads "Giggles/Designed and copyrighted/Rose O'Neill/Cameo Doll Co."

Marcie: painted hair; painted eyes staring to side; closed slightly puckered mouth; dressed in original young girl's French-style outfit (copied from clothing in Lord and Taylor's); molded and painted socks and shoes.

Sissy: painted hair; painted eyes; smiling mouth; wearing original printed percale dress.

Little Annie Roonie: one-piece head and torso, jointed shoulders and hips, long thin legs with molded-on shoes; orange yarn hair; big oval painted side-glancing eyes; small nose; closed smiling mouth; wearing original green dress, black coat, and red tam.

R.C.A. Radiotrons: separate neck piece attached by hook to wood segmented body; molded boots; molded and painted top hat in shape of radio tube; painted facial features. Marked "R.C.A. Radiotrons" across hat and on band across chest.

Pop-Eye: faithful reproduction of cartoon Popeye; wooden segmented body, finished in bright colors; molded sailor cap, no hair showing; painted small eyes; very full cheeks; wooden pipe in closed mouth; wood painted to represent clothing. Marked "King Features/Syn. Inc. 1932" on foot.

Bandmaster: (also known as Drum Major or Bandy); wooden segmented body (twenty segments assembled with coil spring); molded high shako head; humorously cheerful painted facial features; red and white painted drum major's uniform; carries wooden baton; composition medal molded around neck. Medal marked "G. E." (General Electric trademark).

Crownie: wooden segmented body; molded and painted long wavy hair with crown on top of head; painted closed eyes; jolly laughing open/closed mouth; brightly painted body representing clothing, wearing felt cape, holding wooden baton.

Baby Blossom: shoulder plate head, cloth body, composition bent-baby limbs; molded and painted hair in short style with lock coming down over forehead; baby-type face with painted side-glancing eyes; pug nose; dimples in fat cheeks; dressed in original short dress. Marked "Baby Blossom" on tag, "Des & Copyright/by J. L. Kallus/Made in USA."

VINYL

Scootles: fully-jointed vinyl body; molded and painted hair; painted eyes; closed smiling watermelon mouth; dressed in original cotton short dress and matching bonnet. Marked "R7234 Cameo JLK."

Miss Peep: all vinyl, pin-hinged joints at shoulders and hips; painted hair; insert, good-quality plastic eyes; nurser/open mouth (drink and wet baby); appropriately dressed. Marked "CAMEO."

Baby Mine: all vinyl, pin-hinged joints at shoulders and hips; painted hair; sleep eyes; open/closed mouth with molded tongue; appropriately dressed. Marked "CAMEO."

Plum: one-piece latex body; two squeakers, one in bottom for spanking, one in tummy for hugging; painted hair; sleep eyes; open/closed mouth; appropriately dressed. Marked "Cameo."

CAMEO VINYL VALUE COMPARISONS:

Size	Scootles	Miss Peep	Baby Mine	Plum
14"	200.00			
15"		175.00		
16"			200.00	
18"		250.00		175.00
19"	350.00		250.00	
21"		300.00		
24"				250.00
27"	700.00			

Campbell® Kids

Various manufacturers have produced Campbell Kids. The Kids were originally designed by Grace Drayton in 1909 for Campbell's advertising cards. They immediately became popular with children. Within a year, dolls were being manufactured not only as premiums but for over-the-counter sales.

The earliest Horsman composition-on-cloth bodies were made with a flange neck. In 1914, a shoulder head was used so the dolls could wear clothes with lower necklines.

In 1929, American Character Company acquired the license for Campbell Kids. Their all-composition version was slightly pigeon-toed when standing. They are marked with raised lettering on the neck "A Petite Doll." Outfits were copies from Campbell Soup advertisements.

Horsman began to manufacture Campbell Kids again in the late 1940s. Although the dolls were unmarked, some do exist with original tags which read "Campbell Kid/A Horsman Doll." The Canadian company of Dee and Cee purchased the rights to the Horsman Campbell Kids in the late 1940s. The Dee and Cee dolls are similar to the Horsman Campbell Kids, but some differences are evident. The composition is not as fine a quality as Horsman's; eyelashes tend to be heavier and thicker; and the hair color is more orange than brown.

Ideal created vinyl and latex Campbell Kids during the 1950s.

It is extremely difficult to find a Horseman Campbell Kid in good condition. Bearing this in mind, look for examples with as little crazing and paint loss as possible. Avoid totally restored and repainted composition as the integrity of the doll is lost, along with more than half its value.

COMPOSITION

All composition Campbell Kids share a similar face with molded and painted hair; round side-glancing eyes; chubby cheeks; pug nose; and closed smiling mouth. Distinguishing characteristics are body types and markings which include:

12" Mint Horsman Campbell Kid. *Courtesy of Gladys Dichter.*

	CAMPBELL KID VALUE COMPARISONS:						
Size	Prenium Campbell Kid	Early Horsman, All Cloth Body	Later Horsman, All Composition	Dee & Cee, All Composition	Am. Char., All Composition	Magic Skin	Bicentennial
10"	250.00	250.00				50.00	175.00
12"		350.00	475.00	450.00	400.00	75.00	
14"		450.00					

Chad Valley, Ltd.

20" Chad Valley Long John Silver. *Courtesy of Gladys Dichter.*

In the 1929-1930 period, the Chad Valley catalog offered hundreds of dolls, but only four were cloth babies. Most of the dolls manufactured by Chad Valley were children. The royal children dolls were extremely popular. They included representation of Princess Elizabeth, Princess Margaret Rose, Prince Edward, and Princess Alexandria.

A series of six Black dolls with outfits representative of different ethnic cultures was also produced. A Black boy was made wearing tweed knicker-type pants, a large cap, and red suspenders. Carolina wears a grass skirt, beads, bracelets, and a head band. Rajah wears an East Indian outfit with turban and full trousers. Nabob and others were also dressed with great detail.

Prices listed are for dolls in good, clean condition, undamaged, and with original clothing. If damaged, faded, or worn, expect to pay half the values given.

Character Dolls: velvet face and body; plush wig, glass or painted side-glancing eyes; painted facial features. Marked with foot label "Hygienic Toys/Made in England by/Chad Valley Co. Ltd.," label on back reads "Chad Valley/Hygienic/Toys/Made in/England/The Seal of Purity."

Child Dolls, Felt Mask: velvet body; good wig; double thickness of felt for ears; glass eyes or painted side-glancing eyes; molded and painted facial features; appropriately dressed. Typically marked with cloth label sewn on foot "Hygienic Toys/Made in England by/Chad Valley Co. Ltd." and celluloid button "Chad Valley/British/Hygienic Toys."

Royals, Felt Mask: velvet body; mohair wig; glass eyes; nicely molded features in portrait likeness; appropriately dressed. Typically marked "HRH (Name)/British Made Doll/By permission of/Her Majesty The Queen/Sole makers/The Chad Valley Co. Ltd./Harbonne/England."

Chad Valley was located in Harbonne, England, and manufactured toys as early as 1897. The company was a part of England's National Scheme for employment of disabled men and contractors for His Majesty's Government. Chad Valley, Ltd. began producing dolls in 1917 and continued into the 1940s. Various types of cloth dolls were made, the earliest predominately with stockinette faces. Around 1924, the company began producing hand-painted felt faces on dolls made of velvet or velveteen.

The quality of Chad Valley Dolls also varied. Cheaper examples were cloth dolls with printed clothes. Better dolls had combable wigs, threaded glass eyes, molded hand-painted faces, and removable fashion clothes. Dresses and suits were extremely short, exposing long legs.

CHAD VALLEY, LTD. VALUE COMPARISONS:

Size	Character Doll, Glass Eyes	Character Doll, Painted Eyes	Child Doll, Glass Eyes	Child Doll, Painted Eyes	Royals
10"		250.00		300.00	
12"	800.00	350.00		450.00	
14"	950.00	450.00	700.00	550.00	
16"	1,200.00	550.00	750.00	700.00	1,700.00
18"	1,600.00	600.00	900.00	800.00	1,900.00
20"	2,200.00				

Martha Chase

Martha Chase Dolls were made in Pawtucket, Rhode Island, from about 1880 to 1938. Chase Dolls were made of stockinette fabric, with material stretched over a mask with raised features. The head and limbs were sized with a coating of glue and paste, dried, and painted with oils. Features were hand painted, the rough brush strokes of the hair providing a realistic texture. Ears and thumbs were applied separately. The earliest Chase Dolls had pink sateen bodies. Later bodies were made from heavy white cotton cloth stuffed with cotton batting. Legs and arms were painted to above the knees and elbows, and an unstuffed area was left at each joint to facilitate movement. Many of the Chase Dolls were jointed at the shoulders, elbows, hips, and knees. Later dolls were jointed only at the hips and shoulders.

Mrs. Chase was quoted in the 1917 issue of *Toys and Novelties*: "I first made the dolls about 28 years ago (1889) as an amusement and to see what I could do. For several years I did this and gave the dolls away to the neighborhood children. Then by chance a store buyer saw one and insisted upon my taking an order. That was about 20 years ago, and since then there has been a gradual increase in the business. The dolls gained recognition by their merits, as I have advertised them very little. Then someone who knew about them asked me to make one adult size to use in the hospital training schools and from that has developed another new industry. Now (1917) we are making dolls that can be immersed in water and used in child welfare work."

A 1911 Gimbles advertisement shows Martha Chase Dolls were twice as expensive as the finest bisque head doll sold.

Prices listed are for dolls with no damage, unless otherwise noted. Normal wear and surface dust is to be expected and does not greatly affect price. Expect to pay less than half the amounts listed for badly worn or repaired dolls and even less for repainted dolls.

16" Chase Girl. *Photo courtesy of McMasters Doll Auction.*

	MARTHA CHASE VALUE COMPARISONS:			
Size	Chase Adult, Female	Chase Adult, Male	Chase Baby	Child
14"	1,600.00	3,200.00	550.00	
16"			700.00	1,700.00
18"	2,200.00	3,500.00	750.00	2,000.00
20"			800.00	2,200.00
22"	2,500.00	3,800.00	850.00	2,300.00
24"			900.00	2,800.00
26"			1,000.00	3,000.00
30"				3,400.00

Adult: stockinette adult face, cloth body; heavy oil paint covering head, arms, and legs; painted hair; painted eyes, heavy lashes; closed mouth; appropriately dressed. Typically marked "Made by Martha Chase" under arm, "Chase Hospital Doll," or with tag which reads "Made by hand/Chase Stockinette Doll."

Baby: stockinette baby face, cloth body; heavy oil paint covering head, arms, and legs; painted hair; painted eyes; chubby cheeks; slightly smiling mouth; appropriately dressed. Typically marked with paper label on back "The Chase Stockinette Doll/Made of Stockinette and Cloth/Stuffed with cotton/Made by Hand/Painted by Hand/Made by Especially Trained Workers" or stamped "Made by Martha Chase" or "Chase Hospital Doll."

Child: stockinette child face, cloth body; heavy oil paint covering head, arms, and legs; painted hair style; attached ears; painted eyes, heavy lashes; painted slightly smiling mouth; appropriately dressed. Typically marked "Chase Hospital Doll" or "Made by Martha Chase."

Portrait Character: stockinette, cloth body, character features raised and painted in oils; good wig or painted hair; painted eyes; attached ears; closed mouth; appropriately dressed. Marked with label on back "The Chase Stockinette Doll/Made of stockinette and cloth."

CHARACTER PRICE COMPARISONS:								
Size	Duchess	Frog Footman	Mad Hatter	Tweedle Dee	Tweedle Dum	Alice in Wonderland	George Washington	Black ethnic
6"	3,200.00	3,700.00	3,500.00	3,700.00	3,700.00			
18"						3,500.00		
23"								9,000.00
25"							6,500.00	
27"								10,000.00

China Heads

China Heads of glazed porcelain were made primarily in Germany from 1840 to the 1920s. Identifying China Heads according to manufacturer is nearly impossible. Facial features vary little. Most China Heads have painted blue eyes with a red line indicating an eyelid, full cheeks, and a small closed smiling mouth.

Prior to 1880, most China Heads were sold separately. The buyer either purchased a body or made one. Some very early China Heads were attached to commercially-made wooden jointed bodies with china limbs.

Some China Heads have painted brown eyes, or glass eyes and pierced ears. Glass-eyed China Heads Dolls were often referred to as "French China." In reality, most were made in Germany. Flesh tone china is known as "pink luster." Flesh colored China Heads with wigs rather than painted hair are often referred to as "English China." Another rare find would be a china socket head attached to a china shoulder plate. China Heads with girls names stamped in gold letters on a molded yoke were known as "Pet Name" dolls. These dolls gave a final boost to the china head market before losing ground to the lovely bisque dolls around the turn-of-the-century.

Lowbrow China doll.

China Head group with Biedermeier, Covered Wagon, Curly Top, Snood, Fancy-style with exposed, pierced ears and glass eyes, and Flat Top with pierced ears.

The common wavy low brow of the late 1800s continued to be produced in Germany through the 1940s, and thereafter in other countries as reproductions. Reproduction China Heads are plentiful and can be difficult to spot. Most China Heads have no markings, making authentication that much more difficult. Although reproductions are very similar in appearance to the originals, some differences are evident. Reproductions usually have a good clean slip, whereas antique China Heads are often found with peppered china (tiny black flecks are called peppering). Antique China Heads often have a red line above the eyes. Reproductions usually do not. Obtaining the doll's history from the seller can also be of help.

The prices listed are for dolls with undamaged porcelain. Normal wear or well-done repairs to the original body do not greatly affect price. If the porcelain is damaged or repaired, expect to pay less than half the amount listed. A china head without a body commands about 65% of the amount listed.

French China Head: glass or beautifully painted eyes, feathered brows; open crown with cork pate and good wig; shapely kid body; appropriately dressed, 1850s.

English China Head: flesh-tinted china; painted features; solid dome head with good wig; appropriately dressed, 1840s.

Lowbrow: common hairstyle, painted blond or black hair; painted eyes; appropriately dressed, c. 1890.

Covered Wagon: hair styled flat on top with sausage curls around head; appropriately dressed, 1840s.

Bun China Head: hair styled in bun, braid, or roll in back; appropriately dressed, 1840s. Add an additional $500.00 for a fancy braided bun.

Biedermeier: bald or solid dome head, some with top of head painted; good wig; appropriately dressed, 1840s.

Flat Top, aka Civil War or High Brow: hair styled with part in middle and short curls around head; appropriately dressed, 1850s.

Alice (In Wonderland): hair styled with molded head band; appropriately dressed, 1850s.

Curly Top: hair styled with ringlet curls over entire head; 1850s.

Exposed Ear: hair style pulled back from face; features exposed ears and hair pulled back in curly bun; appropriately dressed, 1850s.

Sophia Smith: hair styled with straight sausage curls not curved to head; appropriately dressed, 1860s.

Jenny Lind: hair style parted in middle and pulled back into bun; appropriately dressed, 1860s.

Mary Todd Lincoln: wearing snood; variations include painted black hair with snood, painted blond hair with black snood, or elaborate decoration at the crown with flowers and ruffles; appropriately dressed, 1860s.

Currier & Ives: hair styled with long bangs and molded head band; appropriately dressed, 1860s.

Adelina Patti: elaborate hairstyle with center part and rolled curls; appropriately dressed, 1860s.

Highland Mary: hair styled with straight top with curls at sides; appropriately dressed, 1860s.

Countess Dagmar: identified by pierced ears and various elaborate hairstyles with molded bow and fine decoration; appropriately dressed, 1840s.

Spill Curl: hair styled with individual curls over forehead and shoulders; appropriately dressed, 1870s.

Dolly Madison: hair styled with curls all over and molded ribbon; 1870s.

Highbrow: very round face and high forehead; hair styled with center part and flat top with sausage curls around head; appropriately dressed, 1870s.

Glass Eyed: painted hair with exposed ears; appropriately dressed, 1870s.

Man or Boy: masculine-styled china head; appropriately dressed, 1870s.

Pet Name China Head: common hairstyle; name printed in gold on front of shoulder plate; appropriately dressed; 1905. Names include Agnes, Bertha, Daisy, Dorothy, Edith, Esther, Ethel, Florence, Helen, Mabel, Marion, Pauline, and Ruth.

CHINA HEADS VALUE COMPARISONS:

Size	French China Head	English China Head	Lowbrow China Head	Covered Wagon China Head	Bun China Head	Biedermeier China Head	Flat Top China Head	Alice in Wonderland	Curly Top	Exposed Ear
12"	3,000.00	1,800.00	225.00	500.00	2,000.00	900.00	250.00			
14"	3,300.00	2,000.00		700.00		1,000.00	300.00		600.00	
16"		2,200.00	250.00	800.00	2,700.00		325.00	500.00	700.00	3,500.00
18"	3,800.00				3,200.00	1,200.00		550.00	850.00	
20"	4,500.00	2,500.00		900.00		1,500.00	350.00	700.00	1,000.00	4,200.00
22"	4,900.00	3,500.00	350.00	1,100.00	5,000.00			900.00	1,200.00	4,800.00
24"				1,200.00		1,800.00	450.00			
30"				1,300.00			650.00			
36"			1,200.00	1,400.00			1,000.00			

CHINA HEADS VALUE COMPARISONS:

Size	Sophia Smith China Head	Jenny Lind China Head	Mary Todd Lincoln	Currier & Ives	Adelina Patti	Highland Mary	China Socket Head	Countess Dagmar
12"		900.00			350.00	250.00	2,400.00	
14"		1,100.00		450.00	500.00	350.00		650.00
16"	2,300.00	1,200.00			550.00	375.00		
18"		1,300.00	800.00	600.00	675.00	425.00	4,300.00	900.00
20"	3,200.00	1,400.00	850.00	650.00		475.00		
22"	3,500.00		1,200.00	700.00	750.00			1,100.00
24"		1,600.00				600.00		
30"				2,200.00				

CHINA HEADS VALUE COMPARISONS:

Size	Spill Curl	Dolly Madison or Highbrow	Glass Eye	Man or Boy	Pet Name
12"					225.00
14"	900.00	450.00	3,800.00	1,200.00	275.00
16"	1,000.00	500.00		1,300.00	325.00
18"	1,200.00	550.00		1,500.00	
20"	1,400.00	600.00	4,500.00	1,700.00	400.00
22"	1,600.00	650.00	4,800.00		
24"	1,800.00	750.00			500.00
28"		900.00			
30"	2,800.00				

Note: For all China Head Dolls, add an additional $300.00 for pierced ears, $800.00 for glass eyes, $800.00 for special decoration, or $500.00 for wooden articulated body.

Cloth Dolls

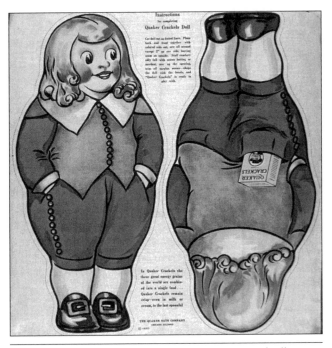

Uncut Crackles Cereal Advertising Doll. *Courtesy of Bill Tyson.*

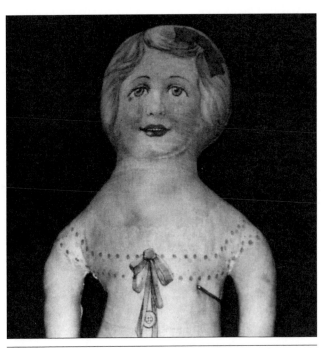

20" Cut and Sew Cloth Doll. *Courtesy of Helen Brooke.*

From the earliest pioneering days until the present, Cloth Dolls of all types have been produced in the United States. The two most popular types are Pillow or Rag dolls and Vintage Folk Art Dolls.

Pillow or Rag dolls were early printed or lithographed Cloth Dolls designed to be cut, sewn, and stuffed at home. Detailed instructions were printed alongside the figures. Most early printed Cloth Dolls were produced in New England, the center of American textile manufacturing in the 1880s.

Many of the early printed Cloth Dolls promoted various products. The inexpensive Cloth Dolls were a perfect advertising medium.

Toy manufacturers were slow to realize the commercial value of Cloth Dolls. Although a few patents were issued in the 1860s and 1870s, it was not until the mid-1880s that patented and perfected Rag Dolls appeared in any great quantity in the United States.

The war years between 1914 and 1920 meant sacrifices for everyone. Doll manufacturing was limited to materials not essential to the war effort. Consequently, Rag Dolls enjoyed a boom.

Vintage Folk Art Dolls handmade by known or unknown crafters are extremely popular with today's collectors. The condition of early "fabric art" dolls is often not as crucial a price determination as it is with other dolls. The charm and personal appeal of these early treasures is often more important. There are vast differences in quality in Folk Art Dolls, depending on the talent and skill of the maker. Uniqueness makes general pricing difficult. Several sample listings are provided here in order to help gauge the current vintage Folk Art Doll market.

Collectors need to be careful when purchasing Cloth Dolls. Craft shows offer hundreds of "aged" Cloth Dolls. Some even have an "attic odor." These charming dolls are made by clever crafters as accent pieces, with no intention of passing them off as antiques. However, they are often very well made and authentic looking, and collectors should be wary. One particular copy that was not intended as a fake, but which has caused some confusion, is the reprint of Palmer Cox Brownies. These convincing reprints even bear the original 1892 copyright date. A clue to spotting these reprints is that they appear paler in color and measure 7". The original Brownies measured 8" and were brightly colored.

When examining a cloth doll, check for stains, fading, holes, tears, or badly soiled areas. Slight overall dust or fading and the normal wear of time is acceptable, and perhaps even adds to the charm of these collectible dolls. Prices listed are for dolls in good, clean condition, showing only normal wear. When a cloth doll is badly worn, faded, soiled, or torn, expect to pay less than half the amount listed.

VINTAGE PILLOW OR RAG DOLL (1880-1930)

American Beauty Doll: Empire Art Company; pretty child with hair ribbon; printed with undergarments, socks, and shoes, separate soles to feet.

Beauty the Cat: Varden Fabric; yellow, tan, and white calico cat print; separate oval bottom with paws.

Brownies: Arnold Print Works; "Irishman" with yellow cap, red band, green jacket, red pants, gray-blue socks, and dark orange slippers. Marked on right foot "Copyrighted 1892 by Palmer Cox."

Buster Brown: Art Fabric Mills/Knickerbacher; printed blond hair in Dutch boy style; happy smiling face; brown suit with knickers, white shirt, blue tie, white stockings, brown ankle strap shoes.

Columbian Sailor Doll: Arnold Print Works; printed brown hair; very attractive face; red cap, blue coat, red striped pants, brown boots. Marked along rim of cap "Arnold Print Works Pat Jan. 13, 1893." This commemorative doll was issued for the Columbian Exposition of 1912.

Darky Doll: Cocheco Mfg. Company; Black boy; unusual feature of seam down center of face gives doll a three-dimensional look; printed tan cap, red jacket, black pants, tan socks, and brown shoes.

Foxy Grandpa: Art Fabric Mills/Knickerbacher; bald head, gray hair at sides, round wire rim glasses; smiling mouth; suit and vest, white shirt, bold tie, pocket watch hanging from side pocket; bunny tucked under his arm; printed spats, black shoes; made to look as though his hands are in his pockets.

Liberty Belle: Annin & Company; silk-screened brown hair; red and white striped hat, blue band with stars and stripes and "Liberty Belle" across front; dressed in jumper in shape of Liberty Bell and "150 Years of American Independence 1776-1926 Sesquicentennial" printed on skirt over red shirt; white star trimmed cuff; red and white striped socks, blue shoes. Marked on back "Pat. Appl'd for Annin & Co. NY."

Little Red Riding Hood: Arnold Print Works; printed blond hair; red hooded cape over cream-colored dress with black trim; white socks, brown shoes; holding daisies in one hand, basket in other; made to look as though doll is standing in grass. Marked on oval base "Patented July 5, 1892 & Oct. 4 1892. Arnold Print Works North Adam, Mass. Incorporated 1876."

Punch & Judy: Art Fabric Mills; complicated cutting and sewing; some seams go down sides and others down front of dolls. Punch has characteristic hooked nose, jutting chin, wide grin; hunched back; lace trimmed plaid jacket, red pants, blue shoes, and blue and red peaked hat. Judy has sharp-featured profile, black hair; smiling character face; plaid gown, white collar, lace trim, and red, blue, and white bonnet.

Roosevelt Bear: Selchow & Righter; bear in sitting position; attached limbs and ears; printed brown wavy fur; open mouth, red tongue.

St. Nicholas/Peck's Santa: New York Stationery and Envelope Company; printed gray beard and hair; closed eyes; red nose; pipe in mouth; pocket watch peeking out from under fur-edged jacket; American flag tucked into belt; holding armful of toys including Chinese doll, pinwheel, hobbyhorse, drum, girl doll, ball, stuffed animal, bell, sword, and wagon. Marked "Patent Applied for Santa Claus" printed under his hand near flag.

Topsy Doll: Art Fabric Mills; Black child with extra piece for foot; short curly hair; exaggerated ethnic features; wearing union suit; printed "Topsy Doll," directions and "Here's something to entertain 'em,/To help 'em in their play./Mama can make 'em,/Baby can't break 'em,/And they will last for many a day."

A general guide for printed Cloth Dolls in very good condition follows. Uncut sheets are valued at twice the amounts listed.

VINTAGE PILLOW OR RAG DOLL COMPARISONS:

Size	Child	Black	Character	Animals	Collectible
8"	150.00				50.00
12"	175.00			250.00	
14"	200.00			300.00	100.00
15"	200.00	300.00		350.00	125.00
16"	225.00	350.00	250.00		150.00
18"	250.00	400.00	275.00		175.00
20"	275.00	450.00	300.00		
24"	300.00		400.00		

COLLECTIBLE AND CONTEMPORARY PRINTED CLOTH DOLLS (1940-1970)

Archie: orange hair, dark thick eyebrows; wide open eyes; freckles across nose; printed red shirt, orange and black bell bottom pants; marked "Archie" c. 1960. . . . . **175.00**

Snow White and the Seven Dwarfs: dwarfs with character faces; Snow White with black hair and red ribbon; the set **150.00**

VINTAGE FOLK ART DOLLS

15": all cloth, handmade, cotton stuffed, one-piece; hands and head completely painted over; facial features embroidered in red and black thread; twisted thread hair knotted to head; original old woolen clothes; hand knitted stockings; appealing face, sweet smile. . .**125.00**

16": all cloth, handmade; face is picture-cut from paper and covered with gauze; poorly proportioned body with long arms and short legs; rather large bosom; wearing original print cotton dress, net and lace bonnet. **125.00**

18": all cloth, handmade, black stockinette limbs; stockinette head shows considerable skill in its making; hand-stitched molded features; red painted lips; black shoe button irises on painted white eyes; black wool wig with red ribbons; brass rings sewn to side of head for earrings; wearing original printed cotton dress with apron; none of the typical "Mammy doll" qualities found on many Black dolls. **250.00**

20": all cloth, handmade, two-piece head and torso (front and back) joined at side seams; legs attached to body at hips; stub hands; painted head, arms, and booted legs; nicely done features; dressed in cotton dress with ruffled trim. **125.00**

21": all cloth, handmade, artistically-made man doll; cotton stuffed body; very long limbs; stitched fingers; oil-painted head, arms, and booted feet; extremely well done facial features, shading and accents giving great charm; original finely-made blue wool suit, brocade vest, white shirt, and red tie; carrying black top hat. **400.00**

26": all cloth, handmade, one-piece; rather naive ink drawn features; touches of red on lips and cheeks; horse hair sewn to head for hair; wearing original brown cotton dress; feather stitched, red satin insert at bodice; white apron, hand-knitted stockings, straw hat. **200.00**

COLLECTIBLE FOLK ART DOLLS

Nancy and Her Doll: Marla Florio; 12", all cloth, one-of-a-kind; stiff cloth legs; clutching armful of cloth minibabies; yarn hair; needle-sculptured features; blue sweater, print slacks, white socks, blue shoes. . .**350.00**

Dolly: 15", all cloth, stuffed body, attached head, arms, and legs jointed to allow movement; yarn hair styled in braids; felt and embroidered facial features; handmade pink dress with rows of lace; white socks, white leather handmade shoes with pink bows; unmarked. **75.00**

Topsy Turvy Doll: Mamie Tyson; 16", all cloth; head at both ends, attached at mid-section—one head is white with yellow yarn hair, embroidered wide awake facial features, nicely stitched fingers, and pink flowered dress with eyelet trim. Doll flips over and dress falls to reveal black doll with black yarn hair, embroidered sleeping facial features, nicely stitched fingers, and white nightie with eyelet trim; exceptional quality and workmanship. **200.00**

Nursing African Doll: Ann Fisher; 24", brown cloth doll; large head; long arms attached to body; well developed bosom; black yarn hair tied up in big red bow; felt eyes, large round white circles with black centers; wide red felt mouth; brass rings sewn on sides of head as earrings; removable twin babies attached to bosom with snaps; brightly colored print skirt. **85.00**

Dewees Cochran

The story of Dewees Cochran's life and doll making career is fascinating yet bittersweet. Dewees was the only child of affluent parents. She was educated in private schools before attending the School of Industrial Art in Philadelphia and the Pennsylvania Academy of Fine Arts. After completing her studies in the United States, she traveled to Europe where she studied and taught art and art history.

Dewees met Paul Helbeck while studying at the International People's College in Elsinore, Denmark. They were married in her parent's home in September of 1924. After the wedding, Paul and Dewees returned to Europe to pursue the artistic life of artist and writer. Situations changed drastically and their ideal life together ended. The stock market crash, the rise of Nazi power in Germany, and the death of her father in March of 1933 made it necessary for the couple to return to America. Dewees' mother was forced to sell her home and furnishings in order to pay off the mortgages. Dewees decided to stay in the United States to help her mother, rather than return to Europe as she and Paul had planned.

Settling in New Hope, Pennsylvania, Dewees began creating dolls. Her first creations were sold at local gift shops. Later, she traveled to New York City to peddle her dolls at fashionable shops such as Saks. Dewees eventually created meticulously sculpted and dressed living portrait dolls. Orders poured in within days of their introduction. The early portrait dolls featured carved balsa wood heads, perfectly proportioned stuffed silk bodies, and beautiful costumes.

Following the success of her portrait dolls, Dewees and Paul moved to New York. Realizing that the wealthy were not alone in desiring her portrait dolls, Dewees set out to produce quality dolls at more affordable prices. In 1936, Dewees developed six basic face shapes and created a less expensive portrait doll. Dewees believed that any child could be captured in a portrait doll through the use of one of these shapes. The six basic Look-Alike heads were: Cynthia, an oval happy smiling face with teeth showing; Abigail, a rather square face with slightly smiling expression; Lisa, with a triangular face barely smiling; Deborah, with heart shaped face slightly smiling; Melanie, a very thin long face with a slight smile; and Jezebel, a round face with slightly pouting mouth. With proper eye and wig coloring, a portrait doll could be likened to nearly any child.

Paul, who had until this point been supportive and a source of inspiration, felt that his own career was being neglected. He desperately wanted to return to Europe to resume his writings. It was decided that Paul would return, and Dewees would join him later. Unfortunately, Dewees' financial situation, coupled with responsibilities to her mother, prevented her reunion with Paul. Although she remained Mrs. Paul Helbeck, Dewees and Paul never saw each other again, a circumstance they came to accept as they concentrated on their individual careers.

The war years all but brought an end to Dewees Cochran doll production. Latex was the culprit, having been requisitioned as a strategic war material. Dewees became Art Director for the R.H. Donnelley Corporation, and later Design Director for the School of American Craftsmen. However, when the war ended and materials were once again available, she formed a small doll company— Dewees Cochran Dolls, Inc. In 1947, a 15" Cindy Doll was introduced.

The contract for the fabrication of the Cindy Doll was awarded to Molded Latex Company of New Jersey, owner of the patented latex process. The doll was transported from the New Jersey factory to the workshop at 10 E. 46th Street, New York City, where it was assembled, wigged, dressed, packed, and shipped. Although originally satisfied with the doll, the Molded Latex Company failed to meet the high standards set by Dewees. After less than one year and 1,000 Cindy Dolls, Dewees withdrew from the company. Authentic Cindy Dolls have a written production number and "Dewees Cochran Dolls" embossed on their torsos. Molded Latex Company continued marketing unmarked dolls of lesser quality following Dewees' departure.

In 1951-52, Dewees developed the famous "Grow-Up" series of dolls. Susan Stormalong (Stormie) had red hair; Angela Appleseed (Angel) had blond hair; and Belinda Bunyan (Bunnie) was a brunette. The three girls were portrayed as grand nieces of famous American folklore characters: Bullhead Stormalong, a Cape Cod fisherman, Johnny Appleseed, and Paul Bunyan. In 1957, two little boys, Peter Ponsett, a blond extrovert, and Jefferson Jones (Jeff) a brunette introvert, joined the Grow-Up family. The Grow-Up Series was an instant success. For the next five years, a new version of each doll was produced with features representing various stages of development. A child of five could watch her doll progress through ages 5, 7, 11, 16, and 20

Dewees Cochran Child. *Photo courtesy of McMasters Doll Auction.*

over the span of five years. Grow-Up Dolls matured from childhood to adulthood in face and figure, growing from 12½ to 18 inches.

When interviewed some years ago by the Valley Press in California, Dewees explained her choices. "I've never wanted to put my art into large production. I suppose I could have made much more money, but your soul gets twisted by the things you have to do for that kind of success. What I do has to do with people, with children, and the love of children. It has nothing to do with the commercial side."

High quality materials made these dolls more durable and less likely to be damaged than their contemporaries. Prices are for dolls in good original condition. Dolls which have slight crazing or which are redressed or undressed command prices only about one-third of the examples listed. Also, beware of the Molded Latex Company Cindy copy, easily recognized by the absence of a Dewees Cochran mark.

See also Artist Dolls and Effanbee.

Look-Alike Portrait Dolls: (1 of 6 faces); Custom Order Portrait Doll, all latex, joined at neck, shoulders, and hips; human hair wig; painted eyes, human hair lashes; open closed mouth; beautifully dressed. Marked "Dewees Cochran Dolls 19＿＿" in script on small of back.

Grow-Up Series Dolls: (Stormie, Angle, Bunnie, Peter, or Jeff, ages 6-20); all latex, jointed at neck, shoulders, and hips; human hair wig; painted eyes, human hair lashes; beautifully dressed. Marked "DC" and signed around initials on back. Typically marked: "D.C./BB-54 #9," "D.C./S.S. 58/1," and "D.C./J.J. 60/2."

Cindy: all latex, jointed at neck, shoulders, and hips; human hair wig; painted brown eyes, human hair lashes; closed slightly smiling mouth. Marked "Dewees Cochran Dolls" within oval. Production number written above mark.

DEWEES COCHRAN VALUE COMPARISONS:			
Size	Look-Alike	Grow-Up Series	Cindy
12½"		2,200.00	
15"			1,500.00
15½"		2,300.00	
17"	2,500.00		
18"		2,400.00	

Columbian Dolls

mma and Marietta Adams, sisters living in Oswego, NY, made and dressed cloth dolls in their home from 1891 until about 1910. Columbian Dolls were named for the Columbian Exposition, the World's Fair held in Chicago in 1893, where the dolls were exhibited. The Miss Columbia Doll traveled around the world as an ambassador of good will and, in 1902, was presented to President William Howard Taft.

Faces on early Columbian Dolls were painted with considerable finesse by Emma. Following her death in 1900, Marietta continued the business for another ten years, hiring less skillful commercial artists to take Emma's place. Columbian Dolls were outfitted by Marietta and wore simple cotton dresses, bonnets or caps, and hand-sewn kidskin slippers or booties.

Although Columbian Dolls were not patented, they do have a rubber stamp identification on the backs of their bodies. Many craft-type cloth and rag doll reproductions have been made, but none are marked with the Columbian Doll stamp.

Prices listed are for dolls with normal wear and no tears, stains, or fading. Expect to pay about half the amount listed for dolls in less than fair condition.

Early Columbian Doll: cloth, stitched joints at shoulders, hips, and knees; stitched fingers and toes; painted flesh-colored lower limbs; painted hair and eyes; heart-shaped nostrils; rosebud mouth; rosy cheeks; appropriately dressed. Marked "Columbia Doll/Emma E. Adams/Oswego Centre/N.Y."

Later Columbian Doll: cloth, stitched joints at shoulders, hips, and knees; stitched fingers and toes; painted flesh-colored lower limbs; painted hair and eyes; rather long mouth; slight blush on cheeks; appropriately dressed. Marked "The Columbian Doll/Manufactured by/Marietta Adams Ruttan/Oswego N.Y." on back.

15" Columbian baby. Photo courtesy of McMasters Doll Auction.

	COLOMBIAN CLOTH DOLL VALUE COMPARISONS:			
Size	Early Mark White	Early Mark Black	Later Mark White	Later Mark Black
15"	5,700.00	7,500.00	3,800.00	6,200.00
18"	6,500.00		4,800.00	
20"	7,000.00	9,500.00		
22"	8,000.00		6,800.00	
24"	10,000.00			
29"	14,000.00		10,000.00	

Composition

Composition Dolls were made by countless manufacturers in various countries from 1912 until about 1940. Many are unmarked and/or unidentified. The earliest composition was made from rags, bones, hides, and other waste materials which were boiled and molded. Later composition was pulp-based.

When World War I halted imports, American doll makers seized upon the opportunity to market dolls without foreign competition. Hundreds of small companies began production and after a year or two quietly went out of business. Thousands of these Composition Dolls with no marks or unknown marks were produced and sold.

The years of Composition Doll production were not particularly happy times for the American people. The Depression and both World Wars are possible explanations for the large quantity of comic characters produced.

Composition Dolls have reached an age in which signs of crazing are acceptable, as are age stress lines at the eyes and mouth openings, and crackling of the eyes. Considering that many of these dolls were manufactured during some of the most difficult and depressed times in this century, it is rather amazing that they have survived as well as they have. Prices listed are for dolls with no damage or showing only slight wear. If the doll is damaged, badly crazed with lifting paint, or extensively restored or repainted, expect to pay about one-fourth of the amounts listed. Mint condition composition doll are rare and can easily command twice the listed amount.

Flange Neck Child: cloth body, composition limbs, painted features; appropriately dressed. Unmarked or marked by a lesser or unknown manufacturer.

Shoulder Head Mama: cloth body, composition limbs; good wig; glass, tin, or glassine eyes; open mouth with teeth; appropriately dressed. Unmarked or marked by lesser or unknown manufacturer.

Socket Head Baby Doll: composition bent-limb baby body; molded hair or wig; sleep or painted eyes; open or closed mouth; appropriately dressed. Unmarked or marked by a lesser or unknown manufacturer.

Socket Head Child: exceptionally good quality dolly-face on composition jointed body; good wig; sleep eyes, at times flirty eyes; open mouth with teeth; appropriately dressed. Unmarked or marked by lesser or unknown manufacturer.

Socket Head Child: standard quality, composition body; good wig; sleep eyes; open mouth with teeth; appropriately dressed. Unmarked or marked by lesser or unknown manufacturer.

Socket Head Loop Type: molded loop for hair bows; all composition body jointed at shoulders and hips or

17" Composition teen doll. *Courtesy of Pat Tyson.*

tightly stuffed cloth torso with composition limbs; painted facial features; appropriately dressed. Unmarked or marked by a lesser or unknown manufacturer.

Socket Head Patsy-type: all composition, jointed at neck, shoulders, and hips; slightly bent right arm; long thin legs, molded and painted bobbed hair, painted or sleep eyes. Unmarked or marked by a lesser or unknown manufacturer.

Socket Head Teen-type: all composition, jointed at neck, shoulder, and hips; good wig; sleep eyes; closed mouth or open mouth with teeth. Unmarked or marked by a lesser or unknown manufacturer.

Monica Studio Doll: highest quality, all composition, jointed at neck, shoulders and hips; implanted human hair with widow's peak; beautifully painted features; appropriately dressed. Unmarked.

Novelty Composition: all composition, various joints, painted features; dramatic foreign costumes, fairy tale, or wedding attire. These dolls were intended as accent dolls and not as play dolls. Unmarked.

18" Composition Dolly-Face Doll.

13" Composition Scottish lassie.

CHARACTER DOLLS

Buddy Lee: 13", all composition; jointed, molded and painted features; large side-glancing eyes; dressed in at least seventeen different outfits:
  Coca-Cola outfit **500.00**
  Other soft drink outfits **300.00**
  Cowboy outfit **350.00**
  Engineer's outfit **300.00**
  Gas Station outfit **250.00**
  John Deere outfit **450.00**

Dennie Dimwit or Bobbi Mae: 11", all composition; molded head on hollow body, mounted on stick fastened to top of legs and attached to body with metal rod; when doll is touched it sways. Marked "Pat. Pending" inside dress; each **135.00**

Famlee Doll: 16", "A Whole Family of Dolls in One," set of at least one body and several interchangeable heads; matching costumes; set with heads, shoulder plates, cloth body; unmarked **1,200.00**

Gene Carr Kids: 14", very character faced; cloth body, composition hands; unmarked.
  Blink: squinting eyes; open/closed mouth; one tooth. **400.00**

Jane: round eyes; freckles; open/closed mouth; two upper teeth. **400.00**

Mike: round eyes; freckles; open/closed mouth; two upper teeth. **400.00**

Skinny: squinting eyes; open/closed mouth; one tooth. **400.00**

Snowball: black, round painted eyes; open/closed smiling mouth; two upper teeth. **550.00**

Jackie Robinson: 20", Black; socket head, jointed at shoulders and hips; molded and painted hair; black side-glancing eyes; open/closed mouth with teeth; wearing Dodger's uniform; no marks **800.00**

Kewpie-Type: 12", jointed at neck, shoulders, and hips; star-shaped hands; no wings on back; molded hair in top knot; painted side-glancing eyes; closed mouth; no marks. **250.00**

Lone Ranger or Tonto: 21", composition swivel head, hands, and feet; cloth body, cloth limbs; molded and painted black hair; painted brown eyes; closed mouth; appropriately dressed; red paper tag reads "The Lone Ranger and Tonto/Manufactured by/Dollcraft Novelty Co./Sole Licensees/New York City" on one side and "Lone Ranger" in rope script and "Official Doll copyright T.L.R.Co. Inc." on other. Doll is unmarked; each **900.00**

Pinocchio: 12", all composition, jointed at neck, shoulders, and hips; molded and painted hair; round eyes; large nose; closed smiling mouth; no marks on doll . **350.00**

Puzzy, Sizzy: 15", "Good Habit" kids; all composition, jointed at neck, shoulders, and hips; molded and painted hair; marked "H of P USA," "Sizzy H of P USA." **450.00**

Trudy: 15", composition head and arms, cloth body; three faces, one smiling, one sleeping, and one crying; knob at top of head turns faces; painted features; appropriately dressed; unmarked **350.00**

Two Face: 16", composition head, cloth body; one face laughing and one crying; molded and painted hair and features; appropriately dressed; unmarked. **300.00**

16" Composition child doll.

COMPOSITION DOLL VALUE COMPARISONS:

Size	Flange Neck Child	Shoulder Head Mama Doll	Socket Head Baby Doll, White	Socket Head Baby Doll, Black	Socket Head Child Doll Exeptional	Socket Head Child Doll Standard	Socket Head Loop-type	Socket Head Pasty-type	Teen-type	Monica Studio	Novelty Costume
12"	250.00	300.00			175.00	250.00				600.00	125.00
14"	200.00				325.00	175.00	200.00	275.00	300.00		
16"		250.00	325.00	400.00			225.00	300.00	350.00	700.00	250.00
18"	300.00		350.00		350.00	200.00		325.00	400.00	750.00	
20"	350.00	325.00	400.00		400.00	250.00			450.00	900.00	
22"	400.00	375.00			450.00	300.00				1,000.00	
24"		400.00			500.00	350.00				1,200.00	
26"	500.00	450.00									

Contemporary Collectible Porcelain Dolls

Yolando Bello's Picture Perfect Babies. Danielle, Emily, Sarah, Jason, Jennifer, Jessica, Amanda, Matthew, Michael, Heather, and Lisa.

This category covers porcelain dolls by various manufacturers such as Danbury Mint, Franklin Mint, Georgetown Collectible, Betty Ball, Marie Osmond, and others. Many dolls offered on the secondary market are valued at much less than their issue price, others at much more.

Certain clues may help determine which dolls will increase in value, but be advised that there is no surefire formula. The first doll in a series often increases in value. Dolls with crossover appeal to other collectibles categories such as Gone With the Wind or Disney are also more apt to show an increase. Finally, dolls that are very pretty and made in limited editions of less than 500 are more likely to escalate. Buying modern dolls as an investment is always a gamble. Buy Contemporary Collectible Dolls because you love them, not for their future investment potential.

Examine Contemporary Dolls carefully for damage or missing accessories. Unless extremely well priced, don't even consider purchasing a less than perfect modern doll.

Prices listed here are for dolls in mint condition, unless otherwise noted. This is by no means an all-inclusive listing. Thousands of collectible dolls are introduced every year. The listings provided are merely a sampling of the contemporary dolls available on the secondary market.

Dream Girl: 7¹/₂", porcelain shoulder head, cloth body, delicately molded porcelain hands and feet, molded high heel shoes; beautifully styled mohair wig; painted eyes, feathered brows; closed mouth; dressed in satin dress, gold trim, lace overlay, beading, and bows; holding porcelain doves; marked "Franklin Heirloom Dolls 1988 E0146," signed "Maryse Nicole." **200.00**

Silver Lining: 8", seated angel; The Cindy McClure Collection; porcelain socket head on separate porcelain shoulder plate, cloth body, porcelain hands and feet; curly wig; blue glass eyes; closed mouth; well dressed in white satin, feather wings; sitting on cloud; marked "1991 Cindy M McClure 5657J." **125.00**

Thorn: 8½", porcelain head, cloth body, porcelain chubby hands, well-molded porcelain bare feet; blond wig; large elf ears; green glass eyes; closed mouth; dressed in very well-made silk shirt and pants; leather shoes, vest, and cap; backpack basket with bird; no marks. **65.00**

Melissa: 9½", Marie Osmond; all porcelain, articulated; medium-length blond curly hair; blue glass eyes; open mouth with upper teeth; mint green and white striped one-piece romper with white lace trim; white shoes, mint green ribbon in hair; carrying three gold wrapped packages; marked "Marie Osmond, 1992." **75.00**

Billy: 11", Linda Steele, Danbury Mint, boy; porcelain head, arms, and legs, cloth body; short blond straight hair; brown glass eyes; open/closed mouth; wearing white two-piece playsuit with bucking bronco appliqué, blue trim, brown felt cowboy hat; bare feet; wooden horse toy; marked "L. Steele O/M 1991 MBI." **75.00**

Savannah: 11", all porcelain, articulated; long blond curly hair with ribbon on top; blue glass eyes; open mouth; blue and white pajamas with white lace trim, kitty cat slippers; box of tissues, holds one in hand; marked "© 1991 Vincent J. DeFilippo/5000." **150.00**

Meagan Rose: 12", Ashton-Drake Galleries, Yolando Bello, Heavenly Scent Babies; porcelain head, hands, and feet, cloth body; painted brown hair; blue glass eyes; open/closed mouth; dressed in one-piece pink sleeper suit, white lace trim, matching bonnet; comes with cotton-stuffed cloud scented with baby powder; edition ended 12-31-94; marked "Yolando Bello 3182FE." **100.00**

Todd: 12½", Ashton-Drake Galleries, Yolando Bello, first issue in "Yolando's Playtime Babies Collection," boy; porcelain head, arms, and legs, cloth body; painted-on blond hair; blue glass eyes looking off to side; open/closed mouth; dressed in striped seersucker playsuit, matching cap, blue trim; bare footed; comes with inflatable toy; edition ended in 1994; marked "Yolando Bello .CB4909." **70.00**

Red Riding Hood: 14", Dianna Effner collection; porcelain socket head on porcelain shoulder plate, cloth body, porcelain arms and legs; auburn curly wig; blue glass eyes; closed mouth, painted to look as saying "Oh;" dressed in plaid dress, white apron, red hooded cape; carrying basket with goodies; marked "Dianna Effner 1724E," first in series. **350.00**
Others in this series include:
Cinderella, at the ball **125.00**
Cinderella, rags **200.00**
Goldilocks **125.00**
Rapunzel **300.00**
Snow White **250.00**

Sweet Cherub: 14", angel by Ellenbrooke; all porcelain, jointed at neck, shoulders, and hips, knees in bent position; blond curly wig; blue glass eyes; open/closed mouth, two teeth; dressed in chiffon dress, gold shorts, feather wings; holding a rose; second in series of four; marked "Ellenbrooke 90" on head and "© Connie Jolls & Co" on back. **650.00**

Susie: 14", Victoria Ashlea doll; porcelain head, hands, and feet, cloth body; long dark brown curly hair; floral headband; brown glass eyes; closed mouth; dressed in ivory dress with pink flowers, lace trim, white stockings, beige shoes with pink bows, musical, plays "The Candy Man;" limited edition of 2,000; marked "Victoria Ashlea Orig. Designed by Bette Ball, Goebel, Inc., 1989." **100.00**

Hansel 14½" and Gretel 13½": porcelain shoulder heads, arms, and legs, cloth bodies; blond mohair wigs; very beautiful faces; high quality blue paperweight eyes; full closed mouths; dressed in quaint regional costumes of blues and reds; marked "1987 Airgail Brahans" price for mint set. **500.00**

Jason: 14½", Yolando Bello, Picture Perfect Babies Series; porcelain head, arms, and legs, cloth body; molded and painted hair; blue glass eyes; open/closed smiling mouth, two teeth; wearing blue nylon clown suit with matching cap; marked "Yolando Bello 3108D;" first in series. **800.00**
Others in this series include:
Amanda **400.00**
Danielle **125.00**
Emily **250.00**
Heather **425.00**
Jennifer **450.00**
Jessica **75.00**
Lisa **300.00**
Matthew **250.00**
Michael **325.00**
Sarah **300.00**

Miss Muffet: 14½", porcelain shoulder head, arms, and legs, cloth body; blond wig in braids; blue glass eyes; open/closed mouth, molded upper teeth; dressed in yellow gingham dress, white apron, matching bonnet; comes with chair, bowl, spoon, and black plush spider; marked "Yolando Bello 3193B." **200.00**

Bettina: 15", Victoria Ashlea doll; porcelain head, hands, and feet, cloth body; blond curly hair pulled on top of head in bun with blue ribbons; blue glass eyes; closed mouth; dressed in blue and pink floral dress, white lace trim, white pantaloons, white stockings, pink shoes; musical, plays "When You Wish Upon A Star;" limited edition of 1,000; marked "Victoria Ashlea Originals, Designed by Bette Ball, Limited Edition of 1,000, Goebel, Inc., 1989." **100.00**

Christmas Angel: 15", porcelain shoulder head with deep plate, porcelain arms and legs, bare feet; full blond curly wig; nicely painted eyes; closed mouth; dressed in white satin dress, gold trim, flowing gold cape, white net wings, gold halo; holding mandolin, marked "Franklin Heirloom Dolls, 1986." **350.00**

Inga Dingle: 15", Dolly Dingle Doll, Norway in the Trip Around the World Series; porcelain head, hands, and legs, cloth body; long blond hair pulled on top of head in golden crown; violet glass eyes looking off to side; closed mouth; dressed in long white dress with gold lamé bow, white boa around neckline and cuffs; holds wand with golden star at top; gold lamé and beaded wings; white stockings and shoes; musical, plays "Minuet;" marked "Dolly Dingle Dolls, Designed by Bette

Ball, Limited Edition of 5000, 1993 Goebel United States." **150.00**

Dinah: 15¹/₂"; Carol Anne doll; porcelain head, arms, and legs, cloth body; long blond curled hair; green glass eyes; closed mouth; mint green dotted Swiss dress, white lace trim, pink floral accents, matching bonnet, white lace trimmed slip and pantaloons; white stockings and shoes; musical, plays "In The Good Old Summer Time;" marked "Carol Anne Dolls, Designed by Bette Ball, Limited Edition of 500, Goebel, Inc. 1989." **150.00**

Candy Corn: 16", Betty Jane Carter Cat, Bette Ball; porcelain cat head and paws, cloth body; calico-painted face; yellow glass eyes; closed mouth; wearing black dress, orange, yellow, and red leaves, ivory apron; dangling spider, matching trim, black painted witch's hat; holding broom; musical, plays "Autumn Leaves;" marked "© Goebel Betty Jane Carter Dolls, Designed by Bette Ball, Limited Edition of 2,000, 1994 United States." **125.00**

Mary Had A Little Lamb: 16¹/₄", porcelain shoulder head, arms, and legs with molded and painted shoes, cloth body; blond wig in long curls; very nicely painted blue eyes; open/closed mouth; dressed in short dress of white and lavender with lace bloomers showing, matching lavender sun bonnet; carrying shepherd's staff; marked "Franklin Heirloom Dolls, 1987." . . **250.00**

Allison: 17", Victoria Ashlea doll; porcelain head, hands, and feet, cloth body; short blond curly hair; blue glass eyes; closed mouth; dressed in navy blue dress with pink floral print, white lace trim, yellow and pink ribbon, matching bow in hair; white stockings and shoes; pink floral accents; musical, plays "Tomorrow;" marked "Victoria Ashlea Originals, Designed by Bette Ball, Limited to 1,000, Goebel, Inc., 1989." **125.00**

Daisy: 17", porcelain shoulder head, arms, and legs with molded and painted white boots, cloth body; blond curly wig; blue glass eyes; closed mouth; wearing green dotted Swiss dress, white overskirt, straw hat; carrying basket of daisies; marked "8340 A Merri 1988;" second in series. **150.00**
Others in series include:
    Rose **200.00**
    Violet **100.00**

Jet: 17", Seymour Mann doll; porcelain head, neck, hands, and feet, cloth body; long straight ash-blond hair with ribbon and floral bow; violet glass eyes; closed mouth; dressed in light blue floral print dress, white lace trim; white stockings, pink shoes; carries basket of pink and blue silk flowers; marked "The Connoisseur Doll Collection, Seymour Mann, Inc., Limited to 2,500." **100.00**

Meredith: 17", Carol Anne doll; porcelain head, hands, and legs, cloth body; long blond spiral curls; blue glass eyes; closed mouth; dressed in white dotted Swiss dress, lace trim, blue embroidered flowers, ribbon accents, blue hair ribbon, white pantaloons; stockings, and shoes with blue satin flowers; musical, plays "I Want To Hold Your Hand;" marked "Carol Ann Dolls, Designed by Bette Ball, Limited Edition of 1,000, 1992 Goebel, United States." **175.00**

16" Christmas Angel from Franklin Mint.

Snow White: 17", porcelain shoulder head, arms, and legs, cloth body; black wig with red ribbon; pale porcelain with round brown glass eyes, single-stroke eyebrows; closed red lips; dress with yellow satin skirt, blue vest, puffed sleeves; white leather shoes with yellow bows; marked "B03 Snow White Golden Anniversary 1987 The Walt Disney Company 4465." **300.00**

Violet: 17", Kingstate doll; porcelain head, hands, and legs, cloth body; long strawberry blond curly hair; blue glass eyes; open/closed mouth; dressed in lavender dress, ivory lace and pink floral ribbon accents, lace slip; ivory stockings and shoes; lavender ribbon trim, matching violet bonnet with lace trim; marked "Kingstate the Doll Crafter, Limited Edition of 3500." **85.00**

Baby: 18", unnamed baby from the Diapers and Diamonds Collection, designed by Rotraut Schrott; porcelain head, arms, and legs, cloth body; short blond straight hair, mohair wig; blue glass eyes; closed mouth, bottom lip tucked under top lip; dressed in ivory antique-style French baby dress with lace trim, Swiss embroidery and pink silk ribbon, matching bonnet; bare footed, big toes bent downward; doll has hand-faceted diamond set into its shoulder plate; marked "The Diamond Collection © 1991 Rotraut Schrott 1703 Limited production to under 5,000." **300.00**

Scarlett: 18", Gone With the Wind Series; porcelain shoulder head, arms, and legs with molded and painted high heel shoes, cloth body; black wig; very nicely painted green eyes; closed mouth; wearing green dress, green velvet ribbon trim, straw hat with velvet ties, white knit shawl; marked "Franklin Heirloom Dolls 1985." **350.00**

Others in series include: Melanie, Rhett, Ashley, and Mammy and their secondary market value is in the $250.00-$300.00 range.

Olivia: 20", porcelain socket head on porcelain shoulder plate, arms and legs with bare feet, cloth body; red curly wig; blue glass eyes; closed mouth; dressed in flowered dress, pink ribbon sash, pink ribbon in hair; marked

"The Diamond Collection 1992 (5682) signed Rotraut Schrott." **300.00**

Gibson Girl: 21½", porcelain shoulder head with deep plate, molded bosom, porcelain arms and legs with molded high heel shoes; brown wig in Gibson rolled style with loose curls framing face; very nicely painted blue eyes; closed mouth; dressed in pink satin gown, cream color lace trim, pink choker; carrying white satin evening bag; marked "Franklin Heirloom Doll 1986 660." **375.00**

Angelica: 22", Marie Osmond baby; porcelain head, hands, and legs; original face, hands, and feet by sculptor Beverly Stoeher; short blond hair pulled up on top with lavender ribbon; blue glass eyes; open mouth; lavender and white lace dress with satin bows, white pantaloons, stockings, and shoes with lavender bows; holds a white all-cloth doll baby accented with white lavender bows; marked "Marie Osmond © 1993, Limited Edition of 5,000." **250.00**

Daniele: 22", Effanbee doll from The Age of Innocence Series; porcelain head, hands, and feet, cloth body; long blond straight hair; blue glass eyes; closed mouth; wearing blue floral print dress, white pinafore, pink and floral embroidery, pink ribbon trim; white stockings and shoes; straw hat with silk flowers; holds a wooden bird cage with two birds inside; marked "Effanbee Doll Co. 1992, © U. Gold." **250.00**

Pistachio: 22", Betty Jane Carter Clown doll; porcelain head, cloth body and limbs; white curly hair with silver strands through it; green glass eyes; white, red, and green clown-painted face; closed mouth; dressed in pink and green two-piece outfit, lace trim and bows; no shoes; musical, plays "Make Someone Happy;" marked "Betty Jane Carter Dolls, Designed by Bette Ball, Limited Edition to 1,000, 1992 Goebel United States." . . .**90.00**

Camille: 23", Marie Osmond doll from the Picture Day Series; porcelain head, hands, and feet, cloth body; original sculpted face by Rita Schmidt; long brown curly hair with pink ribbon; gray-blue glass eyes; closed mouth; dressed in pink, white, violet, and green floral dress, white embroidered collar, on which she wears a locket bearing her photo inside, white pantaloons; white, ruffled socks; "Knickerbocker Creations, Lt." on wrist tag; marked "Marie Osmond 1992, Limited Edition of 2,500." **200.00**

Gibson Bride: 23", porcelain shoulder head, cloth body, porcelain arms with lightly painted nails and gold band, legs with molded high heel shoes with ribbon roses on toes; dark blond wig in Gibson rolled style; painted green eyes with thick eye lashes; closed mouth; dressed in cream satin wedding gown with lace trim; wearing double row of pearls; carrying roses; marked "Franklin Heirloom Dolls, 1987." **350.00**

Nathan: 23", Marie Osmond doll from the Twin Series; porcelain head, hands, and feet on cloth body, articulated head; original Ann Jackson face; short strawberry blond straight hair; blue glass eyes; freckled face; closed mouth; wearing white shirt and mint green knickers with embroidered anchor, matching beret; white stockings and shoes; marked "Ann Jackson Marie Osmond © 1992 Limited Edition/2000." **75.00**

Queen Galadril from Lord of the Rings: 23", porcelain shoulder head on cloth body, porcelain arms, right hand molded to hold a crystal, gold band painted on left; porcelain legs with bare feet; long blond wig done in waves; painted blue eyes; closed mouth; wearing long white gown, chain belt, yard long gold cape; marked "Franklin Heirloom Dolls 1987." **350.00**

Victorian Bride: 23½", porcelain shoulder head on cloth body, porcelain arms and legs with molded high heel shoes; brown wig in rolled style; big painted brown eyes; closed mouth; wearing beautifully made wedding dress with net veil, gold plated locket; carrying silk roses; marked "Franklin Heirloom Dolls, 1987 Edition" on marked wooden stand; edition limited to 2,500. . . . .**800.00**

Gloriana Fairy Princess: 23½", porcelain shoulder head on cloth body, porcelain arms molded to hold tiny all-porcelain fairy in right hand and wand in left hand; porcelain legs with bare feet; long blond wig; blue glass eyes; closed mouth; dressed in pink satin dress with layers of netting, blue under skirt, flowers hanging from dress with pearls dangling from dress; marked "1989 Brigette Deval Farrie Princess." **325.00**

Amber: 24", Marie Osmond doll, Autumn from the Four Seasons Collection; original face sculpted by Vincent J. DeFilippo; articulated porcelain head, arms, and legs, cloth body; long brown curly hair; brown glass eyes; open mouth; dressed in black cotton print dress, ivory eyelet pinafore, white stockings, black shoes; wreath of autumn leaves in hair; carries fall bouquet; marked "Vincent J. DeFilippo © 1991 Maris Osmond 1993 Limited Edition/2500." **300.00**

Cinderella: 24", porcelain shoulder head on cloth body, porcelain arms and legs; very blond wig in up-sweep with jeweled crown; blue glass eyes; closed mouth; wearing blue satin dress, silver trim, attached blue velvet cape; holding glass slipper; marked "Cinderella, 1987, MBI." **200.00**

Amanda: 28", Terri DeHetre doll; articulated porcelain head, hands, and legs, cloth body, poseable wire limbs; long blond curly hair; blue glass eyes; closed mouth; white dress with lace trim and pantaloons; bare feet; marked "Signed by Terri DeHetre, QA/50, Limited Edition of 50." **600.00**

Andrea: 28", Terri DeHetre doll; articulated porcelain head, hands, and legs, cloth body, poseable wire limbs; long auburn curly hair with pink ribbon; dressed in ivory dress with lace trim and pink ribbon, ivory pantaloons with lace trim; bare feet; marked "Signed by Terri DeHetre QB/50." **600.00**

Tammy: 30", Betty Jane Carter doll, one of Four Seasons series by Bette Ball; porcelain head, hands, and legs, cloth body; long blond hair; violet glass eyes; open/closed mouth, painted teeth; pink, lavender, green, yellow, and white plaid dress with faux pearl buttons, white jacket, crystal butterfly pin, white pantaloons and stockings, lavender shoes with pink bows, white hat with matching plaid trim; carries floral bouquet; musical, plays "Primavera;" marked "Betty Jane Carter Dolls, Designed by Bette Ball, Limited Edition of /500, © 1993 Goebel United States." **500.00**

Dean's Rag Book Co.

Dean's Rag Book Co., founded in England in 1903, made cloth books, toys, and dolls since it's conception. Founder Samuel Dean claimed that he started the company for "children who wear their food and eat their clothes." In 1920, the company introduced the first molded, pressed, and painted three-dimensional dolls called "Tru-To-Life" rag dolls.

Prices listed are for dolls in good clean condition. Normal wear is to be expected. If badly faded, soiled, stained, or torn expect to pay less than half the amount listed.

Child Doll: all cloth, felt head and arms, dark pink cloth body, long slender legs; mohair wig; painted eyes, white spot at upper left of eye; two tone closed mouth; appropriately dressed. Marked "Hygenic Al Toys"/picture of two dogs having a tug-of-war over a book/"Made in England/Dean's Rag Book Co. Ltd." within an oval on bottom of foot.

Printed Flat Face Doll: stuffed cotton bodies. Marked "Hygenic Toys/Dean's Rag/Made in England" within an oval.

SPECIAL INTEREST DOLLS

Wolley Wally: Dean's Golliwog.
Dancing Boy and Girl: hugging, bobs up and down on a golden string.
Filly on a Trike: velvet arms, legs, and dress which is part of the body; mohair wig; beautifully painted eyes; attached to metal tricycle.

Mickey Mouse: brown velvet; brown velvet pants with buttons on front; large white felt hands.

Minnie Mouse: brown velvet, large white felt hands.

Peter Pan: molded felt face; velvet body; wearing gold velvet suit.

Wendy: molded felt face; velvet body; wearing white nightgown.

17½" Dean Rag Book Co. Boy. *Courtesy of Judy Ries.*

				DEAN'S RAG DOLL VALUE COMPARISONS:					
Size	Child Doll	Flat Face	Golliwog	Dancing Doll	Filly on Trike	Mickey	Minnie	Peter Pan	Wendy
9"		150.00							
10"	400.00								
12"			400.00	800.00	1,500.00				
14"									
15"	750.00	250.00							
16"						2,900.00	2,700.00		
17"	1,000.00	300.00						2,500.00	2,300.00
20"	1,200.00	350.00							

DEP Dolls

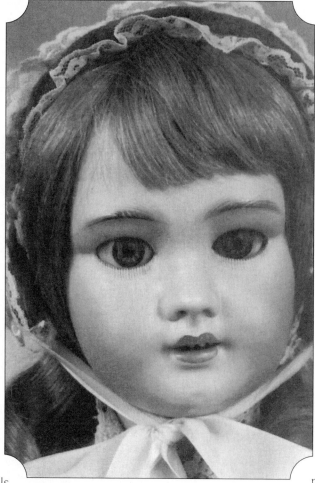

27" DEP French Doll. *Photo courtesy McMasters Doll Auction.*

DEP Dolls originated in the 1880s. These bisque dolls should not be confused with dolls commonly found with the addition of the letters "DEP" to a registered mold number. In the case of many dolls made in France, the DEP stands for "Depose," in Germany it stands for "Deponirt." In both instances, "DEP" indicates a claim of registration and will be found with a mold number, manufacturer, or both. The DEP Dolls described here are marked only with "DEP" and a size number incised into the bisque.

The early closed-mouth DEP Dolls are made with exceptionally fine bisque and delicately applied decoration showing great artistry. Later open-mouthed DEP Dolls, although generally very good in quality, lack the striking beauty of the earlier dolls. These later dolls will be found with real-hair upper lashes and painted lower lashes.

DEP Dolls are generally accepted as being French, largely because of the presence of French bodies. In fact, early DEP Dolls resemble Jumeau Bébés in appearance. Some are even stamped with the Jumeau mark. Later DEP Dolls are widely considered to be German, most probably Simon & Halbig, as indicated by the deeply molded and cut eye socket.

Prices listed are for dolls with no damage to the bisque. Normal wear, slight damage, or well-done repairs to the body do not greatly affect price. If the bisque is damaged or repaired, expect to pay less than half the amount listed. It is

perfectly acceptable to show a missing or repaired finger or joint to the body.

Closed Mouth: bisque socket head, composition-and-wood jointed body; good wig; paperweight eyes, heavy feathered brows, long thick eye lashes; pierced ears; closed mouth; appropriately dressed. Marked "DEP."

Open Mouth Bisque Socket Head: composition-and-wood jointed body; good wig; paperweight eyes, painted lower lashes, real hair upper lashes, feathered brows; pierced ears; open mouth with upper teeth; appropriately dressed. Marked "DEP."

DEP DOLLS VALUE COMPARISONS:

Size	Closed Mouth	Open Mouth	Black
12"		950.00	
14"		1,000.00	
16"	3,200.00	1,100.00	2,900.00
18"	3,800.00	1,200.00	
20"	4,000.00	1,300.00	
22"	4,800.00	1,400.00	
24"	5,200.00	1,700.00	4,200.00
28"		2,400.00	
30"		2,900.00	
34"		3,400.00	

Doll House Dolls

5¹/₂" and 6" German Doll House Couple. *Courtesy of Helen Brooke.*

3" German Doll House Child. *Courtesy of Helen Brooke.*

Petite dolls made to roam the halls of Victorian doll houses originated in the 1880s for the enjoyment of both adults and children. Most doll houses boasted of a wife, husband, several children, two or three maids, a butler, and at least a few visiting friends. Early bisque Doll House Dolls were made in Germany. They are often unmarked or marked with a number or letter only.

Qualities to consider when purchasing a Doll House Doll are condition, visual appeal, and costuming. Prices listed are for desirable and charming dolls with no damage.

Adult or Child: bisque head, cloth, composition, or bisque body; mohair or molded and painted hair; painted or glass eyes; appropriately dressed.

Adult or Child: china head, cloth body, china stub arms, high heel feet, painted shoes; molded and painted common hairstyle; painted eyes; closed mouth, rosy cheeks; appropriately dressed; unmarked.

Size	Painted Eye, Adult or Child	Glass Eye, Adult or Child	China Head	Black	Elderly Character	Molded Military Figures
4"	145.00					
5"	175.00					
6"	250.00	400.00	175.00			
7"	300.00	500.00	200.00	700.00	800.00	900.00
8"	250.00	450.00	175.00			

DOLL HOUSE DOLLS VALUE COMPARISONS:

Door of Hope Dolls

Door of Hope Kindergarten Child. *Courtesy of Carolyn Johnson.*

Door of Hope Dolls were made from 1901 to 1949 in Shanghai and Canton, China. A Protestant mission called the Door of Hope was founded in Shanghai in 1901 to rescue destitute children and slave girls.

At the Door of Hope Mission, the girls were taught needlework, embroidery, knitting, and other skills. These skills were put to good use in the dressing of the Door of Hope Dolls. A girl working five days a week could make only one doll a month. The head, hands, and arms to the elbow were carved of pearwood. Men in Ning Po probably did the doll carving. The wood was as smooth as satin and needed no paint or varnish to mirror the ivory-yellow Chinese skin color. The hair, eyes, and lips were painted. A few of the dolls had fancy buns or flowers carved into their heads. Most dolls have hands with rounded palms and separate thumbs, although some have been found with cloth stub hands. Cloth bodies were stuffed with raw cotton donated to the Mission by local textile factories. The handmade elaborate costumes are exact copies of clothing worn by the Chinese people.

Examples of Door of Hope Dolls include:

Boy in Silk: wearing velvet sleeveless jacket and brocaded silk outfit with tunic and trousers. The long full sleeves ended well below the hands, indicating a member of the upper class who did not work with his hands.

Manchu Lady: wearing carved headdress.

Grandmother: wearing winter hat.

Grandfather: dressed as well-to-do elderly man.

School Boy, Table Boy, and School Girl: all dressed in cotton.

Young Lady and Husband: dressed as members of the upper class.

Small Boy: wearing holiday dress of silk.

Young Man: dressed for father's funeral, three balls on his hat to catch tears, paper wand for driving off evil spirits.

Widow: wearing sack cloth, bonnet acts as veil covering her face.

Bridegroom: wearing official dress with embroidered squares on robe's front and back.

DOOR OF HOPE VALUE COMPARISONS:

Size	Child/Adult	Amah with Baby	Bride, Groom/Manchu Lady	Priest
6"	800.00			
7½"	750.00			
10½"		900.00		
11½"	850.00			1,200.00
16"			1,400.00	

Bride: wearing traditional red hand-embroidered old-style costume.

Farmer: with grass raincoat for working in wet weather.

Buddhist Priest: long yellow gown with no buttons; shaved head.

Municipal Policeman: Shanghai police dress.

Kindergarten Child: wearing cap with ears and "cat" slippers.

Cantonese Amah: nurse with baby on her back; Amah are also found without babies.

Special orders were also filled by the Mission workers and other examples may exist. Condition and costuming are important factors when determining value. Prices listed are for undamaged dolls wearing original clothing. If the doll is undressed or redressed, expect to pay only 30% of the amounts listed.

Door of Hope: carved head, cloth body, carved or cloth hands; painted hair, eyes, and mouth; original clothing. Unmarked or labeled "Made in China."

Door of Hope Dolls. *Courtesy of Mary Jane Brummer.*

Cuno & Otto Dressel

The Dressel family operated a toy business in Sonneberg, Germany from the 1700s until 1942. It is oldest toy manufacturer for which there are conclusively accurate business records. The firm passed from one generation of Dressels to the next, and in 1873 it became known as Cuno & Otto Dressel. The toys sold by Cuno and Otto Dressel were not all original products. The company purchased bisque doll heads from Armand Marseille, Simon and Halbig, Ernst Heubach and Gebruder Heubach. It also depended upon cottage industries to help stock the incredible assortment of 30,000 different toys and dolls in its inventory.

The partnership of the Dressel brothers proved to be immensely successful. They expanded to three factories: one in Sonneberg for dolls; one in Nurnberg for the production of metal toys; and one in Grunhainichen for wooden toys.

Mold numbers known and attributed to Cuno & Otto Dressel are: 93, 1348, 1349, 1468, 1469, 1776, 1848, 1849, 1893, 1896, 1898, 1912, 1914, 1920, 1922, and 2736. Additional trademarks registered by Cuno & Otto Dressel include Holz-Masse (wooden composition), Admiral Dewey, Admiral Sampson, Bambina, Die Puppe de Zukunft (Doll of the Future), Fifth Ave. Doll, Jutta, Jutta-Baby (named for Countess Jutta, the Patroness of Sonneberg), McKinley, M. Miles, Poppy, Uncle Sam, and Victoria.

Reputable doll makers have made reproductions of many Cuno & Otto Dressel Dolls, especially character dolls. Most of these reproduction are marked with the artist's name and

25" C.O.D. Child Doll. *Photo courtesy of McMasters Doll Auction.*

date. A careful inspection should be sufficient to distinguish an authentic Cuno & Otto Dressel Doll from a reproduction.

Prices are for dolls with no damage to the bisque. Normal wear, slight damage, or well-done repairs to the body do not greatly affect price. If the bisque is damaged or repaired, expect to pay less than half the amount listed. It is perfectly acceptable to show a missing or repaired finger or joint to the body. Dolls made from other material may show slight wear. Signs of age are to be expected. Avoid a badly crazed or repaired doll unless the price reflects its condition.

BISQUE

Child Dolly-Face: shoulder head on kid body or socket head on jointed composition body; good wig; glass eyes, feathered brows; open mouth; appropriately dressed. Typically marked "COD 93DEP," "AM 1893COD," "1896," "1898," "1776," or "COD1912."

Character Baby: bent-limb baby body or cloth body; molded and painted hair or good wig; painted or glass eyes; appropriately dressed. Typically marked "COD341," or "Neubach Koppelsdorf 1922/Jutta Baby/Germany."

S & H Jutta Character Baby: socket head, bent-limb baby body; good wig; glass eyes; open mouth; appropriately dressed. Marked "Jutta 1914," or "Jutta 1920." Simon and Halbig Jutta Character babies are marked with either mold number "1914" or "1920." Other Jutta babies were produced by Ernst Heubach and Armand Marseilles and are valued somewhat lower.

S & H Jutta Child: socket head, jointed composition body; good wig; glass eyes; pierced or unpierced ears; open mouth; appropriately dressed. Marked "1349/Jutta/S & H," "S & H/1348/Jutta," or "1348 Dressel." Simon & Halbig Jutta Child dolls are marked with mold numbers "1348" or "1349."

Cuno and Otto Dressel's Character Dolls were produced by prominent German manufacturers such as Gebruder Heubach and Simon & Halbig. They can be whimsical and charming, or simply beautiful. Their three main categories include:

Character Portrait: sculptured and molded to represent famous military, political, or legendary figures; socket head, jointed composition body; glass eyes; appropriately dressed. Typically marked "S," "D," "R," or "A."

Character Child: socket head, jointed composition body; molded and painted hair or wig; painted or glass eyes; closed mouth; appropriately dressed. Typically marked "Germany," "C.O.D.," or "C.O.D./S.H." Open mouth Character Child marked "C.O.D."

Character Lady: lovely slim young woman; socket head, shapely jointed composition lady's body with graceful arms and legs; feet molded for high heel shoes; good wig; glass eyes; closed mouth; appropriately dressed. Marked "1469/ C O Dressel Germany," "1468 COD," "SH1468," or "S & h/COD/1469."

15" C.O.D. Character Flapper. *Courtesy of Elizabeth Frame.*

COMPOSITION

Character Lady: shoulder head, cloth body, composition limbs; good wig; glass eyes; closed mouth; appropriately dressed. Typically marked "C.O.D."

Character Child: socket head, jointed composition body; painted hair with brush marks; glass or painted eyes; closed puckered mouth; appropriately dressed. Typically marked "C.O.D." or stamped "Holz-Masse."

Child Dolly-Face: socket head, jointed composition body; good wig; glass eyes; open mouth; appropriately dressed. Typically marked "M & S," "C.O.D.," or "Jutta."

C. O. D. Bisque Value Comparisons:

Size	Open Mouth, Child Dolly Face, Kid Body	Open Mouth, Child Dolly Face, Composition Body	Heubach/ C.O.D Character Baby	S & H Jutta Baby 1914/1920	S & H Jutta/ C. O. D. Child 1348/ 1349	Uncle Sam/ Admiral Dewey	Old Rip Farmer Buffalo Bill	Closed Mouth Character, Painted Eye	Closed Mouth Character, Glass Eye	Character Lady
12"	400.00		400.00	600.00		1,300.00	1,000.00	2,000.00	2,700.00	3,800.00
14"	425.00	500.00	500.00	700.00	750.00	1,600.00	1,200.00	2,400.00	3,000.00	4,500.00
16"	450.00	550.00	600.00	800.00	800.00	1,800.00		2,600.00	3,600.00	5,000.00
18"	500.00	600.00	700.00	900.00	850.00			3,000.00		5,800.00
20"	600.00	650.00	800.00	1,400.00	900.00			3,400.00		6,200.00
22"	650.00	700.00	900.00		1,000.00				4,100.00	
24"	700.00	750.00	1,000.00	1,700.00	1,200.00				4,500.00	
26"	750.00	800.00		1,900.00	1,600.00					
28"	850.00	900.00	1,500.00		2,000.00					
30"		1,000.00			2,200.00					
36"		2,400.00			3,200.00					
40"					3,800.00					

Note: add an additional $300.00 for Toddler or Flapper

C. O. D. Composition, Papier-mâché, and Wax Value Comparisons:

Size	Composition Lady	Composition, Closed Mouth, Character Child	Composition, Open Mouth, Dolly-Face	Papier-mâché Painted Eye	Papier-mâché Glass Eye	Reinforced Wax Dolls	Wax-Over Composition
14"	900.00		450.00	350.00	300.00	900.00	
18"	1,400.00	1,800.00	475.00	475.00	350.00	1,200.00	500.00
20"		2,200.00		525.00	375.00	1,700.00	
24"		2,500.00	600.00	700.00	450.00	1,800.00	600.00
26"				800.00	500.00		
28"						2,000.00	
30"							

PAPIER-MÂCHÉ

Papier-mâché is made from powdered or torn bits of paper and paste molded and hardened to form a doll. Turn-of-the-century composition was often merely a papier-mâché base with additives. Collectors refer to earlier dolls as papier-mâché and later dolls as composition.

Shoulder Head: cloth body, papier-mâché limbs; molded and painted hair or good wig; painted or glass eyes, feathered brows; closed mouth; entire head and shoulder plate with varnish-like coating; appropriately dressed in vintage materials with vintage leather boots. Typically marked with winged helmet and "HOLZMASSE."

REINFORCED WAX

Reinforced Wax: rare, usually poured and reinforced with plaster or composition; child shoulder head, cloth body, wax over composition arms; good wig; glass eyes; appropriately dressed. Marked with winged helmet and "ED," body stamped "HOLZMAASE," or "Dressel."

Wax-Over Composition: composition head coated with wax; shoulder head, cloth body, wax-over composition limbs; good wig; painted eyes; closed mouth; appropriately dressed. Typically marked "ED Patent DE HOLZ-MASSE" inside back shoulder plate and "XXXVIII" painted in gold.

Eden Bébé

E den Bébé, a trade name, is a more familiar term to collectors than the Fleischmann and Bloedel Doll Factory, its manufacturer. The company was established in 1873 in Fürth, Bavaria and Paris, France. In 1899 Saloman Fleishmann formed and became director of the S.F.B.J. (Société Francaise de Fabrication de Bébés & Jouets), making the Fleischmann and Bloedel Doll Factory its first charter member.

Unwilling to forfeit his German citizenship, Fleischmann left France during World War I and returned to Germany. He died soon after in Spain. Consequently, the firm changed directors and ownership many times and eventually claimed bankruptcy in the early 1920s.

Reproduction Eden Bébés surface occasionally. Examine dolls carefully for the reproduction crafter's name, initials, and/or date in the marking. Also, look at the quality of the bisque. Eden Bébés will not have the satin smooth finish of most reproductions.

Prices listed are for dolls with no damage to the bisque. Normal wear, slight damage or well-done repairs to the body do not greatly affect price. If the bisque is damaged or repaired, expect to pay less than half the amount listed. It is perfectly acceptable to show a missing or repaired finger or joint to the body.

Eden Bébé: socket head, five-piece composition body; good wig; cork plate; paperweight eyes, feathered brows, long eyelashes; closed mouth or open mouth with or without slight molded tongue; appropriately dressed. Marked "Eden Bébé" or "Eden Bébé Paris."

18" Eden Bébé.

EDEN BÉBÉ VALUE COMPARISONS:

Size	Closed Mouth	Open Mouth	Black	Composition
11"	2,000.00	1,400.00		
12"	2,200.00	1,500.00		
14"	2,500.00	1,600.00		
16"	2,800.00	1,800.00	3,700.00	600.00
18"	3,000.00	2,000.00		
20"	3,200.00	2,200.00		
22"	3,500.00	2,400.00		
24"	3,800.00	2,600.00		
26"	4,000.00	2,800.00		
28"	4,400.00	3,000.00		
30"	5,200.00	3,400.00		
34"		3,800.00		

Eegee

This famous doll company was founded in 1917 in Brooklyn, New York, by Mr. and Mrs. E. Goldberger. The trademark EEGEE was adopted in 1923. Eegee is one of longest-running continuously operating manufacturers of dolls in the United States. Although the company never achieved the level of fame acquired by many other doll companies, Eegee constantly strove to introduce innovative and appealing quality dolls.

Prices listed are for dolls in good condition. If badly crazed, cracked, peeling, damaged, or repaired, expect to pay less than half the amount listed.

10" Eegee Child.

COMPOSITION

Child: socket head, jointed composition body; molded and painted hair or good wig; painted or sleep eyes; open/closed mouth; appropriately dressed. Typically marked "EEGEE," "E. Goldberger," or "E. G."

Baby: flange neck, cloth body, composition limbs; molded and painted hair or good wig; tin sleep eyes; open/closed mouth with two molded and painted teeth; appropriately dressed. Typically marked "E. Goldberger," "E. G.," or " EEGEE."

HARD PLASTIC

Gigi Perreaux (child actress): vinyl head, jointed hard plastic body; dark brown synthetic wig; brown sleep eyes, feathered brows; open/closed mouth with painted teeth; appropriately dressed. Marked "E. G."

Child/Teen: socket head, jointed hard plastic body (may be walker body); rooted saran hair; sleep eyes; closed mouth; appropriately dressed. Typically marked "E. G." or "EEGEE."

EARLY VINYL/LATEX

Child: early vinyl head, wooden neck flange, one-piece latex body; molded and painted hair; sleep eyes; open or closed mouth; appropriately dressed. Typically marked "EEGEE" or "EE-GEE."

LATER VINYL OR PART VINYL (1960s)

Baby: socket head, molded plastic body; rooted hair; painted or sleep eyes; closed mouth; appropriately dressed. Typically marked "Eegee."

Teen: all vinyl, socket head, jointed at shoulders and hips; rooted hair; painted or sleep eyes; closed mouth; appropriately dressed. Typically marked "20/25M," "EEGEE," or "20 HH."

MODERN DOLLS

Musical Dimples: vinyl head and hands, cloth body; rooted hair; painted eyes; open/closed mouth; body and clothing as one; music box inside. Marked "14 BD/Eegee Co."

Dolly Parton: vinyl head, jointed plastic woman's body; painted eyes; open/closed mouth with molded teeth; dressed in original gown. Marked "DOLLY PARTON/EEGEE CO./HONG KONG" on back of head, "Goldberger Mfg. Co." on back.

Granny: plastic and vinyl; rooted long gray hair pulled into bun; painted facial features; closed mouth; dressed in original cotton dress. Marked "Eegee/3" on back of head.

EEGEE VALUE COMPARISONS:

Size	Child	Composition Baby	Gigi Perreaux	Gigi Child/Teen	Early Vinyl Child	Vinyl Baby	Vinyl Teen	Musical Dimples	Dolly Parton	Granny
10"						25.00				
12"						45.00	75.00	20.00	45.00	
14"		225.00		65.00	65.00	50.00				100.00
16"	300.00	250.00								
18"	350.00	300.00	700.00			65.00	100.00	45.00	75.00	
20"	500.00			75.00	85.00					
22"		350.00		100.00						
28"				150.00	100.00		135.00			
36"							175.00			

Effanbee Doll Company

Effanbee is an acronym for Fleischaker & Baum, who founded this great company in New York City around 1910. Effanbee has consistently been one of the pioneers in the American doll industry, responsible for many of the most significant innovations in the industry. Patsy was the first realistically proportioned American-made doll designed to resemble a real child. She was also the first doll for which doll companions were created, and the first to have a wardrobe and fan club. Patsy's fan club reportedly had over 275,000 members. In 1934 Effanbee enhanced its image of being on the edge of innovation with the introduction of "Dydee," the first drink-and-wet doll.

Effanbee babies will be the keepsakes of future generations. While maintaining its excellence in the play doll field, Effanbee became a leader in the collector dolls phenomena by introducing talented doll artists, initiating the Limited Edition Doll Club, and producing realistic celebrity dolls.

Prices listed are for dolls in very good to excellent condition. Well-loved dolls which are soiled, cracked, or badly crazed command less than half the amount listed.

COMPOSITION

Character Doll: distinct and memorable face; examples include Chubby Boy Bud, Baby Grumpy, Pouting Bess,

8" Composition Tiny Dutch Twins. *Photo courtesy of McMasters Doll Auction.*

Coquette, Harmonica Joe, Katie Kroose, and Whistling Jim; cloth body; sewn-on shoes; nicely molded and painted features; appropriately dressed. Typically marked "Effanbee," "176," "Deco.," "172," "174," "Baby Grumpy," "166," or "162."

Child and Baby Face: examples include Baby Dainty, Sweetie Pie, Mickey, Baby Bright Eyes, Lovums, Rosemary, and Marilee; shoulder head, cloth body, composition limbs; molded hair or wig; painted or tin sleep eyes; open or closed mouth.

Dolly-Face (Mary Jane): socket head, jointed wood-and-composition body, some with cloth or kid body; good wig; sleep eyes; open mouth; appropriately dressed. Marked "Effanbee."

Mama: examples include Bubbles and Lambkin; cloth body, composition limbs; molded hair or good wig; sleep eyes; open or closed mouth, most say "Mama;" appropriately dressed. Typically marked "Effanbee/Bubbles/Corp 1924/Made in U.S.A.," "Effanbee/Dolls/Walk,Talk,Sleep/.Made in USA," "1924/Effanbee/Dollys/Walk,Talk, Sleep/Made in USA.," or "EFFANBEE."

Patsy and Patsy Family: one of the most popular 20th century dolls; all composition, jointed at neck, shoulders, and hips; painted and molded hair or wig; painted or sleep eyes; closed mouth; appropriately dressed. Marked "EFFANBEE PATSY DOLL," "EFFANBEE PATSY BABY," or with other variations of the Patsy family.

Skippy: newspaper character drawn by Percy Crosby and produced as playmate for Patsy; cloth body with composition limbs or all composition; molded and painted hair; painted round side-glancing eyes; closed mouth; appropriately dressed. Marked "Patsy Pat./Pending" or "Effanbee Skippy/P. L. Crosby," original pin reads "I am Skippy The All American Boy."

Ventriloquist Doll: typically marked "Lucifer/V. Autsin/EffanBEE," "Fleischer & Baum," "W. C. Fields/EffanBEE," or "EDGAR BERGEN CHARLIE McCARTHY EFFANBEE." Because these dolls were expensive to produce, transport, and display, relatively few were made. Today they are a rare find. Puppeteer Virginia Austin designed and patented a number of Effanbee's puppets. She also gave marionette demonstrations and founded the "Clippo Club" as part of the Effanbee marionette promotion.

American Children: composition socket head, jointed composition body; human hair wig; beautifully painted, detailed eyes; closed mouth; wearing original well-made outfit. Typically marked "Effanbee/American Children" or "Effanbee/Ann Shirley." Composition dolls designed by Dewees Cochran. Dewees met Bernard Baum and Hugo Fleischaker, owners of EffanBee Doll Company, in 1935. They were impressed with her work and commissioned her to produce six dolls for the upcoming 1936 Toy Show. Effanbee signed a three-year contract with Dewees to produce the designs of her American Children portrait dolls. Due to global circumstances, when the three-year contract expired, it was not renewed.

21" composition Ann Shirley.

Child/Lady: examples include Suzanna, Tommy Tucker, Ann Shirley, and Little Lady; all composition, jointed at neck, shoulders, and hips; good wig; sleep eyes; closed mouth; appropriately dressed. Typically marked "EFFANBEE USA" or "EFFANBEE/ANN SHIRLEY."

Unmarked Child: part of the American Children series, often called "Open Mouth American Children;" examples include Barbara Joan, Barbara Ann, Barbara Lou, and Peggy Lou; all composition, jointed at neck, shoulders and hips; human hair wig; sleep or painted eyes; open mouth; original well-made outfit. Unmarked or marked "EffanBEE/Anne Shirley."

Historical/Historical Replica Dolls: designed by Dewees Cochran. Effanbee produced three sets of thirty dolls depicting changing American lifestyles. These 20" dolls were exhibited around the country. The original 20" dolls used Ann Shirley bodies and American Children heads. They had painted eyes and were dressed in satins, velvets, and silks. Effanbee produced a smaller and less elaborately costumed 14" version known as a Historical Replica Doll. They were accurately detailed and had painted eyes and costumes made from cotton.

15" Dy-Dee Baby.

OTHER COMPOSITION DOLLS:

Doll House Doll: 6", composition head, cloth body, wire armatures, composition hands, molded and painted shoes; molded and painted hair, painted blue eyes; closed mouth; wearing original felt black tuxedo with white felt vest, tiny glass bead buttons; marked "EFFanBEE" on back of head; 1950 . . . . **75.00**

Button Nose: 8", all composition, jointed at neck, shoulders, and hips; molded and painted hair; painted round side-glancing eyes; closed slightly smiling mouth; dressed in original Dutch Girl outfit with blue dress, white apron, Dutch cap, and wooden shoes; marked "Effanbee" on back; 1938 . . . . **250.00**

Little Sister and Big Brother: 12" and 16", composition socket head, composition shoulder plate, cloth body, cloth limbs, composition hands; embroidery floss hair; painted eyes; small closed mouth; Little Sister dressed in original pink and white check blouse with pink skirt; Big Brother dressed in original blue and white checked shirt with blue coveralls, white socks, tie shoes; marked "Effanbee" on back of head; 1943
    Little Sister: 12" **200.00**
    Big Brother: 16" **250.00**

Candy Kid: 13", all composition, jointed at neck, shoulders, and hips; chubby child figure; molded and painted hair; painted eyes, pointed eyebrows; closed mouth; dressed in original red and white checked gingham outfit; holding small stuffed monkey; 1946 . . . . **325.00**

HARD PLASTIC

Hard plastic collectible Effanbee dolls appeared on the market soon after World War II. With the successful introduction of Howdy Doody in 1947, other hard plastic dolls soon followed.

Howdy Doody: hard plastic character head, cloth body, hard plastic hands; molded and painted hair; sleep eyes; open/closed mouth; wearing original cowboy costume with scarf printed "Howdy Doody;" marked "Effanbee."

Honey: all hard plastic, jointed at neck, shoulders, and hips; synthetic wig; sleep eyes; closed mouth; appropriately dressed. Marked "Effanbee," tag on gown reads "I am Honey An Effanbee Durable Doll." The Honey Series of dolls include famous characters such as Cinderella and Prince Charming, and elaborately costumed dolls such as those from the Schiaparelli Collection, designed by famous Paris designer, Madame Schiaparelli. These dolls command higher prices than their more common counterparts.

HARD RUBBER

Dy-Dee Baby: hard rubber drink-and-wet doll; hard rubber or plastic socket head, hard rubber body, jointed at shoulders and hips, attached soft rubber ears; molded and painted hair; sleep eyes; open nurser drink and wet mouth; appropriately dressed. Marked "Effanbee/DyDee Baby/U. S. Pat. 1-857-485/England-880-060/France-723-980/Germany-585-647/Other Pat. Pending." The hard rubber heads (and later the hard rubber bodies) were replaced with hard plastic.

VINYL

Vinyl Effanbee dolls have been produced by the thousands. The following examples will help in determining comparable values.

Fluffy: 8", all vinyl, jointed at neck, shoulders, and hips; molded and painted hair with long curls molded around back of head; sleep eyes; closed mouth; appropriately dressed. **85.00**

Happy Boy: 10", all vinyl, jointed at neck and shoulders; character face; molded and painted hair; molded and painted closed eyes; open/closed mouth, molded upper tooth; freckles; appropriately dressed; marked "1960/Effanbee" on back of head and "Effanbee." .**65.00**

Half Pint: 11", all vinyl, jointed at neck, shoulder, and hips; rooted short hair; large side-glancing sleep eyes; closed grinning mouth; appropriately dressed; marked "IOME/Effanbee/19©66." **75.00**

Mickey The All American Boy: 11", all vinyl, jointed at neck, shoulders, and hips; molded hat and hair; painted eyes; closed smiling mouth; freckles; appropriately dressed; marked "Mickey/Effanbee." **150.00**

Patsy Ann: 15", all vinyl, jointed at neck, shoulders and hips; rooted hair; sleep eyes; closed smiling mouth; appropriately dressed; marked "Effanbee Patsy Ann/1959." **200.00**

Mae West from Legends Series.

Rootie Kazootie: 19", vinyl character flange neck, cloth body, vinyl hands; molded and painted hair, long curl coming down forehead; round painted eyes; open/closed laughing mouth; appropriately dressed; marked "Rootie/Kazootie/Effanbee." **200.00**

Candy Ann: 20", all vinyl, jointed at neck, shoulders, and hips; rooted hair; sleep eyes; closed smiling mouth; appropriately dressed; marked "Effanbee." **150.00**

Honey Walker: 20", vinyl head, hard plastic body, jointed at shoulders, hips, just above knees, and at ankles; feet molded for high heel shoes; walking mechanism turns head; rooted hair; sleep eyes; pierced ears; closed mouth; appropriately dressed; marked "EFFanBEE." **400.00**

Lil' Darling: 20", vinyl flange neck head, cloth body, vinyl limbs; molded and painted hair; small slit-like painted eyes, molded underlying pouches, wrinkled brow; pug nose; open/closed mouth, molded tongue; appropriately dressed. **200.00**

My Fair Baby: 21", all vinyl, jointed at neck, shoulders, and hips; rooted hair; sleep eyes; open nurser mouth; body has crier; appropriately dressed; marked "EFFanBEE/1960." **100.00**

Precious Baby: 21", vinyl flange neck head, pink cloth body, vinyl limbs; rooted hair; sleep eyes; open/closed mouth; appropriately dressed; marked "Effanbee 19©69." **100.00**

Mary Jane: 30", vinyl socket head, plastic body, jointed at shoulders and hips; rooted hair; sleep/flirty eyes; closed slightly unsmiling mouth; freckles over nose; appropriately dressed; marked "Effanbee/Mary Jane." **350.00**

LIMITED EDITION DOLLS

Effanbee produced dolls in series, collections, and clubs. Initiated in 1975, the Effanbee Limited Edition Doll Club introduced a new doll each year. A unique feature of the Effanbee Club is that each doll is produced in a pre-announced limited quantity and is accompanied by a numbered certificate. The dolls were not available in any retail stores, but only through Effanbee's Limited Edition Doll Club.

DOLL CLUB SERIES

Precious Baby: 1975 . . . .**550.00**
Patsy: 1976 . . . .**450.00**
Dewees Cochran Self Portrait: 1977 . . . . .**225.00**
Crowning Glory: 1978 . . . .**200.00**
Skippy: 1979 . . . .**375.00**
Susan B. Anthony: 1980 . . . .**175.00**
Girl with a Watering Can: 1981 . . . .**175.00**
A Royal Bride: Diana, 1982 . . . .**200.00**
Sherlock Holmes: 1983 . . . .**150.00**
Bubbles: 1984 . . . .**150.00**
Red Boy: 1985 . . . .**150.00**
China Head: 1986 . . . .**100.00**

Twinkie: 15", all vinyl, jointed at neck, shoulders, and hips; rooted hair or molded and painted hair; sleep eyes; open nurser drink and wet mouth; appropriately dressed; marked "Effanbee/1959." **150.00**

Sugar Plum: 16", vinyl head, cloth body, vinyl limbs; rooted hair; sleep eyes; closed smiling mouth; appropriately dressed; marked "141 Effanbee/1969/1949." **75.00**

Honey (later called Suzie Sunshine): 18", all vinyl, jointed at neck, shoulders, and hips; rooted hair; sleep eyes; closed pouty mouth; freckles; appropriately dressed; marked "Effanbee/1961." **85.00**

Miss Chips: 18", all vinyl, jointed at neck, shoulders, and hips; rooted hair, full bangs; very large side-glancing sleep eyes; closed mouth; appropriately dressed; marked "Effanbee/19©65/1700." **60.00**

Sugar Plum: 18", vinyl flange neck head, cloth body, vinyl limbs; rooted hair; blue eyes; closed mouth; appropriately dressed; marked "F & B/1964." **65.00**

Thumbkin: 18", vinyl head, cloth body, vinyl limbs; rooted short hair; round side-glancing eyes; open/closed mouth; appropriately dressed; marked "Effanbee/1965/9500 UI." **100.00**

LEGENDS SERIES

W.C. Fields	300.00
John Wayne: soldier	225.00
John Wayne: cowboy	225.00
Mae West	150.00
Groucho Marx	125.00
Judy Garland as Dorothy	125.00
Lucille Ball	125.00
Liberace	150.00
James Cagney	100.00

PRESIDENTS SERIES

George Washington	75.00
Abraham Lincoln	75.00
Theodore Roosevelt	60.00
Franklin D. Roosevelt	75.00
John F. Kennedy	85.00
Dwight D. Eisenhower	60.00

GREAT MOMENTS IN HISTORY

Winston Churchill	85.00
Eleanor Roosevelt	75.00

GREAT MOMENTS IN LITERATURE

Huck Finn	75.00
Mark Twain	75.00
Becky Thatcher	60.00
Tom Sawyer	65.00

GREAT MOMENTS IN MUSIC

Louis Armstrong	75.00

GREAT MOMENTS IN SPORTS

Babe Ruth	100.00
Muhammed Ali	75.00

INTERNATIONAL COLLECTION

Grand Dames Collection	75.00
Currier & Ives Collection	75.00
Soft & Sweet Collection	45.00
Keepsake Collection	65.00
Age of Elegance Collection	75.00
Gigi Through the Years Collection	100.00
Passing Parade Collection	75.00
Day by Day Collection	60.00
Innocence Collection	60.00

STORYBOOK COLLECTION

Dorothy	75.00
Cowardly Lion	75.00
Tin Man	75.00
Straw Man	75.00
Santa Claus	60.00
Mrs. Claus	50.00
Old Woman in the Shoe	50.00
Little Milk Maid	45.00

CRAFTSMAN CORNER COLLECTIBLE DOLLS

Jan Hagara: Christian	225.00
Jan Hagara: Laurel	175.00
Edna Hibel: Contessa	100.00
Edna Hibel: Flower Girl of Brittany	100.00
Joyce Stafford: Little Tiger	125.00
Joyce Stafford: Lotus Blossom	100.00
Faith Wick: Scarecrow	120.00

DISNEY LICENSED DOLLS

Prince Charming	65.00
Cinderella	65.00
Poor Cinderella	65.00
Mary Poppins	65.00

PATSY & HER FAMILY VALUE COMPARISONS:

Size	Wee Patsy	Baby Tinette	Patsy Babyette	Patsyette*	Patsy Baby/Babykins*	Patsykins/ Patsy Jr.	Patsy/ Patricia	Patsy Joan	Patsy Ann	Patsy Lou	Patsy Ruth	Mae	Skippy
6"	400.00												
7"		350.00											
8"			400.00										
9"				450.00									
10"					400.00								
11"						450.00							
14"							550.00						650.00
16"								550.00					
19"									600.00				
22"										650.00			
27"											1,000.00		
30"												1,000.00	

* Add an additional $200.00 for black dolls.

Eisenmann & Co.

The firm of Eisenmann & Co., known as Einco, was located in Bavaria and London from 1881 until 1930. Einco produced and distributed dolls for which Gebrüder Heubach supplied the bisque heads. Joe Eisenmann, the founder the company, was called "King of the Toy Trade."

There are reproduction dolls which are very similar to the character dolls made by Einco. They do not bear the Einco markings. A careful examination should eliminate any doubt you may have concerning an Einco doll's authenticity.

Normal wear, slight damage, or well-done repairs to the body do not greatly affect price. If the bisque is damaged or repaired, however, expect to pay less than half the amount listed. It is perfectly acceptable to show a missing or repaired finger or joint to the body.

Socket Head: composition bent-limb body; molded and painted hair; intaglio painted eyes; open/closed mouth; appropriately dressed. Marked "Germany Einco."

15" Character EINCO Baby.

EINCO VALUE COMPARISONS:	
Size	**Character Baby**
12"	800.00
15"	900.00
18"	1,000.00
20"	1,200.00

Joel Ellis

Joel Ellis operated the Co-Operative Manufacturing Company in Springfield, Vermont, from 1873 to 1874. Ellis patented and manufactured wooden dolls and employed about sixty people, most of them women. The Joel Ellis Doll is considered one of the first commercially-made American dolls. It embodies many technical innovations. The doll's unique mortise-and-tendon construction allowed it to have complete range of movement. Pewter hands and feet fit into the rock maple limbs. The wood for the heads was cut into a cube, steamed until softened, and compressed in a hydraulic press with steel dies to form the features. The bodies and limbs were turned on a lathe and the head fastened with a dowel. The hair was molded in a prim 1860s-style and painted either black or blond. Joel Ellis Dolls can be found in three sizes: 12", 15", and 18". Many collectors prefer to display the dolls undressed, as this is how they were originally sold.

Although Joel Ellis Dolls are unmarked, their unique body construction, metal hands, and distinct facial features make them easy to identify. The numerous copies that have been made do not have the same joint construction as the originals.

Few Joel Ellis Dolls have withstood the test of time. Peeling and flaking paint is a common problem. Sadder yet,

many have been repainted. Because of this, collectors tend to be a bit more forgiving. The desirability of a Joel Ellis Doll rests in the doll's design and historical

JOE ELLIS WOODEN DOLL VALUE COMPARISONS:	
Size	**Price**
12"	1,200.00
15"	1,400.00
18"	1,900.00

significance rather than the artistry applied to the head. Prices listed are for dolls in fair to good condition with normal wear to the head. A well preserved example may command double the price given.

Joel Ellis Doll: wooden head and body, painted metal hands and feet; molded and painted hair; painted eyes; closed mouth; undressed; no marks.

15" Joel Ellis doll. *Courtesy of Helen Brooke.*

J.K. Farnell & Company

The J.K. Farnell & Company was founded in 1871 in England. In the 1920's Farnell's Alpha Toys began producing dolls made of felt, velvet, stockinette, and other cloth materials. Farnell Dolls are found with a cloth label sewn to the foot.

Farnell's chubby dolls feature felt faces, side-glancing eyes, and smiling mouths. Stockinette bodies have seams at the front, back, and sides of each leg. Hair consists of mohair sewn in a circular pattern on the head or a human hair wig. Dolls with velvet faces and bodies, usually native dolls, were also made.

Farnell produced a King Edward VIII Coronation Doll which was quickly withdrawn from the market following his abdication. Today, this rare doll commands double or even triple the price of other Farnell dolls of comparable quality. Farnell also marketed a King George VI Doll, but it does not enjoy the same status awarded the Edward VIII Doll.

Prices listed are for dolls in very good to mint condition. Dolls which are faded, dirty, worn, or torn will command only half these amounts.

Child Doll: pressed felt mask, pink cotton body, velvet arms and legs, seam joints only; painted facial features; good wig; appropriately dressed. Tagged "Farnell's/Alpha Toys/Made in England."

Novelty and International Tourist Doll: clothing is part of body construction, stitched joints, velvet face; slightly molded painted features; appropriately dressed. Tagged "Farnell/Alpha Toy Co./Made in England."

Portrait Doll: pressed felt mask face, stockinette body, jointed at neck, shoulders and hips; painted facial features; appropriately dressed. Tagged "H.M. The King/(or character name)/Made in England/J. K. Farnell & Co./Acton London."

10" Alpha Toys Scottish doll. *Photo Courtesy of McMasters Doll Auction.*

J. K. FARNELL VALUE COMPARISONS:

Size	Child Doll	Novelty	Portrait	King Edward*
8"		100.00		
12"		200.00		
13"			1,300.00	2,400.00
14"	550.00	300.00		
15"	600.00	400.00		
16"	700.00		1,500.00	
20"		600.00		
22"		800.00		

French Bébés

There are several different French socket-head Bébés found in the marketplace today that were produced by small manufacturers or not attributed to any specific maker. They all have very good quality bisque socket heads on wood-and-composition bodies, with paperweight eyes, pierced ears, and closed mouths.

Bébé: good quality bisque, socket head, wood-and-composition body; good wig; paperweight eyes; pierced ears; closed mouth; appropriately dressed. Marks are listed below. The # indicates a size number.

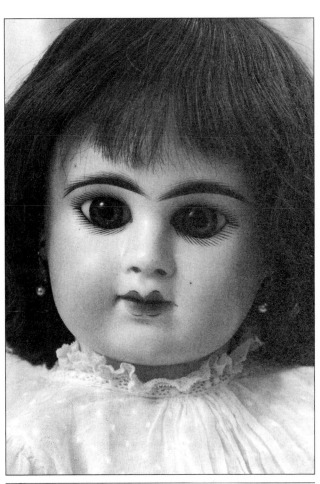

20" E D Bébé. *Photo courtesy of Cobbs Doll Auction.*

A. Marque. *Courtesy of Ellen Schroy.*

		A. Thiuller		B. L.	E D	H. Mold			
Size	A. Marque	A#T	B F	B#L	Deposé	#H	J	M#	JM
15"									
20"		50,000.00	4,900.00	4,700.00	4,800.00	80,000.00	4,500.00	4,500.00	23,000.00
22"	65,000.00								

BÉBÉ VALUE COMPARISONS:

Size	Mothereau BM#	PAN	Paris	P. D.	Pintel & Godchauex PG	R#R	Van Rozen
15"		12,000.00					14,000.00
20"	22,000.00		4,800.00	22,000.00	3,800.00	4,700.00	
22"							

French Fashion-Type

French Fashion-Type Dolls, known as Poupée de Mode, were manufactured between 1860 to 1930. Whether produced in France, Germany, or Austria, collectors use the term "French Fashion" or "Fashion Doll" for these lady dolls with fashionably formed cloth, kid, and/or wooden bodies. There is ample evidence that this type of doll was intended to be a play doll. However, quoting from an 1869 *Harper's Bazaar*, "The chief French toy is a doll—not a representation of an infant—but a model of a lady attired in the heights of fashion." Additional documentation hints that these lovely ladies were also used to model the latest fashions. An advertisement from "Hannah Teats of Boston" states "The mannequin dolls could be seen at her shop for 2 shillings or could be dispatched to a lady's home for 7 shillings, seeing the newest fashions of dress, nightdress and everything pertaining to women's attire, lately arrived on the Captain White from London."

According to the United Federation of Doll Clubs (U.F.D.C.) "The term French Doll is to be applied only to dolls made entirely in France—according to this definition any doll with an unmarked or unrecognizably marked head cannot be called French." To further the controversy is the argument that a fashion doll is not a type of doll, but rather describes a functional use. Nearly any type of doll could be dressed in the latest adult or child's fashions. Although many dealers and collectors apply the term "Fashion" to this type of doll, serious students reject it. Whether mannequin, milliner, lady doll, fashion doll, or play doll, the little Poupée de Mode present a perfect example of the beauty and splendor of Parisian life and fashionable attire.

Reproductions frequently surface. Study the doll carefully. If marked, examine the markings closely. If the bisque has a bit of a shine, it is a clue that the doll may not be authentic. Study the eyes. The French Fashion-Type Dolls have good quality paperweight eyes. The brows should have a nice even feathered look. If the body is kid, look carefully at the seams. Beware of snowy white seams. The dolls measuring 15 to 17 inches are a favorite with those wishing to pass off a reproduction French Fashion Doll as the real thing. Look for subtle differences in markings. For example, F. G. should not be F+G. Finally, if the deal is too good to be true, it probably is. Something is wrong when a $5,000.00 doll is offered for $1,000.00. Spotting a reproduction French Fashion Doll often entails piecing together several minute clues. Seldom are there obvious clamoring signs of a fake. One must learn to recognize the subtle clues—differences which will distinguish authentic dolls from reproductions.

When considering a French Fashion-Type doll, check condition carefully. The prices listed below are for dolls with no damage to the bisque. Normal wear, slight damage, or well-done repairs to the body do not greatly affect the price. If

18" Poupée de Mode.

the bisque is damaged or repaired, expect to pay half the amounts listed. It is perfectly acceptable to show a missing or repaired finger or a repaired or patched joint to the body.

Wooden Body Poupée de Mode: pale fine bisque swivel head, kid-lined bisque shoulder plate, attached with kid to fully articulated wooden body with wooden peg joints; good wig; paperweight eyes finely lined with black and painted with long lashes, softly feathered brows; pierced ears; small closed mouth; appropriately dressed. Unmarked, or marked with size number.

Kid Body Poupée de Mode: pale fine bisque swivel head, kid-lined bisque shoulder plate, fine gusseted kid body, occasionally with bisque arms; good wig; exquisitely painted or paperweight eyes, black eyeliner, finely painted eyelashes and feathered brows; pieced ears; closed mouth; appropriately dressed. Unmarked, or marked with size number.

See-through Necklace-type: bisque shoulder plate, kid body, bisque lower arms; photographic scenes of Paris and religious figures can be seen through glass jewels of necklace when opening in back of doll's shoulder is held to light; good wig; stationary eyes, fine black eyeliner, short lashes, thin feathered brows; closed mouth; appropriately dressed. Marked "Ed. Rochards Brevete S.G.D.G. France Patented 1867." Unmarked dress with ribbon "Ed. Rochards Brevete S.G.D.G. France Patented 1867."

ACCESSORIES

Accessories to complete the Poupée de Mode's wardrobe include tiny parasols, reticules, kid gloves, toilette sets, opera glasses, embroidered handkerchiefs, corsets, stationery, watches, tea sets, and even a miniature all-bisque French doll of her very own.

Album à photographies pour poupées (photo album for dolls) . . . .**200.00 – 450.00**
Boites à chapeaux (hat box) . . . .**150.00 – 350.00**
Buvard (writing case) . . . .**100.00 – 300.00**
Cartes de bureau (business cards) . .**100.00 – 300.00**
Cartes de Toilette (social cards) . . . .**50.00 – 150.00**
Courroies pour châles et waterproofs (straps to carry rain covers) . . . .**100.00 – 150.00**
Cerceau (hoop) . . . .**150.00 – 300.00**
Complet costume sur mesure (tailor made men's suit) . . . .**1,000.00 – 3,500.00**
Cordes à sauter (jump rope) . . . .**75.00 – 175.00**
Cravaches (horse whip) . . . .**200.00 – 350.00**
Damier (checker-board) . . . .**150.00 – 300.00**
Démêloirs (large hair comb) . . . .**75.00 – 200.00**

20" Poupée de Mode. *Photo courtesy of Sotheby's.*

Des Bas (stockings) . . . .**100.00 – 200.00**
Des Bottinés (boots) . . . .**350.00 – 800.00**
Dominos (dominos) . . . .**100.00 – 250.00**
Epingles à cheveux (hairpins) . . . .**35.00 – 65.00**
Eventails (fans) . . . .**125.00 – 350.00**
Formes, tulle pour chapeaux (forms and stands for hat) . . . .**150.00 – 300.00**
Gants peau et fil (leather gloves) . . . .**125.00 – 300.00**
Hamac (hammock) . . . .**45.00 – 100.00**
Jarretières (garters) . . . .**50.00 – 150.00**
Jeu de loto (Loto game) . . . .**200.00 – 350.00**
Jeu de nain-jaune (Pope Joan card game) . . . .**250.00 – 350.00**
Livre de messe (book of Mass) . . . . .**200.00 – 350.00**
Lunettes, lorgnons, binocles (eye glasses, longnette, opera glasses) . . . .**150.00 – 400.00**
Malles pour Poupée (trunk for doll) .**200.00 – 700.00**

	FRENCH FASHION-TYPE (POUPÉE DE MODE) VALUE COMPARISONS:			
Size	Wooden Body Poupée de Mode	Kid Body Poupée de Mode	Black Poupée de Mode on Kid	See-through Necklace Poupée de Mode
12"	5,300.00	2,700.00		
14"	5,500.00	2,900.00		
15"	6,000.00	3,200.00	4,000.00	
16"	6,500.00	3,400.00		
18"	7,000.00	3,600.00	6,000.00	45,000.00
20"	7,500.00	3,800.00		
22"	9,000.00	4,200.00		
24"	9,500.00	4,800.00		
30"	12,000.00	6,200.00		
34"	18,000.00	8,800.00		

Malles pour trousseaux (trunk for trousseau) . . . . .175.00 – 450.00

Médaillon (locket) . . . . .75.00 – 250.00

Montres avec chaîne (watch and chain) . . . . .250.00 – 600.00

Moufle (mittens) . . . . .80.00 – 200.00

Nécéssaires de toilette (toiletries) . .150.00 – 300.00

Ombrelles et En-tou-cas (umbrellas and parasols) . . . . .250.00 – 600.00

Paniers de voyage (baskets for travel) . .150.00 – 300.00

Pantoufles (slippers) . . . . .100.00 – 200.00

Papeterie (stationery) . . . . .75.00 – 250.00

Peignes à chigons (combs with trim) . .100.00 – 250.00

Peignes, brosses (combs and brushes) . . . . .100.00 – 200.00

Perruque (wig) . . . . .200.00 – 700.00

Pied ou support pour la poupée (vintage doll stand) . . . . .75.00 – 200.00

Resilles (hairnet for a Spanish comb) . .75.00 – 150.00

Sacs à ouvrage (work bag) . . . . .125.00 – 250.00

Souliers (shoes) . . . . .250.00 – 500.00

Un Chapeau (hat) . . . . .200.00 – 600.00

Un corsage blanc (white waist) . . . . .150.00 – 350.00

Un Costume de Fantaisie (a fancy outfit) . . . . .700.00 – 3,500.00

Un jupon (petticoat) . . . . .125.00 – 300.00

Un pantalon (drawers) . . . . .75.00 – 200.00

Une chemise (chemise) . . . . .75.00 – 200.00

This is not a complete list of all the accessories available. Hopefully, it will serve as a guide to help the reader get a feel for prices commanded by quality Poupée de Mode accessories. Values are given as ranges. Consider each accessory carefully, and evaluate its individual appeal and condition.

16" B3S French Fashion Doll. *Photo courtesy of McMasters Doll Auction.*

Poupée de Mode's accessories.

Ralph A. Freundlich, Inc.

Ralph A. Freundlich, Inc., was founded in 1929 in New York City. The company is best known for its composition novelty-type dolls.

Most Freundlich dolls are not marked, therefore accurate identification is difficult. Collectors researching the company have relied largely on old advertisements and catalogs for positive identification. Listed below are dolls that have been attributed to Freundlich. In time, more dolls will probably be identified and added to the list. The quality of the dolls produced over the years varies from very good to very poor. Recently, Freundlich character dolls have become extremely collectible and prices have risen sharply.

Prices listed are for dolls with no damage, in very good condition, with original clothing. Although it is getting increasingly more difficult to find composition in perfect condition, avoid badly crazed, cracked or repainted dolls, unless priced accordingly. Normal wear and slight crazing will not necessarily affect the price. When found in poor or repainted condition, expect to pay less than half the amount listed. By the same token, if a doll is found in mint condition with wrist tags, the value could easily be doubled.

Quintuplets and Nurse: 6³/4", 9", all composition, jointed at neck, shoulders, and hips; molded and painted hair; painted eyes; appropriately dressed; no markings on dolls; advertised in the November 1935 *Playthings*. **900.00**

Baby with Scale: 9¹/2", all composition, jointed at neck, shoulders, and hips; molded and painted hair and facial features; wearing diaper; unmarked; in basket on working scale; advertised in June 1934 *Playthings* **200.00**

Red Riding Hood, Grandma, and Wolf: 10", all composition, jointed at neck, shoulders, and hips; molded and painted hair; painted eyes; closed mouth. Grandma has a nicely molded character face, white mohair at front of scarf tied to head; painted side-glancing eyes; and a closed mouth molded to look as though she has no teeth. Wolf has molded and painted fur; character wolf face with face and body painted brown; painted eyes; and closed mouth. All appropriately dressed; advertised in 1934 Sears & Roebuck. **900.00**

Little Orphan Annie and Sandy: 11¹/4", 6³/4", all composition. Annie is jointed at neck, shoulders, and hips and has molded and painted hair, painted round eyes, closed mouth, and is appropriately dressed. Sandy is molded and painted with no joints, and has a character face with painted large round eyes. Unmarked, advertised in 1938 store catalog. **500.00**

Goo Goo Eva: 15", composition head, pink cloth body and limbs, square hands with no finger details; mohair wig

19" Freundlich's General MacArthur. *Photo courtesy of McMasters Doll Auction.*

with stitched side part; round celluloid googly-type eyes with floating disks within; closed mouth; wearing original flowered percale dress and matching bonnet; no marks; advertised in 1938 Sears & Roebuck catalog **200.00**

Douglas MacArthur: 18", all composition, right arm bent to salute; molded hat; character face with painted features; dressed in beautifully detailed full military uniform; unmarked; original paper tag pinned to uniform reads "General MacArthur/The Man of the Hour/Manufactured by Freundlich Corp., New York." **400.00**

Other Military Dolls: 18", Marine, Sailor, Soldier, W.A.A.C., or W.A.V.E. **300.00**

Baby Sandy: 19¹/2", all composition, jointed at neck, shoulders, and hips; molded and painted hair; tin sleep eyes; open mouth with two upper teeth, felt tongue; appropriately dressed. Marked "Baby Sandy." . . . **800.00**

Baby Sandy: 7¹/2" **250.00**

Baby Sandy: 11" **350.00**

Baby Sandy: 16¹/2" **500.00**

Princess: 22", all composition, jointed at neck, shoulders, and hips, longer and slimmer limbs; mohair wig; sleep eyes; open mouth with teeth, felt tongue; appropriately dressed; advertised in July 1937 Toys and Bicycles. **700.00**

Feather Weight Doll: 28", composition head, cloth body, composition limbs; crier box in body; molded and painted hair; painted eyes; closed mouth; appropriately dressed; advertised in February 1930 *Playthings*. . **400.00**

Fulper Pottery Company

The Fulper Pottery Company, founded in 1805 and located in Flemington, New Jersey, is well known for its art pottery and utilitarian wares. Due to import shortages around World War I, the company began producing bisque dolls and doll heads from 1918 to 1921. The quality of Fulper Dolls ranges from very poor to very good. Their historical value is as important as their aesthetic value to today's doll collector.

Fulper made doll heads using German molds, as well as dolls for American companies such as Amberg and Horsman. The American companies had their own molds and it is not uncommon to find dolls marked with the Fulper name alongside the specific company for which the heads were produced.

When considering the purchase of a Fulper bisque doll, in addition to checking condition carefully, consider the quality of the bisque and workmanship of the decoration. Prices listed are for dolls with no damage to the bisque. Normal wear, slight damage or well-done repairs to the body do not greatly affect price. If the bisque is damaged or repaired, expect to pay less than half the amount listed. It is perfectly acceptable to show a missing or repaired finger or joint to the body.

Bisque Socket Head: jointed composition body; good wig; glass eyes; open mouth, two large upper teeth; appropriately dressed. Marked "Fulper Made in USA."

Bisque Shoulder Head: kid body, bisque lower arms; good wig; glass eyes; open mouth with two large upper teeth; appropriately dressed. Marked "Fulper Made in USA."

25" Fulper Child. *Courtesy of Helen Brooke.*

Bisque Character Baby, composition body; good wig; celluloid, metal, or glass sleep eyes; open mouth with two upper teeth; appropriately dressed. Marked "Fulper Made in USA."

	FULPER BISQUE DOLL VALUE COMPARISONS:					
Size	Bisque Socket Head, Composition Body, Exceptional	Bisque Socket Head, Composition Body, Standard	Bisque Shoulder Head, Kid Body, Exceptional	Bisque Shoulder Head, Kid Body, Standard	Character Baby Exceptional*	Character Baby Standard*
13"	450.00	250.00	375.00	200.00		200.00
14"	475.00	265.00	400.00	225.00		
15"	500.00	275.00	425.00	250.00	650.00	400.00
16"	550.00	300.00	450.00	275.00		
18"	650.00	350.00	550.00	300.00	700.00	500.00
20"	750.00	425.00	600.00	400.00	800.00	550.00
22"	850.00	450.00	650.00	450.00	1,000.00	650.00
24"	950.00	500.00	750.00	500.00	1,200.00	750.00
26"	1,300.00	700.00	850.00	600.00		

* Add an additional 300.00 for toddler body.

Francois Gaultier

Francois Gaultier, along with Jumeau, Bru, and Steiner, earned a reputation as a manufacturer of some of the most refined and exquisitely crafted bisque French dolls of the time. As a result of this reputation, Gaultier produced bisque doll heads for several well-known doll companies including Gresland, Jullien, Rabery & Delphieu, Simonne, and Thiller. The 1860 Francois Gaultier factory was located in St. Maurice and Charenton in the province of Seine, on the outskirts of Paris, France. Francois Gaultier continued to produce dolls up until at least 1916, the later years as a part of S.F.B.J. (Societe Française de Fabrication de Bébé s & Jouets).

A Francois Gaultier's Bébé is much harder to find than a Poupée de Modes. Because of their elusiveness, Bébés are priced substantially higher. They are characterized by their subtle pale complexions, delicately blushed eyelids, large wide-set lustrous paperweight eyes, plump cheeks, and fully outlined slightly parted lips, a feature highly valued by collectors.

Reproductions can be spotted with little difficulty. Check the markings. Most copies made of antique dolls were not intended to fool anyone. Therefore, they will be marked with the doll artist's name and possibly a date. Exceptions do

18" F.G. Bébé. *Courtesy of Ellizabeth Frame.*

GAULTIER VALUE COMPARISONS:

Size	Fashion Type Poupée de Mode, Glass Eyes*	Fashion Type Poupée de Mode, Painted Eyes	Block Letter Bébé, Composition Body	Block Letter Bébé, Kid Body	Scroll Mark, Closed Mouth, Exceptional	Scroll Mark, Closed Mouth, Standard	Open Mouth Bébé
8"	1,400.00	900.00				1,500.00	
10½"	1,900.00	1,200.00					
11½"	2,200.00	1,400.00	4,700.00	5,600.00	3,800.00	2,300.00	
13½"	2,500.00	1,700.00	4,700.00	6,000.00	4,000.00	2,700.00	1,800.00
15"	2,700.00	1,900.00	4,900.00	6,400.00	4,500.00	3,000.00	2,000.00
17"	2,800.00	2,200.00	5,100.00	6,700.00	4,800.00	3,400.00	
19"	3,300.00		5,300.00				2,400.00
20"	3,500.00		5,500.00	7,100.00	5,200.00	3,700.00	2,700.00
21"			5,700.00		5,400.00		3,000.00
23"	3,700.00		6,000.00	7,800.00		4,000.00	
25"	4,000.00		6,500.00		5,800.00	4,300.00	3,300.00
27"			7,800.00		6,000.00	4,500.00	3,500.00
29"					6,200.00	4,700.00	3,600.00
31"			8,400.00		6,700.00	5,000.00	3,800.00
35"			9,500.00		7,000.00	5,200.00	4,200.00

* Add an additional $1,200.00 for fully articulated wooden body

exist. Be on the lookout for Fashion-Type Dolls marked F ± G.—they are reproduction Gaultiers and intentional frauds. Check seams of the kid body. Reproductions will be snowy white at the seams. If doubt still exists, lightly run your finger over the doll's cheek. Avoid very smooth, perfectly clean bisque, for although Gaultiers have fine quality bisque, it is not as smooth as the porcelain used in today's reproductions.

Prices listed are for dolls with no damage to the bisque. Normal wear, slight damage, or well-done repairs to the body do not greatly affect price. If the bisque is damaged or repaired, expect to pay less than half the amount listed. It is perfectly acceptable to show a missing or repaired finger or joint to the body.

French Fashion Poupée de Mode: bisque swivel head, kid-lined bisque shoulder plate, kid lady body, bisque lower arms; good wig; paperweight or beautifully painted eyes, black eyeliner, long lashes, feathered brows; pierced ears; closed mouth; appropriately dressed. Marked "F. G."

Block Letter Bébé: socket head with jointed composition French straight-wrist body or socket head with kid-lined shoulder plate kid body; good wig; paperweight eyes; pierced ears; slightly parted closed mouth; appropriately dressed. Marked with early block letters "F.G."

Scroll Mark Bébé: socket head, composition jointed French body; good wig; paperweight eyes, black eyeliner, long lashes, feathered brows; pierced ears; closed mouth; appropriately dressed. Marked "F. G." within a scroll.

Open Mouth Bébé: socket head, composition jointed French body; good wig; paperweight eyes, long lashes, feathered brows; pierced ears; open mouth with teeth; appropriately dressed. Marked "F. G." within scroll.

German Bisque

Various unknown German doll manufacturers operating after 1880 produced bisque dolls. The questions and mysteries concerning a doll are endless. Who made it? What does the mark mean? Where does it come from? How old is it? What is it worth? In an industry that is really only a little over a hundred years old, you would think that we could easily answer these questions. Unfortunately, this is not the case. Obstacles to identification include an ocean to limit our research, two world wars responsible for the destruction of many records; a country which had been divided for years and whose vital information was often on the wrong side of the wall; language barriers; and the fact that hundreds of dolls were produced with little or no documentation ever recorded. All of these reasons help explain why it is virtually impossible to answer all the questions and clear up all the mysteries. We must be forever grateful to the pioneers in doll research, the Cielsliks, the Colemans, the Smiths, the Foulkes, St. George, Theriaults, Leuzzi, King, Johnson, Fraser, Miller, and countless others, who have spent years pursuing the curriculum of dolls.

In building a doll collection, one often encounters a bisque doll with no markings or with an unidentified mark. If you have fallen in love with the doll, don't be discouraged simply because you cannot put a label on it. This section will help you place a value on unidentified or unlisted German bisque dolls. You be the judge—evaluate both the workmanship and condition.

32" German Child.

Prices listed are for dolls with no damage to the bisque. Normal wear, slight damage, or well-done repairs to the body do not greatly affect price. If the bisque is damaged or repaired, expect to pay less than half the amount listed. It is perfectly acceptable to show a missing or repaired finger or joint to the body.

Open Mouth Child: standard or good quality bisque head, jointed composition or kid body; good wig; glass eyes; open mouth; appropriately dressed. Typically marked "G.B.," "L. H. K.," "101,GS," "B.J.," "GKN," "AeM/Austria," or "Girlie", "My Dearie."

Closed Mouth: good quality bisque head, jointed composition body or kid body; good wig; glass eyes, finely painted long lashes, feathered brows; pierced or unpierced ears; closed mouth with white space between lips and two-tone painting, delicate coloring; appropriately dressed. Typically marked "R 806," "50," "132," "51," or "136."

Character Baby: bent-limb baby body or cloth body; molded and painted hair or good wig; glass eyes; appropriately dressed. Typically marked "Made in Germany," "44611," "HVB," or "Melitta."

Character Child: bisque socket head, jointed composition body; molded and painted hair or good wig; glass or painted eyes, no eyelashes, line above eyes to indicate lid; closed mouth with parted lips; appropriately dressed. Typically marked "HJ 1," "GK 223," "216," or "230."

Molded Hair/Bonnet: shoulder head, cloth body; painted or glass eyes; closed mouth; appropriately dressed. Typically unmarked or with a size number only.

Tiny/Doll House: cloth or composition body; molded hair or good wig; painted or glass eyes; closed or open mouth; appropriately dressed. Typically unmarked or marked "Germany" or a size number.

GERMAN BISQUE VALUE COMPARISONS:

Size	Open Mouth Child, Kid Body, Standard	Open Mouth Child, Kid Body, Very Good	Open Mouth Child, Composition Body, Standard	Open Mouth Child, Composition Body, Very Good	Closed Mouth, Kid Body	Closed Mouth, Composition Body	Character Child	Character Baby
10"							900.00	450.00
12"	450.00	700.00	550.00	800.00	1,000.00	1,900.00		500.00
14"	500.00	800.00	600.00	900.00	1,400.00	2,100.00		550.00
16"	600.00	850.00	700.00	950.00	1,700.00		1,400.00	650.00
18"	650.00	900.00	750.00	1,000.00	2,000.00	2,400.00	1,800.00	750.00
20"	700.00	1,000.00	800.00	1,100.00		2,700.00	2,200.00	950.00
22"	750.00	1,050.00	850.00	1,150.00	2,400.00	3,300.00	2,400.00	
24"	800.00	1,100.00	900.00	1,200.00	2,800.00	3,800.00	2,700.00	1,400.00
26"	900.00	1,200.00	1,000.00	1,300.00		4,300.00		
28"	1,100.00	1,400.00	1,200.00	1,500.00				
30"	1,300.00	1,600.00	1,400.00	1,700.00				
34"	1,400.00	1,800.00	1,500.00	1,900.00				
36"			2,000.00	2,400.00				

GERMAN BISQUE VALUE COMPARISONS:

Size	Molded Hair/Bonnet Painted Eye	Molded Hair/Bonnet Glass Eye	Tiny/Doll House Standard	Tiny/Doll House Very Good
4"			145.00	300.00
6"			250.00	400.00
8"	250.00		250.00	450.00
10"	300.00	600.00	275.00	600.00
12"	350.00	700.00		
14"	400.00	800.00		
16"	450.00	900.00		
18"	500.00	1,100.00		
20"	600.00	1,300.00		

7" Gebruder Knoch Child. *Courtesy of Helen Brooke.*

12" German Bisque "American Schoolboy." *Courtesy of Helen Brooke.*

15" Solid Dome Bisque Shoulder Head.

7" German Military Doll. *Courtesy of Phyllis Bechtold.*

E. Gesland

E. Gesland produced, exported, distributed, and repaired bisque dolls from about 1860 until 1928. Gesland advertised that from his Paris factory he could "repair in ten minutes bébés and dolls of all makes and replace broken heads." Gesland purchased most, but not all, of its bisque heads from F. Gaultier. Gesland dolls can also be found with heads by Verlingue, Rabery & Delphieu, and possibly others.

Early Gesland Dolls had outstanding body features. The body and limb frame was steel covered with tin. Joints were riveted to facilitate movement. The framework was wrapped with kapok or cotton to give it a natural shape, and then covered with stockinette or fine lambskin. Hands and feet were either bisque or painted wood. The dolls could be posed in a variety of lifelike positions.

Gesland doll bodies have not been reproduced. Most are marked with the Gesland stamp or a label on the body. The head may bear a different marking, proof again that when speculating upon the purchase of any doll a thorough examination is a wise practice. Bisque heads should always be inspected as many have been reproduced.

Prices listed are for dolls with no damage. Normal wear, slight pulls or tears, or well-done repairs to the body do not greatly affect price. If significant damage to the body has occurred, or the bisque is damaged or repaired, expect to pay less than half the amount listed. It is perfectly acceptable to show a missing or repaired finger or, in the case of the composition bodies, a repaired joint.

Poupée de Mode: swivel head, kid-lined bisque shoulder plate, Gesland body; good wig; paperweight eyes with black eye liner, long painted lashes, feathered brows; pierced ears; closed mouth; appropriately dressed.

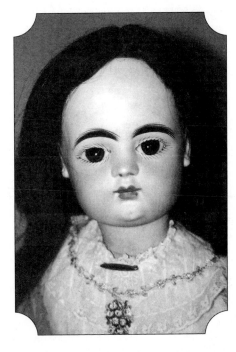

24" Gesland Bébé. *Courtesy of Billie Nelson Tyrrell.*

Typically stamped "E. Gesland Bte F. G." on shoulder plate and "E. Gesland Bte S.G.D.G./Paris" on body.

Bébé: socket head, jointed composition French body; good wig; paperweight eyes, long painted lashes, feathered brows; pierced ears; closed mouth; appropriately dressed. Typically marked "R # D," "A. Gesland Fave De Babes/& Tetes incassables, Bte. S.G.D.G./Reparations en tous genres/5 & 5 Rue Beranger/En Boutique/Paris," or "F.G."

E. GESLAND VALUE COMPARISONS:

Size	Poupée de Mode	Bébé	Exceptionally Beautiful Face
10"		3,700.00	
13"	3,500.00	3,500.00	
14"	3,800.00	3,600.00	5,900.00
15"	4,000.00	3,700.00	6,700.00
17"	4,200.00	3,900.00	
19"	4,500.00	4,300.00	
21"	4,700.00	4,500.00	7,500.00
23"	5,000.00	4,900.00	
25"	5,500.00	5,200.00	8,000.00
27"	6,000.00	5,700.00	
29"	6,400.00	6,200.00	
31"	7,000.00	6,800.00	

Godey Lady Dolls

Although several different dolls have enjoyed the title of Godey Dolls, in fact not many years ago collectors referred to most China Head Dolls as "Godey Dolls." The Godey's described here are the charming dolls made by Ruth Gibbs and the Charlotte Eldridge originals.

The term Godey Lady Doll comes from the popular *Godey's Lady's Book*—the "Victorian Bible of the Parlor"—which generations of American women depended upon for guidance in how to be real ladies. "The aim of a real lady" Godey's told them, "is always to be natural and unaffected and to wear her talents, her accomplishments, and her learning as well as her newest and finest dresses, as if she did not know she had them about her." It could truly be said that *Godey's Lady's Book* was the *Harper's Bazaar*, *Vogue*, and *Newsweek* for women of the 1840s.

Charlotte Eldridge's Godey Lady Dolls of the 1940s are very rare. Each doll was an individual creation. Papier-mâché heads were painted by Ms. Eldridge. Wigs were made from embroidery floss caught with small stitches and with tightly wound curls. The dolls also had a cloth body, wire armatures in legs and arms, and individually sculptured ceramic hands. They were elaborately costumed with authentic details which faithfully followed sketches from *Godey's Lady's Book*. Ms. Eldridge's mother, Susan Blakley, also helped with the costuming. Occasionally, a paper label signed "Frances Jennings" will be found attached to clothing. This was a name Charlotte Eldridge was fond of using.

Ruth Gibbs' Godey's Little Lady Dolls are probably more familiar to collectors. These sweet little china head dolls were designed by Herbert Johnson and made by Ruth Gibbs in Flemington, New Jersey, during the 1940s. Ruth Gibbs' Godey's Little Lady Dolls have a pink or white china head, a cloth body, and rather crude china limbs. Most have lightly molded and painted hair, although occasionally one will be found wearing a wig. Their painted facial features show very little detail. They are usually marked with an incised "R.G." on the back or inside the shoulder plate. They may also have a paper label attached to the clothing which reads "Godey's Little Lady Dolls."

Charlotte Eldridge's Godey's.

Ruth Gibbs Godey's Doll.

GODEY'S LITTLE LADY DOLLS VALUE COMPARISONS:

Size	Edlrige's Godeys	Eldrige's Diorama 2 Dolls	Eldrige's Diorama 4 Dolls	Ruth Gibbs Godey's	Ruth Gibbs with Skin Wig	Ruth Gibbs 5 Little Woman Set	Ruth Gibbs Fairy Tale Doll
7"				125.00			
10"	2,500.00	4,200.00	6,500.00	175.00	350.00	900.00	600.00
12"				250.00			

William Goebel

Franz D. Goebel founded a factory in Oesleau, Bavaria, in 1781 to make ornamental objects from porcelain and earthenware. William Goebel became sole owner of the factory in 1893, changing the name to William Goebel.

Early Goebel bisque objects were marked with a triangle and a quarter moon. After 1900, a crown above an intertwined "W & G" was introduced. Mold numbers include 30, 34, 46, 54, 60, 73, 77A, 77B, 80, 91, 92, 102, 106, 107, 110, 111, 114, 120, 121, 123, 124, 125, 126, 317, 319, 320, 321, 322, 330, 340, 350, 501, and 521.

Prices listed are for dolls with no damage to the bisque. Normal wear, slight damage, or well-done repairs to the body do not greatly affect price. If the bisque is damaged or repaired, expect to pay less than half the amount listed. It is perfectly acceptable to show a missing or repaired finger or joint to the body.

Child: bisque shoulder head, kid body, bisque arms; good wig; glass eyes, feathered brows; open mouth; appropriately dressed. Typically marked with Goebel trademark and "36," "350," or "521."

Child: bisque socket head, jointed composition body; good wig; glass eyes; open mouth, four teeth; appropriately dressed. Typically marked with trademark on back of head and "120," "89," or "330."

Character Baby: bisque character baby socket head, composition bent-limb baby body; good mohair wig; glass eyes; open mouth, two upper teeth; appropriately dressed. Typically marked with trademark, "B5/Germany," "120," "123," or "124."

Cabinet Doll: socket character head, five-piece papier-mâché body; molded and painted hair, may have

14" William Goebel Child. *Courtesy of Helen Brooke.*

molded flowers; painted eyes; open/closed mouth; appropriately dressed. Typically marked trademark "/S/13/0" and "73."

WILLIAM GOEBEL VALUE COMPARISONS:

Size	Child Open Mouth, Kid Body	Child Open Mouth, Composition Body	Character Baby, Bent-Limb Baby Body	Cabinet Dolls
4"				250.00
7"				400.00
12"	400.00		450.00	
14"	425.00	500.00	550.00	
16"	450.00	550.00	600.00	
18"	475.00	600.00	650.00	
20"	500.00	650.00	700.00	
22"		700.00	800.00	
24"		750.00	1,200.00	
26"		850.00		

Googly-Eyed Dolls

Most of the early 20th century doll manufacturers produced Googly-Eyed Dolls between 1912 and 1938. The term "Googly-Eyed" is probably from the German "Guck Augen," meaning eyes ogling to one side.

The mere mention of a Googly-Eyed Doll can easily bring any doll collector to their knees. These small comedians demonstrate their youthful exuberance with their snub noses, rounded faces, and wide alert eyes. They seem to have their own humorous sparkle, and their laughing dimples create the charming expressions that make their appeal so obvious.

Reproductions abound in the Googly-Eyed Doll market. Thoroughly examine a doll before purchase. Check first for marks. Be meticulous in your examination. Often a name or date is hidden under the wig or below the neck socket. Keep the time period in which Googly-Eyed Dolls were manufactured in mind. The quality of the bisque made at that time (1912-1938) ranged from mediocre to good quality. Very clean and smooth bisque may suggest a reproduction. Examine and evaluate.

Prices listed are for dolls with no damage to the bisque. Normal wear, slight damage, or well-done repairs to the body do not greatly affect price. If the bisque is damaged or repaired, expect to pay less than half the amount listed. It is perfectly acceptable to show a missing or repaired finger or joint to the body.

Googly-Eyed: bisque socket head, composition body; molded and painted hair or good wig; round googly eyes; impish mouth; appropriately dressed.

Strobel and Wilken
250 Googly.
*Courtesy of Ellen
Schroy.*

Googly-Eyed Value Comparisons:

Armand Marseille:

Size	200 G.E.	200 P.E.	210 P.E.	240 P.E.	240 G.E.	241 G.E.	252 P.E.	253 G.E.	254 P.E.
7"	1,700.00		2,200.00	900.00	1,800.00	1,200.00	1,000.00	1,100.00	
10"									1,000.00
12"		2,500.00	3,000.00	1,500.00	4,000.00	2,500.00	2,200.00	1,800.00	

Armand Marseille:

Size	255 P.E.	257 G.E.	310 G.E.	322 P.E.	323 G.E.	324 P.E.	325 G.E.
7"	1,000.00	1,200.00	1,200.00	800.00	1,300.00	800.00	900.00
12"	1,700.00	2,000.00	2,200.00	1,200.00	2,000.00	1,200.00	1,300.00

BÄHR PROSCHILD:

Size	686 G.E.
7"	2,200.00
12"	3,800.00

DEMALCOL GbH.:

Size	Demacol GbH.
10"	1,000.00
15"	1,300.00

BUTLER:

Size	179 G.E.
9"	1,500.00

MAX HANDWERK:

Size	Elite Bellhop. G.E.	Elite 2 Face G.E.	Elite Molded Hat G.E.	Elite Uncle Sam G.E.
12"	2,500.00	2,800.00	2,500.00	2,500.00
16"	4,200.00	4,500.00	4,200.00	4,200.00

GOBEL 82/83/84/85/86/87/88:

Size	Molded Gap P. E.
10"	1,000.00

HANSI GRETEL:

Size	LaPrialytine Paris P.E.
8½"	3,000.00

8" S&W Googly Eyed Doll. *Courtesy of Helen Brooke.*

HERTEL, SCHWAB & CO.:

Size	163 G.E.	165 G.E.	172 Toddler G.E.	173 Baby G.E.	175 Winking one G.E.	178 Open Mouth G.E.	222 P.E.	222 G.E.
10"							1,700.00	2,200.00
12"	3,200.00	3,200.00	5,200.00	3,200.00				
14"				4,200.00			2,300.00	2,700.00
15"	5,800.00		7,200.00		5,000.00	6,200.00		
16"		5,500.00						
20"		6,200.00						

GEBRÜDER HEUBACH:

Size	Einco G.E.	8589 P.E.	8606/8729 P.E.	8995 P.E.	9056/ 9081 P.E.	9085 P.E.	9141 P.E.	9513/9572 G.E.	9578 G.E.	9594 G.E.
9"	5,000.00	1,100.00	1,000.00	3,200.00	1,100.00	1,500.00	1,100.00	1,700.00	1,900.00	1,100.00
15"	7,500.00									
17"	8,500.00									
9"	1,900.00	1,100.00								

ERNEST HEUBACH, KÖPPELSDORF:

Size	219/260/261/262/ 263/264 P.E.	289 P. E.	318 P.E.	319 Tearful P.E.
7"	700.00	900.00	800.00	1,000.00

KÄMMER & REINHARDT:	
Size	S & H/KR131 G.E.
9"	2,800.00
14"	7,500.00

KESTNER:		
Size	111/122/208/217/G.E	221 G.E.
7"	700.00	
12"		5,500.00
15"		7,500.00

REINECKE P. M.:		
Size	255 G.E.	950 G.E.
7"	900.00	1,300.00
12"		1,800.00

SCHIELER (AUGUST):	
Size	G.E.
10"	2,700.00

KLEY & HAHN:	
Size	180 G.E.
9"	2,400.00
16"	4,000.00

RECHNAGEL:	
Size	R47A P.E.
7"	700.00

S.F.B.J.:	
Size	245 G.E.
7"	1,900.00

13" E. Heubach 310 Googley. *Courtesy of Elizabeth Frame.*

HERM STEINER:		
Size	133 G.E.	223/242/247 Disc. Pupils
7"	900.00	
10"		1,200.00
14"		1,400.00
17"		1,700.00
20"		2,000.00

COMPOSITION FACE:			
Size	Composition Hug-Me G.E.	Composition 94-7/AM 323	Black Composition, Unmarked, Disc Pupils
10"	900.00		
12"	1,100.00	1,200.00	
20"			900.00

G.E. = Glass Eyes
P.E. = Painted Eyes
Disc Pupils = Insert movable disc pupils under glass

Ludwig Greiner

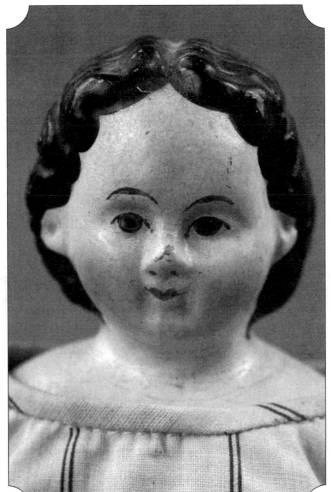

Early Greiner. *Courtesy of Elizabeth Frame.*

Records show Ludwig Greiner was listed as a toy maker in Philadelphia, Pennsylvania, as early as 1840. In 1858, Greiner received the first known United States patent for a papier-mâché doll's head. The patent reads: "1 pound of pulped white paper, 1 pound of dry Spanish Whiting, 1 pound rye flower, [sic] and 1 ounce of glue reinforced with linen...painted with oiled paint so that children may not pick off the paint." The last step in Greiner's production was the reinforcing of the head. Strips of linen or silk lined the inside of the head so as to add strength. When inspecting a Greiner head, these strips are quite easily seen.

The labels on most Greiner Dolls are intact because they are under the layer of varnish. A doll with a label bearing the '58 patent date is known as "Early Greiner." A doll whose label also bears the 1872 extension date is known as a "Later Greiner."

Greiner papier-mâché heads are easy to identify. The molded wavy hair gives the appearance of a high forehead and rather broad face. A snub nose and unsmiling mouth give a sober expression.

Prior to purchasing a Greiner doll, check the dates on the label along with the condition. Prices listed are for dolls in good to very good condition. Normal wear, slight damage, well-done repairs to the body, or a rub to the nose or chin does not greatly affect price. If damaged or repainted, expect to pay less than half the amount listed.

Early Greiner: papier-mâché shoulder head glued to cloth body, cloth legs, kid arms, stitched fingers; molded and painted hair parted in center and drawn back to expose ears; painted black eyes; closed mouth; appropriately dressed. Marked with label on back of shoulder plate "Greiner Improved Patent Heads/Pat. March 30th '58."

Late Greiner: papier-mâché shoulder head glued to cloth body, cloth legs, kid arms, stitched fingers; molded and painted hair with center part; painted eyes; closed mouth; appropriately dressed. Marked with label on back of shoulder plate "Greiners Patent Doll Heads, No. 7 Pat. Mar. 30 '58, Ext. '72."

Pre-Greiner: papier-mâché shoulder head glued onto cloth body, leather arms and legs; molded and painted hair with center part; black pupil-less glass eyes; closed mouth; appropriately dressed. Unmarked.

Hamburger & Company

Hamburger & Company was founded in New York City in 1889 as an importer of dolls and toys. The company later opened offices in Berlin and Nuremberg, Germany. Although dolls made for and imported by Hamburger & Company are quite well known to collectors, they are usually attributed to their respective manufacturers.

Prices listed are for dolls with no damage to the bisque. Normal wear, slight damage, or well-done repairs to the body do not affect price. If the bisque is damaged or repaired, expect to pay less than half the amount listed. It is perfectly acceptable to show a missing or repaired finger or joint to the body.

Dolly Dimple: character dolly-face with molded dimples by Gebrüder Heubach; bisque socket head on jointed composition body or bisque shoulder head on kid body; good wig; glass eyes; open mouth with teeth; appropriately dressed. Typically marked "Dolly Dimple," the Heubach trademark, and "5777."

Santa: character dolly-face by Simon & Halbig (Gebruder Heubach may also have supplied Santa dolls); bisque Santa socket head, jointed composition body; good wig; glass eyes; open mouth with teeth; appropriately dressed. Typically marked "S & H 1248/Germany."

Dolly-Face: socket head bisque dolly-faced child; jointed composition body; good wig; glass eyes, many with real lashes; open mouth with teeth; appropriately dressed. Typically marked "H & Co.," "Viola," or "Marguerite."

HAMBURGER & CO. VALUE COMPARISONS:

Size	Dolly Dimple, Kid Body	Dolly Dimple, Composition Body	Santa	Dolly-Face
14"			1,100.00	400.00
15"	1,200.00			
16"		3,300.00	1,300.00	450.00
17"	1,600.00			
18"		3,500.00	1,400.00	500.00
19"	2,000.00			
20"		3,900.00	1,500.00	500.00
21"	2,700.00			
22"			1,700.00	600.00
24"		4,200.00	1,900.00	700.00
26"			2,100.00	
28"		4,700.00	2,300.00	900.00
30"			2,500.00	1,100.00
32"			2,700.00	
36"			3,300.00	
38"			3,600.00	

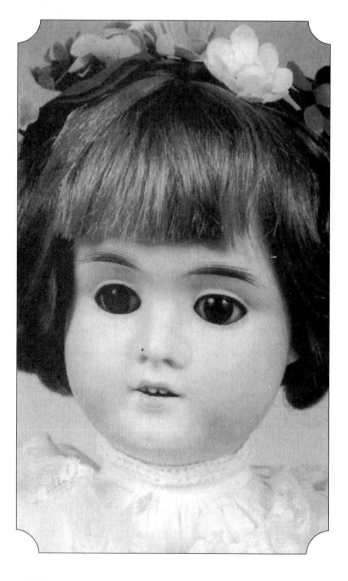

25" Viola Dolly-Face Child. *Photo courtesy McMasters Doll Auction.*

Heinrich Handwerck

einrich Handwerck, Sr., and his wife Minna started producing dolls amidst humble beginnings in Gotha, near Waltershausen, Thüringia, Germany, in 1876. They managed to build one of the most prolific firms in Germany during the flourishing years of the doll industry before closing in 1930.

Early on, they developed a working relationship with Simon & Halbig, which supplied them with doll heads of Handwerck's own designs. The pretty dolly-faced child dolls and babies became Heinrich Handwerck's forte. Character dolls apparently were not included in their repertoire. Consistently meeting the highest standards, Handwerck's dolls are made from an exceptionally fine quality of bisque and have deeply sculptured features and realistically modeled bodies.

Heinrich Handwerck, Sr., suffered from an incurable disease and passed away in 1902 at the age of forty-four. The business was purchased by Kammer & Reinhardt of Walterhausen, following the guidelines set and left by Heinrich. This acquisition made Kammer & Reinhardt world famous. It also afforded K & R the opportunity of obtaining a business contract with the prestigious porcelain factory of Simon Halbig of Gräfenhain.

To the delight of today's collectors, Heinrich Handwerck marked the majority of his dolls with the name "Heinrich Handwerck" alone, or with a two or three digit mold number ending in "9." These are considered the most desirable. Mold numbers include 69, 79, 89, 99, 109, 119, 139, and 189. Other marks include "W" at the top of the forehead, "Hch H.," "Baby Cut," "Bébé Cosmopolite," "Bebe de Reclame," Bébé Superior," "La Belle," "La Bonita," and "Lotti."

Prices listed are for dolls with no damage to the bisque. Normal wear, slight damage, or well-done repairs to the body do not affect price. If the bisque is damaged or repaired, expect to pay less than half the amount listed. It is perfectly acceptable to show a missing or repaired finger or joint to the body.

28" Henrich Handwerck child doll. *Courtesy of Mr. and Mrs. Adam Condo.*

Dolly-Face: shoulder head, kid body, bisque arms; good wig; glass eyes; open mouth with teeth; appropriately dressed. Typically marked "Hch H Germany," or "139."

Un-Numbered Dolly-Face: socket head, jointed composition body; good wig; glass eyes, feathered brows; pierced ears; open mouth with teeth; appropriately dressed. Typically marked "Heinrich Handwerck," "W," or "HANDWERCK."

Numbered Dolly-Face: socket head, jointed composition body; good wig; glass eyes, feathered brows; pierced ears; open mouth with teeth; appropriately dressed. Typically marked "HandwerckGermany/99," "109," "89," "69," 119," or "W."

Closed Mouth: socket head, jointed composition body; good wig; glass eyes, feathered brows; pierced ears; closed mouth with slight space between lips; appropriately dressed. Typically marked "89" or "79."

Character Baby: socket head, bent-limb baby body; good wig; glass eyes; open mouth; appropriately dressed. Typically marked "Germany H W," "LaBelle," or "Baby Cut."

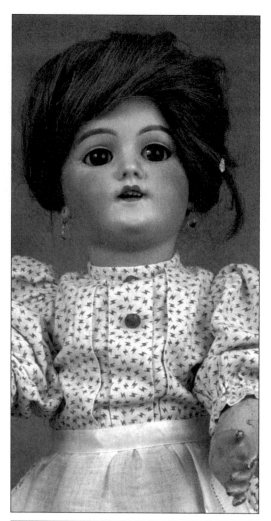

25" Henrich Handwerck Mold 69. *Courtesy of Margaret Ferree.*

22" Handwerck Mold 109. *Courtesy of Leah and Gene Patterson.*

HEINRICH HANDWERCK VALUE COMPARISONS:

Size	Open Mouth, Dolly-Face, Kid Body	Open Mouth, Dolly-Face, Composition Body No Mold #	Open Mouth, Dolly-Face, Composition Body With Mold #	Closed Mouth, Child Doll	Character Baby	Black Dolly-Face
10"		500.00	600.00			
12"		575.00	700.00			
14"	400.00	650.00	750.00			
16"	450.00	700.00	800.00		1,200.00	
18"	500.00	750.00	850.00	2,800.00	1,500.00	
20"	550.00	800.00	900.00	3,000.00		
22"	600.00	900.00	1,000.00	3,500.00	2,200.00	
24"		1,000.00				3,600.00
26"		1,200.00	1,400.00	4,200.00		
28"		1,400.00	1,600.00			
30"		1,600.00	1,800.00			
36"		2,500.00	2,700.00			
42"		4,200.00	4,500.00			

Max Handwerck

24" Max Handwerck Dolly-Face doll.

15" Bébé Elite by Max Handwerck.

he firm of Max Handwerck, located in Walterhausen, Thüringia, Germany, was originally owned by Heinrich Vortmann and Max Handwerck in 1899. Heinrich Vortmann left in 1902 and, after Max Handwerck's death, the business was owned by his widow, Anna.

Max Handwerck doll company created its own facial molds, many of which were produced as bisque doll heads by William Goebel. One of the most popular character babies was Bébé Elite. Poured by Goebel, the head bears the Goebel trademark of a triangle within a half moon, in addition to the name "Bébé Elite." This combination suggests that these heads were produced around 1900 or before, since Goebel changed its trademark after 1900. The doll industry did not start mass production of character babies until 1910. Credit for the origination of the character baby, which is usually given to Kämmer & Reinhardt, may actually belong to Max Handwerck. Either way, Bébé Elite is unquestionably a darling character baby that is actively sought by collectors.

In addition to "Elite," other mold markings include "283," "285," and "296."

Prices listed are for dolls with no damage to the bisque. Normal wear, slight damage, or well-done repairs to the body do not greatly affect price. When the bisque is damaged or repaired, expect to pay less than half the amount listed. It is perfectly acceptable to show a missing or repaired finger or joint to the body.

See also Googly-Eye Dolls.

Bébé Elite Character Baby: socket head, bent-limb baby body; good wig; glass eyes, finely painted lashes, feathered brows; open mouth with two upper teeth; appropriately dressed. Marked with trademark of triangle with moon, and "Max Handwerck Bébé Elite Germany."

Dolly-Face Child: socket head, jointed composition body; good wig; glass eyes, painted lashes, feathered brows; open mouth with teeth; appropriately dressed. Marked "283 Max Handwerck Germany," "285."

MAX HANDWERCK VALUE COMPARISONS:

Size	Baby Elite	Dolly-Face
16"	650.00	500.00
18"	700.00	550.00
20"	750.00	
22"	850.00	650.00
24"		700.00
26"	1,400.00	
28"		850.00
30"		1,200.00
34"		1,800.00
38"		2,500.00
40"		2,700.00

Carl Hartmann

Founded by Carl Hartmann in Neustadt, near Coburg, Germany, in 1899, this firm was an exporter of dolls.

Hartman registered the trade names Erika, Globe-Baby, Hanson, Palodian Baby, and Thuringia. Of these, the small bisque Globe-Babies, often dressed in regional costumes, are the most readily found. Many of the doll heads were supplied by Kämmer & Reinhardt. Hartman advertised that he could supply and export "dolls without the brand mark and without any hint of the producer," which may help to explain the origin of at least some of the many unmarked dolls found.

Size	Globe Baby
5"	400.00
7"	450.00
9"	500.00

CARL HARTMANN VALUE COMPARISONS:

Prices listed are for dolls with no damage to the bisque. Normal wear, slight damage, or well-done repairs to the body do not affect price. When the bisque is damaged or repaired, expect to pay less than half the amount listed. It is perfectly acceptable to show a missing or repaired finger or joint to the body.

Globe Baby: child socket head, five-piece composition body; good wig; glass eyes; open mouth with tiny teeth; appropriately dressed. Typically marked "Globe Baby/DEP/Germany/C3H."

8" Carl Hartmann Child. *Courtesy of Helen Brooke.*

Karl Hartmann

Karl Hartmann operated a doll factory and was also an exporter in Stockheim, Upper Franconia, Germany, from 1911 until 1926. Hartmann's lovely bisque dolls have a sophisticated worldly look, going a step beyond the delicate, wholesome expression often found on German dolly-faced dolls. This cosmopolitan look may be the reason Karl Hartmann dolls are a favorite with so many collectors.

Prices listed are for dolls with no damage to the bisque. Normal wear, slight damage, or well-done repairs to the body do not greatly affect price. When the bisque is damaged or repaired, expect to pay less than half the amount listed. It is perfectly acceptable to show a missing or repaired finger or joint to the body.

Child Doll: socket head, jointed composition body; good wig; glass eyes, feathered brows; open mouth with teeth; appropriately dressed. Typically marked "K" inside "H."

Size	Child Doll
14"	450.00
16"	500.00
18"	600.00
22"	650.00
24"	750.00
26"	850.00
28"	1,000.00
30"	1,100.00

KARL HARTMANN VALUE COMPARISONS:

28" Karl Hartman child. *Courtesy of Joyce McKeague.*

Hasbro®, Inc.

Hasbro, Inc., originally known as Hassenfeld Bros., was founded by Henry and Hillel Hassenfeld in Pawtucket, Rhode Island, in 1923. The family owned and operated toy business adopted the familiar Hasbro name following a division in the company. One branch went into the pencil box business, the other into the toy business.

Although Hasbro was primarily a toy manufacturer, its journey into the doll world was an interesting one. The extremely popular G.I. Joe®—called an action figure by manufacturer, consumers, and collectors—has developed an almost cult following among male collectors. Along with the well-known G.I. Joe and other dolls, Hasbro also manufactured Playskool Toys and Milton Bradley games.

When considering a Hasbro doll, as with all modern collectible dolls, there is little forgiveness for less than perfect examples.

G.I. Joe: The first G.I. Joe was introduced in 1964. In 1962, Hasbro's creative director, Don Levin, was approached by a television producer to develop a line of toys based on a pending television program about soldiers. The first G.I. Joe had twenty-one movable parts and realistic hair. He was named after the title character in the movie "The Story of G.I. Joe." From the beginning, realism, simplicity, price, and an endless supply of play accessories contributed to the success of the G.I. Joe figures. There are reportedly more than five hundred G.I. Joe figures, vehicles, and auxiliary items. Production was discontinued in 1978 due to an increase in the price of petroleum, a major component in the manufacturing of G.I. Joe. Kirk Bozigian Hasbro's Vice President of Boys' Toys Marketing, offers an explanation for G.I. Joe's collectible appeal: "Joe has become a timeless classic because he stands for heroism and the power of imagination."

Sequence of development and changes in G. I. Joe:

1st Series: 1964, 11½", identified by letters "TM" in mark. Marked on lower back:

    G. I. Joe TM
    Copyright 1964
    By Hasbro®
    Patent Pending
    Made in U.S.A.

2nd Series: 1965, 11½", "TM" replaced by "®." First black G.I. Joe introduced. Marked on lower back:

    G. I. Joe®
    Copyright 1964
    By Hasbro ®
    Patent Pending
    Made in U.S.A.

Little Miss No Name. *Courtesy of Trina Miller.*

3rd Series: 1966, 11½", identified by the lack of scar. Same mark as 2nd Series.

Nurse Jane: only female member of series; green eyes; blond wig. Marked "Patent Pend. 1967 Hasbro Made in Hong Kong."

4th Series: 1967, 11½", identified by lack of scar and addition of patent number. Marked:

G. I. Joe®
Copyright 1964
By Hasbro ®
Pat. No. 3,277,602
Made in U.S.A.

5th Series: 1968, 11½", identified by return of scar with same patent number marking. Mark remains the same as 4th Series.

6th Series: 1970, 11½", peace time adventurers in response to anti-war feelings, flocked hair introduced. Same mark as 4th and 5th Series.

7th Series: 1974, 11¾", new "Kung Fu Grips" allows G.I. Joe to grasp objects. Same mark as 4th, 5th, and 6th Series.

8th Series: 1975, 11½", Mike Power model only; identified by see-through right arm and leg and mark on back of head "Hasbro Inc. 1975/Made in Hong Kong." Mark on lower back same as 4th, 5th, 6th, and 7th Series.

9th Series: 1975, 11¾", more muscular body with molded on swimming trunks. New mark introduced:

1975 Hasbro®
Pat. Pend. Pawt. R.I.

10th Series: 1976. Same mark as Series 9, or "Hasbro Ind. Inc. 1975 Made in Hong Kong."

11th Series: 1977, 8" Action Figures.

OTHER DOLLS FROM HASBRO:

Dolly Darling Series: 4½", plastic and vinyl; molded hair; painted eyes; closed mouth; molded-on shoes. Marked "1965/Hasbro/Japan." **15.00**

Peace Series: 9", all vinyl, jointed at neck, shoulders, and hips; bendable knees; rooted hair; painted eyes; closed mouth; red, white, and blue knit pantsuit. Marked "6/Hong Kong/Hasbro/US Patented." **35.00**

Leggy Jill Series: 10", red hair Kate, brunette Nan, Black Sue with Afro; plastic and vinyl, very long legs; rooted hair; painted eyes; closed mouth; dressed in shorts, top, hat, and high boots. Marked "1972/Hasbro/Hong Kong." **45.00**

Little Miss No Name: 15", vinyl and hard plastic; jointed at neck, shoulders, and hips; rooted hair; very big plastic eyes, real tears; closed sad mouth, dressed in burlap dress with patches. Marked "1965 Hasbro" **145.00**

Sweet Cookie: 18", plastic and vinyl; rooted hair; painted eyes; freckles across nose; open/closed mouth, molded and painted teeth; dressed in short dress with white pinafore with "Sweet Cookie" printed across front. Marked "Hasbro, Inc./Pat. Pend. 1972" on head and "Hasbro/Made in USA" on back. **65.00**

That Kid: 21", talking, plastic and vinyl, jointed, battery operated; reposition arm to repeat phases; built-in sling shot in hip pocket; rooted hair; sleep eyes; freckles; open/closed mouth, two upper teeth; cotton shorts outfit. Marked "Hasbro/1967" on head and "Patent Pending/1967 Hasbro." **145.00**

G.I. JOE VALUE COMPARISONS:

SERIES 1, 11½", MINT CONDITION:

Action Soldier, molded black hair, blue eyes . . .**500.00**

Action Sailor or Marine, molded brown hair, brown eyes **650.00**

Action Pilot, molded blond hair, brown eyes . . .**950.00**

SERIES 2, 11½", MINT CONDITION:

Action Soldier, molded black hair, blue eyes . . .**500.00**

Action Sailor or Marine, molded brown hair, brown eyes **650.00**

Action Pilot, molded blond hair, brown eyes . . .**700.00**

Black Action Soldier, molded black hair, brown eyes **650.00**

SERIES 3, 11½", MINT CONDITION:

Action Soldier, molded black hair, blue eyes . . .**500.00**

Action Sailor or Marine, molded brown hair, brown eyes **650.00**

Action Pilot, molded blond hair, brown eyes . . .**700.00**

Black Action Soldier, molded black hair, brown eyes **650.00**

Talking Commander, blond molded hair, brown eyes **550.00**

Nurse Jane, blond wig, green eyes **2,400.00**

Australian Jungle Fighter, molded hair **1,100.00**

British Commando, molded hair **1,900.00**

French Resistance Fighter, molded hair **1,400.00**

German Soldier, molded hair **1,800.00**

Japanese Imperial Soldier, molded hair **2,200.00**

Russian Infantry man, molded hair **1,800.00**

SERIES 4, 11½", MINT CONDITION:

Action Soldier, molded black hair, blue eyes . . .**500.00**

Action Sailor or Marine, molded brown hair, brown eyes **650.00**

Action Pilot, molded blond hair, brown eyes . . .**650.00**

G.I. JOE VALUE COMPARISONS:

Black Action Soldier, molded black hair,
brown eyes **700.00**
Talking Commander, molded blond hair,
brown eyes **700.00**

SERIES 5, 11½", MINT CONDITION:

Action Soldier, molded black hair, blue eyes . . . **300.00**
Action Sailor or Marine, molded brown hair,
brown eyes **250.00**
Action Pilot, molded blond hair, brown eyes . . **250.00**
Black Action Soldier, molded black hair,
brown eyes **300.00**
Talking Commander, molded blond hair,
brown eyes **700.00**

SERIES 6, 11½", MINT CONDITION:

Adventure Team Talking Commander, flocked
blond hair and beard **800.00**
Black Adventure Team Talking Commander,
flocked black hair and beard **800.00**
Adventure Team Talking Commander, flocked
blond hair, no beard **1,000.00**
Land Adventurer, flocked brown hair, no beard . . **400.00**
Sea Adventurer, flocked red hair and beard . . . **400.00**
Air Adventurer, flocked blond hair and beard . . . **400.00**
Black Adventurer, flocked black hair, no beard . **400.00**
Astronaut, flocked blond hair, no beard **600.00**
Talking G.I. Joe **400.00**

SERIES 7, 11¾", MINT CONDITION:

Adventure Team Talking Commander, flocked
brown hair and beard **350.00**
Black Adventure Team Talking Commander,
flocked black hair and beard **350.00**
Land Adventurer, flocked black hair and beard . . . **300.00**
Sea Adventurer, flocked red hair and beard **300.00**
Air Adventurer, flocked blond hair and beard . . . **300.00**
Black Adventurer, flocked black hair, no beard . **350.00**
Man of Action, flocked black hair, no beard . . . **300.00**
Talking Man of Action, flocked brown hair,
no beard **350.00**

SERIES 8, 11½", MINT CONDITION:

Mike Power Atomic Man, molded brown hair,
no beard, blue eyes **600.00**

SERIES 9, 11¾", MINT CONDITION:

Life-Like Talking Commander, flocked brown
hair and beard, blue eyes **400.00**

Life-Like Talking Man of Action, flocked brown
hair, no beard, blue eyes **400.00**
Life-Like Black Talking Commander, flocked
black hair and beard, brown eyes **400.00**
Life-Like Land Adventurer, flocked brown hair
and beard, blue eyes **300.00**
Life-Like Sea Adventurer, flocked red hair
and beard, brown eyes **300.00**
Life-Like Air Adventurer, flocked blond hair
and beard, brown eyes **300.00**
Life-Like Black Adventurer, flocked black hair,
no beard, brown eyes **300.00**
Life-Like Man of Action, flocked brown hair, no
beard, blue eyes **300.00**

SERIES 10, 11½", MINT CONDITION:

Eagle Eye, Bullet Man, The Intruder **250.00**
The Defender **300.00**

SERIES 11, 8", MINT CONDITION: **100.00**

ACCESSORIES, MINT IN BOX THE CONDITION:

Armored Car **300.00**
Desert Jeep **1,800.00**
Foot Locker **75.00**
General's Jeep **500.00**
Helicopter **600.00**
Motorcycle with Side Car **700.00**
Space Capsule **700.00**
Tank **400.00**

OUTFITS, UNOPENED PACKAGES, COMPLETE WITH CLOTHING AND ALL ACCESSORIES:

Action Sailor **500.00**
Air Cadet **1,500.00**
Annapolis Cadet **1,500.00**
Astronaut **350.00**
Deep Freeze with sled **300.00**
Dress Parade Uniform **450.00**
Fire Fighter **350.00**
Frogman **575.00**
Green Beret **600.00**
Marine Jungle Fighter **1,200.00**
Military Police, blue **1,500.00**
Military Police, brown **500.00**
Rescue Diver **400.00**
Shore Patrol **400.00**
Ski Patrol **350.00**
West Point Cadet **1,500.00**

Hertel Schwab & Company

15" Hertel Schwab 152 Character Baby.
Courtesy Rachael Bowser Herlocher.

Hertel, Schwab & Company operated a porcelain factory in Stutzhaus, near Ohrdruf, Thüringia, Germany, from 1910 until at least 1930. The company was founded by sculptors August Hertel and Heinrich Schwab, who designed the dolls, and porcelain painter Hugo Rosenbush, who was a minor partner in the company.

Several molds were produced exclusively for the American market, including the Bye-Lo Baby made for Borgfeldt; Our Baby and Our Fairy made for Louis Wolf; and the Jubilee Dolls made for Strobel & Wilken.

Mold numbers registered by Hertel, Schwab & Company include: 125, 126, 130, 132, 133, 134, 135, 136, 138, 140, 141, 142, 143, 147, 148, 149, 150, 151, 152, 157, 158, 159, 160, 161, 162, 163, 165, 166, 167, 169, 170, 172, 173, 175, 176, 179, 180, 181, 200, 208, 217, 220, and 222. Many Hertel, Schwab & Company dolls had character faces.

Most dolls are marked with their mold number and either "Made in Germany" or the mark of the company for whom the head was made, such as Louis Wolf or Kley & Hahn.

Prices listed are for dolls with no damage to the bisque. Normal wear, slight damage, or well-done repairs to the body do not greatly affect price. If the bisque is damaged or repaired, expect to pay less than half the amount listed. It is perfectly acceptable to show a missing or repaired finger or joint to the body.

Character Baby: socket head, bent-limb baby body; molded and painted hair or good wig; painted or glass eyes, winged eyebrows; open/closed mouth with tongue and two upper teeth; appropriately dressed. Typically marked "130," "132," "136," "142," "150," "151," or "152."

Child: socket head, jointed composition body; good wig; glass eyes, feathered brows; open mouth with teeth; appropriately dressed. Typically marked "Made in Germany 136/."

Character Child: socket head, jointed composition body; painted or glass eyes; open or closed mouth; appropriately dressed. Typically marked "148," "143," "125," "126," "127," "134," "141," "169," "154," or "140."

HERTEL, SCHWAB & CO. CHARACTER BABY VALUE COMPARISONS:

Size	Character Baby	Child Dolly-Face	Open/Closed Mouth Character 148	Closed Mouth Character 143	Open/Closed Mouth Character 140	Open Mouth Character 154,125, 126,127	Closed Mouth Character 134,149
10"	550.00						
12"	600.00						
14"	650.00		3,200.00				
16"	750.00	600.00		1,700.00	5,000.00	1,500.00	6,000.00
18"	800.00	650.00					
20"	900.00	700.00					
24"	1,200.00	850.00					
26"	1,500.00	1,100.00					

HERTEL, SCHWAB & CO. CHARACTER CHILD VALUE COMPARISONS:

Size	Open/Closed Mouth Character 141	Closed Mouth Character 169	Open Mouth Character 169	Closed Mouth Character 154
18"	7,500.00	4,000.00	1,200.00	2,800.00

Hertwig & Company

Hertwig & Company produced Snow Babies and "Nanking Dolls" in its porcelain factory in Katzhütte, Thüringia, Germany. Nanking Dolls have bisque heads and limbs, and cloth bodies stuffed with cotton (nanking). The company also made the "Pet Name" china heads exclusively for the United States market.

Many Hertwig & Company dolls have molded clothing and are either unmarked or marked only "Germany." These dolls are often among the first acquisitions made by doll collectors, partly due to the fact that they are relatively easy to find. Also, their charming vintage appearance makes them a logical first step in the "antique doll collecting" journey.

Prices listed are for dolls with no damage to the bisque, unless otherwise noted. Normal wear, slight damage, or well-done repairs to a cloth body do not greatly affect price. If the bisque is damaged or repaired, expect to pay less than half the amount listed.

See also All Bisque, China Heads and Snow Babies.

Molded Clothing: all bisque, jointed at shoulders; molded and painted features; molded clothing. Typically unmarked.

Bisque Shoulder-Head Child: cloth body, bisque arms and legs; well-molded and painted hair and facial features; closed mouth; appropriately dressed. Typically marked "104, Germany," "150," "175," "3 85" or "3 86."

HERTWIG & CO. VALUE COMPARISONS:

Size	Molded Clothing	Bisque Shoulder-Head Child
5"	185.00	
8"	200.00	200.00
10"		250.00
12"		275.00

8" Hertwig All Bisque. *Courtesy of Susan Metzger.*

Ernst Heubach

In 1887, Ernst Heubach began manufacturing bisque dolls in his porcelain factory in Köppelsdorf, near Sonneberg, Germany.

The structure of the European doll industry at the end of the 19th century was shaped by the traditions of an earlier day, when businesses were bound by strong family ties and intricate interconnections. Ernst Heubach's company is a classic example of this system. Undoubtedly related to the Heubach porcelain factory in Thüringia, Ernst Jr. added to this complexity by marrying Beatrice Marseilles, daughter of Armand Marseilles, who was unquestionably one of the leading doll manufacturers of the time. One of Ernst Heubach's sculptors was Hans Homberger, whose brother was a sculptor for Armand Marseillse. These family connections help explain similarities found in early bisque character dolls made by these manufacturers.

In 1919, Ernst Heubach and Armand Marseilles merged companies to become "Vereinigte Köppelsdorfer Porzellanfabrik vorm Armand Marseilles und Ernst Heubach" (United Porcelain Factory of Koppelsdorf). The new company split into two separate entities once again in 1932.

Most dolls with the trade name "Heubach Köppelsdorf" included in their marks were produced after 1919. Other marks include a horseshoe, the initials "E. H.," and various mold numbers—most often three digit numbers.

Prices listed are for dolls with no damage to the bisque. Normal wear, slight damage, or well-done repairs to the body do not greatly affect price. If the bisque is damaged or repaired, expect to pay less than half the amount listed. It is perfectly acceptable to show a missing or repaired finger or joint to the body.

See also Googly-Eyed Dolls.

Character Baby: socket head, bent-limb baby body; some with pierced nostrils; good wig; glass eyes; open mouth; appropriately dressed. Typically marked "300," "320," or "342."

Infant Character Baby: flange neck, cloth body, composition or celluloid hands; painted hair; glass eyes; closed mouth; appropriately dressed. Typically marked "Heubach/Köppelsdorf/Germany," "338," "339," "340," "349," "350," or "399" (white).

Child Dolls: shoulder head, kid body; good wig; glass eyes; open mouth; appropriately dressed. Typically marked with horseshoe and "1900," "1901," "1902," "1906," or "1909."

Child Doll: socket head, composition body; good wig; glass eyes; open mouth; appropriately dressed. Typically marked "Heubach/Köppelsdorf," "250," "251," "302," or "312."

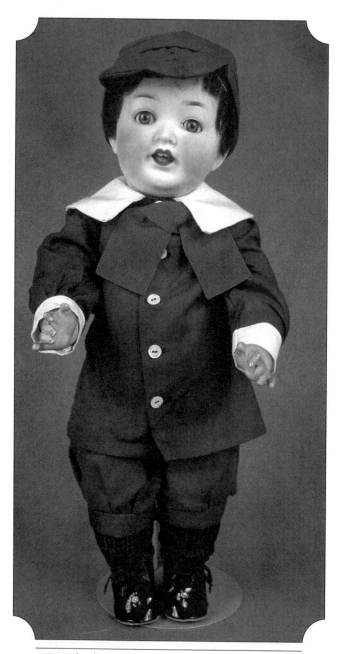

16" Heubach Koppelsdorf 342. *Courtesy of Phyllis Bechtold.*

Character Child: bisque socket head, jointed composition body; molded and painted hair or good wig; glass eyes; open or closed mouth; appropriately dressed. Ethnic dolls and charming characters. Appropriately dressed. Typically marked "Heubach/Köppelsdorf/Germany," "399," "414," "444," "463," "452," "445," or "312."

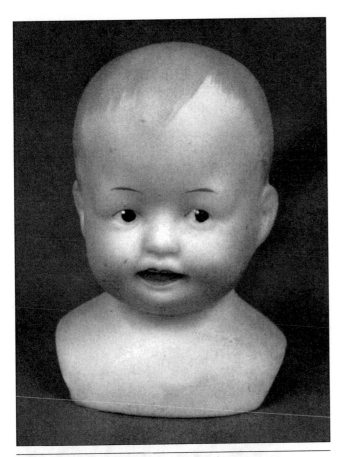

Ernest Heubach Character Shoulder Head.

Ernest Heubach boxed pair.

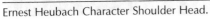

ERNST HEUBACH VALUE COMPARISONS:

Size	Character Baby*	Solid Dome Infant	Child Doll, Kid Body	Child Doll, Composition Body	Gypsy Oriental #452	2-Face Doll #445	Character Clown	Black 399, 414,452*	Black 444	Black 463
6"	300.00									
8"	325.00			250.00				600.00	700.00	800.00
10"	350.00			275.00				650.00	750.00	850.00
12"	400.00	700.00	250.00	300.00				700.00	800.00	900.00
14"	450.00	700.00	275.00	350.00						
16"	500.00	1,000.00	300.00	400.00	1,400					
18"	550.00		325.00	450.00						
20"	600.00		350.00	525.00		2,200.00				
22"	700.00		400.00	600.00						
24"	900.00		500.00	650.00						
26"	1,000.00			750.00						
28"				850.00						
30"				1,000.00			3,200.00			

* Add an additional $300.00 for Toddler body.

Gebrüder Heubach

The Heubach family bought an established porcelain factory in Lichte, Thüringia, Germany, in 1840 and began producing porcelain figurines shortly thereafter. Heubach is not known to have made doll heads until around 1910. With the introduction of character dolls, doll makers in both America and Europe seized upon this new interest to create dolls that would satisfy a growing taste for the exotic. Rarely could other manufacturers compete with the skill and attention to detail used to produce the amusing and extraordinary Gebrüder Heubach character dolls.

One secret to Heubach's success was the location of an art school for sculptors located near the factory. The school turned out especially skilled artists and sculptors responsible for creating beautiful porcelain figurines and dolls. Several of the artists known to have modeled doll heads for Gebrüder Heubach were Zitzmann, Zeiller, Holwein, Krieger, Niemeyer, and Wera von Bartels. Often, their initials appear with the markings.

The Gebrüder Heubach doll factory manufactured such an enormous quantity and range of character doll heads that positive identification is difficult. Due to their heavy use, molds became worn, causing mold numbers to become unreadable. Consequently, identification of some molds has caused considerable misunderstanding. Adding to the confusion is the fact that many heads never had mold numbers. They were simply marked "S" for sun or "Q" for square. No logical system has been deciphered, impeding attempts to precisely identify many dolls.

Heads were either socket or shoulder heads, had either molded hair or wigs, and the famous intaglio eyes or sleeping glass eyes. Size numbers range from 14/0 to 8 and perhaps beyond, heights from at least four inches to twenty-six inches. Mold numbers appear to go from 5,625 to 12,386. Most mold numbers in the 5,000s, 6,000s, and 7,000s have the sunburst mark, while the mold numbers in the 8,000s and beyond are more likely to have the square mark. Far too numerous to list are the thousands of mold numbers in the series from the 5,600s to the 12,000s. In fact, the porcelain factory had a production rate so great that more than ten thousand different models were offered. Many of the firm's doll heads were made for other German companies as well, including Cuno & Otto Dressel, Eisenmann, Hamburger & Company, Gebrüder Ohlhaver, and Wagner & Zetche. Several small doll factories in and around Sonneberg also used Gebrüder Heubach heads.

Reproductions are numerous. Check markings first. A legitimate copy of a Gebrüder Heubach doll will be marked with the artist's name and date. It may also have the name of the company that produced the mold. Examine the doll's patina. Does the doll appear old? Inspect the body. Authentic Gebrüder Heubach bodies are often rather crude.

10" Gebrüder Heubach 8192 Flapper.
Courtesy of Pat Tyson.

While Gebrüder Heubach dolls were charming character dolls, their bisque does not have the satiny smoothness so often found in reproductions.

Prices listed are for dolls with no damage to the bisque. Normal wear, slight damage, or well-done repairs to the body do not greatly affect price. If the bisque is damaged or repaired, expect to pay less than half the amount listed. It is perfectly acceptable to show a missing or repaired finger or joint to the body.

It is hoped that this listing will enable the reader to evaluate mold numbers not listed by using comparables. With thousands of dolls made by Gebrüder Heubach, it is impossible to list each. These examples are indicative of the character dolls currently available in the marketplace and should allow the reader to get a feel for the demand and quality of Gebrüder Heubach dolls.

GEBRÜDER HEUBACH CHARACTER VALUE COMPARISONS:

Size	5626 O/CM Laughing Glass Eyes	5636 O/CM Laughing Intaglio Eyes	5636 O/CM Laughing Glass Eyes	5689 OM Smiling Glass Eyes	5730 OM Smiling Glass Eyes	5777 OM Smiling Glass Eyes	6692 CM Shoulder Head Intaglio Eyes
9"		900.00	1,300.00				
12"	1,600.00	1,200.00	1,800.00				700.00
14"					1,500.00		
16"	2,200.00			2,400.00		3,300.00	1,000.00
20"				3,400.00		3,900.00	

Size	6736 Laughing Intaglio Eyes	6774 CM Whistling Intaglio Eyes	6894 CM Pouty Intaglio Eyes	6969 CM Pouty Glass Eyes	7109 O/CM Intaglio Eyes	7246 CM Glass Eyes	7550 O/CM Molded Tongue, Glass Eyes
8"	1,000.00		400.00		500.00		
10"			500.00				
12"		900.00		2,800.00	700.00	2,800.00	1,300.00
16"	1,900.00	1,500.00		3,900.00		3,900.00	1,800.00
22"				5,700.00		5,700.00	

Size	7602 CM Pouty Intaglio Eyes	7604 O/CM Laughing Intaglio Eyes	7616 O/CM Molded Tongue, Glass Eyes	7620 O/CM Protruding Ears, Intaglio Eyes	7622 CM Pouty Intaglio Eyes	7623 O/CM Molded Tongue, Intaglio Eyes	7631 CM Intaglio Eyes
8"	500.00						600.00
10"		800.00					700.00
12"	900.00				900.00	900.00	
14"		1,200.00	1,700.00	1,300.00			
16"			2,200.00		1,500.00	1,400.00	
20"				1,600.00			

Size	7644 O/CM Intaglio Eyes	7661 O/CM Crooked Mouth, Squinting Eyes	7665 O/CM Smiling/ Glass Eyes	7669 O/CM Molded Tongue, Glass Eyes	7679 O/CM Whistler, Intaglio Eyes	7684 O/CM Screaming, Intaglio Eyes	7686 O/CM Wide Mouth, Glass Eyes
10"	800.00				1,000.00		
12"			1,600.00	2,100.00		1,800.00	
14"					1,400.00		2,800.00
16"		5,000.00	2,000.00			2,700.00	
18"							4,200.00
20"		7,000.00					

Size	7701 CM Pouty, Intaglio Eyes	7711 OM Glass Eyes	7743 O/CM Protruding Ears, Glass Eyes	7745 O/CM Molded Teeth, Intaglio Eyes	7746 O/CM Lower Teeth, Intaglio Eyes	7748 Wide O/CM Fatty Neck/Teeth, Intaglio Eyes	7751 O/CM Squinting Glass Eyes
8"				900.00			
12"				1,500.00			
14"		1,000.00	4,000.00		1,600.00		3,500.00
16"						6,300.00	
18"			6,500.00		2,400.00		4,300.00
20"	2,300.00						
22"		1,400.00					

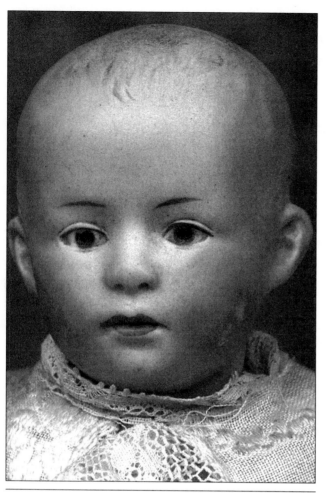

8" Gebrüder Heubach 7802 Character baby.

14" Heubach 7368 Boy. *Photo courtesy of Judy Ries.*

Size	7759 CM, Pouty, Intaglio Eyes	7761 O/CM, Squinting, Painted Eyes	7764 CM, Singing, Intaglio Eyes	7768 CM, Hair Molded in Bun, Intaglio Eyes	7781 O/CM, Yawning, Painted Eyes	7788 CM, Smiling, Intaglio Eyes	7802 CM, Pouty, Intaglio Eyes
8"	475.00				1,000.00		
10"	500.00					850.00	
12"				1,200.00	1,600.00		
14"			8,000.00	1,400.00			2,000.00
16"		6,800.00	10,000.00			1,400.00	
18"		7,000.00	12,000.00				
20"		7,500.00					

Size	7843 O/CM, Yawning, Squinting	7849 CM, Intaglio Eyes	7851 CM, Molded Hair Bow, Intaglio Eyes	7852 CM, Coiled Braids, Intaglio Eyes	7853 CM, Downcast Painted Eyes	7862 CM, Coiled Braided, Intaglio Eyes	7877 CM, Molded Bonnet, Glass Eyes
10"	1,100.00	600.00					
12"			1,300.00		1,500.00	1,800.00	
14"		900.00		2,200.00			2,600.00
16"	2,000.00		1,600.00		2,000.00	2,500.00	
18"				3,000.00			3,400.00

Size	7911 O/CM, Grinning, Intaglio Eyes	7925 OM, Smiling Lady, Glass Eyes	7926 OM, Smiling Lady, Painted Eyes	7959 O/CM, Molded Bonnet, Intaglio Eyes	7975 CM, Removable Bonnet, Glass Eyes	7977 CM, Molded Bonnet, Intaglio Eyes	8107 CM, Pouty, Intaglio Eyes
8"							700.00
12"	1,200.00				2,200.00	1,500.00	1,100.00
14"		4,000.00	3,700.00			2,300.00	
16"	1,500.00	4,500.00	4,000.00		2,700.00		
18"				3,700.00			
22"				4,900.00			

Size	8035 CM, Full Lips, Intaglio Eyes	8050 O/CM, Laughing, Intaglio Eyes	8053 CM, Glancing, Intaglio Eyes	8058 O/CM, Rows Teeth, Intaglio Eyes	8145 CM, Side-Glancing, Intaglio Eyes	8191 O/CM, Laughing Boy, Intaglio Eyes	8192 OM, Child, Glass Eyes
12"						1,100.00	
14"		6,200.00	7,000.00		1,700.00	1,300.00	700.00
16"		6,700.00	9,000.00	9,000.00			
18"						1,900.00	900.00
20"	9,000.00						

Size	8197 CM, Molded Hair Loop, Glass Eyes	8306 O/CM, Molded Teeth, Intaglio Eyes	8316 O/CM, Molded Teeth, Glass Eyes	8381 CM, Exposed Ears, Intaglio Eyes	8420 CM, Pouty, Glass Eyes	8459 O/CM, Laughing, Glass Eyes	8467 CM, Character, Indian
12"		1,300.00			2,800.00	2,700.00	
14"	7,800.00	1,500.00					
16"	8,500.00		3,900.00		3,900.00	3,200.00	4,800.00
18"				14,000.00			
20"			4,800.00				

Size	8469 O/CM, Laughing, Glass Eyes	8550 CM, Protruding Tongue, Intaglio Eyes	8555 CM, Bulging Eyes Painted	8556 O/CM, Molded Hair, Ribbon and Teeth	8590 CM, Puckered Mouth, Intaglio Eyes	8596 CM, Smiling, Intaglio Eyes	8648 CM, Very Pouty, Intaglio Eyes
10"	2,200.00						
12"		1,400.00	3,000.00				
14"	3,000.00				1,500.00	1,000.00	
16"			5,000.00			1,200.00	2,200.00
18"					2,000.00		2,800.00
22"				9,000.00			

Size	8724 CM, Smiling, Intaglio Eyes	8774 O/CM, Whistling, Intaglio Eyes	8793 CM, Slight Dimple, Intaglio Eyes	8868 CM, Short Chin, Glass Eyes	8991 O/CM, Molded Tongue, Intaglio Eyes	9189 O/CM, Hair Bow, Intaglio Eyes	9355 OM, Shoulder Head, Glass Eyes
10"		800.00					
12"						1,300.00	
14"		1,100.00	2,000.00		2,800.00		
16"			2,400.00	2,400.00			
18"	1,900.00						1,200.00
20"				3,000.00			
22"							1,800.00

Size	9457 CM Wrinkled Character	9891 CM Aviator, Intaglio Eyes	9891 CM Farmer, Intaglio Eyes	9891 CM Sailor, Intaglio Eyes	10532 OM Character, Glass Eyes	10586 Baby, Glass Eyes	10633 OM Shoulder Head, Glass Eyes
12"	2,400.00	1,800.00	1,400.00	1,500.00		750.00	
14"					900.00		850.00
20"							1,000.00
22"					1,500.00		

Size	11173 Tiss Mes Indented Cheeks, Glass Eyes	11173 Tiss Me Indented Cheeks, Intaglio Eyes	Animals, Bisque Body	Animals, Bisque Heads, Composition Body	Black Character, Molded Curly Hair, Intaglio Eyes
8"	2,200.00		1,400.00	1,200.00	
12"	2,500.00	1,700.00			2,500.00

O/CM = Open/Closed Mouth

OM = Open Mouth

CM = Closed Mouth

E.I. Horsman & Company

E. I. Horsman & Company was founded in New York City by Edward Imeson Horsman in 1865. In 1859, at the age of sixteen, Edward Horsman worked as an office boy for $2.00 a week. Just six years later he opened a company that was to become a leader in the doll industry.

Beginning in the early 1900s, Horsman produced a variety of popular composition dolls. Although most of these dolls had painted hair, some had wigs. The majority had painted eyes looking to the side. However, some dolls had eyes painted looking straight ahead, while others had either tin or glassine sleep eyes. Several examples had open/closed mouths, with or without teeth. As time went on, even more variations were incorporated. Often, one doll was manufactured with a concoction of parts, entirely different from the norm. Occasionally, the same mold will have more than one name. Consistency was not one of Horsman's virtues.

Around 1890 a Russian inventor, Solomon D. Hoffmann, had brought his formula for "unbreakable" composition doll heads to America. Doll manufacturers of the day showed little interest in his formula, overlooking one of the biggest opportunities in the doll industry. To his credit, Horsman was the only manufacturer to take advantage of this innovation. He used this miracle composition in the creation of the Billiken doll, and gave it the catchy trade name of "Can't Break 'Em."

Knowing how the teddy bear had won the hearts of children and recognizing the appeal of the Billiken character, Horsman reasoned that a doll made of a combination of the two would be irresistible to the public. How right he was! It

Horsman Mama Baby. *Courtesy of Helen Brooke.*

is reported that during the first six months of production, Horsman sold more than 200,000 Billikens. It should be mentioned that the Billiken was originally created by Florence Pretz of Kansas City, who patterned him after Joss, the Chinese god of "things as they ought to be."

Prices listed are for dolls with no damage, unless otherwise noted. If damaged or repaired, expect to pay less than half the amount listed.

See also Babyland Rag, Campbell Kids.

BISQUE

Tynie Baby: flange neck, cloth body, composition head; molded and painted hair; glass eyes; closed mouth; appropriately dressed. Marked "1924/E.I. Horsman Co./Made in Germany/U."

COMPOSITION

Billiken: composition head, beige plush body, jointed at shoulders and hips; brown thread claws on hands and feet; molded and painted hair coming to peak at top; slanted slit eyes, slanted brows, almost forming a "V;" pug nose; closed mouth; impish watermelon grin. Marked with label on chest "Licensed Stamp Copyright 1909 by The Billiken Company."

Baby Bumps: flange neck, cloth body, sateen arms and legs; spray painted hair; painted blue eyes; open/closed mouth; appropriately dressed. Unmarked.

Character Baby: jointed cloth body, composition hands; molded and painted hair; painted eyes; nicely molded closed mouth; appropriately dressed. Marked "1910 by E. I. Horsman Co."

Baby Butterfly: composition head, cloth body, composition hands; painted black hair; painted Oriental facial features; appropriately dressed. Marked "E. I. H."

Peterkins: all composition; molded and painted hair with forehead curl on left side; painted eyes with large pupils, tiny arched eyebrows; tiny closed watermelon mouth; appropriately dressed.

Raggedy Man Character Doll: composition, well-molded head, cloth body, nicely shaped hands; molded and painted hair; painted brown eyes; closed mouth; wearing original costume of patched pants, shirt, jacket, and floppy hat. Marked "The Raggedy Man/Trademark/Under License From L. P. Tucks/Mfgd by E. I. Horsman."

Mama Doll: composition head, cloth body, composition limbs; good wig; tin sleep eyes; open mouth with two upper teeth and felt tongue; appropriately dressed. Typically marked "E. I. H. Co./Horsman."

Child Doll: composition socket head on composition shoulder plate with cloth body and composition limbs, or all composition; good wig; tin sleep eyes; open mouth; appropriately dressed. Typically marked "Horsman, Rosebud."

Jackie Coogan: shoulder head, cloth body, composition limbs; molded and painted brown hair; painted brown

	HORSMAN VALUE COMPARISON:							
Size	Bisque Tynie Baby	Billiken	Baby Bumps, White	Baby Bumps, Black	Mama Dolls	Child Dolls	Jackie Coogan	Baby Dimples
9"			175.00	200.00				
10"	700.00		200.00	250.00	200.00			
12"		475.00	300.00	350.00	225.00	250.00		
13"								700.00
14"	900.00				250.00	300.00		
16"		600.00			300.00	325.00	900.00	350.00
18"			400.00	500.00	325.00	350.00		400.00
20"					350.00	400.00		425.00
22"						450.00		
24"						500.00		500.00

Size	Whatsit Doll	Baby Chubby	Character Baby	Butterfly Baby	Peterkins	Raggedy Man	Ella Cinders	HeBee/ SheBee
10"								700.00
11"			350.00		700.00			
13"				900.00				
14"	500.00	225.00						
16"	600.00					900.00		
18"		250.00					750.00	
24"		300.00						

HORSMAN PLASTIC VALUE COMPARISONS:

Size	Hard Plastic Child	Mary Poppins	Patty Duke	Ruth's Sister	Zodiac Baby	Black Character	Poor Pitiful Pearl	Couturiers Renee Ballerina
6"					20.00			
12"		50.00	85.00			300.00	100.00	
15"	550.00							
16"		100.00					175.00	
17"	450.00							
19"								175.00
26"		250.00		125.00				

Size	Jackie	BiLo	Pippi Longstocking	Squalling Baby
14"		75.00		
17"			85.00	
19"				150.00
25"	225.00			

side-glancing eyes; closed mouth; appropriately dressed. Marked "E. I. H. Co./19©21."

Ella Cinders: cloth body, movable composition limbs; molded and painted black hair with center part; painted wide eyes; freckles; closed mouth; appropriately dressed. Marked "©/1925/M.N.S."

Hebee and SheBee: all composition, large head; spray-painted hair; painted eyes; rosy cheeks and nose; tiny closed mouth; molded chemise and booties, holes in booties for ribbon ties. Marked with paper label on foot "Trademark Charles Twelvetrees/Copyrighted 1925."

Baby Dimples: flange neck, cloth body, composition limbs; molded and painted hair; tin sleep eyes; open mouth with two teeth and molded tongue, dimple on each side of mouth; appropriately dressed. Marked "E. I. H. Co., Inc."

Whatsit Doll: all composition, jointed at neck, shoulders, and hips; molded and painted hair; side-glancing eyes; open/closed mouth with molded tongue; appropriately dressed. Marked "Naughty Sue/©1937, Roberta/1938 Horsman."

Baby Chubby: cloth body, composition limbs; molded and painted hair; glassine sleep eyes, real lashes; closed mouth; appropriately dressed. Marked "A/Horseman."

HARD PLASTIC

Child: all hard plastic, jointed at neck, shoulders, and hips; saran wig; sleep eyes; open mouth with upper teeth; appropriately dressed. Typically marked "170;" "170 Made in USA;" "Bright Star;" "Horsman/All Plastic."

PLASTIC AND VINYL

Mary Poppins: vinyl head, plastic body with rooted hair; painted side-glancing eyes; slightly open/closed mouth; appropriately dressed. Marked "H."

Patty Duke: vinyl head, plastic body, poseable arms and legs; rooted blond hair with bangs; painted blue eyes; closed mouth; appropriately dressed. Marked "Horsman Doll/6211."

Ruth's Sister: vinyl head, plastic body, plastic legs, vinyl arms; rooted hair; sleep eyes with lashes; open/closed mouth; appropriately dressed. Marked "Horsman/T-27."

VINYL

Zodiac Baby: all vinyl, jointed at neck, shoulders, and hips; long rooted pink hair; black eyes; open/closed mouth; wearing star-shaped dress and charm bracelet with signs of zodiac; comes with booklet "Your Individual Horoscope." Marked "Horsman Dolls Inc./1968."

Black Character: vinyl head, one-piece stuffed vinyl body; molded hair; painted squinting eyes; open/closed mouth. Marked "Horsman" on back of head.

Poor Pitiful Pearl: vinyl head, one-piece stuffed vinyl body; rooted long straight hair; sleep eyes; closed, slightly smiling thin line mouth; protruding ears; wearing original cotton dress and scarf. Marked "©1963/Wm. Steig/Horsman."

Couturier's Renee Ballerina: all vinyl, poseable soft stuffed vinyl body, unusual ball joints at neck, shoulders, and elbows; individual fingers; long neck; high heeled feet; rooted pink hair; sleep eyes, real lashes; closed mouth; wearing original white ballerina costume with lace net skirt and collar; satin bodice; long nylon stockings, and pink vinyl ballerina shoes. Marked "82/Horsman."

Jackie: soft vinyl head, rigid vinyl body, jointed at neck, shoulders, and hips; rooted black hair; sleep eyes, pronounced arched eyebrows; pierced ears; closed mouth; wearing original white Schiffli embroidered dress, cotton batiste shawl, pearl earrings, necklace, and bracelet. Marked "Horsman/19©61/JK/25/4."

VINYL AND CLOTH

BiLo: vinyl head, cloth body, swivel vinyl limbs; molded and painted hair; painted blue eyes; open/closed mouth; wearing long gown with lace inserts and matching cap. Marked "Horsman Doll/1972."

Pippi Longstocking: vinyl head, cloth body, vinyl limbs; rooted braided orange hair; painted eyes; freckles; open/closed mouth. Marked "25-3/Horsman Dolls Inc./1972."

Squalling Baby: soft vinyl head, cloth body, vinyl limbs; softly molded hair; painted squinting blue eyes; wide open/closed yawning mouth; appropriately dressed. Marked "Corp. Lastic Plastic 49."

Mary Hoyer Doll Manufacturing Company

The Mary Hoyer Doll Manufacturing Company was named for its founder and located in Reading, Pennsylvania, from 1925 until the 1970s. Mary Hoyer owned and operated a yarn shop. She sold a wide variety of yarns and craft supplies through her mail order business. As a designer of knit and crochet fashions for infants and children, it was a natural transition to begin designing costumes for dolls. Mary Hoyer wanted a doll to use as a model for her clothing designs. She felt that a small, slim doll would be most flattering. Hoyer then conceived the idea of a doll that could be sold along with a pattern book of instructions for a knitted and crocheted wardrobe.

While the Ideal Novelty & Toy Company showed initial interest in marketing Hoyer's idea, nothing was accomplished. Instead, the company offered to supply large quantities of dolls directly to the Hoyers at wholesale prices. These early dolls bear only the Ideal Doll markings. In 1937, Ideal ended this arrangement. Mary Hoyer then approached Bernard Lipfert, a well-known doll sculptor, to design a doll for her. Following Hoyer's specifications, Lipfert created the "perfect" doll. The Fiberoid Doll Company in New York produced these composition dolls until 1946, when hard plastic became available.

The Mary Hoyer Doll Manufacturing Company ceased production in the 1970s, closing the door on an American success story. Recently, the Mary Hoyer family reintroduced a beautiful vinyl Mary Hoyer Doll. This doll was warmly embraced by contemporary doll collectors and caused a renewed interest and demand for the original Mary Hoyer dolls.

Many collectors reject some Mary Hoyer Dolls because they assume that the doll has been given a hair cut. This is a mistake. Hoyer produced a boy doll which had either a fur wig or a regular wig with a ragged hair cut. For positive identification of fashions, see Mary Hoyer's book *Mary Hoyer and Her Dolls* (Hobby House Press, Inc.). It is an invaluable source of information.

Prices listed are for dolls with no damage.

Composition: jointed at neck, shoulders, and hips; slim body; mohair wig; sleep eyes, real lashes, painted lower lashes; closed mouth. Marked "The/Mary Hoyer/Doll."

Hard Plastic Mary Hoyer. *Courtesy of Helen Brooke.*

Hard Plastic: jointed at neck, shoulders and hips; synthetic wig; sleep eyes, real lashes, lower painted lashes; closed mouth. Marked "Original/Mary Hoyer/Doll."

MARY HOYER VALUE COMPARISONS:

Size	Composition	Hard Plastic	Boy Doll
14"	550.00	650.00	700.00
18"		800.00 (Gigi)	

Adolf Hülss

The Adolf Hülss doll factory began operating in Waltershausen, Germany, in 1913. It is generally accepted that the bisque heads were supplied by Simon and Halbig.

These excellent quality dolls are modeled either as child dolls or character babies. Markings include the AHW trademark, which was registered in 1925, "Germany," and possibly a mold number.

Prices listed are for dolls with no damage to the bisque. Normal wear, slight damage, or well-done repairs to the body do not greatly affect price. If the bisque is damaged or repaired, expect to pay less than half the amount listed. It is perfectly acceptable to show a missing or repaired finger or joint to the body.

Character Baby: socket head, bent-limb baby body; good wig; glass eyes; open mouth with upper teeth; appropriately dressed. Typically marked "Simon & Halbig/AHW" within a circle/"Made in Germany 156."

Child: socket head, jointed wood-and-composition body; good wig; glass eyes; open mouth with upper teeth; appropriately dressed. Typically marked "A7H/Germany/AHW" within a circle/"Made in Germany."

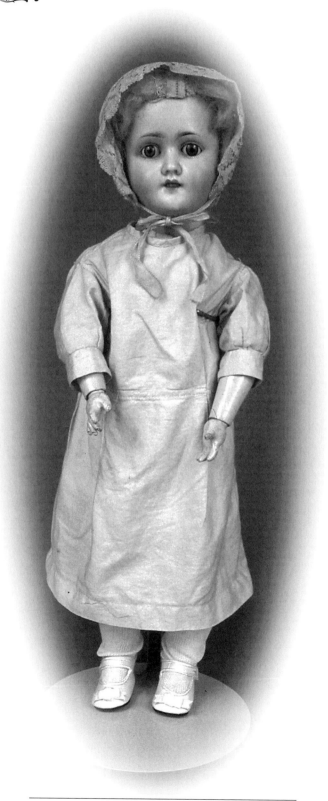

ADOLF HÜLSS VALUE COMPARISONS:

Size	Character Baby*	Child Doll**
10"	550.00	
12"	650.00	
14"		800.00
16"	750.00	850.00
18"	850.00	900.00
20"	1,000.00	950.00
22"	1,400.00	1,100.00
24"	1,600.00	
28"		1,500.00
30"		1,800.00

*Add an additional $300.00 for a jointed toddler body.
** Add an additional $100.00 for flirty eyes. Add an additional $300.00 for a flapper-type body with high knee joints.

20" Hulss Child. *Courtesy of Helen Brooke.*

Maison Huret

ocated in Paris, France, Huret was already an established toy company when, in the 1850s under the creative force of Mele Calixte Huret, it emerged as a French doll manufacturer. Huret was known for its beautifully made, gusseted kid bodies and articulated wooden bodies. The firm pioneered numerous patented innovations including the important socket swivel neck, patented in 1861.

Huret reportedly produced about 1,500 dolls a year, a rather modest figure when compared to other doll makers. Although child dolls were produced, Maison Huret is best known for its Calixte's lady dolls.

Huret Dolls have a full, somewhat youthful face made from either bisque or china, with glass or painted eyes. Bodies are composition, gutta-percha, kid, or wood with hands of bisque, china, composition, or metal. Huret first used astrakhan fur for wigs, later switching to the more satisfactory mohair. Dolls were dressed as ladies or children in a workshop on the Rue de Choiseul.

Huret Dolls can often be dated by their markings. Those made in the 1850s bear the address "2 Bouvelard des Italienos." Dolls produced from the mid- to late-1860s are marked "22 Boulevard Montmartre." After 1870, they are marked "68 Rue de la Boetie." Unfortunately, these stamped markings are sometimes worn away.

Reproduction Hurets have been reported. Check markings first. Ask questions. The doll's owner may know its history. Examine both the inside and the outside of the head. Many Huret Dolls have pressed, rather than poured, bisque heads. Beware of bisque that is very clean and silky smooth. The bisque on an authentic Huret Doll will have a slightly textured feeling.

Prices listed are for dolls with no damage to the bisque. Normal wear, slight damage, or well-done minimal repairs to the body do not greatly affect price. Huret Dolls hold the unique distinction of having an extremely valuable body as well as an artfully produced head. Therefore, if either the head is damaged or repaired, or the integrity of the body has been compromised, expect to pay half the amount listed.

Bébé: socket head, wooden body, wooden limbs joined with kid, metal hands; excellent tongue-and-groove joints; two-piece torso jointed at waist with kid strips; good wig; painted eyes, soft shadow above eyes; rouged cheeks; closed mouth; appropriately dressed. Typically marked "Huret 68 Rue De La Boetie" or other Paris address.

Huret China Fashion. *Photo courtesy of McMasters Doll Auction.*

Lady: shoulder head, kid body, kid hands with stitched fingers; good wig; beautifully painted or paperweight eyes, finely drawn feathered brows and lashes; delicately tinted face; closed mouth; appropriately dressed. Typically marked "Brevet D. Inv: SGCG/Maison Huret/Boulevard Montmarte, 22/Paris," or other Paris address.

Lady: swivel head, wooden body and limbs joined with metal springs, swivel waist, metal hands; good wig; paperweight or beautifully painted eyes, softly feathered brows; rosy cheeks; closed mouth; appropriately dressed. Marked "Huret 68 Rue de la Boetie" or other Paris address.

HURET VALUE COMPARISONS:

Size	Bébé	Lady on Kid Body	Lady on Gutta Percha Body	Swivel-Head Lady on Wooden Body
15"		17,500.00		
16"			22,000.00	35,000.00
17"		19,000.00		
18"				37,000.00
18½"	37,000.00			
19"		20,000.00	25,000.00	
22"		21,000.00		39,000.00

Ideal® Novelty and Toy Company

*I*n 1902, Morris Mitchom and A. Cohn founded the Ideal Novelty and Toy Company for the express purpose of producing Mitchom's teddy bears. Mitchom had his wife make a pair of hand-made stuffed bears for a window display for the small stationery story he owned in Brooklyn, New York, after seeing a newspaper cartoon concerning President Theodore Roosevelt's 1903 hunting trip in Mississippi. The cartoon featured a frightened bear cub that had stumbled into Roosevelt's camp. Mitchom sent the President a sample of his "Teddy" and asked permission to name his stuffed bear after him. The President answered in a handwritten note: "I doubt if my name will mean much in the bear business, but you may use it if you wish." The rest is Teddy Bear history. The Ideal Novelty and Toy Company was off to a tremendous start, and this was only the beginning.

The 1930s were prime years for Ideal. The issuance of the Shirley Temple, Judy Garland, and Deanna Durbin dolls placed the company firmly in the forefront of popularity.

Ideal was one of the few large companies that made its own composition dolls. The company was a pioneer in making "unbreakable" dolls in America. It was so proficient that it supplied other manufacturers in addition to meeting its own needs. American Character, Arranbee, Eugenia, and Mary Hoyer were several of Ideal's customers.

Ideal began experimenting with hard plastic in 1936 and was the first in the industry to market a hard plastic doll. Soon the wonderful Toni Dolls and the Play Pal Family of dolls brought as much recognition to Ideal as its earlier attempts at perfection. Play Pal children were sculpted according to measurements issued by the U.S. Bureau of Standards of Specifications. They could wear actual clothing of a child at the age of 3 months, 1 year, 2 years, 3 years, and an older child of 10 or 11 years.

Prices listed are for dolls with no damage.

Also see Shirley Temple.

Ideal Compostion Deanna Durbin. *Photo courtesy of McMasters Doll Auction.*

CLOTH

Cloth Character (Seven Dwarfs, Queen of Hearts, Snow White, Bo Peep, or Oz's Scarecrow): pressed oil cloth mask, cloth body; wool hair; painted facial features; appropriately dressed. Typically marked with character's name printed on clothing.

COMPOSITION

Many composition dolls were made for various themes such as patriotism, comedy, literature, and the theater. These composition dolls have reached an historical point where signs of crazing and the crackled look to the eyes is not only to be expected, but has become acceptable. If the doll is badly crazed, cracked, or repaired, expect to pay half the amount listed.

Deanna Durbin: all composition, jointed at neck, shoulders, and hips; very dark brown human hair wig; brown sleep eyes, dark gray eye shadow; dimples on cheeks; open mouth with five teeth; appropriately dressed. Marked "Deanna Durbin/Ideal Toy Co."

Betty Jane: all composition, jointed at neck, shoulders, and hips; mohair wig; sleep eyes; open mouth with five teeth; appropriately dressed. Marked "Ideal 18."

13" Composition Snow White. *Courtesy of Marilyn Merry.*

Mortimer Snerd. *Courtesy of Billy Grant Miller.*

Judy Garland: all composition, jointed at neck, shoulders, and hips; dark brown human hair wig; brown sleep eyes; open mouth with six teeth; appropriately dressed. Marked "Ideal Doll" on back of head, "18/Ideal Doll/Made in USA" on back, "11/18" on upper left arm, "10" on upper right arm, and "18" on inside of both legs.

Snow White: all composition, jointed at neck, shoulders, and hips; black mohair wig; brown flirty eyes; open mouth with four teeth; appropriately dressed. Marked "Shirley Temple/18."

COMPOSITION AND CLOTH

Snow White: composition shoulder head on cloth body with composition limbs; molded and painted black hair with molded blue bow; painted side-glancing eyes; closed smiling mouth. Appropriately dressed.

Mama Doll: composition head, cloth body, composition limbs; good wig; tin sleep eyes; closed mouth; appropriately dressed. Typically marked "Ideal" with diamond and "U.S.A." or "Ideal Doll/Made in USA."

Uneeda Biscuit Boy: composition head, cloth body, composition limbs; molded and painted hair; painted blue eyes; closed mouth; wearing original yellow sateen rain slicker and hat, and striped romper; molded and painted black rain boots. Marked with label on cuff of raincoat which reads: "Uneeda Biscuit/pat'd Dec 8, 1914/Mfd by Ideal Novelty & Toy Co."

Snoozie: composition head, cloth body, composition lower limbs; molded and painted hair; celluloid over tin eyes; open yawning mouth with molded tongue; appropriately dressed. Marked "B. Lipfert."

Gorgeous: composition head, composition shoulder plate, cloth body, composition limbs; good wig; sleep eyes, black eye shadow; closed mouth; appropriately dressed. Marked "Ideal."

Flossie Flirt/ Pretty Peggy: composition head, cloth body, composition limbs; good wig; sleep eyes; closed mouth; appropriately dressed. Marked "Ideal US of A, "Ideal" within a diamond and "U.S.A."

COMPOSITION AND RUBBER

Betsy Wetsy: composition (Idonite) head on rubber (Tru-flesh) drink and wet body; molded and painted hair; sleep eyes; open nurser mouth; appropriately dressed. Marked "Ideal."

COMPOSITION AND WOOD

Wood Segmented Character (8¼" Jiminy Cricket, 10½" Pinocchio, 11" Gabby, 13" Superman, and 14" King Little): composition heads on bodies made from wooden spools; bodies painted to represent the character's costume; occasionally, felt ornamentation added to the doll's appearance.

Flexy Character (soldier or Mortimer Snerd): composition head, wooden body, flexible spring construction, composition hands and feet; molded and painted hair; painted eyes; closed smiling mouth; appropriately dressed. Marked "Ideal Doll."

HARD PLASTIC

The first plastic doll was manufactured by Ideal in 1940, but was discontinued shortly thereafter due to war restrictions on materials. Ideal was a leader in the doll industry during the Hard Plastic era. Ideal's patent number for hard plastic was #2252077, and many different dolls can be found marked with this number.

Toni Dolls (Miss Curity nurse, Mary Hartline, Harriet Hubbard Ayer, and Betsy McCall): hard plastic body; synthetic wig; sleep eyes with real upper lashes and painted lower lashes; nice flesh tones. Typically marked with a "P" number, such as "P90-14," "P91-16," "P92-16," "P93-21," and "P94-22 1/2." The least sought after doll in the Toni family is Harriet Hubbard Ayer.

Another member of the Toni family was Sara Ann. She is identical to Toni in every way—without the original box it would be impossible to tell the dolls apart. Ideal manufactured Sara Ann in an attempt to save the royalties that went to the Toni Home Perm Co. for each Toni Doll sold. Sara Ann demanded no such royalties.

Saucy Walker: all hard plastic, walker body, jointed at neck, shoulders, and hips; synthetic wig; flirty sleep eyes; open mouth with two upper teeth; appropriately dressed. Marked "Ideal Doll."

Plassie: hard plastic head, cloth body, latex limbs; good wig; sleep eyes; open mouth with two upper teeth and felt tongue; appropriately dressed. Marked "P-50/Ideal/Made in U.S.A."

MAGIC SKIN

Ideal also manufactured dolls with "Magic Skin," an early synthetic material that looked and felt like human skin. Over time, Magic Skin becomes unstable and deteriorates, becoming badly discolored. Early vinyl dolls produced in the late 1940s were a bit more stable, but still a far cry from the durability of today's vinyl.

CLOTH AND COMPOSITION VALUE COMPARISONS:

Size	Cloth Character	Deanna Durbin	Betty Jane	Judy Garland	Snow White, All Composition	Snow White, Composition and Cloth	Mama Doll	Uneeda Biscuit
12"	325.00				650.00			
13"						350.00	225.00	
14"		600.00						
15"		700.00	400.00			450.00		600.00
16"	700.00			1,500.00				
17"		800.00						
18"			550.00	1,900.00	900.00		400.00	
19"		900.00						
21"		1,000.00						
22"							425.00	
24"		1,200.00						900.00

Size	Snoozie	Gorgeous	Flossie Flirt and Pretty Peggy	Betsy Wetsy	Wood Segmented	Flexy Characters
8 1/4"					550.00	
10 1/2"					550.00	
11"				150.00	500.00	
12"						350.00
13"					600.00	
14"				200.00	500.00	
16"	400.00			250.00		
17"		450.00				
21"	500.00		400.00			

Baby/Sparkle Plenty: hard plastic head on Magic Skin (latex) body, arms attached with metal disc at shoulders; yellow yarn or molded and painted hair; sleep eyes; closed mouth; appropriately dressed. Marked "Made in U.S.A./Pat. No. 2252077."

ALL VINYL

Miss Revlon: vinyl head, solid vinyl body, jointed at neck, shoulders, hips, and waist; rooted hair; sleep eyes; pierced ears; closed unsmiling mouth; polished fingernails and toenails. Marked "Ideal Doll/VT" and size number.

VINYL AND CLOTH

Thumbelina: vinyl head, cloth body, vinyl hands; rooted hair; painted eyes; open/closed mouth; appropriately dressed; mechanism in center back makes her wiggle. Marked "Ideal Toy Corp/©TT-19."

Cuddly Kissy: vinyl head, cloth body; rooted hair; sleep eyes; open/closed mouth; appropriately dressed; press stomach and hands come together, head tilts forward, lips pucker, and doll makes a kissing sound. Marked "Ideal Toy Corp/KB-17-E."

Sara Lee: black vinyl head, cloth body, vinyl limbs, life-like features; molded and painted hair; brown sleep eyes; open/closed mouth; appropriately dressed. Marked "Ideal Doll." Doll was named after designer Sara Lee Creech.

Kiss Me: vinyl head, cloth body, vinyl limbs; molded brown hair; painted squinting eyes; frowning expression with wide open/closed mouth, mouth opens and closes when back is pressed; appropriately dressed. Marked "S3/ideal Doll/Pat. Pending."

Little Lost Baby: three-faced vinyl head, foam stuffed suit encased body; one face smiling awake, one sleeping, and one crying, all with molded and painted features; lever at base of neck turns head. Marked with tag "Little Lost Baby/1968 Ideal Toy Corp."

Judy Splinters: vinyl head, cloth body, vinyl limbs; yarn hair; large painted eyes; wide open/closed smiling mouth; appropriately dressed. Marked "Ideal Doll."

HARD PLASTIC VALUE COMPARISONS:

Size	Toni/ Sara Ann	Betsy McCall and Miss Curity	Mary Hartline	Harriet Hubbard Ayer	Saucy Walker	Plassie	Magic Skin	Play Pal Family
14"	450.00	400.00	450.00	300.00			125.00	
15"					150.00		150.00	
16"	500.00		500.00	325.00	175.00			
17"						175.00	175.00	
18"					200.00			
19"	600.00			350.00		200.00		
20"					225.00		200.00	
21"	650.00			375.00				
22"						225.00	225.00	
22½"	800.00		900.00					
24"								200.00
25"								450.00
32"								300.00
36"								450.00
38"								500.00
42"								1,000.00

Size	Growing Hair Crissy	Black Growing Hair Crissy	Cinnamon	Cricket/ Tara	Kerry/ Brandi/ Tressy	Mia & Dina	Velvet	Baby Crissy
11½"			75.00					
15½"				60.00		100.00	75.00	
17½"	125.00	145.00			80.00			
24"								75.00

VINYL AND HARD PLASTIC

Bonnie Braids: 13", vinyl head, hard plastic body, jointed at shoulders and hips; molded and painted hair with saran braids coming from holes on side of head; blue sleep eyes with real lashes; open mouth with three painted teeth; wearing original dress. Marked "1951/Chicago Tribune/Ideal Doll" on back of head. **250.00**

Dorothy Hamil: 11½", vinyl head, plastic body, vinyl arms and bendable legs; rooted hair; painted eyes; open/closed mouth with painted teeth; appropriately dressed. Marked "1977 DH/Ideal" within oval, "H-282/Hong Kong" on head, "1975/Ideal" in oval on hip, and "U.S. Pat. No. 3903640/Hollis NY 11423/Hong Kong P." **75.00**

Tammy: 12", vinyl head, plastic body, vinyl arms, jointed at neck, shoulders, and hips; rooted hair; painted side-glancing eyes; closed mouth; appropriately dressed. Marked "Ideal Toy Corp./B-5 12" on head and "Ideal Toy Corp/B-5 12-1/2." **100.00**

007 James Bond: 12½", vinyl head, plastic body and legs, vinyl arms; molded and painted hair and facial features; appropriately dressed. Marked "Ideal Toy Corp/B-12-1/2-2." **100.00**

Tiffany Taylor: 14", vinyl head, shapely plastic body, jointed at neck, shoulders, and hips; swivel cap wig which spins to change hair color from blond to brunette; painted eyes; closed mouth; appropriately dressed. Marked "1974/Ideal" in an oval, "Hollis, NY 11423/2M 5854 01/2" on lower back, and "1973/CG-19-H-230." **85.00**

Bye-Bye Baby: 25", vinyl head, plastic body, nicely molded life-like hands and feet; softly molded and painted hair; sleep eyes; open nurser mouth; appropriately dressed. Marked "Ideal Toy Corp./HB-25." **400.00**

Play Pal Family (24" Susy, 25" Miss Ideal, 32" Penny, 36" Pattie, 38" Peter, and 42" Daddy's Girl): vinyl head, plastic body; rooted hair; sleep eyes; smiling mouth; appropriately dressed. Marked "Ideal Doll O.E.B.-24-3-" on head and "Ideal" or "Ideal Toy Corp./SP-#" (# = height of doll). See chart.

Growing Hair Crissy: vinyl head, plastic body; rooted auburn hair with center ponytail, hair can be lengthened by pulling on ponytail; big dark brown eyes; smiling open/closed mouth with molded teeth; appropriately dressed. Marked "1968/Ideal Toy Corp/GH-17-H 129" on back of head and "1969/Ideal Toy Corp/Gh-18 US Pat Pend. # 3,162,976." Crissy series includes her cousins, Velvet and Cinnamon; her friends Cricket, Tara, Kerry, Brandi, and Tressy; Velvet's friends Mia and Dina; and Baby Crissy. See Chart.

14" Toni.

	VINYL AND VINYL COMBINATION VALUE COMPARISONS:							
Size	**Miss Revlon**	**Thumbelina**	**Black Thumbelina**	**Cuddly Kissy**	**Sara Lee**	**Kiss Me**	**Little Lost Baby**	**Judy Splinters**
10"	150.00		60.00					
11"		65.00	85.00					
15"		75.00						
17"		85.00	150.00		300.00			
18"	250.00				400.00	225.00		200.00
20"		100.00						350.00
21"						250.00		
22"	275.00						100.50	
36"	300.00							450.00

Japanese Dolls

*I*n Japan, the art of doll making is a tradition that has been handed down from one generation to the next. Many dolls are created to be more than just children's playthings. There are more than three hundred different types of Japanese dolls, some of which were commercially produced as early as the 16th century. Most Japanese dolls originally had a ritual significance with religious associations and were made for decorative purposes. For example, the Boys' Day and Girls' Day Festivals are part of the Japanese cult of chivalry, and symbolized bravery and loyalty to country and emperor.

The Girls' Day Festival (Hina Matsuri), celebrated as early as the 1400s, was intended to instill the virtues of patriotism and domesticity in young girls and to honor the Imperial family. The holiday is still celebrated in Japan on March 3rd, the peak of the peach blossom season. Several days before the festival, mothers and daughters take their dolls out of storage and display them on steps (hina dan) covered with red silk. A set of these dolls traditionally consists of fifteen figures. The Emperor and Empress are placed on the top step with the court musician, ladies in waiting, guard, and dancers on lower steps.

The Boys' Day Festival (Tanono Sekka) is celebrated on May 5th and was called the Feast of Flags. On this day, banners in the shape of a carp—the fish signifying fortitude—are flown outside the houses of young boys. Inside, an array of fierce-looking dolls symbolizing strength, valor, and adventure are displayed on a cloth-covered tiered stand. The dolls represent warriors such as Monotaro, Yoshitsumen and Kato Kiyomasa, as well as commanders, generals, and wrestlers. Each year a boy receives a new doll to add to his set, reminding him of the vestiges of Japanese chivalry and the Samurai.

While antique Festival Dolls are treasured family heirlooms, newer versions are also popular because of their invocation of a long gone era. Children's play dolls (Ichimatsu) and child dolls (Yamato Ningyo) are also loved by today's collectors.

These exceptionally beautiful unmarked Japanese dolls have perfect white faces. Their porcelain-like finish is made from polished gofun, a fine white paste composed of pulverized oyster shell and glue. It is not unusual for a doll's head to have twenty to thirty coats of gofun. All are gorgeously costumed in non-removable clothing made from materials specially woven in miniature patterns. When appropriate, they are equipped with armor and weapons. These traditional glass-eyed Japanese dolls portray three distinct classes: the Royal group, the Samurai, and the peasants.

In the early years of the 20th century, many dolls with Oriental-type faces and clothing were made in Europe and

8" Japanese Traditional Papier-Mâché Doll. *Courtesy of Helen Brooke.*

the United States. These dolls should not be confused with the Japanese dolls made in Japan.

Later Yamato Ningyo of standard quality are frequently found on the secondary market. In 1927 alone more than 10,000 examples were sent to the United States as part of a good-will exchange. These dolls depict children ages 6 or 7, and are dressed in costumes representing different regions of Japan.

Reproduction Japanese dolls are not a problem. The labor-intensive workmanship needed to achieve the look of the gofun, combined with the dolls' intricate costuming, make them unsuitable for the reproduction market. However, there are different levels of quality of authentic Japanese dolls.

Prices listed below are for dolls with no damage.

Early Hina-Ningyo (Festival Dolls): c. 1870, composition coated with several layers of gofun, highly polished, straw body, long fingered composition hands painted white to match face; silk thread hair; glass eyes; closed mouth; wearing original elaborate robe, obi, and headdress; seated on cut-out and lacquered wooden platform.

Later Hina-Ningyo (Festival Dolls): c. 1920, composition coated with gofun, paper-wound body in permanent position; long fingered composition hands painted white; silk thread hair; glass eyes, feathered brows, finely painted lower lashes; closed mouth; wearing original silk robes and tin headdress; seated on cut-out painted wooden platform.

Early Ichimatus (Play Dolls): c. 1850, papier-mâché socket head coated with gofun, papier-mâché shoulder plate extending to chest area, papier-mâché hips, lower legs, and lower arms connected with cloth (floating joints); fine human hair wig; black glass eyes, finely painted feathered brows, no lashes; pierced ears and nostrils; closed mouth; elaborate costume; wooden painted sandals with silk tassels.

Later Ichimatus (Play Dolls): c. 1920, papier-mâché socket-head coated with gofun, composition body, composition limbs painted pink, jointed at shoulders and hips; black silk hair; brown glass eyes, feathered brows, no lashes; pierced nostrils; closed mouth; wearing original multi-colored floral kimono with large obi and silk slippers.

Early Sakura-Ningyo (Cherry Dolls/Traditional Lady Statue Dolls): c. 1890, oyster shell composition with layers of highly polished gofun socket head, well-shaped torso with rounded belly and molded bosom, composition lower limbs painted to match head, cloth upper arms and thighs; floor length human hair wig styled around gilt metal comb adorning hair; inset glass eyes with painted eyebrows, no lashes; closed mouth finely outlined with deeper red; wearing original long silk kimono over white damask shorter kimono; carrying wooden fan with hand-painted decorations.

Later Sakura-Ningyo (Cherry Dolls/Traditional Lady Statue Dolls): c. 1920, oyster shell composition coated with gofun socket head, slim straw stuffed body, graceful hands with long fingers; black silk wig in elaborate style with ornate combs in hair; black glass eyes, feathered brows, very fine lower lashes; closed

Traditional Japanese Warrior in Case.
Courtesy of Bill Miller.

mouth; wearing original silk kimono with long sleeves, wide obi, and silk jacket; holding painted umbrella or fan.

Modern Sakura-Ningyo (Cherry Dolls/Traditional Lady Statue Dolls): silk mask-type face, wire armature body padded with strips of cotton; black floss wig in upsweep style; painted eyes; closed mouth; wearing original kimono with wide sleeves; holding red disk-type hat; affixed to varnished block of wood stamped "Made in Japan."

Early Warrior: Benkei, c. 1875, papier-mâché head, coated with several layers of gofun and painted flesh color, straw and paper body; long fingered composition hands painted to match face; molded feet; glass eyes, winged brows; long black silk beard; closed mouth; wearing original silk brocade kimono, silk obi, and hooded brocade headdress; holding weapon.

Later Warrior: c. 1900, composition head coated with gofun and painted flesh color; body with padded non-removable costume as part of construction of doll; black silk wig; glass eyes; winged brows with nice detail around eyes; closed mouth; padded silk brocade robes; holding weapons; cut-out, painted and lacquered wooden stand.

Size	Hina-Ningyo Early	Hina-Ningyo Later	Ichimatus Early	Ichimatus Later	Sakura-Ningyo Early	Sakura-Ningyo Later	Sakura-Ningyo Modern	Warrior Early	Warrior Later	Yamato Ningyo Early	Yamato Ningyo Later	Baby
10"	900.00	300.00	400.00	175.00			70.00					
12"			500.00	200.00	500.00	250.00	80.00					250.00
14"	1,300.00	450.00	600.00	250.00	600.00	300.00	90.00	800.00	400.00	1,700.00	250.00	300.00
16"	1,500.00	500.00	700.00	275.00	700.00	350.00	100.00	900.00	475.00	1,800.00	300.00	350.00
18"	1,700.00	550.00	800.00	300.00	800.00	400.00		1,100.00	500.00	1,900.00	325.00	
20"			950.00							2,000.00	350.00	
22"			1,100.00	350.00				1,600.00		2,400.00	400.00	
24"			1,300.00	400.00								
26"			1,500.00	425.00								
28"				450.00								
30"			2,000.00	500.00								

Note: Add an additional $50.00 - $100.00 for dolls found in custom-made glass case.

Early Yamato Ningyo (Japanese Child) Mitsuore: c. 1890, composition socket head coated with gofun and painted flesh color, composition body, and arms; molded male sex organs portrayed in detail; hair delicately painted with fine writing brush; brown inset glass eyes; closed mouth; large molded ears; wearing original brocade kimono tied with silk obi.

Later Yamato Ningyo (Japanese Child) Mitsuore: c. 1920, composition head coated with gofun and painted flesh color, composition body, lower arms, and legs connected to body with cloth (floating joints); black silk hair; brown inset glass eyes; closed mouth; wearing original kimono with large obi and silk tie sandals.

Baby: c. 1920, composition socket head coated with gofun and painted flesh color, bent-limb baby body with joints at shoulders and hips; short silk wig; glass inset eyes; pierced nostrils; open/closed mouth with molded tongue; appropriately dressed.

Jullien

The beautiful Jullien Bébés were made in Paris, France, from about 1863 until 1904. Research concerning Jullien Bébés is inconclusive. There appears to have been more than one factory which operated under the name "Jullien." They were more than likely interconnected, perhaps one was the porcelain factory, another decorated the heads, and yet another assembled the dolls. It is also unclear exactly when Jullien began to produce bisque doll heads, although it is assumed that Jullien was one of the early French doll makers. Records confirm that Jullien purchased at least some doll heads from Francois Gaultier. These lovely bisque heads are marked "Jullien." Dolls have also been found marked with a "JJ" mark, but it is not known whether these are Jullien, Jeune, Jules Jeanson, or Joseph Joanny Dolls.

JULLIEN BÉBÉ VALUE COMPARISONS:

Size	Closed Mouth	Open Mouth
15"	3,800.00	1,500.00
17"	4,000.00	1,800.00
19"	4,400.00	2,000.00
21"	4,800.00	2,200.00
23"	5,000.00	2,400.00
25"	5,300.00	2,700.00
27"		3,000.00
29"		3,500.00

10" Bébé. *Photo courtesy of McMasters Doll Auction.*

While reproductions of French Bébés abound, Jullien Bébés do not seem to be as plagued by this misfortune as other dolls. A routine inspection should be sufficient to dispel any doubt.

Prices listed are for dolls with no damage to the bisque. Normal wear, slight damage, or well-done repairs to the body do not greatly affect price. If the bisque is damaged or repainted, expect to pay less than half the amount listed. It is perfectly acceptable to show a missing or repaired finger or joint to the body.

Closed Mouth Bébé: socket head, jointed wood-and-composition body; good wig; paperweight eyes, long painted lashes, feathered brows; pierced ears; closed mouth with slight white space between lips; very softly blushed; appropriately dressed. Marked "Jullien."

Open Mouth Bébé: socket head, jointed wood-and-composition body; good wig; paperweight eyes, long painted lashes, feathered brows; pierced ears; open mouth; appropriately dressed. Marked "Jullien."

Jumeau

*ierre Francois Jumeau began manufacturing dolls in Paris and Montreuil-sous-Bois, France, about 1842, in a partnership called Belton & Jumeau. Although the death of Belton brought the partnership to an end, Jumeau continued creating one of the most exquisite bisque Bébés in the world. Pierre Jumeau planned to have his eldest son, George, take over the business upon his retirement. However, George died very suddenly, and when Pierre retired in 1877-78, his second son, Emile Jumeau, took over as head of the company. Emile had studied to be an architect, but when forced to take over the family doll making business, he resolved to make France the world leader in the doll industry. Today, collectors eagerly seek his magnificent Bébés—true works of art worthy of admiration. The Metropolitan Museum of Art defines 'art' as "including objects that had a true sense of time and place." According to this definition, antique dolls can be considered perfect examples.

When attempting to date or authenticate a doll, remember that bisque doll heads made prior to 1890 were pressed, after that date they were poured.

During the past years collectors have heightened the distinction between spectacular and mediocre examples. Hence, prices for seemingly identical dolls can vary a great deal. When evaluating a Jumeau Bébé or Poupee de Modes, remember the "visual appeal factor."

Jumeau doll head markings vary considerably. The most commonly found mark is the "Tete Jumeau" stamp, a red artist check mark. Earlier Jumeaus can be found marked "E. J." with a size number. The rare, long faced Jumeau, as well as other portrait Jumeaus, are marked only with a size number. Recent reports indicate that Maison Jumeau released Bébés which did not meet his impeccable standards of excellence. These lesser-quality Bébés were sold as "seconds" and are unmarked. It is also reported that in the 1890s Paris stores sold cheaper dolls made by Jumeau which were unmarked.

Reproduction Jumeaus do show up from time to time. Being armed with some basic information should be helpful. Check the marking first for a doll artist's name, initials, or a date. Copies were often made for the enjoyment of the crafter, rather than as a fraud, and will be well marked. Markings on the body should match those on the head. Examine the inside of the doll's head. Early examples were pressed, not poured. In the case of early dolls which were larger than 20", the ears should be applied, not molded. When inspecting an antique doll, attention must be paid to details.

Prices listed are for dolls with no damage to the bisque. Normal wear, slight damage, or well-done repairs to the body do not greatly affect price. If the bisque is damaged or repaired, expect to pay less than half the amount listed. It is

28" very rare portrait. *Courtesy of Ellen Schroy.*

27" Long Face Jumeau. *Courtesy of Ellen Schroy.*

32" Jumeau 1907 Bébé. *Courtesy of Leah and Gene Patterson.*

15" Tete Bébé. *Courtesy of Helen Brooke.*

perfectly acceptable to show a missing or repaired finger or joint to the body.

Poupée de Modes (Fashion Dolls): socket head on kid-lined shoulder plate, kid body, slender waist, kid arms with stitched fingers; good wig; paperweight eyes; finely feathered brows; pierced ears; closed mouth; appropriately dressed. Body may be stamped with blue "JUMEAU/Medaille D'Or PARIS." The head is marked with a size number only, or a red artist check mark.

Portrait Jumeau Bébé: pressed bisque socket head, French straight-wrist wood-and-composition body, eight separate balls at joints; good wig; large almond-shaped paperweight eyes, often with tri-color irises, feathered brows; pierced ears; chubby cheeks; closed mouth; appropriately dressed. Body stamped in blue "JUMEAU/Medaille D'Or/PARIS." Head marked with a size number only.

Portrait Deposes Jumeau Bébé: may have less dramatic expression and more rounded eyes; may be marked "DEPOSES" in addition to size number.

Long Face Triste: pressed bisque socket head, French straight-wrist wood-and-composition body, eight

separate balls at joints; good wig; luminous oval paperweight eyes, wide-spaced feathered brows; applied pierced ears; closed mouth; appropriately dressed. Typically marked with size number and body stamped with blue ink "JUMEAU/Medaille D'Or/PARIS." Fuller lower cheeks give this doll an almost square-shaped face. Referred to by collectors as "Triste" because of the doll's sad, pensive expression. Commonly found in sizes of 24" or more.

E. J. Jumeau Bébé: socket head, jointed wood-and-composition body; good wig; beautiful paperweight eyes, feathered brows; pierced ears applied on larger sizes; closed mouth; appropriately dressed.

Early: pressed bisque, substantial, almost chubby; straight wrists; eight separate balls at joints. Marked with size number above "E.J.," body stamped with blue ink "Jumeau/Medallioe D'Or/Paris."

Mid: most are poured bisque, although a few are pressed bisque; trimmer French bodies with jointed wrists and attached ball joints. Marked with size number between the "E" and "J.," body stamped in blue ink "Jumeau/Medaille D'Or/Paris," or with oval paper label "Bébé Jumeau/Diplome d'Honneur."

Late: poured bisque, trimmer French bodies, straight or jointed wrists, attached ball joints. Marked with "DEPOSE" above the E. J., with an oval paper label reading "Bébé Jumeau Diplome d'Honneur," or body stamped in blue ink "Jumeau/Medaille D'Or/Paris."

E. J. A. Bébé: earliest and rarest of the Bébés; composition-and-wood chubby bodies with straight wrists; narrow almond-shaped eyes; closely resembles the portrait Jumeau; 25 to 26". Marked "E.J.A.;" body stamped "JUMEAU/Medaille D'Or/PARIS."

Depose Jumeau Bébé: socket head, French straight or jointed-wrist wood-and-composition body, separate balls at joints; good wig; paperweight eyes with deeper sockets, softly feathered brows; pierced ears; closed mouth with slight space between lips; appropriately dressed. Marked "DEPOSE/JUMEAU" on head, body stamped in blue ink "JUMEAU/Medaille D'Or/PARIS."

Tete Jumeau Bébé: poured bisque socket head, French straight- or jointed-wrist wood-and-composition ball-jointed body, good wig, large lustrous paperweight eyes, heavy feathered brows, pierced ears, closed mouth, appropriately dressed. Marked with red stamp "Depose Tete Jumeau Bte SGDG" on head and body marked with oval label "Bébé Jumeau/Diplome D'Honneur," or blue ink stamp "JUMEAU/Medaille D'Or/Paris." Adult-faced Tete Jumeau, shapely composition woman's body; stamped with red "Tete Jumeau" mark.

Open Mouth Bébé: poured bisque socket head, French wood and composition ball-jointed body with jointed wrists; good wig; large paperweight eyes, heavy feathered brows; molded pierced ears; open mouth with molded upper teeth; appropriately dressed. Marked with red stamp "Tete Jumeau," "Depose Tete Jumeau Bte SGDG," and/or incised "1907" on back of head; body may have paper label "Bébé Jumeau/Diplome D'Honneur."

S.F.B.J. Dolls: (such as 221, 230, and 306); may be marked "Jumeau."

Jumeau Character Doll: expressive character face, glass eyes, French jointed composition body. Most are marked with the red Tete stamp. Dolls numbering from 201 to 225 are assumed to be of German origin, but were released as Jumeau Character Dolls. Characters date to the period following Jumeau's joining S.F.B.J. Character dolls with mold numbers higher than 226 are marked "S.F.B.J." Jumeau characters include a mischievous child, a laughing child, a gorgeously sculpted lady with a heart-shaped face, an African woman with worry lines, and so on.

JUMEAU VALUE COMPARISONS:

Size	Poupée de Modes (Fashion Dolls), Kid Body*	Poupée de Modes (Fashion Dolls), Kid Body, Extraordinary*	Portrait Bébé, Closed Mouth, Jointed Body Size # Only	Portrait Bébé, Closed Mouth, Jointed Body, Marked Deposes	Portrait Bébé, Closed Mouth, Very Pale Bisque, Extremely Almond Eyes	Long Face Triste, Closed Mouth, Jointed Body	Early E. J. Jumeau Bébé, Closed Mouth, Jointed Body	Mid E. J. Jumeau Bébé, Closed Mouth, Jointed Body	Later E. J. Jumeau Bébé, Closed Mouth, Jointed Body
10"	2,000.00		8,500.00					6,000.00	4,800.00
11"									
12"	2,800.00		9,000.00				9,000.00	6,200.00	5,000.00
13"									
14"	3,400.00	5,000.00					9,500.00	6,700.00	5,400.00
15"	3,500.00		14,000.00	7,000.00					
17"	4,400.00	6,000.00	18,000.00	8,000.00			11,000.00	7,200.00	6,000.00
19"	4,800.00	7,200.00		9,000.00	25,000.00		13,000.00	7,800.00	6,500.00
20½"			25,000.00			20,000.00	14,000.00	8,000.00	6,700.00
22"	5,000.00		29,000.00				19,000.00	8,800.00	7,000.00
23"					35,000.00				
24"	5,500.00					24,000.00	24,000.00	10,000.00	7,800.00
25"					42,000.00	42,000.00			
26"		11,000.00						11,000.00	8,500.00
28"						28,000.00			
30"						30,000.00		13,000.00	9,500.00
32"						32,000.00			
34"						35,000.00			

*Add an additional $1,500.00 for Jumeau Poupée de Modes with a stamped wooden body.

25" Tete Bébé. *Courtesy of Helen Brooke.*

25" Tete Bébé. *Courtesy of Mr. and Mrs. Adam Condo.*

JUMEAU VALUE COMPARISONS:										
Size	E.J.A. Bébé	Depose Jumeau, Closed Mouth, Jointed Body	Tete Jumeau Bébé, Closed Mouth	Black Tete Jumeau Bebe, Closed Mouth	Tete Lady	Open Tete or 1907	S.F.B.J. 221	230/306	203/211 2-Face Character	200 Series Extreme Character
11"		6,000.00	3,400.00				800.00			
12"			3,600.00							
13"			3,800.00							
14"		6,500.00	4,000.00			2,700.00				
15"			4,200.00			2,800.00				
16"								1,800.00		
17"		7,000.00	4,400.00	8,700.00		3,000.00				
19"		7,500.00	4,500.00			3,300.00			22,000.00	
20½"			4,700.00		6,200.00	3,500.00		2,200.00		
22"		8,000.00	5,000.00	11,000.00		3,700.00				
24"		8,500.00	5,200.00		8,000.00	3,900.00		2,500.00		75,000.00
26"	35,000.00	9,500.00	5,800.00			4,000.00				100,000.00
28"			6,000.00			4,200.00				
30"			6,700.00			4,500.00		3,000.00		
32"			7,500.00			4,700.00				
34"					4,900.00			3,500.00		

K & K Toy Company

K & K Character Child.
Courtesy of Helen Brooke.

K & K Toy Company was founded in New York City in 1915. Like many other doll makers of the time, the company imported its bisque heads from Germany. K & K also supplied cloth and composition bodies to several doll manufacturers, including George Borgfeldt. Composition bodies were often marked "bisquette" or "fiberoid." Many K & K dolls were distributed by Butler Bros.

While most bisque doll heads marked K & K are found on cloth bodies with composition limbs, occasionally one is found on a kid body with bisque arms. The dolls' happy smiling faces and big shining eyes make them irresistible to doll collectors.

Prices listed are for dolls with no damage to the bisque. Normal wear, slight damage, or well-done repairs to the body do not greatly affect price.

Bisque Character Child: shoulder head, kid or cloth body, bisque or composition arms; good wig; glass eyes; open smiling mouth with two upper teeth and felt tongue; appropriately dressed. Typically marked "K & K Made in Germany" or "K & K Germany/Thuringia."

Composition (Rose Marie): shoulder head, cloth body, slim legs; good wig; sleep eyes; open mouth with upper teeth and felt tongue; appropriately dressed. Marked "K & K/Fiberoid/USA."

K & K TOY COMPANY VALUE COMPARISONS:		
Size	Bisque	Composition
18"	500.00	
20"	550.00	375.00
22"	650.00	400.00
23"	700.00	
24"	750.00	450.00
25"	800.00	

Kamkins

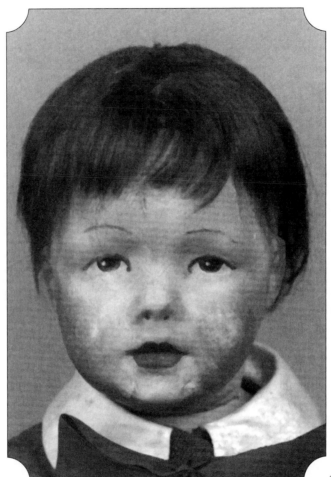

18" Kamkin Boy Doll. *Photo courtesy of of McMasters Doll Auction.*

The Louise R. Kampes Studio of Atlantic City, New Jersey, produced dolls from 1919 until 1928. Kamkins were charming art dolls that were sold on the boardwalk at Atlantic City. Patented in 1920, these dolls were made of heavy cloth treated with rubber, a combination which made the face appear similar to composition. The production of Kamkins was conducted as a cottage-type industry. The studio supplied patterns and materials to home sewers. It also designed a line of doll clothing that could be purchased separately.

The most common characteristic shared by all Kamkins is the heavy molded mask-type face. Most of these character doll faces are painted a deep healthy color and seldom have eye lashes. The stuffed cloth bodies usually have seams down the front of the legs. Kamkins range in size from 18 to 20 inches. Because many Kamkins were marked with only a heart-shaped paper label on the chest which was often lost, Kamkins art dolls are often found with no markings. Other Kamkins are stamped "Kamkins A Dolly Made To Love" or signed "Kamkins Studio."

Reproduction Kamkins do not seem to be a problem. The heavy rubberized mask-type face is difficult to duplicate.

Avoid dolls with excessive wear. Normal aging is to be expected, but if the doll is badly discolored or worn, expect to pay about half the amount listed.

Kamkins Art Doll: heavy molded and painted mask-type face, flange neck, solidly stuffed cloth body jointed at shoulders and hips; good wig; painted eyes; closed mouth; appropriately dressed. Typically marked with paper heart-shaped label on chest "Kamkins A Dolly Made to Love/Patented from L. R. Kampes Studios/Atlantic City N.J.," stamped "Kamkins A Dolly Made to Love," or signed "Kamkins Studio."

KAMKINS VALUE COMPARISONS:	
Size	Price
18"	1,500.00
19"	1,500.00
20"	1,600.00

Kämmer & Reinhardt

Max and Moritz.

Kämmer & Reinhardt was founded by Ernst Kämmer and Franz Reinhardt in 1886 in Waltershausen, Thüringia, Germany. Ernst Kämmer was a designer and modeler. When he died in 1901, Karl Krausser took over his position. At about the same time another great German doll manufacturer, Henrich Handwerck, also passed away. Shortly thereafter, in 1902, the company bought the Handwerck factory. Kämmer & Reinhardt designed doll heads, but did not actually make them. This fact surprises many doll collectors. Simon & Halbig made most of the bisque heads, and was a part of the company by 1920. Scheutzmeister & Quendt also supplied bisque heads for them around 1918.

From 1886 to 1909, Kämmer & Reinhardt made only dolly-face dolls. They claimed they were the first company to include teeth in doll heads. While teeth had been used on dolls produced much earlier, they may have been among the first to use them in bisque doll heads. The "W" found on the forehead of some Kämmer and Reinhardt dolls is probably a reference to the Waltershausen region. Another point of confusion to some collectors is a number between 15 and 100 found low on the doll's neck. This is actually a size number, not a mold number.

Kämmer & Reinhardt has long been credited with popularizing character dolls, though the company was undoubtedly influenced by Marion B. Kaulitz, the instigator of the 1908 "Puppen Reform." Kämmer & Reinhardt caused quite a stir when it introduced its K★R character dolls on bent-limb

baby bodies at the 1909 Munich Exhibit. The company later boasted to the media that it "had brought out our one model and influenced the market with it." The development of character dolls, which were modeled after real children, was an innovative progression of the German doll industry. While Kämmer & Reinhardt may have been the first company to commercialize the character doll, other firms soon joined in.

Reproduction Kämmer & Reinhardt are produced. While many are legitimate copies whose express purpose is to add visual excitement to a collection, others are made as frauds. As always, check the markings carefully. Look for names and dates which would not be present on an authentic doll. Next, inspect the bisque. It should not be creamy smooth. The texture of the bisque of the Kämmer & Reinhardt character dolls is of very good quality, but it does not have a satiny smooth finish, nor is the decoration precisely executed. Many times a reproduction will have an "exact" look, whereas a doll that was produced as a plaything does not.

Prices listed are for dolls with no damage to the bisque. Normal wear, slight damage, or well-done repairs to the body do not greatly affect price. If the bisque is damaged or repaired, expect to pay less than half the amount listed. It is perfectly acceptable to show a missing or replaced finger or joint to the body.

Closed Mouth Child: bisque socket head, jointed wood-and-composition body; good wig; glass eyes, feathered brows; pierced ears; closed mouth; appropriately dressed. Typically marked "K & R 191" or "K & R 192."

32" Kämmer and Reinhardt Child. *Courtesy of Leah and Gene Patterson.*

Kämmer and Reinhardt 403 on a Walker Body. *Courtesy of Helen Brooke.*

KÄMMER & REINHART VALUE COMPARISONS:

Size	Closed Mouth Child*	Open Mouth Child*	Open Mouth Child/Kid Body
5"		550.00	
6"	700.00	600.00	
8"	900.00	650.00	
9"	1,200.00	700.00	
12"	2,000.00	800.00	
14"	3,000.00	900.00	
16"	3,200.00	1,000.00	500.00
18"	3,600.00	1,100.00	700.00
20"	3,800.00	1,200.00	800.00
22"	4,000.00	1,400.00	850.00
24"	4,200.00	1,500.00	900.00
28"		1,700.00	
30"		2,000.00	
32"		2,300.00	
34"		2,700.00	
36"		3,200.00	
40"		4,000.00	
42"		4,500.00	

* Add an additional $100.00 for flirty eyes or $300.00 for flapper.

Open Mouth Socket-Head Child: bisque socket head, jointed wood-and-composition body; good wig; glass eyes, feathered brows; pierced ears; open mouth; appropriately dressed. Typically marked "K★R Simon & Halbig 403," "Halbig/ K★R," "K★R 191," or "192."

Open Mouth Shoulder Head Child: bisque shoulder head, kid body with bisque arms; good wig; glass eyes; open mouth; appropriately dressed. Typically marked "SH/ K★R."

Character Baby: bisque socket head, composition bent-limb baby body; molded and painted hair or good wig; sleep eyes; closed or molded open/closed mouth; appropriately dressed. Typically marked "K★R."

CLOTH

Kämmer & Reinhardt also made cloth dolls. Their wire armature bodies were covered with cloth and had painted features. They were authentically dressed in perfect miniature costumes representing various professions and stations in life such as dude, bum, porter, clerk, bellhop, professor, chauffeur, gentleman, cook, and servant. About twenty-five male character dolls were created. These dolls are very rare, and their value is as much dependent upon visual appeal as condition. A typical example in generally good condition would be valued at $300.00 or more.

CHARACTER BABY VALUE COMPARISONS:

Size	100 O/MC, Solid Dome, Painted Eyes	115 CM, Solid Dome, Glass Eyes	115A CM, Wig, Glass Eyes	116 O/CM, Solid Dome, Glass Eyes	116A O/CM, Wig, Glass Eyes	118-118A OM, Wig, Glass Eyes	119 O/CM, Wig, Glass Eyes	121 OM, Solid Dome, Glass Eyes
12"	800.00	5,800.00	4,500.00	4,200.00	2,400.00	2,200.00	3,500.00	1,000.00
15"	1,000.00	6,200.00	5,000.00	4,700.00	2,900.00	2,700.00	4,000.00	1,200.00
20"	1,500.00	6,700.00	5,500.00	6,000.00	3,800.00	3,200.00	5,500.00	1,700.00

Size	122 OM, Wig, Glass Eyes	126 OM, Wig, Glass Eyes	127 OM, Solid Dome, Glass Eyes	128 OM, Wig, Glass Eyes	135 OM, Wig, Glass Eyes	171 O/CM, Solid Dome, Glass Eyes	200 Cloth Body, Solid Dome, O/CM, Painted Eyes	926 Composition Socket Head, OM, wig, Sleep Eyes	175 Painted Bisque, Cloth Body Sleep Eyes
12"	1,100.00	650.00	1,700.00	1,200.00	1,500.00	3,300.00	600.00		1,400.00
15"	1,300.00	800.00	2,000.00	1,400.00	2,000.00	3,800.00			
18"								850.00	1,700.00
20"	1,600.00	1,200.00	2,700.00	1,700.00	3,000.00				
24"			3,400.00					950.00	

Note: add an additional $500.00 to any Character Baby with Toddler Body.

CHARACTER CHILD VALUE COMPARISONS:

Size	101 CM, Wig, Painted Eye	101 CM, Wig, Glass Eye	102 CM, Solid, Dome, Painted Eye	103 CM, Wig, Painted Eye	104 CM/Laughing, Wig, Painted Eyes	105 O/CM, Wig, Painted Eyes	106 CM, Wig, Painted Eyes	107 CM, Wig, Painted Eyes
12"	3,300.00	11,000.00	38,000.00	58,000.00	60,000.00	100,000.00	58,000.00	19,000.00
14"	4,200.00	17,000.00	45,000.00	65,000.00	80,000.00	150,000.00	65,000.00	25,000.00
20"	6,500.00		60,000.00	78,000.00	100,000.00	200,000.00	78,000.00	50,000.00

Size	108 CM, Wig, Painted Eyes	109 CM, Wig, Painted Eyes	109 CM, Wig, Glass Eyes	112-112X, O/CM, Wig, Painted Eyes	112A, O/CM, Wig, Glass Eyes	114 CM, Wig, Painted Eyes	114CM, Wig, Glass Eyes	117-117A, CM, Wig, Glass Eyes
12"		6,000.00		16,000.00		3,800.00		
14"		12,000.00	19,000.00	18,000.00	24,000.00	5,100.00	12,000.00	
19"								4,500.00
20"		18,000.00	25,000.00	24,000.00		7,200.00	16,000.00	5,800.00
23"								7,200.00
25"	29,000.00							

Size	117 NoN, OM, Wig, Glass Eyes	117 N, OM, Wig, Glass Eyes	123,124, Laughing, CM, Wig, Glass Eyes	201 CM, Cloth Body, Wig, Painted Eyes
14"		1,300.00		2,100.00
15"			20,000.00	
16"				2,500.00
17"			24,000.00	
19"	3,000.00			
20"		1,600.00		
22"			36,000.00	
23"	4,500.00			
24"		1,800.00		

Kenner Parker Toys, Inc.

Purple Pie Man and Strawberry Short Cake. *Courtesy of Maribeth Herlocher.*

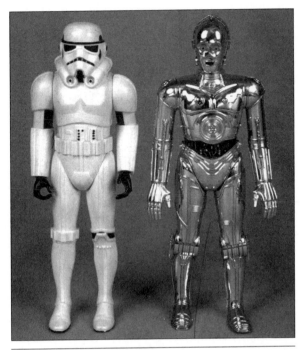

Star Wars C-3P0 and Imperial Stormtrooper. *Courtesy of Ty Herlocher.*

In 1985, Kenner became an independent company with two divisions: Parker Brothers and Kenner products. Kenner was once a subsidiary of General Mills. They produced many dolls as well as popular figures.

Prices listed are for dolls in mint condition. There is little forgiveness for modern dolls in less-than-perfect condition.

DOLLS

Boy Scout: vinyl and plastic; black skin and features; molded and painted hair; painted eyes; closed smiling mouth; beautifully costumed in authentic Boy Scout uniform; gives Boy Scout salute when right arm is raised. Marked "1974 G.M.F.G./Kenner Prod/Cinti. Ohio/NO 7000/Made in Hong Kong."

Blythe: oversized hard plastic head, tiny fully-jointed body; rooted hair; eyes change color as ring is pulled, green, blue, brown, purple (some Blythe dolls have amber in place of purple) eye colors; closed mouth; dressed in original "mod"-type dress and high plastic boots. Marked "Blythe TM/Kenner Products/Cincinnati, Ohio/1972 General Mills/Fun Group Inc./Patents Pending/Made in Hong Kong."

Baby Alive: all vinyl, jointed at neck, shoulders, and hips; rooted blond hair; painted blue eyes; open mouth; wearing original romper and disposable diaper; comes with nine packets of food, bottle, dish, and spoon which activates chewing motion; doll smacks her lips after spoon or bottle is removed from mouth; bubbles like a real baby, and fills her diaper; requires two batteries. Marked "1973G.M.F.G. Inc./KENNER PRODUCTS DIV/Cinti,O/Made in Hong Kong."

Gabbigale: vinyl head, fully-jointed plastic body; rooted blond hair; painted blue eyes; open/closed smiling mouth; pull string in chest; battery operated, repeats spoken words; dressed in original red jumper-type dress. Marked "1972 Kenner Products Co/99" on head and "Gabbigale/1972 Kenner Products/General Mills/Fun Group Inc./Patents Pending."

FIGURES

Star Wars: large size. Marked "GMFGI 1978" on head and "GMFGI 1978 Kenner Prod/Cincinnati, Ohio 45202/Made in Hong Kong."

KENNER VALUE COMPARISONS:

Size	Boy Scout	Blythe	Baby Alive	Gabbigale	C-3PO	Chewbacca	Darth Vader	Boba Fett
9"	40.00							
12"		50.00			175.00			
13"								300.00
15"						150.00	200.00	
16"			75.00					
18"				65.00				

Size	Han Solo	IG 88	Jawa	Leia	Luke Skywalker	Obi Wan Kenobi	R2-D2	Stormtrooper
7½"							175.00	
8½"			85.00					
11½"				175.00				
12"	175.00					225.00		250.00
13"					225.00			
15"		400.00						

Size	Yoda	Small Figures	Strawberry Shortcake and Other Typical Figures	Sour Grapes, Purple Pieman
3"		60.00 - 100.00		
5"			35.00	
9"	125.00			
15"				60.00

J. D. Kestner

ohann Danie Kestner, the charismatic founder of the Kestner empire, started in business by trading with the soldiers of the Napoleonic wars as early as 1805. He traded small necessary items in exchange for the wastes from their slaughtered cattle, such as kid, fat, horns, and bones. This operation was so successful that he opened his own factory in 1816. Originally intended to be a manufacturer of papier-mâché notebooks, he soon expanded to shirt buttons. Needing a lathe to make buttons, it only seemed natural to him that he could also make wooden jointed dolls. By 1820, Kestner was manufacturing a complete line of toys and dolls made from both wood and papier-mâché. In 1840, Kestner participated in the Leipzig Fair as the first toy maker of Waltershausen, an impressive feat when one considers the toy capital that area was to become.

J.D. Kestner was granted a monopoly on the production of papier-mâché by the German government. In exchange for this exclusive right, and being charged a nominal annual tax of only 3 Taler, Kestner agreed to provide food and employment to the poverty stricken people of Waltershausen. The arrangement must have been successful, for he held the monopoly for more than 25 years and

14" JDK Character Toddler. *Courtesy of Phyllis Bechtold.*

employed over three-quarters of the total population in and around Waltershausen. The doll industry was of utmost importance in Germany, and J.D. Kestner was the head of this industry, thus he was bestowed the nickname "King Kestner." Kestner's influence was so great and far reaching that he received permission to practice polygamy by the Ducal Government, and kept two wives at his home. An obituary gives credibility to this story by stating: "His two women continue the business." Upon his death in 1858, the company kept operating until his grandson Adolf (J.D.'s only son had preceded him in death by ten years) was old enough and trained to assume the responsibilities of running the company

Kestner Dolls, as we think of them today, were introduced following Kestner's acquisition of the Ohrdug porcelain factory in 1860. Kestner was one of the few firms which produced its complete doll, parts and all. The company also supplied doll heads to several other doll manufacturers.

The century-old firm used a wide assortment of markings, including its name, initials, various mold numbers, and a series of letters. Some dolls have been attributed to Kestner simply because the marking "Made in Germany" is written in a manner similar to a Kestner practice which was started in 1892, when mold numbers were assigned. Another familiar word associated with Kestner is "Excelsior," which is a trade name for Kestner dolls distributed in the United States. These dolls can be found with various body types and bisque heads.

Reproductions do occasionally surface. There are several characteristics to watch for. Always check the markings first. Look for names, initials, and dates that should not be there. Kestner dolls did not have pierced ears and their painted eyebrows appear heavy and somewhat shiny. The upper lip has a high "bow" and is upturned at each end. On closed-

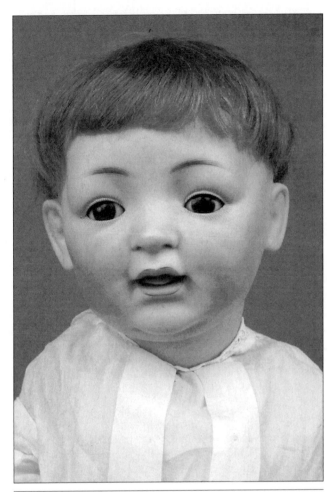

18" JDK 211 Character Baby.

KESTNER VALUE COMPARISONS:

Size	Closed Mouth, Kid Body, Normal#	Closed Mouth, Composition Body	Closed Pouty Mouth, Composition Body	Closed Mouth, French Look	Open Mouth, Carved Square Teeth, Kid Body	Open Mouth, Turned Head, Kid Body	Tiny Doll	Dolly-Face, Open Mouth, Composition Body
7"							950.00	
8"							1,100.00	
10"	900.00	2,200.00	3,100.00					
12"	1,000.00	2,400.00	3,300.00		1,000.00	600.00		1,000.00
14"	1,200.00	2,600.00	3,500.00		1,200.00	700.00		1,000.00
16"	1,400.00	2,800.00	3,800.00	6,500.00	1,300.00	800.00		1,100.00
18"	1,500.00	2,900.00	4,000.00		1,400.00	900.00		1,200.00
20"	1,700.00	3,200.00	4,400.00	7,500.00	1,500.00	1,000.00		
22"	3,600.00				1,600.00	1,100.00		1,400.00
24"	2,000.00	4,000.00	4,700.00	9,000.00	1,700.00	1,200.00		1,500.00
26"	2,200.00	4,700.00			1,800.00			
28"			5,000.00					1,700.00
32"		5,500.00						1,900.00
36"								3,000.00
40"								4,500.00
42"								4,900.00

mouth dolls, a darker line separates the lips. The nostril dots and the dots at the inner corner of each eye should be a soft orange, as opposed to red or pink. These dots usually match the lip color. Kestner dolls have good quality blown glass eyes with threading. A great many early Kestner dolls were originally fitted with blond mohair wigs; therefore, their coloring should compliment the lighter hair color. The crown opening usually is covered by a plaster pate, rather than a cardboard or cork pate. Check carefully for the size letter/number.

Prices listed are for dolls with no damage to the bisque. Normal wear, slight damage, or well-done repairs to the body do not greatly affect price. When the bisque is damaged or repaired, expect to pay less than half the amount listed. It is perfectly acceptable to show a missing or replaced finger or joint to the body.

See also All-Bisque and Googly-Eyed Dolls.

Closed Mouth Shoulder Head: bisque shoulder head, kid body, bisque forearms; good wig; brown eyes, long eyelashes, heavy brows; closed mouth; appropriately dressed. Typically marked "Germany" and a letter or size number.

Closed Mouth Socket Head: bisque socket head, jointed wood-and-composition body, straight wrists; good wig; glass eyes, feathered brows; closed mouth; appropriately dressed. Typically marked "3," "X," "128," "169," or a letter or size number only.

Closed Pouty-mouth Socket Head: bisque socket head, jointed wood-and-composition body, straight wrists; good wig; glass eyes, heavy feathered brows; closed pouty mouth; appropriately dressed. Typically marked "XI" or "103."

22" Kestner with Square Cut Teeth. *Courtesy of Leah and Gene Patterson.*

KESTNER VALUE COMPARISONS (CONTINUED):

Size	Unique Dolly-Face, Composition Body	Dolly-Face, Open Mouth, Kid Body	Character Baby Solid Dome Bent-Limb Body*	Character Baby, Kid Body	Character Baby, Bent-Limb Body*	Hilda Character Baby*	Cunning Character Baby	Flange-Neck Baby
8"		400.00						
10"		450.00			700.00	3,000.00	1,100.00	1,700.00
12"	1,200.00	500.00	800.00	900.00	800.00	3,700.00	1,400.00	1,900.00
14"	1,300.00	550.00	900.00	1,000.00	900.00	4,200.00	1,800.00	2,200.00
16"	1,400.00	650.00	1,000.00		1,000.00	4,600.00	2,200.00	2,400.00
18"	1,500.00	700.00	1,200.00		1,200.00	5,000.00		
20"		750.00	1,400.00			5,300.00	2,400.00	
22"	1,600.00	800.00		1,400.00	1,500.00	5,900.00		
24"	1,700.00	1,000.00	1,700.00	1,600.00	1,700.00	7,000.00	2,500.00	
26"	1,100.00				2,000.00	8,000.00	2,700.00	
28"	1,900.00	1,200.00				9,000.00		
30"		1,400.00			2,400.00	10,000.00		
32"	2,300.00	1,600.00						
36"	3,200.00	2,200.00						
40"	4,700.00							
42"	5,400.00							

* Add an additional $500.00 for Toddler Body

Closed Mouth French-Look: jointed body; good wig; large glass eyes, long lashes, feathered brows; full slightly parted lips with a hint of a molded tongue; appropriately dressed. Marked with a letter or size number only.

Open Mouth, Carved Square-Tooth, Shoulder Head Child: kid body, bisque forearms; good wig; glass eyes, feathered brows; open mouth with carved square teeth; appropriately dressed. Typically marked "Made in Germany" and/or with a letter or size number only.

Open Mouth, Turned Shoulder Head: kid body, bisque forearms; good wig; glass eyes, feathered brows; open mouth with upper teeth; appropriately dressed. Typically marked "Made in Germany" and/or with a letter or size number only.

Tiny Doll: bisque socket head, five-piece composition body; molded and painted shoes; good wig; glass eyes; open mouth with tiny teeth; appropriately dressed. Typically marked "155" or "170."

Dolly-Face: socket dolly-face doll; wood-and-composition body; good wig; glass eyes, feathered brows; open mouth with upper teeth; appropriately dressed. Typically marked "Made in Germany " and "136," "141," "142," "144," "146," "152," "156," "160," "164," "167," "168," "171," "174," or "196" on back of head.

Unique Dolly-Face: socket dolly-face with unique, almost character face, ball-jointed wood-and-composition body; good wig; glass eyes, feathered or fur brows; open mouth, chubby cheeks; appropriately dressed. Typically marked "Made in Germany JDK/" and "129," "143," "149," "161," "214," or "215."

Dolly-Face Shoulder Head: kid body, bisque forearms; good wig; glass eyes, feathered brows or fur brows; open mouth with upper teeth; appropriately dressed. Typically marked "Made in Germany" and "145," "147," "148," "154," "156," "159," "166," or "195."

Solid Dome Character Baby: bent-limb baby body; softly painted hair; glass eyes, feathered brows, open or open/closed mouth; appropriately dressed. Typically marked "J. D. K." and size number only.

Character Baby Shoulder Head: rivet-jointed kid body, composition limbs, solid dome; glass eyes; open/closed mouth; appropriately dressed. Typically marked "Made in Germany/J.D.K./" and "210," "234," "235," or "238."

Character Baby Socket Head: composition bent-limb baby body; good wig; glass eyes, winged feathered brows; open mouth with teeth; appropriately dressed. Typically marked "Made in Germany J.D.K./" and "211," "226," "236," "260," "262," or "263."

Hilda Character Baby: bent-limb baby body; softly molded and lightly painted hair or good wig; glass eyes; open mouth with two upper teeth; appropriately dressed. Typically marked "J.D.K./ges.gesch K 14 1070/Made in Germany," "237," "245," and "Hilda." The marking on the head of a Hilda Baby does not have to read "Hilda" for her to be authentic. The wigged version must be marked "237" or "245." The solid dome may be marked "1070;" the wigged version may also have the "1070" in addition to "237" or "245." 1070 may possibly be a registration number.

Cunning Character Baby: exceptional character face with beautiful molding; socket head, bent-limb baby body; good wig; glass eyes; open mouth with two upper teeth, appears to have a slight overbite; appropriately dressed. Typically marked "Made in Germany/J.D.K.," "247," (at times referred to as "Baby Jean") or "JDK."

Flange Neck Character Baby: character face, cloth body, solid dome with painted hair; glass eyes; appropriately dressed. Typically marked "255/O.I.C." or "Siegfried 272."

Character Child: wood-and-composition body; good wig; glass or painted eyes. Typical mold numbers include "175," "176," "177," "178," "179," "180," "181," "182," "183," "184," "185," "186," "187," "188," and "190."

Lady Character Face: very shapely composition woman's body, cinched waist, molded bosom; good wig; glass eyes; open mouth with teeth; appropriately dressed. Marked "162."

Gibson Girl: kid body, bisque forearms; good wig in Gibson style; glass eyes; closed mouth; head with very stylish regal bearing and upward-glancing eyes, appropriately dressed. Marked "172."

KESTNER VALUE COMPARISONS (CONTINUED):

Size	Character Children, Glass Eyes	Character Children, Painted Eyes	191	206	208	241, 239, or 220	249	162 Lady	172 Gibson Girl
10"		1,700.00							
12"	3,700.00	2,500.00		5,600.00			1,200.00		
14"			4,800.00		7,200.00	4,800.00			
16"	4,900.00	3,900.00			8,700.00		1,600.00	1,800.00	3,100.00
18"	5,700.00	4,700.00			10,000.00		2,000.00	2,000.00	
19"			6,700.00						
20"					15,000.00		2,200.00	2,200.00	
22"							2,500.00		4,800.00
24"					18,000.00	8,000.00			

Kewpies

13" Bisque Kewpie. *Photo courtesy of McMasters Doll Auction.*

12" Composition Kewpie.

These sweet little elfin-like creatures made their debut in the December 1909 issue of *Ladies Home Journal*. Famous illustrator Rose O'Neill designed the Kewpies and held the design patents for them until her death in 1944. According to O'Neill, Kewpies first danced across her bed and shared their name with her while she was napping in her art studio—The Bird Café—on the third floor of her family home. O'Neill always maintained that she did not invent Kewpies; she only introduced them.

George Borgfeldt held the manufacturing rights for many years, eventually passing them to Joseph Kallus, who retained them until 1984 when Jesco took possession of the rights to the Kewpie trademark and copyright. Over the years there have been many legal battles fought over the manufacturing of Kewpies without consent of the copyright.

Kewpies were so popular that it was inevitable that a Kewpie Doll would be born. The first Kewpie Doll was designed by Joseph Kallus, a friend of Miss O'Neill. Early Kewpies were made of bisque and came from Germany. It is reported that at the peak of the Kewpie craze, thirty German factories were producing Kewpies in order to meet demand. Although imports from Germany ceased during World War I, Kewpies continued to be made in the United States. The Cameo Doll Company of Port Allegheny, Pennsylvania, manufactured composition Kewpies, and later plastic and vinyl. Again the demand for Kewpies was too great for a single company to supply. Kallus, president of Cameo Doll Company, licensed several other doll companies to aid in the manufacturing of Kewpie, including Effanbee, Stombecker, Knickerbocker, and Amsco. To maintain quality control, Joseph Kallus required each licensed company to affix a Cameo label, in addition to its own marking, on all their Kewpie dolls.

Rose O'Neill passed away more than a half century ago, but she and her immortal Kewpies are by no means forgotten. There is a collectors' club exclusively for Kewpies, as well as the Bonniebrook Historical Society, the home and final resting place for Rose O'Neill. Bonniebrook, located near Branson, Missouri, is a wonderful place to visit. The Bonniebrook Historical Society is rebuilding O'Neill's home, striving to establish a lasting memorial to her genius.

Collectors avidly seek all forms of Kewpies. Determining an authentic O'Neill Kewpie can sometimes be tricky. The first area of concern should be the marking. O'Neill's signature is often found incised in the bisque. Check the bottom of the foot. Factory markings are often obscure because, with the absence of clothing, there was no place for it to be hidden. A paper label with a clear protective covering was attached to the doll; however, it is often removed. In the absence of markings, collectors should rely on the following clues:

1. Licensed Kewpies were never made in Japan. A "Nippon" or "Japan" mark indicates that the Kewpie is not authentic.
2. Rose O'Neill and Joseph Kallus both insisted on top

quality. If a doll is made of poor quality materials or the application of decoration is inferior, the Kewpie is not authentic.
3. All Kewpies have blue tipped wings.
4. Authentic Kewpies have star-shaped hands.

Prices listed are for dolls and figurines with no damage. When damaged or repaired, expect to pay about half the amount listed.

DOLLS

All Bisque: jointed at shoulders only; molded, painted top-knot hair; painted round side-glancing eyes with

KEWPIE VALUE COMPARISONS:

Size	All Bisque, Painted Eyes*	Bisque Head, Composition Body, Glass Eyes	Bisque Head, Cloth Body, Painted Eyes	Bisque Head, Cloth Body, Glass Eyes	Celluloid Shoulder Joints, Painted Eyes	Composition Head and Body, Painted Eyes	Composition Head, Cloth Body
2"	200.00				60.00		
3"	225.00				75.00		
4"	250.00				85.00		
5"	300.00				100.00		
6"	350.00				150.00		
7"	450.00						
8"	600.00				250.00	250.00	
9"	750.00						
10"	1,000.00	5,000.00			300.00		
12"	1,600.00	6,000.00	2,200.00	3,200.00	400.00	350.00	350.00
14"		7,000.00					
15"					450.00		
16"		8,000.00					
20"		10,000.00					

Size	Black, All Composition	Cloth, Kuddle Kewpie	Hard Plastic, No Joints	Hard Plastic, Fully Jointed	Vinyl Jesco	Vinyl, Pin Hinged	Vinyl Ragsy	Plush Knickerbocker
6"								50.00
8"			150.00				75.00	
9"					80.00			
10"		250.00	175.00				100.00	
12"	500.00	275.00	250.00	550.00	125.00			75.00
14"		325.00		600.00	175.00			
16"			350.00	650.00	200.00	250.00		
18"		375.00			225.00	300.00		
20"		425.00			250.00			
22"					275.00			
24"					300.00			
27"					350.00			

* Add an additional $400.00 - $500.00 for jointed hips or molded and painted shoes and socks.

white dot highlights; closed watermelon mouth; blue wings. Typically signed "O'Neill" on sole of foot; may also have German manufacture marking.

Bisque Head: composition body, jointed at shoulders, hips, and knees, extended arms, starfish hands; long torso with rounded tummy; light brown molded and painted top-knot; round glass side-glancing eyes, single dot brow; closed smiling watermelon mouth; tiny blue wings on sides of neck. Typically marked "Ges.gesch/O'Neill J.D.K."

Bisque Head: flange neck, cloth body; molded and painted light brown top-knot; painted or glass side-glancing eyes, single dot brow; closed, smiling watermelon mouth; appropriately dressed. Marked "A.B. & G 1377/O'Neill."

Celluloid: straight-standing doll or action figure; jointed arms; painted side-glancing eyes; blue wings.

Composition: jointed at shoulders, and occasionally hips, arms extended, starfish hands; molded and painted top-knot; painted side-glancing round eyes, single dot eyebrows; closed smiling watermelon mouth; blue wings on back. Marked with red paper heart-shaped label "Kewpie/Des & Copyright/by/Rose O'Neill."

Black Composition Head: flange neck; cloth body.

Cloth Kuddle Kewpies: all cloth, plush body with mask-type Kewpie face. Typically marked with cloth label with Kruegar or King Pat. number 1785800.

Hard Plastic Kewpies: one-piece head, body, and legs; jointed at shoulders only; painted features.

Hard Plastic Kewpies: fully jointed at neck, shoulders, and hips; sleep eyes.

Vinyl Jesco: made using Cameo's original molds; molded and painted top-knot hair; side-glancing eyes; wearing original clothing. Typically marked "Jesco."

Vinyl Pin-Hinged Limbs: painted features; original one-piece pajama outfit. Typically marked "Cameo" on head and body, and "SI/61C2/63" on doll's bottom.

Vinyl Ragsy Kewpie: blue vinyl molded to resemble stitching; painted features. Typically marked "Cameo 65 JLK" on head and "Cameo 6S" on back.

Red Plush Kewpie: plush body; vinyl face; painted features. Typically marked with cloth label "Knickerbocker Toy Co. Inc./N.Y. U.S.A./Kewpie/Designed and Copyrighted/by Rose O'Neill/Licensed by Cameo Doll Co. 1964."

Bisque Kewpie Figurines (known as "Action Kewpies"): Typically marked with a paper label; marked on the bottom of the foot; or unmarked.

KEWPIE FIGURINES VALUE COMPARISONS:

Figurine	Size	Value	Figurine	Size	Value
Blunderboo*	4"	$600.00	Soldier & Nurse	6"	$2,000.00
Bride & Groom	4"	750.00	Thinker	4"	500.00
Driving a Chariot		2,800.00	Traveler with suitcase	3½"	450.00
Farmer	4"	750.00	Two Kewpies hugging	3½"	350.00
Gardener	4"	750.00	Two Kewpies reading book	3½"	1,000.00
Governor	4	750.00	Wearing Helmet	6"	800.00
Guitar Player	3½"	650.00	With Broom or Mop	4"	650.00
Holding Cat	4"	750.00	With Butterfly	4"	800.00
Holding Pen	3" h	650.00	With Dog Doodle	3½"	1,500.00
Hottentot (Black Kewpie)	3½"	500.00	With Ink Well	3½"	800.00
Hottentot (Black Kewpie)	5"	600.00	With Ladybug	4"	650.00
In a Basket with Flowers	3½"	1,200.00	With Outhouse	3"	1,400.00
In a Draw String Bag	4½"	750.00	With Pumpkin	4"	550.00
Kewpie Doodle Dog	1½"	900.00	With Rabbit	2½"	600.00
Kewpie Doodle Dog	3"	2,000.00	With Rose	2"	500.00
On Bench with Doodle Dog	4"	4,200.00	With Tea Table	4"	2,200.00
On Stomach		550.00	With Teddy Bear	4"	1,000.00
Reading a Book	3½"	1,000.00	With Turkey	2"	500.00
Sitting in High Back Chair	4"	650.00	With Umbrella	3½"	600.00
Soldier	4½"	800.00	With Umbrella and Doddle Dog	3½"	1,400.00
Buttonhole Kewpies Attached to wooden disk to fit into button hole.	1¾"	175.00	Kewpie Mountain or Tree		48,000.00

* Tumbling Kewpies are also known as Blunderboo. They have less rounded eyes and wider smiles.

Kley & Hahn

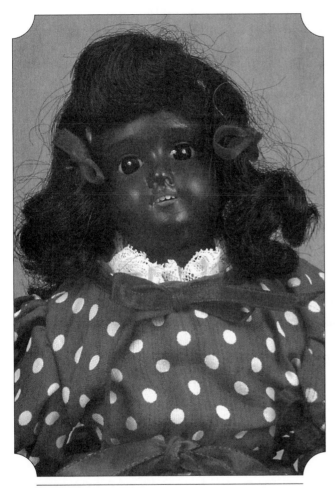

18" Black Bisque Walküre.

Kley and Hahn Walküre Child Doll.

Founded in Ohrdruf, Thüringia, Germany, by Albert Kley and Paul Hahn in 1902, Kley & Hahn began operations with just fifteen employees. They devoted most of their efforts to capitalizing on the character doll boom in the American market.

Mold numbers on Kley & Hahn doll heads indicate to doll historians that several different porcelain factories contributed to the Kley & Hahn inventory. It is widely accepted that molds in the 200 series, 680, and the Walküre were made by J.D. Kestner. The 100 series characters were produced by Hertel, Schwab & Company. Bähr & Pröschild was responsible for the 500 series characters. In addition to mold numbers, the following trade names registered by Kley & Hahn may be found on the heads: Dollar Princess, Durable, K, Majestic, Mein Einziges Baby (My Only Baby), Mein Einzige (My Only One), Princess, Schneewittchen (Snow White), Special, and Walküre.

Reproduction Kley & Hahn dolls are not a problem, although there are molds available for artists' enjoyment. Reproductions should be marked with the artist's name and sometimes a date. Inspect the body and neck socket button for signs of age. Although Kley & Hahn used a good quality of bisque, it is not as smooth as new bisque. Authentic Kley & Hahn eyebrows are very difficult to reproduce.

Prices listed are for dolls with no damage to the bisque. Normal wear, slight damage, or well-done repairs to the body do not greatly affect price. If the bisque is damaged or repaired, expect to pay less than half the amount listed. It is perfectly acceptable to show a missing or replaced finger or joint to the body.

Named Child: socket head, jointed wood-and-composition body; good wig; glass eyes, feathered brows; open mouth; appropriately dressed. Typically marked "Special 65 Germany," "Dollar Princess," "Majestie," or "Princess."

Walküre: child doll attributed to Kestner; socket head, jointed wood-and-composition body; good wig; glass eyes, molded feathered brows; open mouth; appropriately dressed. Typically marked "Walküre Germany," "250," or "282."

Character Baby: socket head, composition bent-limb baby body; solid dome with molded and painted hair or good wig; painted or glass eyes; open or open/closed mouth; appropriately dressed. Typically marked "Germany K & H" within a ribbon and with mold number "133," "135," "138," "158," "160," "162," "167," "176," "292," "458," "525," "531," "554," "568," "571," or "680."

Character Child: socket head, jointed composition body; molded and painted hair or good wig; painted or glass eyes; appropriately dressed. Typically marked with mold number "154," "159," "166," 169," "520," "526," "536," "546," "547," "549," or "567."

19" Kley and Hahn 536 Character. *Photo courtesy of McMasters Doll Auction.*

KLEY & HAHN VALUE COMPARISONS:

Size	Named Child, Dolly-Face	Walküre 250/282, Child Doll	Character Baby*	154 Closed Mouth, Glass Eyes*	154 Open Mouth, Glass Eyes	159 2-Faced Doll, Glass Eyes*	159 2-Faced Doll, Painted Eyes*	166 Closed Mouth, Glass Eyes
12"			650.00			2,300.00	2,300.00	
14"			700.00			2,500.00	2,500.00	2,700.00
16"		650.00	800.00	2,800.00		2,700.00	2,700.00	
18"		700.00	850.00	3,100.00	1,700.00			
20"	500.00	750.00	950.00					3,700.00
22"	550.00	800.00	1,050.00					
24"		850.00	1,200.00		2,300.00			
26"	700.00	950.00	1,500.00					
28"	750.00	1,050.00	1,800.00					
30"	800.00	1,200.00						
34"		1,700.00						
36"		1,800.00						
40"		3,100.00						
42"		3,300.00						

KLEY & HAHN VALUE COMPARISONS (CONTINUED):

Size	166 Open Mouth, Glass Eyes*	169 Closed Mouth, Glass Eyes*	169 Open Mouth, Glass Eyes*	520 Closed Mouth, Painted Eyes*	526 Closed Mouth, Painted Eyes*	536/546 Closed Mouth, Glass Eyes*	547 Closed Mouth, Glass Eyes*	549 Closed Mouth, Painted Eyes	567 Multi-Face, Glass or Painted Eyes*
12"									
14"	1,600.00	2,500.00		3,600.00				4,000.00	2,700.00
16"				4,400.00		4,500.00	6,500.00		2,900.00
18"		3,600.00		4,800.00	4,500.00	5,200.00	6,800.00	4,700.00	3,200.00
20"			1,400.00		4,800.00				
22"	2,000.00				4,800.00			5,800.00	
24"			1,700.00						

* Add an additional $500.00 to any above value for a toddler body.

Knickerbocker Doll & Toy Company

The Knickerbocker Doll & Toy Company was established in New York City in 1925. Leo L. Weiss was the president of the Knickerbocker Doll & Toy Company, and A.S. Ferguson was the company's representative. Disney characters are among the premium products of this well-known American firm. Value is not only based on the condition of the doll, but upon the popularity of the character portrayed.

Reproductions of Knickerbocker Dolls do not seem to be a problem. The company had exclusive rights to very few dolls; most were also made by another toy company.

Prices listed are for dolls with no damage. The early dolls of composition and cloth may show some slight crazing. It is getting increasingly more difficult to find perfect examples and, therefore, collectors recently have not only been accepting, but sometimes even expecting signs of aging. The later modern dolls should be in very good condition as there is little forgiveness for less-than-perfect dolls. Slight wear or surface dust does not greatly affect value. If an early doll is badly crazed, cracking, or peeling, or if the composition has been repainted, expect to pay less than half the amount listed. Cloth dolls which are badly soiled, stained, faded, or degraded are also worth less than half the amount listed.

See also Raggedy Ann & Andy.

CLOTH DOLLS

Dwarf: heavy oil cloth-type pressed mask face, seam at sides of head; velveteen body in various colors with clothing being part of the body structure; cardboard in bottom of feet, arms stitched on at shoulders, cotton gauntlet hands; mohair wig and beard; painted expressive face; extra piece of velveteen at bottom of coat and for belt at waistline; slightly pointed brown velveteen feet curved upwards; wearing original cap with name printed in front in all capital letters, some letters printed on a slant. Marked with wrist

Knickerbocker's Ferdinand the Bull and Jiminy Cricket. *Photo courtesy of McMasters Doll Auction.*

tag only, "Walt Disney's/Snow White and/The Seven Dwarfs" on one side and on reverse "American's/Premier Line of/Stuffed Toys/Walt Disney's/Mickey Mouse/and/Donald Duck/Manufacturers/Knickerbocker Toy Co. Inc./New York City."

Disney Characters: all cloth, stuffed body; applied oil cloth eyes; appropriately dressed. Marked with tag "(Character Name) Mfg. Knickerbocker." All characters are comparable in quality. Value is largely based on the popularity of the character.

Katzenjammer Kids (Hans, Mama, Captain, or Inspector): all cloth; applied and painted hair; cloth stitched on ears; glass button bug-eyes; bulbous stuffed nose, painted facial accent features and closed mouth; appropriately dressed. Marked with wrist tag only, "Katzenjammer/Kids/Fritz/Knickerbocker/Toy Co. Inc./New York Toy Co. Inc./New York/Licensed by King Features Syndicate, Inc."

Holly Hobbie: stitched at shoulders and hips, mitt-type hands; yellow yarn hair; printed facial features with blue eyes and lashes; small smiling mouth; dress and matching bonnet. Marked with tag sewn into dress "Holly Hobbie/ Knickerbocker Toy Co. Inc." Tags may vary.

COMPOSITION

Dwarf: all composition, jointed at neck and shoulders; painted hair and beard; painted eyes and expressive facial features; dressed in velvet plush outfit; name printed on front of cap in all capital letters, some letters slanted. Marked "Walt Disney Knickerbocker Toy Co." on back.

Snow White: all composition, jointed at neck, shoulders, and hips; mohair wig or molded and painted black hair with molded and painted blue ribbon; painted brown eyes looking to side; closed mouth; wearing original satin and velvet dress with matching cape. Marked "Snow White Walt Disney" on head and "Knickerbocker Toy Co." on body.

Girl: all composition, jointed at neck, shoulders, and hips; mohair wig; sleep eyes, light gray eye shadow; open mouth; appropriately dressed. Marked "Knickerbocker Toy Co./New York" on back.

VINYL

Annie: vinyl head, plastic body, rigid vinyl limbs; rooted hair; painted eyes; smiling mouth; dressed in original red cotton dress with white collar, white socks and black shoes. Marked "1982 CPI Inc. 1982 CTNYNS, Inc/1982 Knickerbocker Toy Co. Inc. H-15."

Little House on the Prairie Child: vinyl head, cloth body, vinyl hands and legs; rooted hair; painted eyes; smiling mouth; wearing original cotton dress with name printed on front pocket. Marked "1978 ED FRIENDLY PRODUCTIONS INC/LIC JLM/Made in Taiwan T-2" on back of head; dress tagged "Little House on the Prairie Made by Knickerbocker Toy Co."

Soupy Sales: vinyl head, cloth body; molded and painted hair; character face with painted eyes and heavy brows; closed smiling mouth; non-removable clothes with polka-dot bow tie. Marked "1965 Knickerbocker" on back of head; tagged "Soupy Sales/1966 Soupy Sales W.M.C."

				CLOTH KNICKERBOCKER VALUE COMPARISONS:						
Size	Cloth Dwarf (each)	Cloth Mickey Mouse*	Cloth Pinocchio	Cloth Donald Duck	Cloth Jiminy Cricket	Cloth Minnie Mouse	Cloth Snow White	Katzenjammer Kid	Cloth Holly Hobbie
10"									50.00
13"	325.00	850.00	550.00	700.00	750.00	700.00	550.00	600.00	
14"								700.00	
16"								900.00	75.00
24"									125.00

*Mickey in original cowboy outfit with sheepskin chaps, guns, lasso and hat is quite rare and valued at $1,500.00 or more.

	COMPOSITION KNICKERBOCKER VALUE COMPARISONS:		
Size	Composition Dwarf (each)	Snow White	Girl
9"	350.00		
14"		500.00	
15"			400.00
20"		700.00	

	VINYL KNICKERBOCKER VALUE COMPARISONS:			
Size	Annie	Daddy Warbucks	Little House Characters	Soupy Sales
7"	25.00	25.00		
12"			40.00	
13"				185.00

Koenig & Wernicke

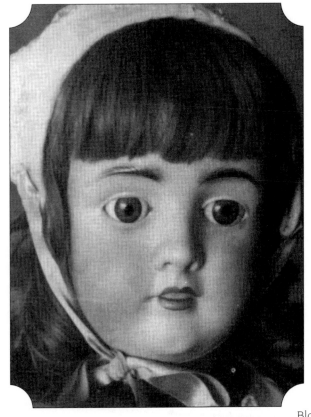

Köenig & Wernicke 4711 character Baby. *Photo courtesy McMasters Doll Auction.*

There are several points of disagreement concerning the Koenig & Wernicke (also spelled König & Wernicke) doll factory of Waltershausen, Thüringia, Germany. Uncertainty exists regarding the identities of the founders and owners, in addition to the spelling of their names. One fact that is undisputed is the date of the company's founding—1911.

Koenig & Wernicke was originally Koenig & Rudolph of Walterhausen. This team was made of up of Max Koenig (König), and Max and August Rudolph. One year later, in 1912, Max and August Rudolph left the company and their share was taken over by Rudolf Wernicke. Some reports state that Max and August retired. However, their names surfaced intermittently in the doll industry over the next ten years. Nevertheless, the Rudolphs were out and Rudolf Wernicke was in.

Koenig & Wernicke's bisque doll heads were poured at the porcelain factories of Bähr and Pröschild, Hertel, Schwab & Company, and Armand Marseille. Koenig & Wernicke supplied dolls under the trade name "My Playmate" to George Borgfeldt, New York. Koenig & Wernicke is best known for its well decorated character babies made from fine quality bisque.

Coincidentally, several mold numbers registered by Koenig & Wernicke are identical to Simon & Halbig mold numbers. There is no known relationship between the two companies.

Prices listed are for dolls with no damage to the bisque. Normal wear, slight damage, or well-done repairs to the body do not greatly affect price. When the bisque is damaged or repaired, expect to pay less than half the amount listed. It is perfectly acceptable to show a missing or replaced finger or joint to the body.

Character Baby: socket head, bent-limb baby body; good wig; glass eyes; open mouth; appropriately dressed. Typically marked "Made in Germany" and mold numbers "98," "99," "170," "179," or "1070," body may also be stamped "Germany/K&W." Blown glass eyes may be reflective, and appear to follow the viewer; however, these eyes do not move except to sleep.

Character Child: very rare character bisque socket head, jointed wood-and-composition body; closed mouth; glass eyes. Usually marked with a "K & W" and no mold number.

KOENIG & WERNICKE VALUE COMPARISONS:

Size	Character Baby*	Character Child
10"	600.00	
12"	650.00	
14"	750.00	
16"	850.00	3,200.00
18"	900.00	
20"	950.00	3,800.00
22"	1,050.00	
24"	1,250.00	4,200.00
26"	1,400.00	

* Add an additional $400.00 for Toddler Body.

Richard G. Krueger Inc.

Two of the Seven Dwarfs, Doc and Sleepy with Ideal's Mask-face Snow White. *Photo courtesy of McMasters Doll Auction.*

Richard Krueger produced cloth dolls in New York City from 1920 through the 1930s. Krueger was also involved with King Innovations, the sole licensed manufacturer of soft-stuffed Kewpie dolls. This license was granted by Rose O'Neill and was fully protected by copyrights, trademarks, and United States patents.

Krueger produced a wide variety of dolls, including stuffed animals and rag dolls. Oil cloth was frequently used for the bodies and or costumes. Most dolls are marked with a cloth label sewn either to the doll or its clothing.

Prices listed are for dolls in very good condition. Look for dolls with good decoration, bright color, high visual appeal, and in original condition. If the doll is well worn, shows rubs or discoloration, is badly faded, stained, or torn, or has been repainted, expect to pay less than half the amount listed. Slight signs of aging and surface dust do not greatly affect price.

See also Kewpies.

Pinocchio: pressed and molded cloth character face, attached ears, cloth body, jointed wooden arms and legs; appropriately dressed. Body labeled "Authentic Walt Disney/R. G. Krueger."

Dwarf: pressed and molded cloth face, side seams, velveteen body, arms stitched on at shoulders, polished cotton gauntlet hands; plush beard, painted facial features; clothing and body as one; extra piece of velveteen at waist; "(Character Name)" stamped on top of hat in capital letters. Marked with cloth body label "Authentic Walt Disney/Character/Exclusive/with R. G. Krueger, New York."

Oilcloth Child: heavy buckram-type, mask face with side seams; flesh tone, soft cotton body and limbs, jointed at shoulders and hips; mitt hands with no stitching to indicate fingers; mohair wig; painted facial features; delicately applied eyelashes; freckles across nose; closed smiling mouth; appropriately dressed. Marked with body label "R Krueger/N.Y.C." and dress tag "Krueger, N.Y./Reg. U.S. Pat. Off./Made in U.S.A."

Cotton Child: mask-type face, cotton body; yarn hair; painted features; appropriately dressed. Body labeled "Krueger, N.Y./Reg. U.S. Pat. Off. Made in U.S.A."

KRUEGER VALUE COMPARISONS:

Size	Pinocchio	Dwarf (Each)	Oilcloth Child	Cotton Child
12"		275.00		
12½"			200.00	75.00
15"	500.00			
16"			250.00	125.00

Käthe Kruse

äthe Kruse Dolls have been in production from 1910 to the present. Formerly located in Bad Kosen, Silesia, and Charlottenburg, Prussia, after World War II they moved to Donauworth, Bavaria. The company was founded by artist Käthe Kruse. Legend tells us that Käthe's husband was not in favor of his children playing with toys purchased at stores. To amuse her daughters, Käthe tied a towel to resemble a doll. The girls were happy for awhile, but eventually the towel came undone. Attempting to amuse her children, Käthe continued to improve her dolls, a task which ultimately developed into a successful business.

Käthe Kruse Dolls were from waterproof treated muslin, cotton wool, and stockinet. The earliest dolls were marked in black, red, or purple ink on the bottom of the foot with the name "Käthe Kruse" and a three- to five-digit number.

Käthe Kruse spent years developing a soft life-like cloth doll that could withstand a child's loving. Daughter Hannah took over the doll manufacturing business after her mother's death in 1968.

Reproduction Käthe Kruse Dolls are not as big a problem as Käthe Kruse copies. Kruse was forced several times to bring litigation on infringement rights against competing doll manufacturers. While records indicate that she was always victorious, many Käthe Kruse-type Dolls were produced before a settlement was reached. Pay particular attention to markings on the bottom of the feet. Also, authentic Käthe Kruse Dolls typically have detailed toes. Sculpturing of the face and a doll's decoration may also provide clues to its authenticity.

Prices listed are for dolls with no damage. If torn, soiled, stained, repainted, or damaged in any way, expect to pay about one-half the amount listed.

Doll I: 1910, all muslin, sturdy toddler body; heavy oil-painted hair; well painted eyes; closed mouth with pensive expression. This series can be identified by three vertical seams on back of head.

Doll II: 1922, Schlenkerchen; all stockinet, arms and legs are supple and loose on soft body; heavy oil-painted hair; nicely painted eyes with upper lashes; smiling open/closed mouth. This series can be identified by one vertical seam on back of head.

Doll V and VI: 1925, all cloth; heavy oil-painted hair; nicely painted facial features; closed, rather sad and pouty mouth; wigs added after 1930. Traumerchen have closed eyes with lashes. Du Mein have open eyes. Both dolls are found in both V and IV sizes. These dolls are often found weighted down with about five pounds of sand.

Doll VII: 1927, all cloth, heavy oil painted hair; nicely painted facial features, pensive face of Doll I or pouty Du Mein face; wigs were added to some dolls after 1929.

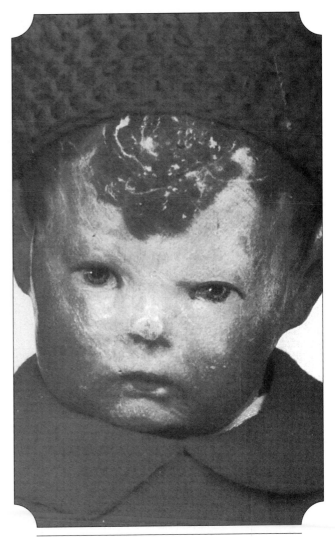

16" Käthe Kruse Type I. *Photo courtesy of McMasters Doll Auction.*

Doll VIII: 1929, all cloth, swivel head; human hair wig; painted facial features; closed mouth. This series can be identified by one vertical seam on back of head.

Doll IX: 1929, same as Doll VIII; smaller 14" size.

Doll X: 1935, swivel head; same type face as Doll I; smaller 14" size.

Celluloid: 1936-1939, all celluloid; same characteristics as earlier cloth dolls.

U.S. Zone/Germany: 1945-1951, very heavily painted; often with turtle mark.

Hard Plastic: 1952, pink muslin body; human hair wig; painted eyes.

KÄTHE KRUSE VALUE COMPARISONS:

Series	Size	Description	Excellent Condition
I, Early	16"	Wide hips	$5,400.00
I, Later	17"	More slender hips	4,200.00
I, 1H	17"	Wigged	3,600.00
I, Bambino	8½"	Special doll	2,600.00
II	13"		5,200.00
V	17½ to 19½"	Du Mein, open eyes	4,200.00
V	17½ to 19½"	Traumerchen, closed eyes	4,100.00
VI	21½ to 23½"	Du Mein, open eyes	4,400.00
VI	21½ to 23½"	Traumerchen, closed eyes	4,200.00
VII	14"	Wide hips	2,900.00
VIII	21"		3,200.00
IX	14"	Swivel head	2,200.00
X	14"		2,000.00
Celluloid	16"		600.00
US Zone/Germany	14"		1,600.00
Hard Plastic	14"		450.00
Hard Plastic	20"		800.00
Contemporary	10"		250.00
Contemporary	14"		350.00

Gerbrüder Kuhnlenz

The firm of Gebrüder Kuhnlenz was founded by brothers Julius, Cuno, and Bruno Kuhnlenz in 1884. The Porzellanfabric (porcelain factory) was located in Kronach, Bavaria. The dolls from this factory were long thought to be from Gebrüder Knoch or Gebrüder Krauss. However, thanks to extensive research by Jurgen and Marianne Cieslik, we now know about Gebrüder Kuhnlenz and its wonderful dolls.

Kuhnlenz Dolls were once advertised as "Doll heads with strange features." Perhaps "strange" is too strong a term to describe a doll that is not easily forgotten. Kuhnlenz Dolls are certainly lovely. The bisque tends to be quite pale; brows are usually heavy and close together. It is not unusual to find good quality paperweight eyes with black outlining and long finely painted lashes. The open-mouth doll has square, unglazed teeth, with lips more orange than red. Closed-mouth dolly-face dolls are of very good quality and are made from a pale bisque with delicate coloring.

Gebrüder Kuhnlenz also produced dolls with less dramatic expressions. Although they are quite pleasing, they do not command as high a price. It is essential that individual dolls be evaluated carefully.

25" Kuhnlenz 54 Character. *Courtesy of Leah and Gene Patterson.*

Many doll collectors believe Gebrüder Kuhnlenz supplied doll heads for the French market. Few can dispute the fact that Kuhnlenz dolls have a touch of "French" in them.

Typical mold numbers now attributed to Gebrüder Kuhnlenz include 13, 21, 27, 31, 32, 34, 36, 38, 44, 54, 68, 71, 72, 75, 76, and 77.

Prices listed are for dolls with no damage to the bisque. Normal wear, slight damage, or well-done repairs to the body do not greatly affect price. If the bisque is damaged or repaired, expect to pay less than half the amount listed. It is perfectly acceptable to show a missing or replaced finger or joint to the body.

Closed Mouth: pale bisque, shoulder head, kid body, often lady-type; bisque arms; good wig; good quality glass or paperweight eyes, softly feathered brows, delicately painted eye lashes; beautifully blushed; closed mouth; appropriately dressed. Typically marked "G K 38."

Closed Mouth: pale bisque socket head, jointed wood-and-composition; good wig; good quality glass or paperweight eyes, heavy feathered brows; closed mouth; appropriately dressed. Typically marked "32" or "31."

French Look: pale bisque socket head, French body; good wig; good quality glass or paperweight eyes, feathered brows; closed mouth; appropriately dressed. Typically marked "34."

Unique Look: socket head, jointed wood-and-composition body; good wig; good quality glass or paperweight eyes, eyeliner, long lashes, heavy brows; open mouth; appropriately dressed. Typically marked "GK," "41," "44," "54," or "56."

Open Mouth Shoulder Head: kid body, bisque arms; good wig; glass eyes with black outlining, heavy brows; open mouth; appropriately dressed. Typically marked "13," "61," or "47."

Typical Dolly-Face, Socket Head: jointed wood-and-composition body; good wig; glass eyes, feathered

7" Kuhnlenz 44 Tiny Child Doll.

brows; open mouth; appropriately dressed. Typically marked "G.K." or "165."

Tiny Doll: socket head, five-piece composition body with molded and painted shoes; good wig; glass eyes; open mouth; appropriately dressed. Marked with sun burst and "44."

Size	Closed Mouth, Shoulder Head, Kid Body	Closed Mouth, Socket Head, Jointed Body	French-Look, Closed Mouth, French Body	Unique-Look, Open Mouth, Jointed Body	Open Mouth, Shoulder Head, Kid Body	Dolly-Face Open Mouth, Jointed Body	Tiny Doll
7½"							350.00
14"	1,300.00		3,800.00				
16"	1,500.00	2,200.00		1,000.00	700.00	550.00	
18"	1,600.00	2,400.00	4,500.00	1,100.00	800.00	600.00	
20"	1,700.00	2,700.00	5,200.00	1,200.00	900.00	650.00	
22"	1,900.00			1,400.00		750.00	
24"	2,100.00			1,500.00			
28"				2,000.00		1,000.00	
30"						1,200.00	
32"						1,400.00	
34"						1,600.00	

GEBRÜDER KUHNLENZ VALUE COMPARISONS:

A. Lanternier et Cie

A. Lanternier et Cie was a late arrival on the French doll scene. Although the company was in operation since about 1855, it was not until 1915 that it began producing doll heads. Many of the dolls produced by Lanternier have an interesting and dramatic face, with distinctive modeling. Others are less appealing. Considering this porcelain factory was located in Limoges, France, a city known worldwide for its porcelain products, the vast difference in the quality of the bisque is startling, ranging from very good to coarse and grainy.

Despite the varying quality of the dolls, particularly when compared to their German counterparts of the same era, Lanternier Dolls command relatively high prices. This is often the result of a collector being overzealous in their desire to own a first (or second or third) French doll and showing little regard for the variations in quality and excellence of production. Be patient and take the time to find a Lanternier doll that will satisfy both your taste and pocketbook. A great variety of markings have been found on dolls attributed to Lanternier et Cie. Marks include trade names such as "Caprice," "Cherie," "Favorite," "La Georgienne," "Lorraine," "Masson," or "Toto," or they may be the initials "CC" of J. E. Masson or the word "Limoges."

Prices listed are for dolls with no damage. Normal wear, slight damage, or well-done repairs to the body do not greatly affect price. If the bisque is damaged or repaired, expect to pay less than half the amount listed. It is perfectly acceptable to show a missing or repaired finger or joint to the body.

Character Child: socket head, jointed wood-and-composition body; good wig; jeweled eyes; open/closed mouth with molded upper and lower teeth;

14" Lanternier Toto Character on jointed Toddler Body. *Courtesy Helen Brooke.*

appropriately dressed. Typically marked "Limoges" with anchor and "Toto."

Child Doll: standard quality, bisque socket head, jointed wood-and-composition body; good wig; glass eyes with black outlining, lower lashes painted straight up and down with no slant; pierced ears; open mouth with molded teeth; appropriately dressed. Typically marked "Fabrication Francaise" with a box/"Limoges" or "Limoges."

Child: better quality, nice decoration, bisque socket head, jointed wood-and-composition body; good wig; very good quality glass or paperweight eyes outlined with black, nicely painted eyelashes; pierced ears; open, slightly smiling mouth with molded teeth; appropriately dressed. Typically marked "Depose Fabrication Francaise" within a box/"FAVORITE/J. E. Masson/AL & Cie/Limoges," "Cherie," or "Caprice."

Lady Lanternier: bisque socket head designed by J.E. Masson; five-piece lady body, long graceful arms and legs, molded and painted high heel pumps; good wig; glass eyes with black outline; open/closed mouth with molded upper teeth; high color to face; appropriately dressed. Marked "J. E. Masson/LORRAINE/No. 0/A. L & Cie/Limoges."

A. LANTERNIER ET CIE VALUE COMPARISONS:

Size	Character Child	Child, Standard Quality	Child, Better Quality	Lady Lanternier
12"	900.00			
14"	1,000.00			
16"	1,200.00	750.00	950.00	1,400.00
18"	1,400.00	800.00	1,000.00	1,600.00
20"	1,500.00	900.00		
22"		1,000.00	1,200.00	
24"		1,100.00	1,300.00	
26"		1,300.00	1,500.00	
28"		1,600.00	1,900.00	
30"		2,100.00	2,400.00	

 Lenci

The Lenci Doll history of Turin, Italy, is well documented and quite interesting. Young Elana Konig Scavini was left alone when her husband, Enrico, went off to the war in 1918. Elana and her brother, Bubine Konig, made the first felt doll in the Scavini's apartment. Bubine steam-pressed the faces and Elana did the artistic work. This was the beginning of the world-famous Lenci doll.

There are at least two versions of the origin of the name Lenci. The more romantic is that Lenci was a nickname given to Elana by her husband before he went off to war. This may be true, as there is evidence of Elana having been known by this name as early as 1915, when a gift of a bronze likeness was given to her with the name "Lenci" engraved on it. However, the Lenci Company itself gives an entirely different explanation. According to the company, the Lenci trademark was registered in 1919 as a child's spinning top with the words "Ludus Est Nobis Constanter Industria (taken from the Latin motto which freely translated means "To Play Is Our Constant Work.") The first letters from the motto spelled out "LENCI."

By the 1920s, the dolls produced by the Lenci factory had achieved worldwide recognition for their artistic beauty. Lenci was the first company to produce dolls using the pressed-felt method to give the faces dimensional character. Collectors and dealers will often refer to a series when speaking of Lenci Dolls, such as Bambino, which is a bent-limb baby, or doll codes such as 110, 500, 109, 950, and 169 which are child dolls. Child dolls with a hollow felt torso belong to the 300 series; pouty-face child dolls in the 1500 series; lady or man dolls in the 165 series; and girl dolls in the 700 series.

Lenci dolls are often marked with a hang tag or clothing label, or a purple or black ink stamped "Lenci" on the bottom of a foot. This stamp has a tendency to wear off easily.

OTHER CHARACTERISTICS OF LENCI DOLLS INCLUDE:

1. Zigzag stitching on back of neck, through tops of arms and legs, and occasionally at crotch.
2. Ears on larger dolls (over 10" tall) are double thickness of felt sewn together and then top stitched.
3. Human hair or mohair is attached in rows or strips.
4. Hollow cardboard bodies covered with felt or cloth; occasionally stuffed.
5. Well-shaped and proportioned arms and legs; slight elbow bend.
6. Nicely formed hands with separate thumb; mitt-type stitched fingers or separate fingers with third and fourth fingers stitched together.

1920s Glass Eyed Lenci. *Courtesy of Glady's Dichter.*

7. Beautifully sculptured face with pleasingly round cheeks and soft expression.
8. Two white dots in each eye; one in upper right hand corner and other in lower left hand corner.
9. Artistically applied two-tone lip color.
10. White milk glass buttons on felt and/or organdy clothing; three or four holes in shoe buttons.
11. Scalloped top socks.

While ostensibly produced as playthings for children, their sophisticated design and high prices resulted in many Lenci dolls being purchased as "playthings" for adults, which explains why so many vintage Lenci dolls are found in near mint condition.

There are many reports of Lenci-type dolls found with "Lenci" stamped on the foot. Rubber stamps are easily duplicated. Fakes can be spotted by using the above characteristics to identify authentic Lenci dolls.

Prices listed are for undamaged dolls in original clothing. If the doll is torn, stained, badly moth eaten, or missing its original clothing, expect to pay about half the amount listed. Character dolls with extremely high visual appeal, elaborate costumes, or which are historically noteworthy may be valued much higher.

Adult, Teenager, or Child: all felt, jointed at neck, shoulders, and hips; mohair wig; painted side-glancing eyes; closed mouth; original clothing. Typically marked with hang tag, clothing label, and "Lenci" stamped on foot, or unmarked.

Bambino: bent-limb baby body, hand in fist position; mohair wig; painted side-glancing eyes; closed mouth; wearing original costume. Typically marked with "Bambino" hang tag or "Bambino" clothing label.

Floppy Limb Felt Dolls: all felt, swivel neck, long arms and legs; mohair wig; felt disk eyes sewn to face; painted rosy cheeks; felt lips; dressed in felt costume. Typically marked with brown cardboard tag attached to clothing.

1930s Painted Eyed Lenci. *Photo courtesy of Sotheby's.*

LENCI VALUE COMPARISONS:

Size	Adult, Teenager, or Child	Bambino	Floppy Limb	Mascotte	Miniature	Fat Sports Character	Brown Islander	Cheeked Child
9"				350.00				
10"					450.00			
12"	1,000.00							
14"	1,200.00	2,400.00						
16"	1,400.00	2,600.00				2,800.00	2,200.00	2,600.00
18"	1,600.00	2,800.00						
20"	1,800.00	3,000.00						
22"	2,200.00							
24"	2,400.00		250.00					
26"	2,600.00							
28"	2,800.00							
30"	3,000.00							
32"	3,200.00							
34"	3,500.00							
36"	3,600.00		350.00					
38"	3,800.00							
40"	4,200.00							

Size	Aviator (Amelia Earhart)	Tom Mix	Oriental	Indian Holding Papoose	Mozart, Bach, and Mendel	Surprised Eyes	Googly Eyes	Rudolph Valentino
17"			3,900.00					
18"	4,000.00	3,800.00		5,500.00	4,000.00			
20"						3,000.00		
24"							3,400.00	
29"								15,000.00

Mascotte: loop at top for hanging; all felt; mohair wig; painted side-glancing eyes, raised sculptured eyebrows; closed mouth, surprised expression; wearing original tagged costume.

Miniature: all felt; mohair wig; painted, round, side-glancing surprised eyes, raised sculptured brows; mouth painted with surprised "oh" expression; wearing original tagged costume.

OTHER LENCI TREASURES

Lenci Head: wearing hat with felt loop for hanging; used for decorative purposes **150.00**

Lenci Head: wrapped in felt petals forming flowers and planted into clay pot; several Lenci flowers in shades of yellow, green, and violet. **700.00**

Lenci Head: with cap on top of basket with lid. . . .**150.00**

Lenci Pan: all green pincushion; beautifully decorated with bright felt. **400.00**

Pocketbook: all felt lady with handle being part of doll; painted face with side-glancing eyes; beautifully dressed. **500.00**

Smooth Face Girl: pressed felt face, finished to resemble composition; painted eyes, rosy cheeks, closed mouth. **1,400.00**

Lenci-Types

So popular and successful were the Lenci dolls that many companies could not resist the temptation to copy them. In many cases they even copied the label designs. A sampling of companies which produced copies of Lenci dolls include: Alma, Alpha, Alexander, American Stuffed Novelty, Amfelt, Averill, Chad Valley, Celia, Davis, Deans, Eros, Fiori, Giotti, La Rosa, Magis, Perotti, Pori, Raynal, and Wellings. Although several Lenci-Type dolls are quite charming and well made, the artistry of authentic Lenci dolls makes them unique.

Prices listed are for undamaged in original clothing. If the doll is torn, stained, moth eaten, or missing its original clothing, expect to pay less than half the amount listed.

Child: all felt or cloth; mohair wig; painted features; nicely dressed in original felt or organdy costume. Typically marked with cloth label, paper tag, wrist tag, or unmarked.

Novelty: all felt; mohair wig; painted features; often dressed in ethnic, military, or comic costumes. Typically marked with cloth label, paper tag, wrist tag, or unmarked.

LENCI-TYPE VALUE COMPARISONS:		
Size	Child	Novelty
7½"		75.00
12"		150.00
14"	650.00	
16"	750.00	
18"	800.00	
20"	850.00	

7½" Eros.

A. G. Limbach

20" Limbach Child Doll.

This factory was founded in 1772 by Gotthelf Greiner near Alsbach, Thüringia, Germany. A.G. Limbach was an early pioneer in the doll industry. The Sonneberg Museum has identified a china shoulder-head doll dating from 1850 as having been made by Limbach. The most beautiful of the Limbach bisque doll heads were produced from 1893 until 1899, when the production of bisque doll heads was discontinued.

Early bisque doll heads are marked only with the clover-leaf trademark and a size number. Most are socket heads on composition bodies, but occasionally a bisque shoulder plate is used with a kid and/or cloth body. The manufacture of bisque doll heads was resumed in 1919 when the trade name of Norma, Rita, or Wally began to appear, along with the cloverleaf and crown mark. During the twenty year interim, Limbach continued to manufacture small jointed dolls, bathing dolls, and all bisque dolls and figurines.

Prices listed are for dolls with no damage to the bisque. Normal wear, slight damage, or well-done repairs to the body do not greatly affect price. If the bisque is damaged or repaired, expect to pay less than half the amount listed. It is perfectly acceptable to show a missing or repaired finger or joint to the body.

See also All Bisque.

Early Child Doll: bisque socket head, full lower cheeks, jointed composition-and-wood or shoulder plate on kid body; good wig; large oval-shaped eyes; closed mouth; appropiately dressed. Typically marked with clover leaf and size number.

Later Child Doll: bisque socket head, jointed wood-and-composition body; good wig; glass eyes; open mouth; appropriately dressed. Typically marked "Wally," "Norma," or "Rita/3/0/crown/cloverleaf/Limbach."

Character Baby: socket head, bent-limb baby body or composition body, solid dome; painted or glass eyes; open/closed mouth; appropriately dressed. Typically marked with mold number "8682." This doll is similar in appearance to character dolls produced by Swaine & Company.

A. G. LIMBACH VALUE COMPARISONS:

Size	Early Closed Mouth	Early Open Mouth	Later "Named" Open Mouth	Character Baby
12"	2,700.00	1,000.00		1,400.00
14"	2,800.00	1,100.00	600.00	
16"	2,900.00	1,200.00	650.00	1,600.00
18"	3,000.00	1,300.00	700.00	
20"	3,200.00	1,450.00	725.00	
22"	3,500.00	1,600.00	750.00	
24"	3,700.00	1,800.00	800.00	

Armand Marseille

Armand Marseille founded this famous doll company in 1885, in Sonneberg and Köppelsdorf, Thüringia, Germany.

Armand Marseille was born in 1856 in St. Petersburg (Leningrad), Russia, where his father was an architect. Around 1860, the Marseille family left Russia, roamed Europe for a time, and eventually settled in Coburg, which was then Thuringia and is now Bavaria. In 1884, Armand Marseille bought the toy factory of Mathias Lambert in Sonneberg, and the next year took possession of the Porcelain Factory of Lidbermann & Wegscher in Köppelsdorf.

From 1900 until 1930, Armand Marseille was one of the largest suppliers of bisque doll heads in the world, reportedly producing a thousand heads a day. Companies which used these heads include Amberg, Arranbee, C.M. Bergmann, Borgfeldt, Butler Bros., Cuno & Otto Dressel, Eckart, Edelmann, Otto Gans, Goldberger, Hitz, Jacobs & Kassler, Illfelder, E. Maar, Montgomery Ward, Emil Pfeiffer, Peter Scherf, Seyfarth & Reinhardt, Siegel Cooper, E.U. Steiner, Wagner & Wetzsche, Wislizenus, and Louis Wolf.

The incidence of reproductions is not as troublesome as in other antique bisque doll categories. Occasionally, a character face will surface on the secondary market which is an intentional fraud. Always inspect the markings. Check for names, initials, and dates that should not be there. Bisque used by Armand Marseille will not be satiny smooth. The decoration, though well done, will not have a perfect art-like application. Many of the reproductions appear to be precisely decorated. This was not the case with the mass-produced dolls of the time.

Prices listed are for dolls with no damage to the bisque. Normal wear, slight damage, or well-done repairs to the body do not greatly affect price. If the bisque is damaged or repaired, expect to pay less than half the amount listed. It is perfectly acceptable to show a missing or repaired finger or joint to the body.

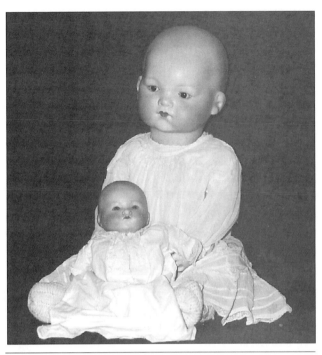

20" and 14" Dream Babies. *Courtesy of Helen Brooke.*

24" Queen Louise.

23" A.M. 400. Character on Flapper Body. *Photo courtesy of Helen Brooke.*

Standard Dolly-Face, Shoulder Head: kid body or imitation kid body; good wig; glass eyes, some with fur brows; open mouth; appropriately dressed. Typically marked "Made in Germany," "A.M.," "Armand Marseille," "270," "309," "370," "376," "920," "957," "2015," "3200," "Alma," "Darling," "Duchess," "Floradora," "Lily," "Lissy," "Mabel," "My Dearie," "My Playmate," or "Rosebud." A shoulder head with an exceptionally pretty face should be priced accordingly

Better Dolly-Face, Shoulder Head: kid body; good wig; glass eyes; open mouth; appropriately dressed. Typically marked "AM/DEP/Made in Germany," "Armand Marseille," "1374," "1890," "1892," "1894," "1895," "1897," "1899," "1900," "1901," "1902," "1903," "1905," "1909," "3091," "3093," "3095," "3200," "3300," "3500," "3700," "4008," "Baby Betty," "Beauty," "Jubilee," "Majestic," "Princess," or "Queen Louise."

Bisque Socket Head: jointed wood-and-composition body; good wig; glass eyes; open mouth; appropriately dressed. Typically marked "Made in Germany/Armand Marseille," "384," "390," "390n," "391," "395," "1894," "1897," "2010," "3600," "Baby Betty," "Floradora," "Queen Louise," or "Rosebud." Note that several dolls share a name with shoulder heads.

22" A.M. 390. One look at this sweet face explains why 390's were and are so popular. *Courtesy of Leah and Gene Patterson.*

ARMAND MARSEILLE VALUE COMPARISONS:

Size	Dolly-Face, Shoulder Head, Open Mouth, Standard Quality*	Dolly-Face, Open Mouth, Better Quality*	Dolly-Face, Open Mouth, Composition Body*	Character Lady	Character Baby, Bent-Limb Baby Body	Infant Cloth Body	Infant Composition Body	Named Character, Flange Neck	Named Character, Shoulder Head
8"					450.00	350.00	400.00	600.00	700.00
10"	200.00	300.00	325.00	1,400.00	500.00	400.00	500.00	700.00	750.00
12"	250.00	350.00	325.00	1,700.00	550.00	450.00	550.00	800.00	600.00
14"	300.00	400.00	350.00	2,000.00	650.00	550.00	650.00	900.00	650.00
16"	325.00	425.00	400.00	2,500.00	850.00	700.00	800.00		700.00
18"	400.00	500.00	450.00	3,100.00	900.00	750.00	850.00	1,000.00	800.00
20"	450.00	550.00	500.00	3,700.00	950.00	800.00	900.00		
22"	500.00	600.00	550.00	4,200.00	1,100.00	900.00	1,000.00		1,000.00
24"	525.00	625.00	600.00	4,800.00	1,200.00				
26"	550.00	650.00	800.00		1,400.00				
28"	575.00	675.00	900.00						
30"	600.00	700.00	1,400.00						
34"			1,900.00						
38"			2,400.00						
40"			2,600.00						
42"			2,800.00						

* Add an additional $100.00 for nice soft coloring, or exceptionally pretty doll.

20" A.M. 1894 Dolly-Face.

17" Scowling Character Indian. *Courtesy of Helen Brooke.*

Character Lady: socket head, wood-and-composition "flapper" body with high knee joints or five-piece slender composition lady's body; good wig; glass eyes, soft brows; closed mouth; appropriately dressed. Marked "400" or "401." Some dolls are found with an "M. H." mark.

Character Baby: various characteristics on bent-limb baby body. Typically marked "Germany A. M. DRGM," "256," "326," "327," "329," "347," "352," "360a," "750," "760," "790," "900," "927," "971," "980," "984," "985," "990," "991," "996," "1330," or "1333."

Infant (Dream Baby, Kiddie Joy, Our Pet): composition bent-limb baby body or flange neck with cloth body. Typically marked "AM Germany," "341" (closed mouth), "351," "342" (open mouth) or "Our Pet." A "K" at the end of the marking designates a composition body.

Named Character Baby, Flange Neck: cloth body, composition arms and straight legs; molded and painted hair; sleep eyes with soft brows; open mouth, dimples; appropriately dressed. Typically marked "Baby Gloria/A Germany M," or "Melitta."

Named Character Baby, Shoulder Head: kid body, composition limbs; molded and painted hair; sleep eyes; tiny closed mouth; appropriately dressed. Typically marked "Phyllis Made in Germany," "Baby Betty," or "Ellen."

Character Baby or Child: molded and painted hair or good wig; glass or painted eyes; open, closed, or open/closed mouth; appropriately dressed. Typically marked "AM" only.

ARMAND MARSEILLE CHARACTER BABY VALUE COMPARISONS:

Size	233 OM, Glass Eyes	251/248 OM, Glass Eyes	251/248 CM, Glass Eyes	328 OM, Glass Eyes	410 OM, 2 Rows of Teeth, Glass Eyes	580/590 O/CM, Glass Eyes	920 OM, Glass Eyes	970 Character
12"		1,000.00		650.00		1,300.00		
14"	650.00	1,200.00	2,000.00	700.00	1,600.00	1,500.00		
16"	750.00		3,000.00	950.00	1,800.00			
18"			3,500.00			2,000.00	900.00	800.00
20"	1,000.00			1,300.00			1,000.00	900.00
22"					2,200.00	2,200.00		

ARMAND MARSEILLE CHARACTER CHILD VALUE COMPARISONS:

Size	255 OM, 2 Rows Teeth, Glass Eyes	230 CM, Wig or Solid Dome, Glass Eyes	231 CM, Wig, Glass Eyes	250/248 G.B. OM, Painted Eyes	300 MH CM, Glass Eyes	340 OM, Glass Eyes	345 CM, Painted Eyes	350 CM, Glass Eyes	372 OM, Glass Eyes
9"					1,700.00				
10"				850.00				1,400.00	
12"				1,200.00			1,800.00		600.00
14"			5,200.00	1,500.00		2,800.00	2,200.00		900.00
16"	3,800.00	6,800.00	6,400.00			3,400.00	2,600.00	2,700.00	
18"	4,200.00	8,800.00	8,500.00						
20"		9,400.00						3,500.00	
24"								4,300.00	

Size	375 OM, Glass Eyes	451 OM, Glass Eyes	500 AM 232 CM, Glass Eyes	520 AM 232 CM, Glass Eyes	550 CM, Glass Eyes	560 AM 232 O/CM, Painted Eyes	570AM 232 O/CM, Glass Eyes	600 AM 234 CM, Painted Eyes
10"				800.00			800.00	800.00
12"			900.00		2,400.00	900.00		
14"		900.00	1,200.00			1,200.00		
16"				1,600.00	3,500.00	1,600.00	1,600.00	1,200.00
18"	1,100.00		1,700.00					
20"					4,200.00			
22"	1,400.00			2,200.00			2,200.00	

Size	620 AM 234 O/CM, Glass Eyes	640a AM 234 CM, Painted Eyes	700 CM, Glass Eyes	700 CM, Painted Eyes	701 CM, Glass Eyes	711 CM, Glass Eyes	800 AM 234 O/CM, Glass Eyes	810 O/CM, Glass Eyes
10"						1,400.00		
12"	900.00		3,500.00	2,800.00	1,800.00			1,800.00
14"	1,200.00		4,000.00	3,600.00	2,600.00		2,200.00	2,000.00
16"	1,500.00	1,500.00			3,400.00		3,000.00	
18"						4,200.00		
20"		1,800.00					3,700.00	

Size	820 O/CM, Glass Eyes	950 CM, Painted Eyes	Marked A.M. Only, Character Face, Painted Eyes	Marked A.M. Only, Character Face, Glass Eyes
12"	1,400.00	900.00		
14"	1,600.00	1,200.00	4,200.00	5,200.00
16"		1,400.00	4,700.00	5,700.00

* Add an additional $400.00 for toddler body on any doll.
OM=Open Mouth
CM=Closed Mouth
O/CM=Open/Closed Mouth

Mascotte

*B*ébés bearing the Mascotte label were the creation of May Freres, Cie. from 1882 through 1901. Records indicate that Jules Steiner purchased May Freres and advertised Bébé Mascotte after 1897, as did Jules Mettais, Steiner's successor.

Reproductions and copies of Bébé Mascottes occasionally surface. Copies often bear a date and the signature or initials of the artist or craft person who created the doll. Inspect the body and its markings. Look inside the thigh and upper arm joints. They should be smooth and not show signs of being turned. The bisque should be creamy, but not satiny. Close your eyes and use your fingers lightly to stroke the cheek of a Bébé Mascotte. If the bisque is satiny smooth, beware. The brows of the Bébé Mascotte are often a bit shiny.

Prices listed are for dolls with no damage to the bisque. Normal wear, slight damage, or well-done repairs to the body do not greatly affect price. If the bisque is damaged or repaired, expect to pay about half the amounts listed. It is perfectly acceptable to show a missing or repaired finger or joint to the body.

Bébé: Socket Head, jointed wood-and-composition body; good wig; large paperweight eyes, heavy feathered shiny brows, long thick eyelashes; pierced ears (may be applied); closed mouth with two-tone paint; appropriately dressed. Typically marked "Mascotte I," stamped "Bébé Mascotte/Paris."

18" Bébé Mascotte. *Photo courtesy of McMasters Doll Auction.*

MASCOTTE VALUE COMPARISONS:	
Size	Bébé
10"	3,500.00
13"	3,700.00
15"	4,000.00
17"	4,400.00
19"	4,900.00
21"	5,500.00
23"	5,900.00
25"	6,300.00
27"	6,800.00

Mattel®

*I*n 1945, Mattel established its headquarters in Hawthorne, California. The company, founded by Harold Matson and Elliot Handler, derived its name from a combination of letters from the two partners' names. Mattel, the world's largest toy manufacturer, is probably best known for its Barbie Doll and her friends and family. Initially a producer of doll house furniture, Mattel's toy line was expanded to include music boxes, guns, and a host of other famous dolls such as Chatty Cathy, Sister Bell, Baby First Step, Cheerful-Tearful, Dancerina, and Talking Mrs. Beasley. Because of the innovative dolls created at Mattel, it is understandable why security is one of Mattel's top priorities. The company's research department, headed by a former missile engineer, is strictly off-limits to all but a few employees.

Mattel dolls have attained collectible status faster than dolls produced by any other company. Their high quality and imaginative concepts have no doubt lead to this phenomena. Mattel Dolls are often action oriented. In addition to the walkers and talkers, there are singers, a bike rider, a doll which plays with puppets, another that juggles, and even one that moves her lips as she tells a secret.

Mattel Dolls are well marked. Prices listed are for dolls in mint to near mint condition. Remember, as with any modern or collectible doll, there is very little forgiveness for less-than-perfect dolls. If found dirty, played with, or missing its original clothing or accessories, expect to pay less than half the amount listed.

Doug Davis, Spaceman: 6", all vinyl, posable; molded and painted hair and features. Marked "Mattel Inc./1967/Hong Kong." **50.00**

Tiny Cheerful Tearful: 6½", all vinyl; rooted hair; painted eyes; open mouth; press tummy to change expression from glad to sad. Marked "1966 Mattel Inc. Hong Kong." **35.00**

Kretor and Zark the Shark: 7" Kretor and 12" Zark; Kretor is vinyl frogman, Zark is plastic shark that swims in water and carries Kretor with him; pull-string activated. Marked "6389-0150/2" on Kretor's left foot; "1970 Mattel Inc./Hong Kong/U.S. U For/Patented/Patented in Canada 1970" on Kretor's right foot; "1970 Mattel Inc./Hong Kong/U. S. Patent Pending" on Zark's underside; the set. **175.00**

Gorgeous Creatures: 7½", animals in very womanly bodies; molded-on undies. Marked "Mattel, Inc. 1979 Philippines."

> **Cow Belle:** lavender and blue. **45.00**
>
> **Ms. Giddie Yup:** (horse), hot pink. **45.00**
>
> **Ms. Heavenly Hippo:** yellow. **45.00**
>
> **Princess Pig:** lavender and black. **45.00**

Talking Woody Woodpecker. *Courtesy of Ellen Schroy.*

The Sunshine Family (9½" Steve, 9" Stephie, and 3" Sweets): vinyl heads and arms, plastic bodies, jointed knees; rooted hair; inset eyes; Marked "1973 Mattel Inc." on heads; "1973/Mattel Inc./Taiwan" on back; wrist tag "The Sunshine Family;" the set. **150.00**

Baby Go Bye Bye: 10", vinyl head, plastic body, vinyl limbs; rooted white hair; painted blue eyes; open/closed mouth with two upper teeth. Marked "1968 Mattel Inc./Hong Kong." **35.00**

Buffie: 10", vinyl head, plastic body, vinyl limbs; rooted hair; painted eyes; open/closed mouth with two upper teeth; freckles across nose; holding 3½" Mrs. Beasley doll. Marked "1967/Mattel Inc./U.S. & For./Pats. Pend. Mexico." **200.00**

Valerie: 10½", vinyl head, plastic body, vinyl limbs; rooted blond hair; painted blue eyes; open/closed mouth with two upper and two lower molded teeth. Marked "1967 Mattel Inc./U. S. & For./Pat. Pend../Hong Kong." . .**25.00**

Baby Beans: 11", vinyl head, bean bag body; rooted blond hair; painted features; pull-string talker. Marked "Mattel/Baby Beans/1970" on tag sewn into seam. .**20.00**

Baby Small Talk: 11", all black vinyl; rooted black hair; painted brown eyes; open/closed mouth with two upper and two lower teeth; pull-string talker. Marked "1967 Mattel/Japan" on head. **35.00**

Baby Walk N Play: 11", vinyl head, plastic body, vinyl limbs; rooted yellow hair; painted eyes; open/closed mouth with two upper and two lower teeth; battery operated to play with yo-yo and paddle ball. Marked "1967/Mattel Inc./Hong Kong" on head; "1967 Mattel Inc./US & Foreign Patented" on torso; dress tag reads "1968 Mattel Inc." **35.00**

Bouncy Baby: 11", vinyl head, plastic body, vinyl limbs; rooted hair; painted eyes; open/closed mouth with two upper molded and painted teeth; spring action arms, legs, and head; giggles. Marked "1968 Mattel Inc./Mexico/U. S. Patent Pending" on back; dress tag reads "Bouncy Baby/1968 Mattel Inc./Hong Kong." **25.00**

Small Talk Cinderella: 11", all vinyl; rooted hair; big, painted eyes looking up. Marked "Japan" on head; "1967 Mattel Inc./US & For/Pats. Pend./Mexico" on back; dress tag reads "Small Talk/1968 Mattel Inc. Hong Kong." **40.00**

Sister Small Walk: 11½", vinyl head, plastic body, vinyl limbs; rooted brown hair; painted blue eyes; open/closed mouth with two upper and two lower molded and painted teeth; molded-on socks and shoes. Marked "1967 Mattel Inc./U.S. & Foreign Patented/Other Patents Pending/U.S.A." **25.00**

Gold Medal Big Jack: 12", all rigid black vinyl, jointed at neck, shoulders, wrists, waists, hips, knees, and ankles; boxer; press back to make right arm move. Marked "1971 Mattel, Inc./Hong Kong U. S. & Foreign Patented." **100.00**

Guardian Goddesses: 12", adult figure, test market dolls only, Moonmystic and Sunspell; arms go up and down when limbs are pulled; gowns fly off and reveal "Super Girl" outfit, 1979-1980. . . . .**250.00**

Guardian Goddesses Outfits: Blazing Fire; Ice Empress; Lion Queen; and Soaring Eagle; each. **175.00**

Talking Twin Kip: 12", vinyl head, cloth body; rooted blond hair; painted eyes; two upper and two lower molded and painted teeth; pull-string talker. Marked "1967 Mattel Inc., Japan" on head; "Mattel/Talking Twins 1970 Mattel Inc." on tag sewn into seam. **35.00**

Baby Pattaburp: 13", vinyl head, cloth body, vinyl limbs; rooted hair; sleep eyes with lashes; open mouth; mechanism causes her to burp when patted on back. Marked "Quality Originals By Mattel/Baby Pattaburp/1963 Mattel Inc." on tag sewn into seam. **45.00**

Little Kiddie. *Courtesy of Trina Miller.*

Cheerful Tearful: 13", vinyl head, plastic body, vinyl limbs; rooted hair; painted eyes; open mouth; moving left arm makes face change from sad to glad expression. Marked "1965 Mattel Inc./Hawthorne Calif., U. S. Patents Pending/3036-014-1." **35.00**

Baby Colleen: 14", vinyl head, cloth body; rooted orange hair; painted blue eyes; pull-string talker. Marked "Baby Colleen/1965 Mattel Inc." on tag sewn into seam, Sears exclusive. **35.00**

Shopping Sheryl: 14", vinyl head, plastic body, jointed at shoulders, hips, waist, left wrist, and thumb; magnetic right hand, buttons on side of body operate thumb; rooted white hair; painted features. Marked "1970 Mattel Inc./Hong Kong" on head; "Mattel Inc./Hong Kong/U.S. Patent Pending" on back. **35.00**

Love n' Touch Real Sisters: 15", vinyl head, cloth body, vinyl hands; rooted hair; painted eyes; good molding around eyes. Marked "Mattel Inc. 1980 Taiwan" on head. **65.00**

Shrinking Violet: 15", all cloth; yellow yarn hair; felt eyes with movable lids; movable mouth, pull-string operates talker and facial movements. Cloth label sewn into seam marked "Mattel Shrinking Violet" and "63 The

Funny Company All Rights Reserved Through Out The World" on reverse side. **125.00**

Baby Play A Lot: 16", vinyl; rooted blond hair; painted features; pull-string and start-switch on back activates doll to comb hair, brush teeth, do dishes, or play with one of twenty toys included in storage tray. Marked "1971/Mattel Inc./Hong Kong/US Patent Pend" on back of head. **45.00**

Saucy: 16", vinyl head, plastic body, vinyl limbs; rooted hair; sleep eyes; rotating left arm causes eyes and mouth to form eight different expressions. Marked "1972 Mattel Inc. Mexico" on head; "1972 Mattel Inc. Mexico/US Patent Pend." on back. **75.00**

Talking Baby Tenderlove: 16", all vinyl; insert scalp with rooted white hair; painted eyes; open nurser mouth; pull-string talker in plastic hair ribbon on back of head. Marked "677K 1969 Mattel Inc./Mexico." **35.00**

Talking Miss Beasley: 16", vinyl head; blue and white polka-dot cloth body with apron; rooted blond hair; painted features; black plastic glasses; pull-string talker. Cloth tag "Mattel Miss Beasley" sewn into seam. . **65.00**

Tippy Toes: 16", vinyl head, plastic body, vinyl arms; rooted hair; painted eyes; open/closed mouth with two lower molded and painted teeth; battery operated to ride plastic tricycle. Marked "Mexico" on head; "1967 Mattel Inc./Hawthorne Calif./Made in USA" on body; came with plastic tricycle. **45.00**

Hi Dottie: 17", vinyl head and left arm, plastic body, plastic right arm; rooted hair; painted features; plug in left hand to connect phone. Marked "1969 Mattel Inc. Mexico" on head; "1971/Mattel Inc./Mexico /U. S. Patent Pend." on back. **45.00**

Peachy and Her Puppets: 17", vinyl; rooted hair; painted features; pull-string to operate and make puppets talk; puppets include clown, girl, dog, and monkey. Marked "1972 Mattel Inc./Mexico" on head; "1964 Mattel Inc./Hawthornee" on back. **45.00**

Sing-A-Song: 17", vinyl head, plastic body; rooted blond hair; painted blue eyes; pull-string singer. Marked "1969/Mattel Inc. Mexico" on head; "1964 Mattel Inc./Hawthorne" on back; dress tag reads "1968 Mattel Inc./Made in Hong Kong." **60.00**

Sister Bell: 17", hard plastic head, cloth body; glued-on yellow yarn hair; large side-glancing painted eyes; pull-string talker, eleven different phrases. Marked "Mattel Inc./Hawthorne Calif." on head; "Mattel Inc. 1961" on tag sewn into seam. **65.00**

Teachy Keen: 17", vinyl head, stuffed cloth body; rooted blond hair; painted features; dressed to teach skills of opening zippers, buckling shoes, tying, and buttoning. Marked "Mattel/Teachy Keen/1966 Mattel Inc." on tag sewn into seam. **45.00**

Baby Secret: 18", vinyl head, cloth body, vinyl hands; rooted hair; painted eyes; open mouth, pull-string talker, mouth moves as she talks. Marked "Japan 1965" on head; "Baby Secret/Mattel Inc." on tag sewn into seam. **50.00**

Beany: 18", vinyl head, cloth body, vinyl hands and feet; molded and painted yellow hair; painted side-glancing blue eyes; open mouth with molded tongue, pull-string talker. Marked "Mattel Inc. Toymakers/Bob Clampett - Hong Kong" on shoe; "Mattel 1969" on tag sewn into seam. **45.00**

Chatty Cathy: 20", vinyl head, plastic body, vinyl limbs; rooted hair; sleep eyes with lashes; open/closed mouth with molded and painted teeth. Marked "Chatty Cathy 1960/Chatty Baby 1961 By Mattel Inc./US Pat. 3017187/Other US and Foreign Pats. Pend/Pat'd in Canada 1962;" dress tag reads "Chatty Cathy, Mattel." **125.00**

Cynthia: 20", vinyl head, plastic body; rooted blond hair; painted features; battery operated, talks with records. Marked "1971 Mattel Inc./Hong Kong" on head; "1971 Mattel Inc./USA/US Patent Pending" on back. **65.00**

Living Baby Tenderlove: 20", one-piece vinyl body; rooted skull cap; painted features; open nurser mouth. Marked "140/1970 Mattel Inc. Mexico/US and Foreign Patented." **25.00**

Scooba-Doo: 21", vinyl head, cloth body; rooted blond hair; blue sleep eyes with eye liner and eye shadow; closed mouth; pull-string on left hip. Marked "Mattel/Scooba Doo 1964" on tag sewn into seam. **95.00**

Doctor Doolittle: 22", vinyl head, cloth body; molded and painted realistic facial features; top hat; pull-string talker. Marked "Dr. Doolittle/MCMLXVII Twentieth Century Fox/Film Corp Inc." on tag sewn into seam. **85.00**

Dancerina: 24", vinyl head, plastic body, vinyl arms; rooted hair; painted eyes; open/closed mouth; battery operated, activated by knob on top of head. Marked "1968 Mattel" on head; "1968 Mattel" on body. . . . **75.00**

Charmin Chatty: 25", vinyl head and arms, plastic body, plastic legs; rooted hair; side-glancing sleep eyes with lashes; closed smiling mouth; record fits into slot on side of doll; pull-string operates talker. Marked "Charmin Chatty 1961 Mattel, Inc." **185.00**

COLLECTOR DOLL SERIES

Classic Beauty: 1977-1978, vinyl head, plastic body; rooted hair; sleep eyes; very pretty facial molding; dolls and clothing in excellent condition with wrist tag:

Cassandra: world-wide production of 2,761. . . **600.00**

Cecelia: world-wide production of 3,005. . . . . . **500.00**

Catherine: world-wide production of 2,799. . . . **500.00**

Cynthia: world-wide production of 3,731. . . . . . **450.00**

La Cheri Collection: also known as "French Country Garden Collection"; 18"; tagged with serial number and date; blue, burgundy, or pink dress:

1982, limited to 1,200 of each color. **650.00**

1983, limited to 2,000 of each color. **500.00**

Mariko Collection: limited to 1,800 world-wide production of each doll; 1983; 14"; ivory complexion:

    Art: floral print dress. **350.00**

    Drama: boy, striped pants. **350.00**

    Mime: yellow dress. **350.00**

    Music: lavender dress. **350.00**

Sekiguchi of Japan: Mattel owned exclusive distribution rights in the United States:

    1982: mint **350.00**

    1983: mint **300.00**

KIDDLES

Dainty Deer Animiddle: 2", all vinyl, fleece covering; deer outfit with antlers; orange hair; painted features. Marked "1967 Mattel Inc." **75.00**

Lolli Lemon: 2", all vinyl; rooted yellow hair; painted features. Marked "Mattel Inc." on back. **50.00**

Low Locket: 2", all vinyl; rooted red hair; painted features. Marked "Mattel Inc.;" came in plastic locket. **50.00**

Calamity Jiddle Kiddle: 2¹/₂", all vinyl; rooted blond hair; painted features. Marked "1965/Mattel Inc./Japan;" came with large cowgirl hat and horse. **75.00**

Violet Kiddle Kologne: 2¹/₂", all vinyl; rooted lavender hair; painted features. Marked "Mattel" on back; came in plastic cologne bottle. **40.00**

Bunson Burnie: 3", all vinyl; rooted red hair; painted features. Marked "1966/Mattel Inc." **35.00**

Rosemary Roadster: 3", all vinyl; rooted blond hair; painted features. Marked "1966/Mattel Inc." **100.00**

Little Red Riding Hiddle: 3¹/₂", all vinyl; rooted blond hair; painted features. Marked "1966/Mattel Inc.;" with chenille wolf. **175.00**

Soapy Siddle: 3¹/₂", all vinyl; brown rooted hair; painted features; wearing bathrobe. Marked "Mattel Inc." on head. **50.00**

Telly Viddle Kiddle: 3¹/₂", all vinyl; rooted hair; painted features. Marked "1965/Mattel Inc./Japan/15" on back; "Mattel/1965" on head. **60.00**

Howard Biff: 4", all vinyl; rooted blond hair; painted features. Marked "1966/Mattel Inc." on back; came with plastic wagon. **95.00**

Suki Skididdle: 4", all vinyl; rooted blond hair; painted features. Marked "1966/Mattel Inc." on back; came with plastic skiddle pusher. **50.00**

PERSONALITY DOLLS

Welcome Back Kotter Series: Marked "Wolper-Komack" on head; "1973 Mattel Inc. Taiwan" on back:

    Barbarino **45.00**

    Epstein **30.00**

    Washington **30.00**

    Horshack **30.00**

    Mr. Kotter **30.00**

Mindy: 8¹/₂", rooted hair, open/closed mouth. Marked "1979 P.P.C. Taiwan" on head; "1973 Mattel Taiwan" on back. **35.00**

Mork: 9", molded hair; closed mouth. Marked "1979 P.P.C. Taiwan" on head; "1973 Mattel Taiwan" on back. . .**35.00**

Lone Wolf: 9¹/₂", Indian; rooted hair. Marked "1975 Mattel Inc." on head; "Hong Kong" sideways, "1971 Mattel Inc./Hong Kong U. S. & Foreign Patents." **65.00**

Grizzly Adams: 10", molded beard. Marked "1971 Mattel Inc./U.S. & Foreign Patents/Hong Kong" on back. .**60.00**

Jimmy Osmond: 10", open/closed mouth and freckles. Marked "22-1209/Mattel Inc./1966/Taiwan" on back. **85.00**

Zeb Mccahan: 10", molded blond hair and mustache. Marked "1975 Mattel Inc." on head; "Hong Kong" sideways, "1971 Mattel Inc./Hong Kong U. S. & Foreign Patents." **45.00**

Julia: 11¹/₂", from TV program Julia starring Dianne Carroll; all black vinyl; bendable knees; rooted black hair; painted brown eyes; closed mouth. Marked "1966 Mattel Inc." **250.00**

Cheryl Ladd: 11¹/₂", bendable knees; green eyes. Marked "Mattel 1966/Korea/13." **45.00**

Debbie Boone: 11¹/₂", open/closed smiling mouth; holding microphone. Marked "RESI Inc. 1978 Taiwan" on head; "Mattel Inc. 1966 Taiwan" on back. **65.00**

Kate Jackson: 11¹/₂", brown hair and eyes; closed mouth. Marked "Mattel Inc./1978" on head; "Mattel Inc./1966 Korea 13" on body. **65.00**

Marie Osmond: 11¹/₂", dark rooted hair; smiling. Marked "Mattel Inc./1966/12 Korea" on back. **75.00**

Twiggy: 11¹/₂", short blond rooted hair; long lashes. Marked "Mattel Inc./1969." **350.00**

Donny Osmond: 11³/₄", molded brown hair and eyes; open/closed smiling mouth. Marked "10-88-0S00S/Mattel Inc., 1968, Hong Kong." **75.00**

Shaun: 12", holds plastic guitar. Marked "Mattel Inc. 1979" on head; "Mattel Inc. 1975/Taiwan" across waist. . .**65.00**

Mego

7" Fonzi. *Courtesy of Ty Herlocher.*

Mego marketed dolls during the 1970s and 1980s until going bankrupt in 1983. Mego is most famous for its well-made and beautifully costumed action figures and accessories, particularly the Super Heroes adapted from the popular D.C. Comics and the personality "stars" of the day. The 8" D.C. Comic figures are actively sought by collectors. The KISS dolls are also very popular. Originally retailing for less than $15.00 each in 1978, today the set of four in original boxes can command $500.00—not a bad investment.

Neal Adams, the well-known comic book artist, was responsible for much of Mego's packaging and toy artwork.

Reproduction Mego dolls/action figures are not a problem.

When considering a Mego doll, check condition carefully; there is little forgiveness for less-than-perfect dolls or dolls missing accessories. Prices listed are for dolls in perfect condition.

MEGO DOLL VALUE COMPARISONS:

Character Name	Size	Value	Character Name	Size	Value
Action Jackson	8"	$200.00	Waltons Mom & Pop, pair	8"	$25.00
Dinah-mite	8"	25.00	Grandma & Grandpa, pair	8"	40.00
Superman	8"	50.00	Fighting Batman	8"	45.00
Batman, 1st, removable cowl-mask	8"	55.00	Fighting Robin	8"	45.00
Batman	8"	45.00	Fighting Riddler	8"	45.00
Robin	8"	45.00	Fighting Joker	8"	45.00
Aquaman	8"	45.00	Jon, Chips	8"	30.00
Captain America	8"	50.00	Ponch, Chips	8"	30.00
Tarzan	8"	40.00	Captain Patch	8"	85.00
Spider Man	8"	50.00	Jean Lafitte	8"	85.00
Shazam	8"	45.00	Long John Silver	8"	85.00
Penguin	8"	50.00	Blackbeard	8"	85.00
Joker	8"	50.00	Mighty Thor	8"	45.00
Riddler	8"	45.00	Conan	8"	45.00
Mr. Mxyzptlk	8"	45.00	The Thing	8"	30.00

MEGO DOLL VALUE COMPARISONS:

Character Name	Size	Value	Character Name	Size	Value
Wonder Woman	8"	$35.00	The Human Torch	8"	$30.00
Super Girl	8"	25.00	Mr. Fantastic	8"	30.00
Bat Girl	8"	25.00	Invisible Girl	8"	30.00
Cat Women	8"	25.00	Neprunain	8"	35.00
Frankenstein	8"	35.00	The Keeper	8"	35.00
Dracula	8"	35.00	The Gorn	8"	30.00
Wolfman	8"	30.00	The Cheron	8"	30.00
Mummy	8"	30.00	Zon, 1 Million BC	8"	25.00
Wyatt Earp	8"	40.00	Trag	8"	20.00
Cochise	8"	40.00	Grok	8"	20.00
Davy Crockett	8"	40.00	Orm	8"	20.00
Buffalo Bill Cody	8"	45.00	Alfalfa	8"	40.00
Wild Bill Hickok	8"	40.00	Spanky	8"	40.00
Sitting Bull	8"	40.00	Darla	8"	40.00
Cornelius, Planet of the Apes	8"	30.00	Buckwheat	8"	40.00
Dr. Zaius	8"	30.00	Mickey	8"	40.00
Zira	8"	30.00	Porky	8"	40.00
Soldier Ape	8"	30.00	Galen	8"	25.00
Astronaut	8"	30.00	General Ursus	8"	25.00
Captain Kirk	8"	65.00	Peter Burke	8"	25.00
Mr. Spock	8"	65.00	Alan Verdono	8"	25.00
Dr. "Bones" McCoy	8"	65.00	Fonzie	8"	45.00
Lt. Uhura	8"	50.00	Richie	8"	30.00
Mr. "Scottie" Scott	8"	65.00	Potsy	8"	30.00
Klingon	8"	50.00	Captain	12"	35.00
Dorothy & Toto	8"	30.00	Tenille	12"	35.00
Tin Woodsman	8"	30.00	Sonny	12"	65.00
Cowardly Lion	8"	30.00	Cher	12"	45.00
Scarecrow	8"	30.00	Diana Ross	12"	75.00
Glinda "The Good" Witch	8"	35.00	Jaclyn Smith	12"	40.00
Wicked Witch	8"	40.00	Joe Namath	12"	85.00
King Arthur	8"	90.00	Laverne	12"	45.00
Sir Galahad	8"	90.00	Shirley	12"	45.00
Sir Lancelot	8"	90.00	Lenny	12"	45.00
Black Knight	8"	90.00	Squiggy	12"	45.00
Ivanhoe	8"	90.00	Suzanne Somers	12"	40.00
Robin Hood	8"	90.00	Wonder Woman	12"	45.00
Little John	8"	85.00	Llia, Star Trek	12"	40.00
Friar Tuck	8"	85.00	Arcturian	12"	25.00
Will Scarlet	8"	85.00	Maddie Mod	12"	10.00
Green Arrow	8"	30.00	Farrah Fawcett	12"	40.00
Green Goblin	8"	35.00	KISS, set	12"	500.00
The Lizard	8"	30.00	Kriss	12"	100.00
The Falcon	8"	30.00	Gene	12"	100.00
The Invincible Iron Man	8"	30.00	Ace	12"	100.00
The Incredible Hulk	8"	25.00	Peter	12"	100.00
Waltons, John Boy & Ellen, pair	8"	40.00			

Metal-Head Dolls

The chief manufacturing center for making Metal-Head Dolls was in Germany at Nossen, Saxony. The most common type of Metal-Head Doll is the familiar tin head, dating from the turn-of-the-century. Though inexpensive, tin heads usually had a pleasant expression. They were stamped out of sheet metal and the two halves were welded together. Heads were sold separately as replacements for the easily broken doll heads of the day. This explains why metal heads are so often found on various bodies.

Buschow & Beck took over a metal doll making firm in 1890, and for the next forty years produced various types of metal dolls. Their "Minerva" trademark is so well known that it became the generic name for all Metal-Head Dolls. Karl Standfuss produced Metal-Head Dolls with the trade name Juno, and Alfred Heller used the trade name Diana. Gebeler-Falk's "Gie-La" metal dolls have aluminum heads and well-made wooden bodies, some with wooden joints. These dolls have attained a level of popularity with collectors.

Prices listed are for dolls with no damage. The painted surface of the metal heads is easily chipped, making these dolls difficult to find in excellent condition. Repainting is another common fault of tin head dolls. Tin heads degrade in value very quickly. Avoid dolls which are badly chipped or repainted. A damaged or repainted tin head decreases the doll's value by at least 80%.

Tin Shoulder Head: kid or cloth body; molded and painted hair or good wig; painted or glass eyes; open or closed mouth; appropriately dressed. Typically marked "Minerva" (over a helmet) "JUNO," or "DIANA."

Aluminum Socket Head: jointed wood or metal body; good wig; tin eyes; open or closed mouth; appropriately dressed. Typically marked "G" (within a star) and "U.S."

METAL-HEAD VALUE COMPARISONS:

Size	Tin Shoulder Head, Painted Eyes, Molded Hair	Tin Shoulder Head, Glass Eyes, Molded Hair	Tin Shoulder Head, Dolly-Face, Glass Eyes Wig	Aluminum Socket Head, Tin Eyes, Wig
12"	125.00	175.00		
14"	150.00	200.00	250.00	
16"	175.00	225.00	275.00	350.00
18"	200.00	250.00	300.00	
20"			325.00	400.00
22"			350.00	
25"				475.00

16" Juno Metal Head. *Courtesy of Cheryl Metzger.*

Molly-'es

Molly-'es is the trade name used by the International Doll Company, founded in 1929 by Marysia (Mollye) Goldman of Philadelphia, Pennsylvania.

Marysia was born in Russia around the turn-of-the-century. As a child, she fled with her parents to the United States. In 1919 she married Myer Goldman and began designing doll clothing shortly thereafter. The International Doll Company was originally a cottage industry, with neighborhood women sewing doll dresses in their homes. Eventually, Mollye opened a factory which reportedly employed as many as 500 people. In addition to designing doll dresses for her own company, she also designed and made doll costumes for other companies, including Horsman, Effanbee, Ideal, and Cameo. Mollye also entered into a contract with Ideal Toy Company to design the Shirley Temple doll's clothing.

In 1937, Molly-'es (International Doll Company) created a Hollywood Cinema Fashion doll series, with dolls dressed to represent such stars and well-known personalities as Irene Dunne, Jeanette McDonald, Betty Grable, June Allison, Olivia deHaviland, Joan Crawford, Queen Elizabeth, and Princess Margaret Rose. Molly-'es also created an entire group of dolls representing the characters from the movie Thief of Baghdad. These dolls are some of Mollye's best work. The Sultan, with his beautifully hand-painted facial features, groomed beard, and satin costume, makes an impressive presentation. Mollye purchased good quality dolls of composition, hard plastic, and vinyl from various manufacturers, dressed them in her original costumes, and sold them under her name. Except for hanging tags, earlier Molly-'es Dolls are unmarked; later vinyl dolls are found marked "Mollye" on the head.

Prices listed are for dolls with no damage. Normal wear, slight crazing, or surface dust does not greatly affect price. If badly worn, crazed, or soiled, expect to pay less than half the amount listed.

See also Raggedy Ann and Andy.

13" Molly-'es International Series.

appropriately dressed. Unmarked or marked with hang tag.

International Children Series: mask-type face, stuffed cloth body; mohair wig; painted facial features; wearing original regional costume. Unmarked or marked with hang tag.

Character Face Mask-Type: cloth body; yarn hair; painted, big, round, side-glancing eyes; smiling watermelon mouth; appropriately dressed. Unmarked or marked with hang tag.

COMPOSITION

Baby: all composition, jointed at neck, shoulders, and hips; molded and painted hair; sleep eyes; closed mouth; appropriately dressed. Unmarked or marked with hang tag.

Lady/Teen: all composition, jointed at neck, shoulders, and hips; good wig; sleep eyes, real lashes; closed mouth; appropriately dressed. Unmarked or marked with hang tag.

Thief of Baghdad Series (Sultan, Thief, or Princess): all composition, jointed neck, shoulders, and hips; good wig, may have mohair beard and eyebrows; detailed painted eyes; closed mouth; wearing original costumes. Unmarked or marked with hang tag.

HARD PLASTIC

Lady/Teen: all hard plastic, jointed at neck, shoulders, and hips; good wig; sleep eyes; closed mouth; appropriately dressed. Unmarked or marked with hang tag.

VINYL

Child/Baby: all vinyl, jointed at neck, shoulders, and hips; rooted hair; sleep eyes; closed mouth; appropriately dressed. Marked "Mollye."

CLOTH

Child Mask-Type Face: stuffed cloth body; yarn hair; painted eyes, long lashes; small closed mouth;

MOLLY-'ES DOLL VALUE COMPARISONS:

Size	Cloth Child	Cloth International	Cloth Character-type	Composition Baby	Composition Lady/Teen	Composition "Baghdad Series"	Hard Plastic Lady/Teen	Vinyl
9"								75.00
12"								85.00
13"	150.00	100.00						
14"				225.00			325.00	
15"	175.00	125.00	225.00	250.00	500.00	700.00		
16"								100.00
17"							350.00	
18"	200.00		250.00	300.00	500.00			
19"						900.00		
20"							400.00	
21"				400.00	650.00			
23"							425.00	
24"	250.00		300.00					
25"							450.00	
27"		200.00			800.00			
28"							475.00	
29"	325.00							

Morimura Brothers

Morimura Brothers, a Japanese import house operating since the 1870s, began producing dolls in 1915. With the outbreak of World War I, the flow of bisque dolls from Europe had virtually ceased. Morimura Brothers stepped in to supply Japanese-made bisque-head dolls to American customers during and immediately following World War I. Bisque doll heads manufactured by Morimura Brothers, while projecting a certain amount of charm, were of surprisingly poor quality. The company demonstrated a lack of the technical knowledge and experience needed to produce fine bisque dolls.

Morimura Brothers unabashedly set out to imitate the much-loved German doll and did, in fact, achieve a certain degree of success. Few modern collectors actively seek Morimura Brothers dolls. However, there are many fine examples available, and as their German and French counterparts continue to escalate in price, Morimura Brothers dolls may become more desirable.

Prices listed are for dolls with no damage to the bisque. Normal wear, slight damage, or well-done repairs to the body do not greatly affect price. If the bisque is damaged or repaired, expect to pay less than half the amount listed. It is

16" Morimura Brothers Character Baby. *Courtesy of Helen Brooke.*

14" Morimura Brothers Sweet Little Character Baby. *Courtesy of Anna Fortney.*

perfectly acceptable to show a missing or repaired finger or joint to the body.

Character Baby: socket head, bent-limb baby body; good wig; glass eyes; open mouth; appropriately dressed. Typically marked "M B" (within a circle), "Japan," "Nippon," "Yamato," "FY," or "MB."

Exceptional Character (such as Hilda Look-A-Like): socket head, jointed composition body; good wig; glass eyes; open mouth; appropriately dressed. Typically marked "M B" within a circle, "JAPAN," "NIPPON," "JW," "Yamato," "FY," or "MB."

Child: standard quality or exceptional quality bisque head, composition or kid body; good wig; glass eyes; open mouth; appropriately dressed. Typically marked "MB" within a circle, "NIPPON," "JW," "Yamato," "FY," or "MB."

MORIMURA BROTHERS VALUE COMPARISONS:

Size	Character Baby, Standard	Character Baby, Exceptional	Child Dolly-Face, Standard	Child Dolly-Face, Exceptional
8"			150.00	325.00
10"	250.00		200.00	350.00
12"	300.00		225.00	375.00
14"	350.00	1,000.00	250.00	400.00
15"	400.00	1,200.00	275.00	425.00
18"	550.00	1,400.00	300.00	450.00
20"	650.00	1,600.00	350.00	500.00
22"	750.00	1,900.00	400.00	550.00
24"			450.00	600.00

Multi-Faced Dolls

V intage Multi-Faced bisque dolls were made by various manufacturers. These dolls have two or more faces on a single head, usually within a molded bonnet which keeps all but one face hidden from view. Better known manufacturers include Carl Bergner, Max Frederick Schelhorn, and Fritz Bartenstein.

Two-faced dolls are usually found with opposing facial combinations: awake and asleep; white and black; youth and old age; or crying and laughing. Combination of faces on three-faced dolls include: awake, asleep, and crying; crying, laughing, and sleeping; black asleep, white awake, and mulatto crying; and even Red Riding Hood, Wolf, and Grandma.

Prices listed are for dolls with no damage. Evaluate any Multi-Face Doll according to its uniqueness and visual appeal, as these factors greatly affect price. Inspecting these dolls can be difficult as one does not have access to the crown opening or the neck socket. Therefore, it is very important to carefully inspect the doll for damage or repairs. Normal wear or well-done repairs to the body do not greatly affect price. If the bisque is damaged or repaired expect to pay about half the amount listed. It is perfectly acceptable to show a missing or repaired finger or joint to the body as the artistry of these dolls are their bisque heads.

Please note that examples of Multi-Faced Dolls may also be found elsewhere in this book, located in the sections devoted to their respective manufacturers.

Multi-Face: bisque socket head, composition body; hood or bonnet with molded and painted hair or wig; painted or glass eyes; appropriately dressed. Typically marked "CB," "HvB," "SH," and "Shl."

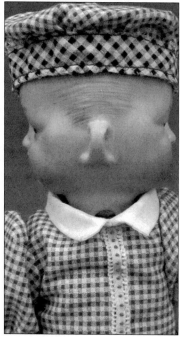

Two-faced Kley & Hahn Doll. *Courtesy of Marilyn A. Merry.*

	MULTI-FACED DOLLS VALUE COMPARISONS:				
Size	2-Faced Character, Standard	2-Faced Character, Unusual	2-Faced Character, Extraordinary	3-Faced Character, Standard	3-Faced Character, Unusual
12"	1,200.00	2,200.00	12,000.00	1,700.00	6,500.00
15"	1,600.00	2,800.00		2,300.00	
18"			17,000.00		

Munich Art Dolls

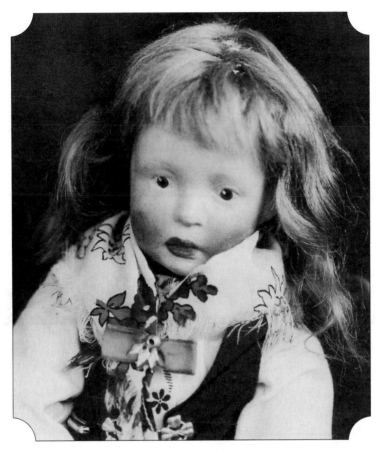

Munich Art Doll.
*Courtesy Pat
Vaillancourt.*

Marion Kaulitz was the undisputed originator of Munich Art Dolls. At an awards ceremony in 1910, Kaulitz was credited with leading the Puppen Reform—a movement in Bavaria towards the creation of realism in dolls. The heads were designed by Marie Marc-Schnur, Paul Vogelsanger and Josef Wacherle. The faces were hand painted by Marion Kaulitz. The dolls were then dressed by Lillian Frobenius and Alice Hagemann. *Studio Talk* is quoted: "when the artistic conscience began to invade the doll industry it fell to some artists of Dresden and Munich to introduce the change." These efforts attracted a great deal of attention in both artistic and commercial circles. In fact, the Munich Art Dolls certainly inspired Kammer & Reinhardt to manufacture character dolls in 1909.

The dolls had molded composition heads with painted eyes and ball-jointed composition bodies. They were commonly dressed to resemble French and German children.

These beautiful Munich Art Dolls are extremely collectible, not only for their appealing avant-garde naturalism, but also for their historical importance in the chronology of doll making.

Prices listed are for dolls with no damage. Normal wear, slight damage, or well-done repairs to the body do not greatly affect price. If the head is damaged or, worse yet, repainted, expect to pay less than half the amount listed. It is perfectly acceptable to show a missing or repaired finger or joint to the body.

Character Doll: composition head, jointed composition body; molded and painted hair or good wig; molded and painted eyes with great detail; rosy cheeks, full pouty closed mouth; appropriately dressed. Typically marked "K III," or "KI." Occasionally signed on neck.

MUNICH ART DOLLS VALUE COMPARISONS:

Size	Munich Art Doll
13"	2,900.00
16½"	4,000.00
17½"	4,700.00
21½"	7,000.00

Nancy Ann Storybook Dolls

Nancy Ann Storybook Dolls were produced by a California-based company founded by Nancy Ann Abbott and her partner, A.L. Rowland, in 1936. These popular dolls were first made in what is referred to as "painted bisque" and then later in hard plastic. Abbott first bought dolls from overseas, but because of the poor quality they often had to be repainted in the United States. By 1938, the Nancy Ann Storybook Doll Company began making its own dolls from clays imported from England.

In the 1960s the company, which at its peak was producing over eight thousand dolls a day, began to experience production problems. Doll production ceased when Abbott passed away in 1964. The dolls and clothing designed by Abbott are among the most outstanding produced during the 1950s and 60s, despite the vast number of fashion dolls on the market at that time. They are highly prized by today's collectors.

When Nancy Ann Storybook Dolls are mentioned, one immediately thinks of the adorable little all-bisque characters which have endeared themselves to virtually every doll collector. Although not truly bisque dolls, these 1940-era American dolls, composed of so-called painted or sprayed bisque, are so avidly sought after today that they belong firmly in the legion of bisque doll collecting.

Characters portrayed by the 5½ to 7 inch Nancy Ann Storybook Dolls from 1936 to 1947 are identified on a wrist tag and/or box and generally incised on the back. Only babies were produced the first year. Dolls had hip joints through 1942, when stiff-legged dolls were introduced. Clues to identifying the 17 to 18 inch all hard plastic dolls include: second and third fingers molded together and curved inwards; excellent details on hands, wrists, and ears; and a slight blush on knees and wrists. Clothing snaps are usually small, with solid tops, and marked on the underside "Grippers SMCO."

Prices listed are for dolls with no damage. Values for these dolls are determined by condition; the scarcity of various models and costumes; originality of costumes; and the presence of a doll's wrist tag and original box.

Painted Bisque Nancy Ann Story Book.

Nancy Ann: 10", all vinyl, jointed at neck, shoulders, and hips; rooted blond hair; blue sleep eyes with lashes; closed mouth; pierced ears; appropriately dressed. Marked "Nancy Ann" **125.00**

Nancy Ann: 17 to 18", all hard plastic (or vinyl heads with rooted hair), jointed at neck, shoulders, and hips; synthetic wig; sleep eyes with real lashes; closed mouth; appropriately dressed. Typically unmarked. Occasionally marked "17B" or "18B" on head or marked with hang tag only. **700.00**

Muffie: all hard plastic, jointed at neck, shoulders and hips; good wig; sleep eyes; closed mouth; appropriately dressed. Typically marked "StoryBook Dolls California/Muffie" or "Muffie."

8" MUFFIE VALUE COMPARISONS (1953-ON):	
Identification	**Value**
Painted lashes, no eyebrows, straight leg, non-walker	$225.00
Molded lashes, painted eyebrows, straight-leg walker	200.00
Vinyl head, rooted saran hair, straight-leg or bent knee walker	185.00
Unmarked, molded lashes, wig, Muffie Around the World re-issue straight leg walker	150.00

5½" TO 7" STORYBOOK DOLL VALUE COMPARISONS:

Date	Child	Baby	Box	Clothing Closures	Identification	Value Estimates
1936		Painted bisque, Mark I	Pink/Blue marbleized or color with starbursts	Silver pin	Gold foil sticker "Nancy Ann Dressed Dolls"	550.00
1937	Painted bisque, Mark I	Painted bisque, Mark I	Colored boxes w/starbursts	Silver pin	Gold Foil sticker "Nancy Ann Dressed Dolls"	450.00
1938	Painted bisque," "AMERICA" or "JUDY ANN USA"		Colored boxes w/starbursts*	Silver pin	Gold foil sticker "Judy Ann"	800.00
1938	Painted bisque, Mark II	Painted bisque, Mark I or II	Colored boxes w/starbursts	Silver or brass pin	Gold foil" sticker "Story Book Dolls"	450.00
1939	Painted bisque, bangs, molded socks, Mark III	Painted bisque, star-shaped hands, Mark III	Colored box, small silver dots	Brass pins	Gold foil sticker "Story Book Dolls"	450.00
1940	Painted bisque, molded socks, Mark III	Painted bisque, star-shaped hands, Mark III	Colored box, white dots	Brass pin	Gold foil sticker "Story Book Dolls	300.00
1940	Painted bisque, molded socks, Mark III	Painted bisque, star-shaped hands, Mark III	Colored box, white dots	Brass pin	Gold foil sticker "Story Book Dolls"	300.00
1941-1942	Painted bisque, transition dolls,** Mark III	Painted bisque, some w/star-shaped hands, some w/fists, Mark III	White box, colored dots	Brass pin	Gold foil wrist tag with name	175.00
1943-1947	Painted bisque, 1 pc. head, torso and legs, Mark III	Painted bisque, fist hands, Mark III	White boxes, colored dots	Dull silver or brass pin or ribbon ties	Gold foil wrist tag with name	150.00
1947-1949	Plastic, painted eyes, Mark IV	Painted bisque body, plastic limbs, Mark III	White box, colored dots, "Nancy Ann Storybook Dolls" printed between dots	Brass snaps	Gold foil wrist tag with name	85.00
1949-1953	Plastic, black sleep eyes, Mark IV	Plastic, black sleep eyes, Mark IV	Same as above	Brass or painted snaps	Gold foil wrist tag with name	85.00
1953	Plastic, blue sleep eyes	Plastic, black sleep eyes	Same as above	Painted donut snaps	Gold foil wrist tag with name	75.00

* Rare red book shaped box, with "Judy Ann in Fairyland," MIB $1,500.00.
** Some with chubby tummies, some slim.

Mark I = "Made in Japan"
Mark II = "STORYBOOK USA" or Story Book USA
Mark III = "StoryBook Doll USA"
Mark IV = "StoryBook Doll USA/Trade Mark Reg."

Gebrüder Ohlhaver

There are conflicting dates as to the founding of the Gebrüder Ohlhaver doll factory in Sonneberg, Germany. Some sources give 1897 and others 1912. Either way, all sources agree that in 1913 Ohlhaver was advertising "ball jointed dolls for sale." The owners of the company, Jonny Paulas Gerhard Ohlhaver and Hinrick Ohlhaver, forever immortalized their names with their famous "Revalo" trademark, derived from the owners' names being phonetically spelled backwards.

The beguiling and quaint faces of the Character Child dolls—not to mention the enchanting Revalo Child with its distinctive slender face—are difficult for collectors to resist. Ohlhaver ordered its doll heads from several porcelain factories including Ernst Heubach, Gebrüder Heubach, and Mengersgereuth—the latter distinguishable by an "X" within a circle mark. Another marking found on Ohlhaver dolls is "Igodi," which refers to a patented swivel head invented by Johann Gottleib Dierich in 1919, and which appears on some heads produced by Ernst Heubach. Additional markings include the Ohlgaver trade names "Revalo," "My Queen Dolland," and "Bébé Princess," along with mold numbers "150," "151," "10727," and "11010."

Prices listed are for dolls with no damage. Normal wear, slight damage, or well-done repairs to the body do not greatly affect price. If the bisque is damaged or repaired, expect to pay less than half the amount listed. It is perfectly acceptable to show a missing or repaired finger or joint to the body.

Character Faced Child: socket head, composition body; molded and painted hair; painted and highlighted intaglio eyes; open/closed mouth; appropriately dressed. Typically marked "Revalo/1/Dep."

22" Revalo Character. *Courtesy of Trina Miller.*

Character Baby: socket head, bent-limb baby body; good wig; glass eyes, winged feathered brows; open mouth; appropriately dressed. Typically marked "Germany Revalo."

Child: slender face, socket head, jointed composition body; good wig; glass eyes; open mouth; appropriately dressed. Typically marked "Germany Revalo."

REVALO VALUE COMPARISONS:

Size	Character Child	Character Baby*	Child
8"	800.00		
10"	900.00		
12"	1,000.00		
14"	1,200.00	700.00	
16"	1,400.00	800.00	700.00
18"		900.00	800.00
20"		1,000.00	900.00
22"		1,100.00	1,000.00
24"			1,100.00
26"			1,200.00
28"			1,400.00

* Add an additional $400.00 for Toddler Body.

Oriental Dolls

Many manufacturers made or handled dolls representing Oriental people. Oriental characteristics were achieved through the use of tinted bisque and by applying appropriate expressions to the face.

Reproductions are not a problem, although several molds are available of the earlier bisque Oriental Dolls. These are generally not made with a deliberate intent to deceive. A thorough inspection of the doll and its markings should be sufficient to identify a copy.

Prices listed are for dolls with no damage. Normal wear, slight damage, and/or well-done repairs to the body do not greatly affect the prices of early dolls. If an early bisque doll is damaged or repaired, or if a composition doll is badly crazed, chipped, or repaired, expect to pay less than half the amount listed. There is little forgiveness for less-than-perfect condition on the more modern dolls. Judge each Oriental Doll individually.

BISQUE

Oriental Socket Head: expressive Oriental features; composition body; good wig; glass eyes; appropriately dressed. Various manufacturers' markings include:

Armand Marseille: typically marked "353, Ellan."

Bähr & Pröschild: typically marked "220."

Belton-Type: typically marked "129" or "193."

Bruno Schmidt: typically marked "500."

Jumeau: closed mouth; typically marked "Tete."

Kestner: typically marked "243."

Schoeneau & Hoffmeister: typically marked "4900."

Simon & Halbig: typically marked "164," "1099," "1129," "1199," or "1329."

COMPOSITION

Composition Head: cloth body with composition limbs or all composition; molded and painted hair or good wig; expressive Oriental face; appropriately dressed. Various markings, or unmarked.

HARD PLASTIC AND VINYL

Ginny Tui: 14", vinyl, plastic body; rooted long black hair, braided style; painted Oriental facial features; open/closed mouth, molded teeth; wearing original aqua two-piece suit with gold frog closures and embroidered figures. Marked "15-5." **200.00**

Puyi & Suzi: 24" and 30", vinyl flange, cloth body, vinyl limbs; black wigs; crystal-like eyes, real upper and lower lashes; full closed mouth; original well-made appropriate clothing. Marked "Rotraut Schrott/Gadco Square;" the set. . . .**800.00**

Suzi and Puyi Designed by Contemporary Artist Robtraut Schrott.

ORIENTAL DOLLS VALUE COMPARISONS:

Size	Armand Marseille	Bähr Pröschild	Belton-Type	Bruno Schmidt	Jumeau Closed Mouth	Kestner	Schoneau & Hoffmeister	Simon & Halbig 164, 1329
8"	1,000.00							
10"	1,200.00		1,800.00				900.00	
12"	1,400.00		1,900.00			4,800.00	1,200.00	2,200.00
14"	1,500.00	3,200.00	2,000.00	2,400.00		5,200.00	1,600.00	2,400.00
16"	1,600.00	3,800.00	2,200.00	2,600.00		5,800.00	2,000.00	2,700.00
18"	1,700.00	4,300.00	2,300.00	2,800.00	57,000.00	6,500.00	2,300.00	3,100.00
20"	1,800.00	4,800.00	2,500.00	3,000.00	65,000.00	7,300.00	2,700.00	3,600.00
22"	1,900.00	5,500.00	2,700.00	3,400.00	70,000.00			
24"	2,000.00				75,000.00			
25"					82,000.00			

12" Lame Beggar Composition Chinaman.

Size	Simon & Halbig 1099, 1129, 1199	Composition
8"		200.00
10"		250.00
12"	2,400.00	300.00
14"	2,600.00	350.00
16"	2,900.00	
18"	3,300.00	
20"	3,800.00	

Simon and Halbig 1329 Bisque Oriental. *Photo courtesy of McMasters Doll Auction.*

Papier-Mâché Dolls

arious German manufacturers made doll heads from the special type of composition known as papier-mâché. A 19th century dictionary defined papier-mâché as "a tough plastic material made from paper pulp containing a mixture of sizing, paste, oil, resin, or other substances or from sheets of paper glued and pressed together." Wood and rag fibers in paper were responsible for much of papier-mâché's strength. The term papier-mâché was adopted by German, French, and English consumers. The French term "carton-pate" and the German "holz-masse" were both used over the years, but neither label achieved lasting recognition.

Papier-Mâché Dolls were produced as early as the 16th century, but they did not become popular until it was discovered that they could be mass-produced. The development shortly before 1810 of a pressure process which used molds enabled a vast number of dolls to enter the marketplace. These pressure-molded papier-mâché dolls, which were allegedly introduced to the Sonneberg area in Germany from Paris about 1807, helped lay the foundation of the great German doll industry.

When considering a papier-mâché doll, check condition carefully. The prices listed are for dolls in good condition.

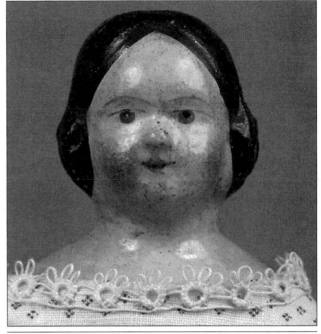
Papier-Mâché Doll.

Group of early Papier-Mâché Dolls.

Normal wear, slight damage or well-done repairs to the body do not greatly affect the price. It is getting increasingly more difficult to find papier-mâché in excellent condition. Therefore, we have come to accept these important early dolls in less than perfect condition. If the head is badly worn, crazed, or has been repainted, expect to pay less than half the amounts listed.

Early Papier-Mâché: shoulder head, adult-shaped kid or cloth body, kid or wooden limbs; molded hair styled close to head and painted black, or top of head painted black with nailed-on wig; painted or glass almond-shaped eyes, single-stroke brows; oval-shaped face; may have pierced nostrils; most with closed mouth, open mouth doll may have bamboo teeth; appropriately dressed. Typically unmarked.

Milliner's Models: molded hair papier-mâché doll; delicate oval face, somewhat long neck, thin tightly-stuffed kid body; wooden limbs with no articulation, many with strips of red, green, or blue paper covering junctures of wooden limbs and kid body; painted flat shoes, stylishly molded black hair; painted eyes; closed mouth; appropriately dressed. Typically unmarked. These dolls share many of the same characteristics of the earlier papier-mâché shoulder-head dolls. Values are determined primarily by hair style. The U.F.D.C. named these demure little ladies, by popular vote, "Molded Hair Papier-Mâché's." The name, although accurate, does not seem popular with collectors. The term "Milliner's Model" apparently originated with the well-known doll historian, Eleanor St. George. According to her own account, there was no real basis for the term other than that she liked it. Evidence suggests that there were Milliner's Model dolls, but there is no reason to believe that they resembled the Molded Hair Papier-Mâché's.

L. Moss Black Papier-Mâché: character head, cloth body; molded and painted tight curly hair; glass eyes; molded tear on cheek; closed mouth; appropriately dressed. Unmarked.

Later Papier-Mâché: shoulder head, cloth body, leather hands; may have molded wavy blond or black hair reminiscent of the styles commonly found on china-head dolls; short neck, rounded face; painted eyes are more rounded than the earlier period dolls, with lightly feathered brows; closed mouth. Typically unmarked, or occasionally marked "M & S Superior."

Milliners Model/Molded Hair Papier-Mâché. *Courtesy Helen Brooke.*

			PAPIER-MÂCHÉ VALUE COMPARISONS:			
Size	Early Glass Eyes	Early Painted Eyes	Molded Hair/ Milliner's Model Fancy Hair Style	Molded Hair/ Milliner's Model Common Hair Style	L. Moss Black Character	Later Papier-Mâché
6"			800.00	500.00		
8"			900.00	600.00		
10"		800.00	1,100.00	700.00		
12"	1,300.00	900.00	1,300.00	800.00		
14"	1,500.00	1,000.00	1,700.00	950.00		400.00
16"	1,700.00	1,100.00	1,900.00	1,100.00		500.00
18"	1,900.00	1,200.00	2,400.00	1,300.00		550.00
20"	2,100.00	1,250.00	2,700.00	1,500.00		600.00
22"	2,300.00	1,300.00	3,100.00	1,700.00	7,500.00	650.00
24"	2,500.00	1,350.00	3,600.00	1,900.00	9,000.00	700.00
26"	2,700.00	1,400.00		2,400.00		750.00
28"	3,200.00	1,600.00				850.00
30"	3,600.00	2,000.00				1,000.00
32"		2,300.00				

Note: Add an additional $200.00 for an unusual hairstyle or glass eyes in later papier-mâché shoulder head models.

Parian-Type Dolls

*V*arious German porcelain factories produced Parian dolls from 1850 on. Parian is a generic term used by collectors for the untinted bisque dolls of the 19th century. The term "Parian" has often been a source of confusion. How do Parian heads differ from other bisque heads? Actually, they don't. All glazed or unglazed "biscuit" mix heads are bisque. It is believed by collectors that the white bisque of the Parian Dolls resembles the marble of Greek statues.

Do not confuse the coarse grayish "stone bisque" with these pale beauties. The almost soapy-feeling porcelain is of the highest quality, with extremely delicate decoration. The Dresden porcelain factories were responsible for most of the early fine Parian heads. The hardness of the paste made it possible to cast it in an intricately detailed mold. Artists were inspired to great flights of imagination when creating detailed laces and ruffles, not to mention the elaborate hairstyles which incorporated braids, ringlets and curls. Even wreaths of flowers and jewels can be found on these detailed beauties. Delicate coloring with touches of gold and luster decorated the exquisite marble-like heads. Although most Parians have painted eyes, some had glass eyes, solid domes with wigs, plain unadorned shoulder plates, pierced ears, and occasionally swivel necks. Any combination of these varieties is a possibility.

Reproduction Parians do surface from time to time. It is believed that the majority of these were not made with an intent to deceive, but rather were meant for the enjoyment of the artist who made them. Any markings at all on a Parian should be reason for concern. Authentic untinted bisque dolls are typically unmarked, or marked only with a number.

Prices listed are for dolls with no damage to the bisque. Normal wear, slight damage, or well-done repairs to the body do not greatly affect price. Slight flakes of the delicate ruffles or petals of a flower could detract from the value in direct correlation to the amount of damage. If the Parian is cracked, or significant damage to the trim exists, expect to pay less then half the amount listed. It is perfectly acceptable to show a missing or repainted finger, or patch to the body, as the artistry is in the Parian head.

17" Parian Solid Dome with Mohair Wig. *Courtesy Helen Brooke.*

18" Beautiful and Ornate Parian (close-up and full view). *Courtesy of Mary Jane Brummer*

PARIAN DOLL VALUE COMPARISONS:

Description & Type of Eyes	Size	Value
Plain hairstyle, no decoration in hair nor on shoulder plate; may or may not have pierced ears; painted eyes	14" 18" 22"	$450.00 550.00 700.00
Men's hairstyle; decorated shirt and tie shoulder plate; painted eyes	14" 18" 22"	800.00 1,500.00 2,200.00
Men's hairstyle; decorated shirt and tie shoulder plate; glass eyes	18" 22"	3,000.00 3,300.00
Molded head band, such as "Alice in Wonderland"-type, no decoration on shoulder plate; may or may not have pierced ears; painted eyes	14" 18" 22"	700.00 900.00 1,200.00
Solid dome, wearing wig, no decoration on shoulder plate; may or may not have pierced ears; painted eyes	14" 18" 22"	900.00 1,200.00 1,900.00
Solid dome, wearing wig, no decoration on shoulder plate; may or may not have pierced; ears glass eyes	14" 18" 22"	1,200.00 1,500.00 1,900.00
Moderately fancy hairstyle, decorated shoulder plate; may or may not have pierced ears; painted eyes	14" 18" 22"	1,000.00 1,400.00 1,700.00
Moderately fancy hairstyle, decorated shoulder plate; may or may not have pierced ears; glass eyes	14" 18" 22"	1,500.00 1,900.00 2,400.00
Moderately fancy hairstyle, decorated shoulder plate; applied flowers or necklaces; may or may not have pierced ears; painted eyes	14" 18" 22"	1,200.00 1,500.00 1,800.00
Moderately fancy hairstyle, decorated shoulder plate; applied flowers or necklaces; may or may not have pierced ears; glass eyes	14" 18" 22"	1,600.00 2,100.00 2,500.00
Elaborate hairstyle and shoulder plate; may or may not have pierced ears; painted eyes	14" 18" 22"	1,400.00 1,800.00 2,000.00
Elaborate hairstyle and shoulder plate; may or may not have pierced ears; glass eyes	14" 18" 22"	1,900.00 2,200.00 2,700.00
Elaborate hairstyle and shoulder plate; swivel neck; may or may not have pierced ears; glass eyes	18" 22"	3,200.00 3,700.00

Patent Washable Dolls

Patent Washable Dolls were made by various German manufacturers after 1880. These composition dolls are seldom found in good condition. The area around the eyes seems particularly susceptible to damage. Occasionally, a Patent Washable will be found with exceptionally fine-quality composition and decoration.

Patent Washable: composition shoulder head, thin cloth body, long cloth limbs, composition forearms and lower legs; good wig; bulgy glass eyes; closed mouth; appropriately dressed. Typically unmarked.

29" Patent Washable Composition Shoulderhead. *Photo courtesy of McMasters Doll Auction.*

PATENT WASHABLE VALUE COMPARISONS:

Size	Standard Quality Patent Washable	Extraordinary Quality Patent Washable
14"	300.00	550.00
20"	350.00	700.00
29"	600.00	1,200.00
38"	800.00	1,500.00

Dr. Dora Petzold

Dr. Dora Petzold's composition character child dolls are another mysterious, but highly sought-after doll. Little information is available about either Dr. Dora Petzold or her dolls. One fact all seem to agree on is that these dolls are rare. The character heads have been variously reported as being silk, layers of paper, composition, and pressed cardboard—all of these may be correct. The bodies are stockinette with rather short torsos, and are jointed at the shoulders and hips. Hands have separate free-form thumbs, with the other fingers being only stitched. Legs have shaped calves.

A 1919 magazine, *Die Post*, reported on the Dora Petzold dolls. The article stated "...These are dolls for the high society, for the elegant world, for the boudoir, for the lady. Worked of velvet and silk...to decorate a room by placing them before an embroidered pillow or having them swing on the handrail of an armchair...." The author thought Petzold dolls were extraordinary—an opinion shared by today's collectors.

Yet another quote, from Dr. Dora Petzold herself: "All Dora Petzold dolls are produced in my workshops under my personal directorship and after my personal designs and models. The body of the dolls consists of high quality knit wear and is stuffed so that all doll joints can be bent to imitate every human movement. The heads of Dora Petzold dolls are of unbreakable non-flammable material and painted with non-toxic colors which makes my dolls washable. The outfit of the dolls is fashioned after the best children's outfits and produced of the first class material. All these characteristics make a practical and at the same time very nice toy of my doll...."

Prices listed are for dolls in good to very good condition. Normal wear and signs of aging, along with well-done repairs to the body, do not greatly affect price. Badly worn, stained, or repainted dolls will command less than half the amount listed.

Petzold Character: composition flange head, pink stockinette body, jointed at shoulders and hips; mitt hands with stitched fingers and separate thumb; mohair wig; painted eyes, single-stroke brows; accent nostrils; closed mouth; molded dimples; appropriately dressed. Stamped "Dora Petzold/Registered/Trade Mark/Doll/Germany."

DORA PETZOLD VALUE COMPARISONS:	
Size	**Petzold Character**
18"	1,000.00
22"	1,100.00
25"	1,300.00

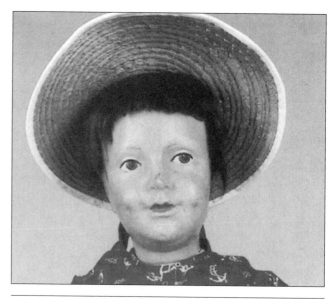

26" Dora Petzald Character Doll. *Photo courtesy of McMasters Doll Auction.*

Sheppard & Co. Philadelphia Baby

The Philadelphia Baby, also known as the Sheppard Baby, is a life-size cloth doll. The dolls were sold at the J.B. Sheppard Linen Store on Chestnut Street in Philadelphia, hence the name. The designer, maker, and dates of origin are unknown. The doll is generally accepted as having been made around the turn-of-the-century. One theory is that the Philadelphia Baby was designed by Elizabeth Washington, a student/artist at the Philadelphia School of Design. Supposedly, J.B. Sheppard's Linen Store held a contest for the best-designed doll which could be used as a model for its baby clothes and also offered for sale. Elizabeth Washington's doll won the contest and the rights were purchased by the Sheppard Store. There is no documentation to either support or discredit this story. However, we can thank U.F.D.C. member Frances Walker for offering this legend through her writings in the 1980s.

Philadelphia Babies range in size from 18 to 22 inches. The head, shoulders, forearms, and legs are painted in

SHEPPARD BABY VALUE COMPARISONS:	
Size	**Sheppard Baby**
18"	4,000.00
21"	4,500.00
22"	4,700.00

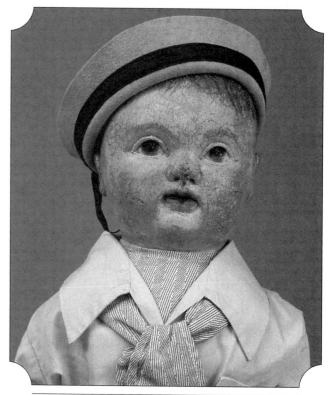

22" Sheppard & Co. Philadelphia Baby. *Courtesy of Carolyn Johnson.*

flesh-colored oil paints. The hair is painted. The face is molded with large deep eyes and well-molded, heavy eyelids. The mouth is a "cupid's bow" with a deep indentation in the center of the lower lip. The chin is quite pronounced. The well-molded ears are applied. The entire face has a rather flattened appearance. The fingers curve slightly inwards, in mitten fashion with separate thumbs. The one-piece arms have no elbow seams. The legs are stitched at the knees, allowing flexibility. The toes are also stitched.

Prices listed below are for a doll in good to very good condition. Normal wear, slight damage, or well-done repairs to the body do not greatly affect price. If the face is badly worn, cracked, or has been repainted, expect to pay less than half the amount listed.

Sheppard Baby: all cloth, oil-painted stockinette head and body, painted lower limbs, jointed at shoulders, hips, and knees; painted hair, matching eyebrows; painted eyes, molded eyelids; accented nostrils; applied ears; closed mouth with center lower lip indentation; appropriately dressed. Typically unmarked.

Rabery & Delphieu

This Paris, France, doll manufacturer produced dolls from 1856 until 1899. After 1899, the company was absorbed by the Societe Française de Fabrication de Bébés & Jouets (S.F.B.J.). Named for founders Alexandre Rabery and Jean Delphieu, the company was primarily interested in the production of doll bodies during its earliest years. By 1878, Rabery & Delphieu was exhibiting its own dressed and undressed dolls at the Paris Exhibition. During the 1880s, Francois Gaultier supplied both bisque heads and arms for Rabery & Delphieu Bébés.

Rabery & Delphieu Bébés were made from both pressed and poured bisque. The markings are "R. D." and a size number. Size numbers range from 6/0 (11") to at least 4 (28").

Rabery & Delphieu Bébés hold their own with the best-of-the-best from the late 19th century. These bébés were developed to be quite distinctive, with very pale creamy bisque and uniquely shaped square facial construction. They have large, dark, almond-shaped paperweight eyes with black eyeliner under widely arched, long, feathered brows, and have pierced ears. The delicately colored, outlined, accented, and shaded lips have a high cupid's bow.

Earlier examples of Rabery & Delphieu Bébés are distinguished by their vary pale smooth bisque. Later examples have rosier and somewhat coarse bisque, and less delicately applied decoration with rather exaggerated lashes, brows, and mouths.

Reproduction Rabery & Delphieu Bébés surface from time to time. As always, inspect the markings. Often a legitimate copy of a doll made by a doll artist will be marked with the artist's name or initials, and possibly its date of production. The texture of the bisque of a reproduction tends to be very smooth and satiny.

Prices listed are for dolls with no damage to the bisque. Normal wear, slight damage, or well-done repairs to the body do not greatly affect price. If the bisque is damaged or repaired, expect to pay less than half the amount listed. It is perfectly acceptable to show a missing or replaced finger or joint to the body.

22" Sheppard & Co. Philadelphia Baby. *Courtesy of Carolyn Johnson.*

Bébé: exceptional or standard quality socket head, jointed wood-and-composition body with straight wrists; good wig; paperweight eyes; open or closed mouth; appropriately dressed. Typically marked "R. D."

RABERY AND DELPHIEU BÉBÉ VALUE COMPARISONS:

Size	Closed Mouth, Extraordinary Quality	Closed Mouth, Standard Quality	Open Mouth
11"	3,400.00	3,600.00	1,700.00
13"	3,200.00	2,500.00	1,800.00
15"	3,400.00	2,600.00	1,900.00
17"	3,600.00	2,800.00	2,100.00
19"	3,900.00	3,000.00	2,400.00
21"	4,200.00	3,300.00	2,500.00
23"	4,600.00	3,500.00	2,700.00
24"	5,200.00	4,000.00	3,000.00
26"	5,700.00	4,600.00	3,400.00
28"	6,000.00	5,000.00	3,600.00

Raggedy Ann and Andy®

*I*n 1915, Johnny Gruelle registered the trademark and patented a Raggedy Ann doll pattern. The story of Raggedy Ann and Andy is probably one of the best loved American folk tales. Johnny Gruelle was born on Christmas Day, 1888. The Gruelle family was unusually gifted. His father and brother were both artists; his sister, Prudence, was a dancer and concert singer. It came as no surprise that Johnny would also make an everlasting and far-reaching impression on the world.

Johnny and his wife Myrtle had three children—a daughter, Marcella, and two sons, Worth and Richard. It is obvious from his stories that Johnny loved children very much and wanted them protected from the harsh realities of an adult world. In his first book, *Raggedy Ann Stories*, Johnny wrote "...Who knows, but that Fairyland is filled with old, lovable Rag Dolls—soft, floppy Rag Dolls who ride through all wonders of Fairyland in the crook of a dimpled arm, snuggling close to childish breast within which beats a heart filled with eternal sunshine." The love and tenderness which inspired such insight could only be that of an adoring father.

Marcella suffered a long and painful illness as a result of complications from a contaminated smallpox vaccination. Johnny spent hours telling his daughter wonderful stories about a land were dolls would come to life. About this same time, an old rag doll was found in his grandmother's attic. It is assumed that Gruelle painted a new face on the old rag doll, giving her a renewed life, and the name "Raggedy Ann." Marcella cherished her Raggedy Ann until her death in 1916. A grieving Johnny took Raggedy Ann to his office, where she became his constant companion. Although she failed to console him, she did inspire him. Whether as a self-prescribed therapy to lessen the pain of losing his daughter, or an attempt to immortalize her, Johnny Gruelle set about retelling the stories that had amused his daughter so. Beginning with *The Raggedy Ann Stories*, published in 1918, he wrote twenty-five books about Raggedy Ann and her adventures before his untimely death in 1938. The Chicago firm of P.F. Volland published Gruelle's Raggedy Ann books and suggested to him that a rag doll could help promote sales.

The first Raggedy Ann Dolls were made by the Gruelle family. It is estimated that about two hundred of these family-crafted Raggedy Anns were produced before the patent rights were given to Volland.

In 1920, Raggedy Ann's faithful companion and brother, Andy, first appeared. According to legend, Johnny was sitting in his office working on an illustration when a prim and proper little old lady suddenly appeared. She told Gruelle that she had been a neighbor and best friend to his mother when they were both little girls. It was her mother that had made the girl rag doll for Johnny's mother, and had also made a boy doll for her. The two best friends had played many hours with their rag doll sister and brother. She pulled

Georgene's Raggedy Ann and Andy.
Courtesy of Rusty Herlocher.

a well-loved, old boy rag doll from her bag and gave it to Johnny, saying she was glad that the old rag dolls were together again. Johnny was touched by the story as he lovingly accepted the doll and turned briefly to place it beside Raggedy Ann. When he turned around, the old woman was gone. He never saw her again, but from that time forward Raggedy Andy has been a constant companion to Ann.

The early hand-crafted Raggedy Ann and Andy dolls are undoubtedly very rare and infrequently found. The first mass-produced Raggedies, made by Vollands, are uncharacteristic of the typical Raggedy Ann and Andy. They stand about 16" high and have rather long faces. Brown yarn hair usually surrounds the face only, which has button eyes and painted facial features. Vollands were stamped on the belly "Patented Sept 7, 1915." Volland also produced other characters from the Gruelle stories, such as Uncle Clem, Beloved Belindy, Johnny Mouse, Eddie Elephant, Percy Policeman, Cleety the Clown, Brown Bear, and Sunny Bunny. In 1934, Volland declared bankruptcy and the Exposition Doll and Toy Company assumed production of Raggedy Ann and Andy dolls.

Exposition Raggedies are nearly as rare as the original hand-crafted version. They are a bit more familiar in appearance, with painted eyes and facial features, and a more triangular nose. Although the company had legal rights to continue producing Raggedy Ann and Andy dolls, they were in business for less than one year. When the Gruelles became embroiled in a legal battle over production of an unauthorized Molly-'es version of Raggedy Ann and Andy, the Exposition Doll and Toy Company backed out of the deal.

Molly-'es Raggedies have their own baffling history. By some accounts, mainly those of Mollye Goldman (owner of Molly-'es), Gruelle and Molly-'es entered into a friendly agreement. Reportedly, Gruelle even paid for a holiday trip for the Goldmans. However, something went wrong and he changed his mind about having them produce Raggedy Ann and Andy. Conflicting stories state that within a year of Volland's filing for bankruptcy, Molly-'es Doll Outfitters began producing Raggedy Ann and Andy dolls without permission from the Gruelle family, which had retained the rights to the dolls regardless of the manufacturer. Despite being confronted with the improper use of the Raggedy Ann name, and her failure to obtain Gruelle's permission, Mollye refused to stop manufacturing the dolls. The court battle lasted for three years and in 1938, the Supreme Court ruled in favor of the Gruelles. A month later, Gruelle died of a heart attack.

The Raggedy Ann and Andys produced by Molly-'es between 1935 and 1938 are among the most desirable Raggedies. Although unconventional in their appearance, few collectors can resist their charm. Ranging in size from 17 to 22 inches, Molly-'es version was the first to print a heart on the chest of the Raggedies. The bodies are more structured, allowing them to sit, and the legs are usually a multicolored striped material. They have dark auburn yarn hair, and the facial features are painted with large black eyes and a triangular nose, outlined in black. In addition to Raggedy Ann and Andy, Molly-'es also made a 14" Baby Ann and Andy. Molly-'es were usually stamped on the chest "Raggedy Ann and Andy Dolls Manufactured by Molly-'es Doll Outfitters."

After winning the suit against Molly-'es, the Gruelle family entered into an agreement with the Georgene Novelties Company. Georgene continued to produce Raggedy Ann and Andy for the next twenty-five years. The earliest and most desirable Georgenes have black outlined noses. Georgenes ranged in size from 15 to 50 inches. The floppy cloth bodies were stitched at the knees and elbows, allowing them to bend. Although they usually have red and white striped legs, a few original Georgenes have been found with legs of different materials. The yarn used for the hair changed color many times, from an almost strawberry blond to a deep orange, and all shades in between. Tin or plastic button eyes were added. The mouth was more defined. Most dolls have a curved line, as opposed to a straight line smile. Georgene also marketed a Beloved Belindy and an Awake/Asleep Raggedy Ann, with one side of the head sleeping and the other side awake. Georgene Raggedies have various cloth labels sewn into the side seam of the doll. Although wordy, all labels read "Johnny Gruelle's Own Raggedy Ann and Andy Dolls/and Georgene Novelties, Inc. New York City/Exclusive Licensed Manufacturer/ Made in U.S.A."

14" Molly-'es Raggedy Ann Baby. *Courtesy of Rusty Herlocher.*

The Knickerbocker Toy Company made a bid to the Gruelle family for the rights to Raggedy Ann and Andy in late 1962. When the contract with Georgene expired, the Gruelles decided to award Knickerbocker the license to manufacture Raggedies and use the Raggedy Ann and Andy names. Although most readily found in 12", 24" and 36" sizes, Knickerbocker Toy Company offered Raggedy Ann and Andy in an impressive range of sizes from a tiny 3 inches to a towering 78 inches. Body construction remained the same, but all known Raggedies made by the Knickerbocker Toy Company have red and white striped legs and a heart imprinted on the chest. The yarn hair is redder, the eyes are black plastic disks, and the mouth is a straight line smile. Knickerbocker Toy Company also produced Beloved Belindy, Camel with the Wrinkled Knees, and Raggedy Arthur. A vast assortment of Raggedy items were introduced, including sleeping bags, marionettes, huggers, dress-me-dolls, musical Raggedies, tote bags, and "Flexies," (bendable Ann and Andy). Knickerbocker Toy Company tagged the clothing of Raggedy Ann and Andy. At least six different types of tags were used in the twenty years that the company manufactured Raggedies. Although wordy, all include "Knickerbocker Toy Co./Raggedy Ann" or "Raggedy Andy"/and country of origin.

In 1982, Warner Communications sold the Knickerbocker Toy Company, and with it the license for Raggedy Ann, to Hasbro Industries. Today Hasbro-Playskool Raggedies are either 12 or 18 inches tall. The faces are silk screened and carry the Playskool label.

In 1993, Applause released a Raggedy Ann, Andy, and Baby Ann, copying the unauthorized Molly-'es as well as the more traditional Raggedy Ann and Andy with embroidered-type stitched features. All the high quality Applause dolls range from 7 to 36 inches and are tagged.

Johnny Gruelle's efforts to pay tribute to Marcella were well rewarded. Raggedy Ann walked into our hearts, hand-in-hand with her faithful Andy, and remains there still.

Reproduction Raggedy Ann and Andy dolls can be a problem. There is a very convincing reproduction Georgene presently circulating. Remember that Georgenes are tagged with a cloth label on the side seam. The reproductions are also made with what appears to be a well-worn tag on the side. Georgene's tags were white, whereas the fakes have peach-colored tags of the same material from which the body is made. Gently check the back of the head. The reproduction Georgene has a coarse, loosely woven red material covering the back of the head, beneath the yarn hair.

Another fake representation uses an authentic Georgene, and outlining the nose with a black marker. A careful inspection is helpful. The black outlining of the nose should show the same amount of wear and fading as the remaining face color. If the outline is darker than the other black details on the face, be suspicious. The worn, vintage look of the face is hard to copy. In addition to a good visual examination, smell the doll. Nothing can duplicate the scent acquired by a rag doll which has been around for sixty years. Several craft-type dolls boast of an "attic" smell, but these are only perfumed and don't have that true "I've been around a long time" smell. Inspect the seams. Recently made dolls have strong seams which lack a worn look.

Finally, be aware of the hand-crafted Raggedy Ann and Andy dolls made from the McCall's pattern. The buying and selling of these dolls is an infringement of the Gruelle copyright, and therefore unlawful.

Prices listed are for dolls in very good condition. Early Raggedies can be forgiven for showing some wear. So rarely is one found in excellent condition that it would easily command three or four times the amount listed. Badly stained, torn, or damaged Raggedies command less than half the amount listed. It is perfectly acceptable to show a repaired seam, settled stuffing, or normal signs of aging.

First Gruelle Family Hand-crafted Raggedy Ann: 1918, body with loosely jointed limbs and stuffed with white cotton; long face with hand-painted features and brown yarn hair; candy heart in body (often sucked on by a child, so look for stains on the chest). Typically marked with rubber-stamped date on tummy or back. Very rare.

Volland Raggedy Ann or Andy: 1920-1934, all cloth, movable arms and legs; brown yarn hair; painted features; button eyes. Typically marked "Patented Sept 7, 1915."

Exposition Doll and Toy Company: 1935, brown yarn hair; painted features. These extremely rare dolls were produced for only a few months. About one dozen dolls are known to be in collections.

Molly-'es Raggedy Ann or Andy: 1935-1938, all cloth, often patterned materials; auburn yarn hair; printed features; black outlined nose; heart on chest. Typically marked "Raggedy Ann and Andy Dolls Manufactured by Molly-'es Doll Outfitters."

RAGGEDY ANN AND ANDY VALUE COMPARISONS:

Company Name	Size	Value
Gruelle Family	16", Ann only	8,000.00
Volland	16", Ann or Andy	2,900.00
	14", Beloved Belindy	3,500.00
	14" - 18" Character	2,500.00
Exposition Doll		9,000.00
Molly-'es	17" to 22" Ann or Andy	1,500.00
	14", Baby	1,700.00
Georgene *	13", Ann, Awake/Asleep	700.00
	14" - 18", Beloved Belindy	2,200.00
	15", Ann or Andy	300.00
	19", Ann or Andy	325.00
	24", Ann or Andy	400.00
	31", Ann or Andy	450.00
	36", Ann or Andy	500.00
	45", Ann or Andy	900.00
	50", Ann or Andy	1,500.00
Knickerbocker Toy Co.	3", Ann or Andy Huggers	75.00
	6", Ann or Andy	45.00
	12", Ann or Andy	85.00
	15", Ann or Andy	100.00
	19", Ann or Andy	125.00
	24", Ann or Andy	225.00
	30", Ann or Andy	250.00
	36", Ann or Andy	300.00
	40", Ann or Andy	450.00
	45", Ann or Andy	600.00
	78", Ann or Andy	800.00
	15", Beloved Belindy	1,000.00
Camel with Wrinkled Knees		400.00
Raggedy Arthur		200.00
Applause	15", Ann or Andy	45.00
	20", Ann or Andy	60.00

* A black outlined nose doubles the value of any Georgene Raggedy Ann or Andy.

Georgene: 1938-1962, all cloth, stitched elbow and knee seams, printed heart on chest, silk-screen printed features; button eyes; orangish-red yarn hair, Ann has a few longer strands on top to which a ribbon can be tied. Typically marked with cloth label sewn into side reading "Johnny Gruelle's Own Raggedy Ann and Andy Dolls.../Georgene Manufacturers/Made in U.S.A."

Knickerbocker Toy Company Raggedy Ann or Andy: 1963-1982, silk-screen printed face; red shades of yarn hair. Typically marked only with clothing label "Raggedy Ann or Andy.../Knickerbocker Toy Co."/country of origin.

Hasbro/Playskool: currently available.

Applause: 1993, embroidered-type face, Molly-'es look alike, currently available.

Ravca Dolls

Ravca Dolls are known as the Real People Dolls. They are the artistic creations of Bernard Ravca, originally of Paris, France, and later the United States. After Bernard Ravca won first prize at the Paris Fair with his two life-size figures of a Normandy peasant and his wife, the French government sent him to the United States. Fate intervened when, in 1939, Bernard arrived to exhibit his famous dolls in the French Pavilion at the New York World's Fair. The winds of war were gathering momentum in Europe, and while representing his country in the United States, France fell under the heel of Nazi oppression, leaving Bernard an exile. He spent the next several years raising money for the Free French War Relief, and doing what he could for orphans of the resistance movement. Tragically, during Hitler's occupation of France, Ravca's entire family was lost, his studio pillaged, and his bank accounts seized. Bernard Ravca began life anew, and he became a United States citizen in 1947.

The sadness and loss that was so much a part of his life can be seen reflected in his work. The peasant with the gnarled hands, stooped from a life of toil; aloof expressions on persons of royalty, far removed from ordinary life; corrupt political figures ridden with greed and ruthlessness—all are preserved in Ravca's life-like soft sculptures. All facets of human nature are conveyed—some unpleasant emotions, to be sure, but also joy and happiness. Ravca Dolls are not dark and sinister, but show tremendous emotion and sensitivity. In the course of viewing and studying many Ravca Dolls while researching this book, it became evident that at least a few of the dolls credited to Bernard Ravca may, in fact, be the creations of his wife, Frances Elinor Ravca. While Ravca Dolls normally portray a realistic view of life, several of the dolls seem to have a more idealized view of how we wish life could be.

Ravca doll heads are made from silk stockings stretched over sculpted cotton, with painted facial features. Wire armatures form the bodies. Occasionally, a composition of bread crumbs was used. Dolls are marked with hang tags which read "Bernard Ravca," and/or with labels sewn into their perfectly accurate costumes.

While reproductions are not a problem, contemporary doll makers influenced by Ravca's creations have imitated his study with varying degrees of success. Since tags are often missing, it may be difficult to distinguish an original Ravca Doll from a copy. There is no sure-fire way to identify an unmarked Ravca. Seek out and examine as many authentic Ravcas as possible in order to learn to evaluate these exquisitely detailed dolls.

Ravca Dolls are especially vulnerable to nose and chin rubs, which result in snags. Prices listed are for dolls in good condition. If damaged, repaired, or redressed, expect to pay less than half the amount listed.

Ravca Stockinette Couple. *Photo courtesey McMasters Doll Auction.*

RAVCA CHARACTER VALUE COMPARISONS:

Size	Ravca Character
10"	250.00
15"	350.00
20"	450.00
30"	750.00
42"	1,700.00

Ravca Character: all cloth, silk stockinette drawn over face and arms, straw-filled wire armature body; wool wig; beautifully painted facial features; original clothing. Typically unmarked, or marked with hang tags with Bernard Ravca's signature and the region or character depicted.

Theodor Recknagel

Recknagel Child.

Production of dolls by Theodor Recknagel, located in Alexandrienthal, near Oeslau, Thüringia, Germany, began about 1893. While Recknagel's porcelain factory was founded in 1886, there is no evidence of doll production before 1893, when he registered two Mulatto doll heads which were tinted rather than painted.

Quality varies. Recknagel Dolls can be of the finest quality with extremely artistic application of decoration, or they can be of very coarse bisque with the facial features rather haphazardly applied.

Mold numbers registered by Recknagel include R1, 21, 22, 23, 24, 25, 26, 27, 28, 29, 30 31, 32, 33, 34, 35, 37, 39, 41, 43, 44, 45, 46, 47, 48, 49, 50, 53, 54, 55, 56, 57, 58, 86, 121, 126, 128, 129, 131, 132, 134, 135, 136, 137, 138, 226, 227, 1907, 1909, 1914, RIV, and R XII.

The four digit mold numbers starting with a 19 do not appear to be a date. For example, mold 1907 was registered in 1910. Often, in addition to, or occasionally in place of, a mold number, you may find an "RA." Supposedly the initials of Recknagel/Alexandrienthal, they are sometimes reversed to "AR." And, "JK," "NG," or "NK" occasionally appears above the reversed "AR" marking. It appears that NG denotes a newborn with a flange neck, and NK denotes a newborn with a socket head.

Prices listed are for dolls with no damage to the bisque. Normal wear, slight damage or well-done repairs to the body do not greatly affect price. If the bisque is damaged or repaired, expect to pay less than half the amount listed. It is perfectly acceptable to show a missing or repaired finger or joint to the body.

See also Googly-Eyed Dolls.

Child Dolly-Face: bisque socket head of either good or fair quality, jointed composition body; good wig; glass eyes; open mouth; appropriately dressed. Typically marked "1909 DEP R/A," "RA1907," or "1914."

Character Baby: flange or socket neck, cloth or composition body. Typically marked "RA," "86," "126," "127," "128," "129," "131," "132," "134," "135," "136," "137," "138," or "1927."

Character Doll: varying characteristics including molded bonnet, cap, and/or hair ornaments, painted eyes, closed or open/closed mouth; appropriately dressed. Typically marked "AR," "RA," " 22," "28," "43," or "55."

Max/Mortiz: molded and painted hair and facial features. Typically marked "31" or "32."

RECKNAGEL BISQUE DOLL VALUE COMPARISONS:

Size	Good Quality, Dolly-Face	Fair Quality, Dolly-Face	Character Baby	Character-face Dolls	Max or Moritz
8"			325.00	550.00	800.00
10"	300.00	150.00	350.00	700.00	
12"	325.00	175.00	375.00	900.00	
14"	350.00	200.00	400.00	1,200.00	
16"	450.00	300.00	450.00		
18"	500.00	350.00	500.00		
20"	550.00	400.00	600.00		
24"	650.00	450.00			

Grace Corry Rockwell

Located in New York City, Grace Corry Rockwell designed dolls for several manufacturers around 1920. Among her most popular dolls are Little Sister and Little Brother, designed for Averill Manufacturing. She also designed dolls for Century Doll Company, such as Fiji Wiji and a number of child dolls.

The most valuable doll designed by Grace Corry Rockwell is a bisque character doll simply marked "Copr. by Grace C. Rockwell Germany." It is assumed by many doll collectors that Kestner produced this doll for Century Doll Company. The very good quality of the bisque and nice application of decoration, coupled with the close association of Grace Corry Rockwell, Century Doll Company, and Kestner makes this a rather safe assumption.

While reproductions have been reported, they are not as commonly found as for other dolls. An inspection of the markings is a must. The addition of any dates or initials other than those listed above is an immediate indication to beware. Let your fingers be the final judge. Lightly run your finger over the cheek. If the bisque is very smooth and satiny soft, the doll may not be authentic. Although Kestner used a very high-grade quality bisque, true Kestners will not feel satiny.

Prices listed are for dolls with no damage. Slight wear or well-done repairs to the body do not greatly affect price. If the bisque is damaged or repaired, or if the composition head is cracked, peeling, or repainted, expect to pay about one half the amount listed. It is perfectly acceptable to show a missing or repaired finger or joint to the body.

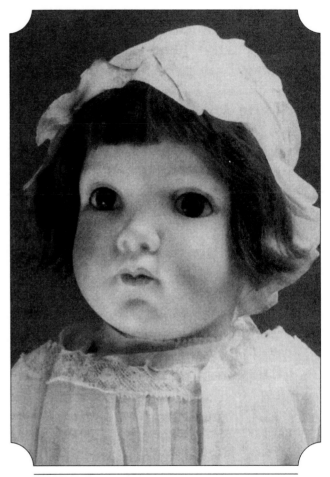

20" Grace Corry Rockwell on a cloth body. *Photo courtesy Cobbs Doll Auction.*

Bisque Character Doll: bisque flange neck character head, cloth body, composition limbs; molded and painted hair or good wig; glass sleep eyes, painted upper and lower short lashes, very soft brows; closed mouth. Typically marked "Copr. by/Grace C. Rockwell/Germany."

Composition Character Doll: composition flange neck character head, cloth body with cryer box, composition arms, composition or cloth legs; molded and painted hair and eyes; closed mouth; when dressed as a boy "Little Brother;" when dressed as a girl "Little Sister;" when dressed as a nursery rhyme character "Kiddie Karakter." Typically marked "©/By Grace Corry."

		Composition Little Brother/Sister*	**Composition Kiddie Karakter***
Size	**Bisque Character**		
14"	6,000.00	700.00	800.00
18"	7,000.00		
20"	8,000.00		

GRACE CORRY ROCKWELL VALUE COMPARISONS:

* The difference in the value of these dolls can only be interpreted by demand, appeal, and availability of the rarer Kiddie Karakter.

Mme. Rohmer

arie Antoniette Leontine Rohmer of Paris, France, operated her doll business from 1857 until 1880. She produced elegant Parisian fashion ladies, Poupée de Mode, of both china and bisque.

During the early years of production, Mme. Rohmer obtained several patents for improvements to doll bodies. The first was for articulated joints on kid bodies, followed by a patent for gutta percha or rubber arms for kid bodies. The final patent was for a new type of doll's head with a cord running through the head, into the body, and coming out riveted holes in the front of the torso. This facilitated turning of the head in any direction and also secured the head to the body. Examples of bodies utilizing the first and last patents are occasionally found. However, bodies with gutta percha arms are seldom seen. One explanation for the absence of these arms may be that they deteriorated and were replaced with bisque. Almost fifty years after Mme. Rohmer registered her patent for articulated joints, Charles Fausel received a patent for a very similar universal joint in the United States.

The doll industry of the 19th century made great strides in manufacturing thanks to leaders such as Mme. Rohmer, who continually sought to improve the appearance and movement of her Poupée de Mode. During a time when most companies were directed by men, Mme. Rohmer was apparently quite successful.

Rohmer Poupée de Modes can be found with either painted or glass eyes—the latter being more rare. All are noted for their sensuous and somewhat dreamy expressions. Look for the oval stamp on the body which reads "Mme. Rohmer/Brevete SGDG Paris."

Reproduction Rohmer dolls appear on the market from time to time. A careful examination of the body and head is essential in order to positively identify a Rohmer. The early date of production of these dolls often results in peppering (minute specks) of the porcelain. The neck flange of an authentic Rohmer doll should have a kid lining at the shoulder plate. Finally, Rohmer eyelids have good detailing. This detailing is often lost in a mold used over for reproductions.

Prices listed are for dolls with no damage to the bisque. Normal wear, slight damage or well-done repairs to the body do not greatly affect price. If the bisque is damaged or

Rohmer Fashion Doll singed body with trunk and accessories. *Photo courtesy Cobbs Doll Auction.*

repaired, expect to pay less than half the amount listed. It is perfectly acceptable to show a missing or repaired finger or a mended kid seam.

Poupée de Mode: china or bisque head, flange neck, kid-lined shoulder plate; kid body may have wooden joints at shoulders and knees; china or bisque arms; good wig; painted or glass eyes; rosy cheeks; closed mouth; appropriately dressed. Stamped "Mme. Rohmer/Brevete SGDG Paris" on chest. May have two eyelet holes at abdomen.

ROHMER POUPÉE DE MODE VALUE COMPARISONS:		
Size	Painted-eye Lady	Glass-eye Lady
14"	4,900.00	5,800.00
16"	6,000.00	6,500.00
18"	7,200.00	8,000.00

Rollinson Doll

Founded in 1916 by Gertrude Rollinson of Holyoke, Massachusetts, this doll company operated until 1929. Mrs. Rollinson originally designed and created cloth dolls. Her first dolls were handmade for crippled children confined to hospitals. These first attempts had flat, painted faces. However, she was unhappy with the effect, and continually experimented with several sculptured techniques until finally achieving three-dimensional features on a stockinette doll. So successful were her efforts that before long there was a great demand for her dolls. In 1916, Mrs. Rollinson commercialized her doll-making talents. A large-scale manufacturer was needed. Utley Company fulfilled that demand by producing thirty-five styles of Rollinson Dolls.

Rollinson Dolls can be found wearing one of three styles of wigs: short curls, long curls, or Dutch boy style; or may have painted blond, or light or dark brown hair. Eyes were painted. The mouths were closed or open/closed with painted teeth. Some dolls have pierced nostrils. During the production of the Rollinson Doll, twenty coats of paint were applied to each stockinette head. After each coat was applied, the head was dried in the sun and smoothed down with sandpaper, resulting in a hard, durable, beautifully polished washable surface.

Rollinson Dolls have a diamond-shaped stamp on the torso with "Rollinson Doll Holyoke Mass." around the border, and a picture of a doll in the center.

Prices listed are for dolls in good condition. Some wear is normal and to be expected, and is acceptable. However, if the paint is chipped, peeling, damaged, or repainted, expect to pay less than half the amount listed.

Rollinson Child: cloth doll, painted shoulder head, sateen covered cloth body, painted lower limbs; stitched at shoulders, elbows, and knees; hands and feet are stitched to show finger and toe details; painted hair or good wig; applied ears; painted eyes; closed mouth; appropriately dressed. Stamped "Rollinson Doll Holyoke Mass" within a diamond on torso.

ROLLINSON CHILD DOLL VALUE COMPARISONS:	
Size	**Cloth Child**
14"	1,100.00
16"	1,300.00
18"	1,500.00
20"	1,700.00
22"	1,900.00
24"	2,200.00
26"	2,400.00
28"	2,600.00

15" Rollinson Doll with a 12" German Cymbaler.
Photo courtesy McMasters Doll Auction.

Sasha Dolls

Sasha Dolls are vinyl dolls designed by Sasha Morgenthaler, an extremely gifted artist. Turning her talents to the creation of dolls, she operated a somewhat limited commercial enterprise. She was finally able to have her dolls mass produced according to her artistic specifications and high standards of quality. The first Sasha Dolls were produced in 1964 by Gotz of Germany. Production problems occurred, prompting Ms. Morgenthaler to grant the licensing rights to Trenton Toy, Ltd., Reddish, Stockport, England, which continued producing Sasha Dolls until the company went out of business in 1986.

All Sasha Dolls are similar in appearance, with wistful serious expressions and a slightly darkened skin tone. The Gotz dolls are marked "Sasha Series" within a circle on the back of the head. Also, the upper eyelids of the Gotz dolls are painted with a curved line, resulting in a somewhat unnatural appearance. Other Sasha eyelids are painted with a straighter eyelid line. All Sasha Dolls have a realistic body construction, allowing for a great range of movement. Later Sasha dolls are unmarked save for a wrist tag.

A limited edition series of dolls was produced between 1981 and 1986. Because Trenton Toy, Ltd., went out of business in 1986, it is unlikely that the last doll of the series ever reached true production quantities.

Reproduction Sasha Dolls are not a problem. However, Sasha Dolls are once again being manufactured by Gotz. These newly introduced Sashas, although very similar in appearance to the earlier dolls, are easily recognized by their markings. The 1995 Sasha Dolls are marked with an incised circular logo between the shoulders, and the neck is engraved with "Gotz."

Prices listed are for dolls in mint to near mint condition. There is little forgiveness for damaged or redressed dolls.

Sasha Series: 16", similar in appearance to early Gotz. Marked "Sasha Series."

Trenton Toys, Ltd.: 16", straight upper eyelid. Marked with wrist tag only.

Bent-Limb Baby: 12", rigid plastic, jointed at neck, shoulders and hips; cup-like hands; rooted hair; painted eyes; closed mouth. Marked with wrist tag only.

20th Anniversary Sasha: 16", black hair; copy of first Sasha doll; made by Trenton Toys, Ltd.; wearing blue corduroy dress.

Limited Edition Series: 16", with certificate and wrist tag.

   Velvet: girl; black hair; gray eyes; blue velvet dress; 1981, limited to 5,000.

   Pintuck: girl; light hair; brown eyes; cotton dress with pintucking; 1982, limited to 6,000.

Sasha "Gregor."

Kiltie: girl; human hair; gray eyes; black watch tartan dress, amethyst necklace; 1983, limited to 4,000.

Harlequin: girl; long hair; straw hat; carrying wooden guitar; 1984, limited to 5,000.

Prince Gregor: boy; dark hair; tunic top; 1985, limited to 4,000.

Princess: girl; long blond hair; blue eyes; pink dress, blue velvet cape; 1986, limited to 3,500.

Sasha Sari: 16", wearing exquisitely made sari from India. Marked with wrist tag only.

Early Morgamthaler Original Sasha: 20", original artist doll.

						Marked "Sasha Series,"	20th Anniversary	1995
SASHA DOLLS LIMITED VALUE COMPARISONS:								
Size	Black Baby	Sexed Baby	White Baby	White Child	Black Child	Boy or Girl	Sasha	Sasha Doll
16"	275.00	325.00	200.00	275.00	350.00	1,200.00	400.00	300.00

	Early Sasha Doll	Velvet (1981)	Pintuck (1982)	Kiltie (1983)	Harlequin (1984)	Prince Gregor (1985)	Princess (1986)	Sasha Sari
SASHA DOLLS LIMITED VALUE COMPARISONS (CONTINUED):								
Size								
16"		400.00	375.00	400.00	400.00	400.00	1,800.00	1,200.00
20"	6,500.00							

Peter Scherf

This doll factory was founded in 1879 by Peter Scherf, and located in Sonneberg, Germany, the famous "Town of Toys." Following Scherf's death in 1887, the business was divided among various family members. Bisque dolls continued to be supplied to the American market bearing Peter Scherf marks, or the trade name "The Fairy Kid," well into the 1920s. Bisque heads were produced at Armand Marseille's porcelain factory.

Prices listed are for dolls with no damage to the bisque. Normal wear, slight damage, or well-done repairs to the body do not greatly affect price. If the bisque is damaged or repaired, expect to pay less than half the amount listed. It is perfectly acceptable to show a missing or repaired finger, joint, or patched kid body.

Dolly-Face Child: bisque shoulder head, composition or kid body, riveted joints, nicely molded bisque lower arms; good wig; glass sleep eyes; open mouth; appropriately dressed. Typically marked "P. Sch Germany."

25" Peter Scherf 1899 Bisque Shoulderhead. *Courtesy of Joyce McKeague.*

PETER SCHERF VALUE COMPARISONS:

Size	Dolly-Face Child	Size	Dolly-Face Child
10"	225.00	22"	650.00
12"	350.00	24"	750.00
14"	400.00	26"	800.00
16"	450.00	28"	850.00
18"	500.00	30"	900.00
20"	550.00		

Bruno Schmidt

*I*n 1900 Bruno Schmidt founded his bisque doll factory in Waltershausen, Germany. Prior to 1900, Schmidt was in partnership with Hugo Geisler. When Geisler left the business, Schmidt changed the name to Bruno Schmidt. Schmidt's doll company manufactured and distributed some of the most desirable character dolls. Two of the best known characters are Tommy Tucker (mold 2048) and his companion Wendy (mold 2033), which is decidedly more rare. Records indicate that Bruno Schmidt's character bisque heads were purchased exclusively from Bähr & Pröschild.

Bruno Schmidt eventually purchased the Bähr & Pröschild company. The heads produced by Bähr & Pröschild often bear both firms' trademarks, namely the heart and crossed swords, as well as two sets of mold numbers. The three-digit numbers were Bähr & Pröschild's, the four-digit mold numbers beginning with a 2 belonged to Bruno Schmidt. Mold numbers used by Bruno Schmidt include 2020, 2023, 2025, 2033, 2048, 2068, 2070, 2072, 2074, 2075, 2081, 2084, 2085, 2092, 2094, 2095, 2096, 2097, 2099, and 2154.

Reproduction Bruno Schmidt dolls surface from time to time. The majority of Bruno Schmidt reproduction dolls were made as legitimate copies by modern doll artists and/or craft persons. Most of these craft persons were proud of their work and signed and dated their creations. A careful examination of the markings is the first clue to authenticating a bisque doll. Also examine the body. Is the body new or does it appear to be of the same age as the head? An inspection of the eyes may also help to determine age. Finally, vintage bisque does not have a creamy appearance or a silky feel.

Prices listed are for dolls with no damage to the bisque. Normal wear, slight damage, or well-done repairs to the

Flirty Eye Bruno Schmidt. *Photo courtesy of McMasters Doll Auction.*

Size	2023, 2025, 2026 CM, Glass Eyes	2023, 2025, 2026 CM, Painted Eyes	2033 CM, Glass Eyes	2048 CM, Glass Eyes	2048, 2094, 2096 OM, Glass Eyes	2072 CM, Glass Eyes	2072 OM, Glass Eyes	2092, 2097, 2099 OM, Glass Eyes
12"			13,000.00					
13"				2,000.00	1,300.00			
15"	5,200.00	4,400.00	19,000.00	3,000.00	1,800.00	3,700.00		750.00
18"	5,600.00	4,700.00	27.000.00		1,900.00	4,100.00	1,800.00	1,000.00
20"				3,800.00	2,000.00			
22"	6,300.00	5,400.00				4,500.00	2,300.00	1,300.00
24"				4,500.00	2,500.00			1,500.00

BRUNO SCHMIDT CHARACTER DOLLS VALUE COMPARISONS:

Note: Add an additional $500.00 for toddler body. Add an additional $200.00 for flirty eyes.
CM = Closed Mouth
OM = Open Mouth

body do not greatly affect price. If the bisque is damaged or repaired expect to pay about one-half the amount listed. It is perfectly acceptable to show a missing or repaired finger or joint to the body.

Character Doll: bisque socket head, jointed composition body; molded and painted hair or good wig; painted or glass eyes; open, closed, or open/closed mouths; appropriately dressed. Typically marked "BSW" within a heart, and a number "2020," "2023," "2025," "2033," "2048," "2068," "2070," "2072," "2074," "2075," "2081," "2084," "2085," "2092," "2094," "2095," "2096," "2097," or "2099." May also include a three-digit number, beginning with "5", such as 524, 537, 538, or 539.

Child Doll: socket head, jointed composition body; good wig; glass eyes; open mouths; appropriately dressed. Typically marked "B.S.W." within a heart, and/or "2154."

BRUNO SCHMIDT CHILD DOLL VALUE COMPARISONS:	
Size	Dolly-Face
16"	600.00
18"	700.00
20"	800.00
22"	900.00
24"	1,100.00
26"	1,200.00
28"	1,500.00
30"	2,000.00
32"	2,500.00

Note: Add an additional $200.00 for flirty eyes.

Franz Schmidt

This bisque doll company was founded by Franz Schmidt in 1890 in Georgenthal, Thüringia, Germany. Franz Schmidt dolls are well-known for their charming modeling and consistently excellent quality. The company also provided many innovations to the doll industry, including improved wooden body joints (1899); pierced nostrils (1912); movable tongue (1913); universal joints (1914); eye bar (1928); and doll voices (1928).

The Simon & Halbig porcelain factory supplied bisque heads to the Franz Schmidt Doll Factory according to designs and specifications of the Schmidt Company. Two of Schmidt's most famous sculptors were Traugott Schmidt and Albin Scheler.

Often, a small "z" will appear along with the marking on a Franz Schmidt Doll. It is assumed that this is an abbreviation for zentimeter—German for centimeter. Franz Schmidt also appeared to have marked earlier bisque heads "S & Co." and later heads "FS & C."

Prices listed are for dolls with no damage to the bisque. Normal wear, slight damage, or well-done repairs to the body do not greatly affect price. If the bisque is damaged or repaired, expect to pay about one-half the amount listed. It is perfectly acceptable to show a missing or repaired finger or joint to the body.

Child Dolly-Face: kid or jointed composition body; good wig; glass eyes; open mouth. Typically marked "269," "293," "1180," "1250," "1253," "1370," "S & Co. Simon & Halbig," or "FS & C Simon & Halbig."

Character Baby: socket head, bent-limb baby body; wig or solid dome; glass eyes; open mouth; often with pierced nostrils; appropriately dressed. Typically marked "FS & C," "1271," "1272," "1295," "1296," "1297," or "1310."

21" Franz Schmidt Toddler 1296. *Photo courtesy McMasters Doll Auction.*

Character Doll: bisque head with molded and painted hair or good wig; glass or painted eyes; open, closed, or open/closed mouth; appropriately dressed. Typically marked "1262," "1263," "1266, "1267," or "1268."

	Size	Child Dolly-Face, Kid Body	Child Dolly-Face, Composition Body	Character Baby	1262 O/CM, Painted Eyes	1263 CM, Painted Eyes	1266 O/CM, Painted Eyes	1267 CM, Painted Eyes	1268 OM, Glass Eyes
	12"	250.00	500.00	700.00					
	14"	300.00	600.00	800.00					
	15"						3,200.00	2,900.00	
	16"	400.00	700.00	900.00	7,000.00	19,000.00			4,200.00
	18"	450.00	750.00	1,000.00					
	20"	500.00	800.00	1,200.00	15,000.00	24,000.00	4,100.00	4,000.00	5,000.00
	22"	600.00	900.00	1,400.00					
	24"	700.00	1,000.00	1,700.00	23,000.00	32,000.00			
	26"	800.00	1,100.00	1,900.00					
	28"		1,200.00	2,500.00					
	30"		1,500.00						
	36"		2,500.00						
	42"		3,800.00						

FRANZ SCHMIDT VALUE COMPARISONS:

Note: Add an additional $500.00 for a toddler or key wound walker body.

OM = Open Mouth
CM = Closed Mouth
O/C = Open/Closed Mouth

Schmitt et Fils

Schmitt et Fils, which translates to Schmitt and Sons, was located at Nogent-sur-Marne, Seine, and Paris, France. Maurice and Charles Schmitt manufactured Bébés from 1863 to 1891.

Schmitt et Fils Bébés usually have pressed rather than poured bisque. The facial modeling consists of either a full, round face or a long-cheeked oval shape. Lamb's wool wigs are not uncommon. Almond-shaped paperweight eyes possess great depth and richness of color. The eyeliner is black and thick, and the lashes are not necessarily long. Blushed eye shadow matches the delicate cheek color, as well as the matching blushed pierced ears. The mouth is closed, with a slender space between the lips and carefully painted outlines and shading. These enchanting facial features help explain why Schmitt et Fils Bébés are numbered among the finest and costliest in today's doll market.

Reproduction Schmitt et Fils Bébés surface occasionally. Inspect the markings, looking carefully for a doll artist's name, initials or date. Examine the body both for construction and a stamp which may be found on the hip. A careful inspection of the inside of the head should provide evi-

Beautiful Schmitt & Fils Bébé. *Photo courtesy Cobbs Doll Auction.*

dence of the earlier pressed bisque. The ears should show a light blush, a detail which is often overlooked on the fakes.

Prices listed are for dolls with no damage to the bisque. Normal wear, slight damage, or well-done repairs to the body do not greatly affect price. If the bisque is damaged or repaired, expect to pay about one-half the amount listed. It is perfectly acceptable to show a missing or repaired finger or joint to the body.

Bébé: bisque socket head, wood-and-composition body, straight wrists, long flat bottom feet; good wig; oval-cut paperweight eyes, black eyeliner, blush eye shadow, thick short lashes, feathered brows; pierced lightly blushed ears; closed mouth with slight space between lips; appropriately dressed. Marked with hammer and "SCH" within a shield on head and hip.

Bébés may also be found with the neck ending in a dome shape that fit up into the neck socket, eliminating the line at the base of the neck. Collectors refer to this arrangement as a "cup and saucer" neck.

Size	Long-face Bébé	Round-face Bébé
12"	9,500.00	14,000.00
14"	13,000.00	
16"	15,000.00	20,000.00
18"	17,000.00	
20"	19,000.00	
22"	22,000.00	26,000.00
26"	27,000.00	

Note: Add an additional $3,000.00 to the above prices for a "cup and saucer" neck.

Schoenau & Hoffmeister

The Schoenau & Hoffmeister porcelain factory was located in Burggrub, Upper Franconia, Germany. Founded in 1901 by Arthur Schoenau and Carl Hoffmeister of Sonneberg, the factory produced bisque doll heads until 1953. By 1907, several disagreements erupted between the partners, the worst concerning the merits of socket versus shoulder heads. Although it seems a trivial thing, Carl Hoffmeister insisted upon producing bisque doll heads in the shoulder head-style, while Arthur Schoenau was equally determined to produce socket head-types. Unable to resolve their differences, the partnership was dissolved; Carl Hoffmeister left the firm, and Arthur Schoenau became sole owner.

In 1909, a new partner was added—Magnus Leube. When Arthur Schoenau died in 1911, his son Hans took over as director of the company. Eventually, the directorship passed to Arthur's widow, Caroline, and to Curt Schoenau. Curt supplied Cäsar Schneider, the sculptor for Schoenau & Hoffmeister, with a photo of Princess Elizabeth. This was used as a model for the famous Princess Elizabeth Doll.

The Princess Elizabeth Doll is only one of the many dolls produced by Schoenau & Hoffmeister. The enviable record of design included child dolly-faces, ethnic faces, and fine portrait dolls. Markings that may be found are "DALABA," initials for Das Lachende Baby (the laughing baby); "Hanna MB" for My Cherub, "Princess Elizabeth," and "Viola." Mold numbers include 169, 900, 914, 1400, 1800, 1904, 1906, 1930, 2500, 4000, 4001, 4500, 4600, 4700, 4900, 5000, 5300, 5500, 5700, and 5800 in conjunction with initials "SHPB" and a five-pointed star. After 1930 the heads were incised with

31" Schoenau & Hoffmeister 1906. *Photo courtesy of McMasters Doll Auction.*

"Porzellanfabrik Burggrub" and perhaps "Special." "NKB" and "WSB" may denote neck style on some babies.

Prices listed are for dolls with no damage to the bisque. Normal wear, slight damage, or well-done repairs to the body do not greatly affect price. If the bisque is damaged or repaired, expect to pay less than half the amount listed. It is perfectly acceptable to show a missing or repaired finger or joint to the body.

Character Baby: socket head, bent-limb baby body; good wig; glass eyes; open mouth; appropriately dressed. Typically marked "S (star)" with "P.B. H," "Porzellanfabrik Burggrub," "900," "169," "769," and "Special."

Solid Dome Infant: bisque flange neck, cloth body; painted hair; small glass sleep eyes; closed mouth; appropriately dressed. Typically marked "N.K.B.," may also have stamp in German. There are conflicting opinions whether N.K.B. denotes flange neck or a factory location.

Hanna Character Baby: bisque socket head, bent-limb baby body; good wig; large somewhat-rounded glass eyes, no painted upper lashes, winged feathered brows; open, slightly smiling mouth; appropriately dressed. Typically marked "S (star with PB) H/Hanna."

Das Lachende Baby (The Laughing Baby): bisque socket head, full face, bent-limb baby body; good wig; glass eyes; open smiling mouth with two upper teeth; molding may resemble a happy baby rather than a laughing one; appropriately dressed. Typically marked "Porzellanfabrik/Burggrub/Das Lachende Baby/1930/Made in Germany/D.R.G.M."

18" Schoenau & Hoffmeister 5800 Child doll. *Photo courtesy of McMasters Doll Auction.*

Princess Elizabeth: bisque socket head, jointed composition body; blond mohair wig; blue sleep eyes cut in oval, slightly squinting; open smiling mouth, rosy cheeks, giving very pretty expression; appropriately dressed. Typically marked "Porzellanfabrik/Burggrub/Princess Elizabeth/Made in Germany."

Character Doll: bisque socket head, composition body; good wig; deeply cut rounded eyes with real upper lashes, no painted upper lashes, winged brows; open mouth with wistful expression. Typically marked "S(pb) within a star," "H," and "OX."

Dolly-Face: bisque head, jointed composition body or kid body; good wig; glass eyes; open mouth; appropriately dressed. Typically marked "SH" and a five-pointed star with "PB" and mold number "1400," "1800," "1904," "1906," "2500," "4500," "4700," "5300," "5700," or "5800."

"Künstlerkopf" (art doll head): child doll; appropriately dressed. Marked "Künstlerkopf," and/or "#4000," "4600," "5000," or "5500."

SCHOENAU & HOFFMEISTER VALUE COMPARISONS:							
Size	Character Baby	Solid Dome Infant	Hanna Character*	Das Lachende Baby	Princess Elizabeth	Character H, OX Doll	Child Dolly-Face	Künstlerkopf (Art Doll) Child
10"		850.00						
12"	400.00	900.00						
14"	500.00	950.00	900.00	1,500.00	2,200.00		400.00	
16"	600.00		950.00	1,700.00	2,400.00		450.00	900.00
18"	700.00		1,000.00	1,900.00	2,500.00	3,000.00	500.00	
20"	750.00		1,100.00	2,200.00	2,700.00	3,400.00	550.00	
22"	800.00		1,300.00	2,500.00	2,900.00	3,800.00	600.00	
24"	1,000.00		1,500.00	2,700.00	3,200.00	4,200.00	700.00	1,400.00
26"	1,200.00		1,700.00			4,500.00	800.00	
28"	1,400.00						900.00	
30"	1,600.00						1,100.00	
32"							1,200.00	
34"							1,600.00	
36"							1,900.00	
38"							2,300.00	
40"							2,700.00	

* Add an additional $400.00 for Toddler body.

A. Schoenhut & Company

Albert Schoenhut founded A. Schoenhut & Company in Philadelphia, Pennsylvania, in 1872, continuing a family tradition of toy makers. Grandfather Anton had carved wooden toys at his home in Württenberg, Germany. His son, Frederick, followed in his footsteps. Albert was destined to become a toy maker!

After venturing to the United States at the age of seventeen, Albert worked at different jobs, but by age twenty-two he established his own toy factory. Schoenhut's first toy was a piano.

The famous Humpty Dumpty Circus, introduced in 1903, probably included Schoenhut's first attempt at dolls. The ringmaster, lion tamer, lady circus rider, and gentleman and lady acrobats are identified solely by their characteristic painting and costuming. At about this same time, Schoenhut introduced the Chinaman, Hobo, Negro Dude, Farmer, Milkmaid, and Max and Mortiz. Rolly-Dollys were patented in 1908, as was Teddy Roosevelt and his "Teddy Adventures in Africa."

In 1909, Albert Schoenhut filed a patent application for his swivel, spring-jointed dolls, but the patent was not granted until 1911. The metal joints had springs that compressed, rather than stretched when pulled. This added to the durability of the Schoenhut doll. In addition to the unique spring joints, the wooden dolls were entirely painted with oil colors. Their solid wood heads came either with mohair wigs or molded hair. Although collectors refer to this type of molded hair as carved hair, only the very crudest of features were carved, then refined and finished by molding under pressure. The feet are of hard wood with two holes drilled into the soles to enable the doll to be placed on its stand and posed. One hole was drilled at an angle and one straight. The oblique hole allows the doll to hold its foot in the tip-toe position. The straight hole allows the doll to hold its foot resting flat.

Following his death in 1912, Albert Schoenhut was succeeded by his six sons, Harry, Gustav, Theodore, Albert Jr., William, and Otto. The new directors introduced an infant doll with curved limbs in 1913. It is identified by the © copyright symbol on its head.

The dolly-faced all-wooden dolls produced in 1915 had rounded eyes, advertised as "imitation glass," as opposed to intaglio eyes, and they had mohair wigs. These dolls came boxed in an accordion-type box with detailed instructions on posing. A round tin doll stand with pins to accommodate the holes in the feet was included. A series of older boy dolls, usually dressed as athletes, was also introduced in 1915. These dolls, called "Manikins" by collectors, are 19" tall and have an additional joint at the waist. Only 1,000 of these finely crafted Manikins were produced, all portraying young men. Another new doll produced in 1915 was the bent-limb baby which had a split joint at the elbows and knees.

Schoenhut's Maggie and Jiggs. *Photo courtesy of McMasters Doll Auction.*

Walking dolls were introduced in 1919. The dolls were jointed at the shoulders and hips only; foot holes and knee and ankle joints were eliminated. In 1921, sleep eyes were added to the Schoenhut babies and dolly-faced dolls.

Cloth bodied mama dolls and a cheaper line of dolls with elastic joints were marketed in 1924, but neither achieved the success of the earlier "All Wood Perfection Art Dolls."

In addition to producing finely crafted toys, A. Schoenhut & Company was a significant contributor to the beginning of the mass-marketed commercial doll industry in the United

States. Although the majority of Schoenhuts are child dolls, none can argue the appeal of the character dolls, Nature Babies, or the desirable Manikins.

Reproduction Schoenhut dolls do not seem to be a problem. However, the accessories—i.e., tin stands, name pins, and Schoenhut shoes—have been reproduced. The pins read "Made in U.S.A. Strong Durable and Unbreakable" around the outer edge, with a shield in the center which reads "Schoenhut All Wood Perfection Doll." The reproductions are quite "yellowed." In an attempt to make them appear old, the coloring has been overdone. The reproduction stands have a rather pressed and rolled look which originals do not. The shoes are difficult to positively identify, as the reproductions are made from vintage doll shoes. One clue is that authentic Schoenhut doll shoes often show slight corrosion around the rivets in the holes.

Prices listed are for dolls with no damage. Be particularly aware of facial painting. Slight rubs and chips are becoming somewhat acceptable to collectors as is very minimal paint touch-up. If there is significant repainting or other damage, expect to pay less than half the amount listed.

Character: all wooden, spring-jointed body; carved molded (possibly with a ribbon or bow) hair or good wig; intaglio eyes; closed or open/closed mouth; appropriately dressed. Typically marked with a paper label reading "Schoenhut Doll/Pat. Jan 17th 1911/U.S.A.," incised on back "Schoenhut Doll, Pat. Jan 17 '11 U.S.A./& Foreign Countries."

Bonnet Girl: molded and painted hair around face, cap molded to head, molded hair in back; intaglio painted eyes; slightly open/closed mouth; cap with floral design; appropriately dressed. Marked with paper label "Schoenhut Doll/Pat. Jan 17th 1911/U.S.A." on back.

Schnickel-Fritz: molded wavy hair; squinting painted eyes; toothy grin; appropriately dressed.

Tootsie Wootsie: lightly molded short hair; small eyes; open/closed mouth; appropriately dressed.

Black Child: molded curly hair; slightly side-glancing eyes; appropriately dressed.

Manikin: pensive expression, mature look; costumed in football, baseball, basketball, or circus outfit, complete with accessories.

Circus and Character Figures: small, comic, jointed characters; good molding; painted features.

Early Humpty Dumpty Circus: complete with tent, animals, and figures. **3,800.00**

Later Humpty Dumpty Circus Parade: #18, complete with tent, animals, and figures. **2,500.00**

Schoenhut Baby: jointed toddler or bent-limb baby body; painted hair; painted eyes; open or closed mouth. Typically marked "©," label reading "C" in center; "H. E. Schoenhut 1913" printed on rim; "Schoenhut Doll/Pat. Jan. 17th 1911/U.S.A." inscribed on shoulder; blue stamped "Patent applied for; Schoenhut Doll."

Dolly-Faced Doll: full spring-jointed body; good wig; painted round eyes; open/closed mouth with painted teeth; appropriately dressed. Typically marked with "Schoenhut/Doll Pat. Jan 17 '11 U.S.A./& Foreign Countries" incised on back.

Walker Body: jointed at shoulders and hips only; arms bent at elbows; no holes in feet; painted features; appropriately dressed. Typically marked with label reading "C" in center; "H. E. Schoenhut 1913" printed on rim; or "Schoenhut Doll/Pat. Jan 17 '11 U.S.A./& Foreign Countries."

Sleep-eye Child: all wood; good wig; sleep eyes; open mouth with teeth; appropriately dressed. Typically marked "Schoenhut Doll/Pat. Jan 17th 1911/USA," "C" in center; "H.E. Schoenhut 1913" printed on rim.

Composition: jointed at neck, shoulders, and hips; molded and painted hair; painted eyes; small closed mouth; appropriately dressed. Typically marked with paper label reading "Schoenhut Toys/Made in/U.S.A."

Cloth Body: hollow wooden head, cloth limbs, wooden hands; mohair wig; painted features; appropriately dressed. Typically marked with Schoenhut stamp on head.

A. SCHOENHUT & COMPANY EARLY CHARACTER VALUE COMPARISONS:

Size	Character, Carved Hair and Intaglio Eyes	Character, Wig and Intaglio Eyes	Bonnet Bonnet Girl	Schnickel-Fritz	Tootsie Wootsie	Black Child	Manikins Men
14"	2,500.00	1,800.00	3,900.00				
16"	2,900.00	2,000.00		3,000.00	3,200.00	3,500.00	
19"	3,100.00	2,300.00	4,600.00				3,500.00
21"	3,500.00	2,500.00					

A. SCHOENHUT & COMPANY CIRCUS AND CHARACTER VALUE COMPARISONS:

Lion Tamer, Rolly Polly, Clown	Farmer, Milk Maid	Ringmaster, Acrobat	Negro Dude, Maggie, Jiggs
350.00	400.00	450.00	550.00

A. SCHOENHUT & COMPANY BABY AND CHILD VALUE COMPARISONS:

Size	Baby with Toddler Body	Baby With Bent-Limb Body	Dolly-Face Child	Walker	Sleep-Eye Child	Composition	Cloth Body
9"		550.00					
11"	1,000.00	650.00		900.00			
13"						700.00	
14"	1,100.00		1,100.00	1,100.00	1,300.00		300.00
16"			1,300.00		1,400.00		350.00
17"	1,300.00			1,300.00			
19"			1,500.00		1,500.00		
21"			1,700.00		1,600.00		

Schuetzmeister & Quendt

Wilhelm Quendt and Philipp Schuetzmeister founded a porcelain factory in Boilstadt, Gotha, Germany, in 1889. In 1908, Wilhelm Quendt left and Philipp Schuetzmeister became sole owner. Following the company's acquisition by the Bing concern of Nürmberg in 1918, Schuetzmeister & Quendt limited its production to bisque doll heads for Welsch & Company and Kämmer & Reinhardt. Those companies were members, along with Schuetzmeister and Quendt, of the holding company known as Concentra.

The firm's intertwined S & Q trademark can be found incised on heads, along with mold numbers 101, 102, 201, 204, 252, 300, 301, and 1376. Mold numbers 79, 80, and 81 were also registered in 1891, but there are no known examples of dolls produced from these molds. According to their registration, they are "dolly face child dolls." Doll collectors everywhere are on the lookout for these mold numbers.

22" Schuetzmeister & Quendt 201.
Photo courtesy Cobbs Doll Auction.

SCHUETZMEISTER & QUENDT VALUE COMPARISONS:

Size	Character Baby*	Dolly-Face Child	Black Child
12"		500.00	
14"	550.00	650.00	
16"	650.00	750.00	
18"	750.00	800.00	
20"	850.00	900.00	
22"	1,000.00	950.00	2,600.00
24"		1,000.00	
26"		1,200.00	
30"		1,500.00	

* Add an additional $300.00 for Toddler body.

Prices listed are for dolls with no damage to the bisque. Normal wear, slight damage, or well-done repairs to the body do not greatly affect price. If the bisque is damaged or repaired, expect to pay less than half the amount listed. It is perfectly acceptable to show a missing or repaired finger or joint to the body.

Character Baby: socket head, bent-limb baby body; good wig; glass eyes; open mouth; appropriately dressed. Typically marked "S & Q" intertwined, "201," "204," "300," and "301."

Dolly-Face: socket head, jointed composition body; good wig; glass eyes; open mouth; appropriately dressed. Typically marked "S & Q" intertwined, "101," and "102."

Simon & Halbig

24" Simon & Halbig 1139 Child Doll.
Courtesy of Helen Brooke.

29" Simon & Halbig Lovely Child Doll.
Courtesy of Leah and Gene Patterson.

24" Very rare Character Mold 989.
Courtesy of Helen Brooke.

The Simon & Halbig porcelain factory was located in Frafenhain and Hildburghausen, near Ohrdruf, Thürginia, Germany. Founded by Wilham Simon and Carl Halbig in 1939, it began producing dolls in the late 1860s or early 1870s.

Early documentation for Simon & Halbig is quite elusive. The company's tinted and untinted bisque shoulder heads with molded hair and delicate decoration are typical of the prodigious output of fine-quality dolls produced by this German manufacturer. Kid-bodied shoulder heads, originally made in the 1880s, followed closely in the French tradition with large, often paperweight eyes, pierced ears, and heavy brows. A number of swivel heads on kid-lined shoulder plates were made completely in the French manner.

Practically all combinations of bisque heads and features have been found with Simon & Halbig's mark, including solid dome and Belton-Type; molded hair and wigs; and painted, stationary, sleep, or flirty eyes. Mouths can be open, closed or open/closed. Ears may be pierced. Often a single mold number will be found with a variety of characteristics.

Simon & Halbig registered several new ideas. These include eyes operated by a lever, movable eyelids, the use of threads for eyelashes, and glazing the neck of a socket-head doll to reduce friction between the neck and the body socket.

Simon & Halbig not only produced a multitude of fine-quality dolls from their own molds, but also produced dolls for several other manufacturers, including C.M. Bergmann, Carl Berger, Cuno & Otto Dressel, Hamburger, Handwerck, Hulss, Kämmer & Reinhardt, Schmidt, and Wislizenus; and the French firms Fleischmann & Bloedel, Jumeau, Roullet & Decamp, and S.F.B.J. It appears that heads marked "DEP" were made for the French market. While many of these manufacturers were supplied heads from different porcelain factories, Kämmer & Reinhardt depended entirely upon Simon & Halbig—a dependency that no doubt led to Kämmer & Reinhardt's acquisition of Simon & Halbig in 1920.

Most Simon & Halbig dolls are fully marked. The ampersand was added to the mark in 1905; consequently, it is assumed that marks without the ampersand were produced before 1905.

Reproduction Simon & Halbig dolls certainly can be found. Inspect the markings first. Remember that doll crafters usually sign and date their dolls made from a Simon & Halbig mold. Check the "fittings." Does the neck plug seem to be new? Also check the body and the facial features, keeping in mind that Simon & Halbig dolls were mass produced. The painting may not be perfectly executed as it often is with reproductions.

Prices listed are for dolls with no damage to the bisque. Normal wear, slight damage, or well-done repairs to the body do not greatly affect price. If the bisque is damaged or repaired, expect to pay about half the amount listed. It is perfectly acceptable to show a missing or repaired finger or joint or a patch to the kid body.

CHARACTER DOLLS

Due to the wide variety of Simon & Halbig character dolls, the following charts are arranged by mold numbers, with pricing of specific molds corresponding to size.

CHARACTER DOLL VALUE COMPARISONS:

Mold #	Description	Size	Value
	Fashion doll; bisque socket head, bisque shoulder plate; kid lady body; good wig; glass eyes; CM	12" 18"	3,000.00 3,800.00
	Fashion doll, bisque socket head, bisque shoulder plate, wood lady's body; good wig; glass eyes; CM	10" 16"	4,900.00 6,700.00
SH	Shoulder head lady; glass eyes; molded hair with bow; pierced ears; CM	12" 16"	2,000.00 3,700.00
SH	Shoulder head lady; painted eyes; molded hair with bow; pierced ears; CM	12" 16"	1,600.00 3,500.00
SV IV	Jointed composition body; good wig; glass stationary eyes; CM	14" 18"	17,000.00 27,000.00
120	Character baby face; glass eyes; OM	12" 24"	1,800.00 3,200.00
150	Jointed composition body; good wig; intaglio eyes; CM	16" 20" 26"	16,000.00 25,000.00 40,000.00
151	Jointed composition body; good wig; dimples; intaglio eyes; O/CM	23"	15,000.00
152	Character face; painted eyes; CM	18" 24"	1,800.00 2,600.00
153	Character face; molded hair; painted eyes; CM	18"	45,000.00
172	Character Baby; molded hair	14"	3,800.00
411	Fashion Lady, bisque shoulder head, cloth lady's body, kid arms; glass eyes; good wig; O/CM with molded teeth	18"	4,500.00
600	Baby; good wig; dimple in chin; glass eyes; OM	16"	1,500.00
616	Baby, good wig; glass eyes; OM	20"	1,200.00
719	Jointed composition body; round face; glass eyes; OM	20" 23"	3,200.00 3,600.00
720	Kid body; glass eyes; CM	20"	2,300.00
739	Black Bisque; good wig; dolly-face; glass eyes; OM	24"	4,800.00
740	Kid body; glass eyes; CM	20"	2,300.00
749	Composition Body glass eyes; CM	20" 24"	3,700.00 4,200.00
905	Jointed composition body; good wig; glass eyes, CM	16"	2,400.00
908	Kid body; good wig; glass eyes; OM	16"	2,400.00
919	Child; glass eyes; CM	20"	8,000.00
929	Child; glass eyes; CM	20"	4,700.00
941	Kid body; good wig; glass eyes; OM	22"	1,600.00
949	Composition glass eyes; CM	16" 20" 24"	2,500.00 3,000.00 3,500.00
950	Kid body; good wig; glass eyes; CM	14"	1,700.00
969	Bisque shoulder head; glass eyes; smiling OM	20"	2,600.00
979	Composition body; glass eyes; OM	18"	3,500.00
989	Composition body; glass eyes; CM	22" 24"	4,000.00 4,800.00

CHARACTER DOLL VALUE COMPARISONS (continued):

1009/1010	Shoulder head; good wig; glass eyes; OM	16"	1,300.00
		20"	1,500.00
1039	Pull-string walker body; good wig; glass eyes; OM	22"	1,600.00
1039	Key-wind walker body; good wig; sleep eyes; OM	22"	2,300.00
1039	Jointed composition body; good wig; glass eyes; OM	16"	1,000.00
		20"	1,200.00
		24"	1,400.00
1139	Composition body; good wig; glass eyes; OM	24"	2,900.00
1159	Lady-type body; good wig; glass eyes; OM	12"	1,800.00
		16"	2,400.00
		22"	3,200.00
1160	Cloth or kid body; fancy mohair wig; glass eyes; CM	6"	500.00
		7"	550.00
		10"	600.00
1269	Composition body; good wig; sleep eyes; OM	18"	1,300.00
1279	Composition body; good wig; glass eyes; OM w/pursed lips, upper teeth	12"	2,100.00
		18"	3,000.00
		24"	5,500.00
1294	Baby; composition body; good wig; flirty eyes; OM	18"	1,100.00
		22"	1,500.00
		24"	1,900.00
1299	Baby; good wig; glass eyes; OM	12"	1,600.00
		16"	1,800.00
1303	Older woman; good wig; glass eyes; CM	14"	14,000.00
1307	Long face lady; glass eyes; CM	20"	22,000.00
1308	Coke Maker; composition body; head painted to show smudges; mohair wig; wearing original costume; glass eyes; smiling, CM*	14"	14,000.00
1339	Glass eyes; OM;"L.L. & S."	18"	1,300.00
		24"	2,000.00
1388	Composition body; good wig; glass eyes; O/CM, wide smile, molded teeth	24"	34,000.00
1398	Composition body; good wig; glass eyes; O/OM, wide smile, molded teeth	24"	24,000.00
1428	Bent-limb Baby body; good wig; glass eyes; O/CM	16"	2,500.00
		21"	3,300.00
		25"	3,900.00
1448	Composition body; good wig; pierced ears; glass sleep eyes; CM	15"	20,000.00
		24"	32,000.00
1468	Child; glass eyes; CM	10"	2,700.00
		12"	2,900.00
1469	Lady's body; good wig; glass eyes; CM	16"	4,600.00
1478	Glass eyes; CM	14"	8,500.00
1488	Character Baby; glass eyes; O/CM	20"	5,200.00
1489	Baby; good wig; glass eyes; OM	22"	4,200.00
1498	Solid dome glass eyes; O/CM	22"	6,600.00

Note: Add an additional $300.00 for an open mouth doll with square teeth. Add an additional $500.00 for Toddler baby.
* Coke Maker's costume consists of a long black coat, black pants, red vest with two rows of brass buttons, and black felt hat.
OM = Open Mouth
CM = Closed Mouth
O/CM = Open/Closed Mouth

CHILD DOLLS

Unique Child: jointed composition body; good wig; glass eyes, feathered brows; pierced ears; open mouth; appropriately dressed. Typically marked "Simon & Halbig," "S & H," "719," "739," "749," "759," "769," "939," "949" and "979."

Santa: jointed composition body; good wig; glass eyes; pierced ears; open mouth; appropriately dressed. Marked "Simon & Halbig," "S & H," "1248," or "1249."

Dolly-Face: jointed composition body; good wig; glass eyes, softer brows; may have pierced ears; open mouth; appropriately dressed. Typically marked "Simon & Halbig," "S & H," "540," "550," "570," "1079," "1078," and "Baby Blanche."

Dolly-Face: shoulder head, kid body, bisque arms; good wig; glass eyes; pierced ears; open mouth; appropriately dressed. Typically marked "Simon & Halbig," "S & H," "1040," "1080," "1250," and "1260."

CHILD DOLL VALUE COMPARISONS:

Size	Pretty Child	Santa	Dolly-Face, Composition Body	Dolly-Face, Kid Body	Little Women
6"					500.00
7"			600.00		550.00
10"			700.00		600.00
12"	1,500.00		750.00		
14"	1,600.00	1,100.00		750.00	
16"	1,800.00		850.00	800.00	
18"	2,200.00		900.00	850.00	
20"		1,500.00	950.00	900.00	
22"			1,000.00	950.00	
24"		1,600.00	1,100.00	1,000.00	
26"	2,900.00		1,250.00	1,200.00	
28"			1,400.00	1,300.00	
30"	3,500.00		1,600.00	1,500.00	
32"		2,700.00	1,800.00		
34"			2,200.00		
36"			2,700.00		
38"			3,000.00		
40"	4,800.00		3,500.00		
42"			4,400.00		

Note: Add an additional $300.00 for an open mouth doll with square teeth.

Ella Smith Doll Company

According to legend, a neighbor girl brought Ella Smith a broken bisque doll to be repaired. When Ella saw how upset the little girl was, she set out to make a doll that could not be broken. She obviously succeeded. At one point, as the story goes, a truck ran over one of the dolls and didn't even crack the paint. These dolls are commonly known as Alabama Indestructible Dolls. They were produced from 1904 until 1924 in Roanoke, Alabama.

In obtaining the patent, Ella Smith describes her dolls as follows: "I make the body or trunk, the arms, hands, legs and feet of stuffed fabric and apply over the feet and hands as high up on the legs and arms as desirable one or more coats of flesh colored and preferably water proof paint. The head, face, neck, and bust are also fabric covered, and the neck or bust is secured to the trunk by suitable stitching. The outer fabric of the face covers and conforms to the curvature of a backing molded to conform to the contour of the human face. The fabric of the head is stitched up and stretched over a stuffed head portion forming a continuation of the stuffed body, and as a means for making the head rigid a rod or stick may be inserted through the head and passed down a suit-able distance into the trunk or body. If desired, the doll may be provided with a wig, I prefer, however, to produce the appearance of hair by paint applied directly to the fabric and to render the head waterproof. The ears are preferably made of stuffed fabric and sewed to the side of the head, after which they are painted."

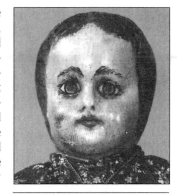

18" Ella Smith's Alabama Indestructible Doll. *Photo courtesy McMasters Doll Auction.*

The Ella Smith Doll Company was housed in a factory built by Smith's husband. Each beautifully hand-crafted doll was stitched and painted by Mrs. Smith or one of her assistants, whose ranks at times numbered twelve or more. At the peak of production, it has been reported that as many as 6,000 dolls a year were made.

Ella Smith Dolls have heavily painted cloth bodies which are jointed at the hips and shoulders. The hair is usually painted in a short style, occasionally wigged. The faces are molded and painted with added ears. Many have bare feet with stitched toes, but dolls with painted on button slippers or low boots are more commonly found. The dolls were made to represent white and Black children and babies. Stuffed through the top of the head, Alabama Indestructible Dolls are easily recognized by a stitched circular crown. Consider these characteristics in authenticating an Ella Smith—Alabama Indestructible doll.

Prices listed are for dolls in good condition. Normal wear with slight crazing or rubs will not greatly affect price. If a doll is badly worn, cracked, or peeling or has been repainted, expect to pay less than half the amount listed.

Early: all-painted cloth child; applied ears; short painted hair or wig; painted shoes or bare feet; appropriately dressed. Marked "Pat. Nov. 9 1912/No. 1/Ella Smith Doll Co." or "Mrs. S. S. Smith Manufacturer and Dealer to/ The Alabama Indestructible Doll/ Roanoke, Ala./ Patented Sept. 26, 1905" (on some dolls the date 1907 will appear on leg or torso).

Later Ella Smith Doll: molded rather than applied ears; typically marked the same as early dolls.

Later Black Ella Smith Doll: with molded ears; typically marked the same as early dolls

ELLA SMITH (ALABAMA INDESTRUCTIBLE DOLL) VALUE COMPARISONS:

Size	Early Applied Ears	Early Applied Ears, Black	Later Molded Ears	Later Molded Ears, Black
12"	1,800.00			
14"	2,000.00	7,000.00		
15"			1,200.00	3,500.00
17"			1,700.00	3,700.00
18"	2,800.00	8,000.00		
19"				4,000.00
21"		10,000.00	2,200.00	
24"	3,500.00			
25"			2,700.00	
38"	10,000.00			

Société de Fabrication de Bébés & Jouets

The Société de Fabrication de Bébés & Jouets—the Society for the Manufacturer of Bébés and Toys—is commonly known as S.F.B.J. In 1899, the society signed an agreement for locations in Paris and Montreuil-sous-Bois, France.

French doll manufacturers struggled against the German competition for many years, finally being forced to economize in an effort to compete. Most of the premier French firms were absorbed by the S.F.B.J. syndicate. Many companies continued to manufacture the same dolls under S.F.B.J. that they previously produced as individual companies. Dolls produced under the amalgamation rarely met the high standards set by the original firms. Vast differences in quality are probably more obvious within S.F.B.J. than within any other doll manufacturer. Good examples are very good, and poor examples are very poor. If you keep in mind that the S.F.B.J. heads were made in several different porcelain factories, with different molds which belonged to different companies, the spectrum of differences seems more logical.

S.F.B.J. 239 Poulbot Character. *Photo courtesy of McMasters Doll Auction.*

Two types of dolls were produced by S.F.B.J. First, the society continued to manufacture the familiar Bébé, similar in concept, if not in quality, to the earlier Bébés. The second thrust was the modeling and production of charming, imaginative character dolls. Character dolls are modeled in the likenesses of real children with portrait-like detail, as opposed to the idealized "dolly face" Bébé. Characters may be pouting, laughing, screaming, or smiling, as they portray both baby and adolescents. After viewing these fascinating characters, it becomes obvious why they enjoy a large audience of collectors, and demand such generous prices.

Reproduction S.F.B.J. dolls can be found for almost every character mold. Most of these were made for the enjoyment of the doll crafter and not intended as frauds. An inspection of the marking should dispel any misgivings. Gently run your fingers over the doll's cheek. Dolls produced by the S.F.B.J. will feel somewhat grainy, as opposed to the silky smooth bisque of today's dolls.

Quality and condition are equally important when considering the purchase of a Société de Fabrication de Bébés & Jouets doll. Prices listed are for dolls of good quality, with nice decoration and no damage to the bisque. Normal wear, slight damage, or well-done repairs to the body do not greatly affect price. If the bisque is damaged or repaired, expect to pay less than half the amount listed. It is perfectly acceptable to show a missing or repaired finger or joint to the body.

SOCIÉTÉ DE FABRICATION DE BÉBÉS & JOUETS (S.F.B.J.) VALUE COMPARISONS:

Size	Jumeau-type	#60 (glass eyes)	#301
10"		550.00	
11"			1,000.00
12"		600.00	1,000.00
14"	1,300.00	650.00	1,100.00
16"	1,500.00	700.00	1,200.00
18"	1,700.00	800.00	1,300.00
20"	1,900.00	900.00	1,400.00
22"	2,300.00	1,000.00	1,500.00
24"	2,400.00	1,200.00	1,700.00
26"	2,600.00	1,300.00	1,900.00
28"	2,800.00	1,400.00	2,000.00
30"	3,000.00		2,200.00
32"			2,400.00
34"			2,700.00
36"			3,000.00
38"			3,500.00

SOCIÉTÉ DE FABRICATION DE BÉBÉS & JOUETS (S.F.B.J.) CHARACTER VALUE COMPARISONS:

Size	60 Painted Eyes	226 O/CM Squinting	227 OM Character	229 OM Molded teeth	230 OM Chin Dimple	233 O/CM Screamer	235 O/CM Squinting Eyes	236 O/CM Laughing
12"	600.00							
14"		2,500.00						
16"				3,900.00				
18"			2,600.00			3,800.00	2,300.00	
20"								2,400.00
26"			3,500.00		2,600.00			

Size	237 OM Flocked Hair	237 OM Walker Body	238 OM Slight Smile	239 CM Street Urchin	242 Nursing Baby	245 O/CM Googly	247 Slight Overbite	248 CM Pouty
14"				8,800.00		4,000.00		7,500.00
16"	2,800.00	3,500.00	3,200.00		3,500.00	4,800.00		
18"							3,000.00	

Size	250 O/CM Smiling Lady	251 OM Deep Molded Eyes	252 CM Pouty	262 OM Lower Lashes Only	287 O/CM Intaglio Eyes	Black Dolly-Face
8"						375.00
12"					2,300.00	1,000.00
14"		2,200.00				
16"			5,200.00			
18"	4,000.00			2,100.00		2,000.00

Note: Add an additional $500.00 to any Character Doll with a Toddler Body.

OM = Open Mouth
CM = Closed Mouth
O/CM = Open/Closed Mouth

Jumeau-Type Bébé: jointed composition body; very pretty, obviously Jumeau-type face; good wig; paperweight eyes; open mouth; appropriately dressed. Typically marked "S.F.B.J." and/or with a size number.

S.F.B.J. Bébé: bisque head, wood-and-composition jointed body; good wig; glass eyes; open mouth. Typically marked "S.F.B.J.," "S.F.B.J./301/Paris," "S.F.B.J./60/Paris," and "Bleuette #301."

Character Dolls: jointed body; molded and painted or flocked hair, or good wig; painted or glass eyes; appropriately dressed. Typically marked "S.F.B.J./PARIS" and with a mold number.

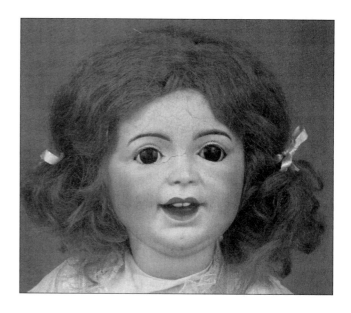

S.F.B.J. 236 Laughing Jumeau.
Courtesy of Helen Brooke

Sonneberg Täufling

Sonneberg Täufling, also known as Motschmann Babies were made by various manufacturers in the Sonneberg area of Germany as early as 1851. Täufling simply means a baby dressed in a shift.

The idea of the Sonneberg Täufling came to Germany by way or Edmund Lindner, a Verleger (a German merchant who buys manufactured goods or places orders). Lindner was in London in 1851 when he spied a new type of doll with oriental facial characteristics and a distinct body construction. The shoulders, lower arms, hip section and lower legs were made of composition and were connected by strips of cloth called floating joints.

Sonneberg Taufling dolls may be found with the name Ch. Motschmann stamped on their bodies, explaining why, for many years, collectors referred to these early dolls as Motschmann Babies. It is now widely known that Ch. Motschmann held the patent for the voice boxes often found within the doll bodies.

By the mid-1850s, doll manufacturer Henrich Stier had done much in the way of improving the Sonneberg Täufling, including covering the head in wax in order to produce a more pleasing doll.

Prices listed are for dolls in good condition. Normal wear and signs of aging are to be expected and do not greatly affect price. A purist doll collector will look past the fine veining of the wax, or slight nose rub, and appreciate the doll for its historical importance and for being an essential link in the historical chain of the doll industry. If badly damaged or repaired, expect to pay half the amount listed.

SONNEBERG TÄUFLING VALUE COMPARISONS:	
Size	**Baby**
6"	800.00
8"	1,000.00
10"	1,200.00
12"	1,400.00
14"	1,600.00
16"	1,800.00
18"	2,000.00
20"	2,200.00
22"	2,400.00
24"	2,700.00
26"	2,900.00
28"	3,200.00

Sonneberg Täufling. *Photo courtesy of Cobbs Doll Auction.*

Sonneberg Täufling: wax over papier-mâché shoulder head, cloth and composition body with floating joints; solid dome with painted wisps of hair above ears on either side of head, or wearing wig; very oval, glass, black pupil-less eyes with no lashes, faint single-stroke brows; closed or open mouth with bamboo teeth; appropriately dressed. Unmarked.

Steiff

The German town of Gienger an der Brenz— the home of Margarete Steiff— dates back to the time of cobblestone streets and gingerbread houses. Born in 1847, Margarete Steiff contracted polio at the age of two, which weakened her legs and right hand. However, this did not dampen her spirits for she was determined to learn to sew in order to support herself. As a young woman she became an accomplished seamstress, having her own workshop where she made women's and children's clothing of wool felt. In 1880, a flash of inspiration changed her life forever. Steiff designed and created a small felt elephant pin cushion. She is quoted as writing in her diary: "...I quite casually came across a picture representing an elephant. Felt is quite the kind of material suitable for making small pattern animals, so I set to work, choosing for the purpose the best wool felt I could lay my hands on. The little elephant will make a lovely pincushion." This little elephant was very popular among the children of the neighborhood, who approached Steiff requesting copies of the little elephant to use as a plaything. It was then that she began commercially producing small stuffed animals.

In 1897, Margarete's nephew, Richard, joined the family business. Richard had studied art in Germany and England. It was while he was at Stuttgart, Germany, that the seeds of the most popular toy of all times were planted. Richard developed a passion for sketching the antics of the brown bears housed at the Nills Animal Show. He was so amused with the playful bears that he filled whole sketchbooks with his drawings. These sketchbooks proved invaluable in 1902 when he designed a small toy bear made of mohair plush with movable joints. This toy made its debut at the 1903 Leipzig Easter Fair.

By coincidence, at about this same time, President Theodore Roosevelt traveled into the backwoods of Mississippi on a hunting expedition. One evening, after several unsuccessful days, a small bear cub wandered into camp. Roosevelt refused to kill the young cub, instead chasing it back to its mother. The *Washington Post's* famous political cartoonist, Clifford Berryman, happened to be a member of the hunting party. Upon returning to Washington, he drew his first cartoon of the President chasing the bear. From that day forward the little bear was in every cartoon that Berryman did of President Teddy Roosevelt. Berryman called him "Teddy's Bear." President Roosevelt obviously enjoyed the kidding he received over the little bear. In 1906 at his daughter's wedding reception held at the White House, the decorations for the table were Steiff bears dressed and equipped as hunters and fishermen—a theme chosen because of the President's love of the outdoors. This unusual wedding reception theme created an unparalleled endorsement for a toy. During the next year, one million Steiff bears were sold, a record which has not been equaled since.

13" Steiff.

Leadership of the Steiff company was passed to Margarete's nephews following her death in 1909. The making of toys at the Steiff factory continues to this day in much the same way as was done some one hundred years ago. Until very recently, the tradition was that of a cottage industry, with women picking up the raw materials at the factory and returning with the finished products.

Markings for Steiff toys have changed over the years. In 1892, a camel was used, but never registered. In 1898, the elephant with his trunk forming the letter "S" was used, but again without being registered. The Teddy Bear, introduced as "Petz," was never registered, explaining why numerous competing firms were able to manufacture "Teddy Bears." Perhaps the failure to register trade names and marks in the past prompted Margarete to make an application in December of 1904 for the "Button in the ear for toy of felt and similar material." She even wrote to her customers to inform them, "...From November 1, 1904 on, each of my products, without exception, shall have as my trademark a small nickel button in the left ear."

Although best known for its animals, Steiff also produced dolls advertised as "jovial lads and buxom maidens" with painstaking attention paid to details of both structure and dress. Their large feet offer a good foundation. Felt pressed heads characterized by a seam down the middle of the face, mohair wigs, and glass eyes express an individuality which continues to endear these dolls in the hearts of collectors.

In 1988, the new line of hard vinyl Steiff dolls became available in the United States. These dolls have hard vinyl heads, cloth bodies with hard vinyl arms, and human hair wigs. They are well-dressed with the familiar button in the ear and a 24 karat gold-plated Steiff brooch.

Reproduction Steiff dolls are not a problem, but copies of Steiff dolls can be. These copies are not reproductions in the true sense of the word, but copies of a very successful doll. They will be found with seams down the face and may even copy the character faces. However, they will not have the button in the ear and most likely will not be of the same high quality. The detailed features on original Steiff dolls are often hand painted or embroidered. Often seams are hand sewn. These qualities, which make Steiff dolls so famous, are frequently missing from copies.

Prices listed are for dolls with no damage. If a doll is soiled, stained, missing original clothing, or has moth holes, expect to pay less than half the amount listed.

Adult Doll: felt, velvet, or plush; seam down center of face; oversized nose; applied ears; many with very large feet; glass button eyes; painted or embroidered features; original costume. Typically marked with button in ear.

Child Doll: felt, velvet, or plush; seam down center of face; jointed body; applied ears; glass button eyes; painted features; original costume. Typically marked with button in ear.

Character Doll: felt, velvet, or plush; seam down center of face; applied ears; large feet; jointed body; glass button eyes; painted and embroidered features; original costume. Typically marked with button in ear.

Tea Cozy: with Steiff Doll topper.

Vinyl Steiff Doll: cloth body, marked with button in ear.

STEIFF VALUE COMPARISONS:

Size	Adult	Child	Military Officer/ Soldier	Mickey Mouse	Minnie Mouse	Clown
10"				1,400.00	1,900.00	
12"	2,000.00	1,400.00				
14"	2,400.00					2,600.00
18"	2,700.00	1,800.00	4,200.00			
21"			4,500.00			
22"	3,400.00					

Size	Golliwog	Max and Moritz (pair)	Comic Characters, Elf/Chef	Tea Cozy	Vinyl Steiff
12"				1,200.00	
14"	4,500.00	7,000.00			
16"			2,900.00		
16½"					350.00
20"					550.00

Edmund Ulrich Steiner

18" E.U. Steiner. *Courtesy of Helen Brooke.*

Edmund Ulrich Steiner manufactured and distributed dolls from 1864 until 1916. Edmund came from a family with roots planted deeply in the doll industry. His father produced a high-grade doll which was one of the first prominent lines to be marketed in the United States. His brother, Albert, was also a well-known personality in the doll business. Edmund, born in Germany, came to America as a young man from Sonneberg, Thüringina, Germany, and reportedly crossed the Atlantic eighty-four times in his career. He maintained a close association with the doll community in both his native country and the United States. He worked with a number of firms including Louis Wolf, Sanstag & Hilder, and Strobel & Wilken. Over the years, he registered several designs for bisque dolls, including Liliput, Daisy and Majestic (Daisy and Majestic are registered trade names of other doll manufacturers, therefore care should be taken not to confuse a praticular doll). Edmund Steiner's designs were manufactured by several companies, among them Armand Marseille. Many of Steiner's bisque-head dolls are marked with his initials within a diamond.

Prices listed are for dolls with no damage to the bisque. Normal wear, slight damage or well-done repairs to the body do not greatly affect price. If the bisque is damaged or repaired, expect to pay less than half the amount listed. It is perfectly acceptable to show a missing or repaired finger or joint to the body.

Dolly-Face Child: bisque socket or shoulder head, jointed composition or kid body; good wig; glass eyes; open mouth; appropriately dressed. Typically marked "Majestic/A M/Made in Germany," "Majestic," or "E. U. St." (within a diamond).

EDMUND ULRICH STEINER VALUE COMPARISONS:		
Size	**Dolly-Face Child, Kid Body**	**Dolly-Face Child, Composition Body**
14"	300.00	
16"	350.00	450.00
18"	400.00	500.00
20"		550.00
22"	450.00	600.00
24"	550.00	650.00
26"		700.00

Hermann Steiner

10" Hermann Steiner Character Baby. *Courtesy of Helen Brooke.*

The factories of Hermann Steiner were located in Sonneberg, Neustadt, Thur, Germany, and in Bavaria. Although the company was founded in 1911, it did not produce dolls until 1920. This explains why the majority of dolls found with the Hermann Steiner mark are the character babies which were so popular and dominated the market at that time. Hermann Steiner had poor timing regarding the manufacture of bisque dolls, entering the market at the end of the era.

Prices listed are for dolls with no damage to the bisque. Normal wear, slight damage or well-done repairs to the body do not greatly affect price. If the bisque is damaged or repaired, expect to pay less than half the amount listed. It is perfectly acceptable to show a missing or repaired finger or joint to the body.

Character Baby: jointed composition or cloth body; solid dome with molded hair or good wig; painted or glass eyes; closed or open mouth; appropriately dressed. Typically marked "Herm Steiner H S Germany," "H S," "246," and "131."

Dolly-Face Child: socket head, jointed composition body; good wig; glass eyes; open mouth; appropriately dressed. Typically marked "H S Germany" or "Herm Steiner Germany."

HERMANN STEINER VALUE COMPARISONS:

Size	Character Baby, Composition Body	Character Baby, Cloth Body	Dolly-Face Child
8"	350.00	300.00	
10"	400.00	325.00	350.00
12"	450.00	350.00	
14"	600.00	425.00	450.00
16"	700.00	600.00	550.00

Jules Steiner

Rare Jules Steiner
C Bourgoin Bébé. *Photo
courtesy of Cobbs Doll
Auction.*

Jules Nicholas Steiner founded his famous doll company in 1855, in Paris. Steiner was succeeded by Amédée La Fosse from 1892-1893 and, following his death, by his widow, who ran the business until 1899. From 1899 to 1901, Jules Mettais headed the company. He, in turn, was succeeded by Edmond Daspres from 1904 until 1908.

Many Steiner dolls are marked with the name "Bourgoin." Bourgoin was a Paris merchant dealing in porcelains and associated with Jules Steiner during the 1880s. Sometime after 1897, the Societe Steiner purchased May Freres Cie., the company responsible for the manufacture of Bébé Mascotte.

It was long believed that Steiner dolls were produced in Germany—a misconception possibly resulting from the Germanic name, or from distorted recollections. These beliefs have long since been abandoned. It is now generally accepted in the doll community that these exquisite creations are unquestionably French. From the early dolls with their round faces and two rows of tiny pointed teeth, to the later Bébés with their captivating beauty, the Societe Steiner produced some of the most distinctively high-quality dolls of the 19th century while under the leadership and creativity of it's founder, Jules Nicholas Steiner.

There is evidence that Steiner pressed its bisque doll heads even after other French manufacturers were routinely using the poured bisque method.

Steiner Bébé have been found in sizes ranging from 8½ to 38 inches. A variety of markings will be found, including some that may seem strange:

Fl, Fire or Figure	=	Face or countenance
Bte	=	registered
Ste	=	Steiner
SUCCe	=	Successor
S.G.D.G.	=	registered but without government guarantee

Markings usually include one of four letters: A, B, C, or D, with A being the most commonly found. A size number is also incorporated into the marking.

Reproduction Jules Steiner dolls often surface on the secondary market. As always, inspect the markings carefully. A legitimate copy of an antique doll will be marked with the artist's name or initials, and sometimes a date. Remember, most Steiner bisque Bébés will have a pressed, rather than poured, head. Check inside the head to verify this important feature. The pates of an original Steiner are usually purple cardboard. The body can also provide clues to authentication. Original Steiner bodies have a purple

Jules Steiner Bébé on signed body. *Photo courtesy of Cobbs Doll Auction.*

undercoat which is sometimes visible at the joints. Hands should have short chubby fingers which are all the same length, except the thumb. On Le Parisien Bébé, the hands are more graceful, with thinner, longer fingers. The big toe is often molded separately. Any of the molds may be found with sleeping eyes that are operated manually by means of a wire behind the ear. Dolls with this type of eye are often marked "J. Steiner."

Markings on Jules Steiner dolls can be confusing as the heads often have both an incised marking and a stamped marking. The incised marking, being in the mold, is the more definitive labeling, although some collectors prefer to use the stamp marking for identification.

Prices listed are for dolls with no damage to the bisque. Normal wear, slight damage, or well-done repairs to the body do not greatly affect price. If the bisque is damaged or repaired, expect to pay less than half the amount listed. It is perfectly acceptable to show a missing or repaired finger or joint to the body.

Early Round Face: 1870s, very pale bisque socket head, jointed wood-and-composition body, stubby fingers; mohair or skin wig; bulgy paperweight almond-shaped eyes, slight pink-mauve eye shadow, thin eyebrows; with or without pierced ears; open mouth with eight upper and seven lower teeth, thin lips; appropriately dressed. Typically with no marks on head. Body may be stamped "J. Steiner fabricante," "J. Steiner fabricate, rue de Saintonge, No. 25 Paris, Prissette, Imp. Pass du Carre 17."

Täufling-type Body: round, very pale bisque shoulder head with molded full shoulders and upper body, bisque lower body/hip and tops of legs, lower arms, and legs; cloth joints (same style of body found on the Sonneberg Täufling); mohair or skin wig; bulgy paperweight oval eyes, slight pink-mauve eye shadow,

thin eyebrows; most without pierced ears, closed mouth; appropriately dressed. Typically unmarked.

Series A or C Stamped Bourgoin: 1880, bisque socket head, jointed wood-and-composition body, short chubby fingers of same length except for thumb, straight wrists; human or mohair wig; round face with wide forehead and full cheeks; slight chin with hint of dimple; excellent-quality paperweight eyes with dark rims, or beautiful glass porcelain-encased sleep eyes operated by lever protruding from back of head; black eyelashes, black outlined eyes, heavy brows with tiny brush strokes, brows are heavier than on early round face, light pink-mauve eye shadow; pierced ears with light blush on rims; almost-pink closed mouth with high cupid's-bow upper lip and upturned corners; appropriately dressed. Typically marked with incised "Ste A" and size number or "Ste C" and size number and stamped in red script "J. Steiner Bte SGDG J. Bourgoin," or "J. STEINER B.S.G.D.G."

Figure A B or C Bébé: bisque socket head, jointed wood-and-composition body, short chubby fingers of same length except for thumb, may have separate big toe, jointed or unjointed wrists; human or mohair wig; original cardboard dyed purple pate; somewhat longer and fuller face, prettier oval-shaped face with lower cheeks and higher forehead, slight chin; beautiful, good quality paperweight eyes, long dark eyelashes beginning in corners of eyes, thick dramatic lashes often have a dot at the base of each lash, black outlined eyes, heavy brows with tiny brush strokes (Steiner Bébé brows do not meet at bridge of nose as on other French dolls, but they tend to be longer at outer corner of eye); nicely detailed pierced ears with deep molding; deep pink colored closed mouth with high cupid's-bow upper lip and upturned corners; appropriately dressed. Typically marked with incised:

Figure C No. #   (or A or B)
J. Steiner Bte. S.G.D.G.
Paris

OR

Figure A#   (or B or C)
J. Steiner Bte. S.G.C.G.
PARIS

OR

J. Steiner
Bte. S.G.D.G.
Paris
FI re A #   (or B or C)
(# = size number)

Stamp may or may not be present on either head or body:
"Le Petit Parisien"
Bebe Steiner
Medaille d'Or
Paris 1889
Body may also have a label with a picture of a girl holding a flag.

Le Parisien Bébé: bisque socket head, wood-and-composition body, longer, thinner, more graceful fingers, big toe molded separately, jointed or unjointed wrists; later Le Parisien may have mediocre-quality composition straight-limb body; human or mohair wig, most with cardboard pates dyed purple, some with cork pate; more rectangular face, slight chin; good quality, large and more oval-shaped paperweight eyes, more pronounced brows; beautifully sculptured pierced ears with intricate folds and canals; somewhat longer nose; deep pink colored open or closed mouth, with high cupid's-bow upper lip and upturned corners; longer neck. Typically marked with incised:

OR   A
Paris   Paris
(# = size number)
Stamped: Le PARISIEN (in red block letters)
Body Stamped (in purple):
Bebe Le Parisien
Medaille D'or
Paris
OR
Marque Deposes
Article
FRANCAIS (within a triangle in black)

JULES NICHOLAS STEINER VALUE COMPARISONS:

Size	Early Round Face	Täufling-Type	Series A or C Stamped Bourgoin	Figure A Closed Mouth Bébé	Figure B Closed Mouth Bébé	Figure C Closed Mouth Bébé	Figure Bébé Open mouth	Le Parisien Bébé, Closed Mouth	Le Parisien Bébé, Open Mouth
8½"					2,900.00	4,300.00			1,700.00
9"				3,200.00					
10"			4,700.00		3,200.00	4,500.00			
11"	5,000.00		5,000.00		3,400.00	4,600.00			2,000.00
12"				3,500.00				4,500.00	
13"	5,500.00		5,500.00	3,600.00	3,600.00	4,800.00	4,000.00	4,800.00	
15"		6,700.00		4,000.00	4,000.00		4,400.00	5,300.00	2,400.00
16"	6,000.00		6,000.00		4,200.00	5,200.00			
17"		7,000.00		5,000.00			4,700.00	5,900.00	2,700.00
18"	6,500.00		6,500.00	5,300.00	4,400.00	5,600.00			
20"	7,000.00	7,400.00	7,000.00	5,700.00	5,000.00	6,400.00		6,600.00	3,000.00
22"			7,500.00	5,900.00	5,400.00	7,200.00	5,000.00	7,200.00	3,200.00
24"			8,000.00	6,400.00	6,000.00	7,900.00	5,500.00	8,000.00	
26"									4,000.00
28"			10,000.00	7,000.00	6,700.00	8,700.00	5,800.00	9,500.00	
30"				7,600.00				10,500.00	4,700.00
32"				7,900.00			6,200.00		5,200.00
34"			14,000.00		8,400.00	11,000.00			
36"				8,700.00		14,000.00			
38"			16,000.00						

Swaine & Company

waine & Company was a porcelain manufacturer in Hüttensteinach, near Sonneberg, Germany. It is believed that the company began producing dolls around 1910. Owned by William Swaine, the factory produced quality dolls for only a brief period of time. Made from high-grade bisque, the dolls were beautifully sculptured with fine molding, and exhibited extraordinary talent in the application of decoration. Faces were delicate, sweet, and uniquely Swaine. Many collectors believe Swaine produced only one doll, Lori, with several expressions. Her expressions have been classified by the letters "DI," "DII," "DIP," and so on. Other collectors contend that the character dolls produced by Swaine & Company were entirely different dolls.

Authentic Swaine & Company creations have a green ink stamp on the back of the head, in addition to the incised markings. The stamp consists of "GESTCHUTZT GERMANY S & Co." within a circle. It is often difficult to read.

Reproduction Swaine & Company character dolls are not a problem. A possible deterrent to reproductions is the small green stamp found on all Swaine & Company dolls.

Prices listed are for dolls with no damage to the bisque. Normal wear, slight damage, or well-done repairs to the body do not greatly affect price. If the bisque is damaged or repaired, expect to pay about one-half the amount listed. It is perfectly acceptable to show a missing or repaired finger or joint to the body.

Character Doll: socket head, jointed composition body; solid dome or good wig; especially fine detailing around

Swaine & Company Character Baby.

painted or glass eyes; open or closed mouth; appropriately dressed. Typically marked with green stamp reading "GESTCHUTZT GERMANY S & Co." within a circle and incised "232," "Lori," "DIP," "VI," "DI," "BP," "BO," "S & C," or "FP."

SWAINE & COMPANY VALUE COMPARISONS:

Size	Lori Open/ Closed Mouth	232/Lori Open Mouth	DIP Closed Mouth	DV Open/ Closed Mouth	DI Open/ Closed Mouth	BP Open/ Closed Smiling Mouth	FP Open/ Closed Mouth	SC Child Doll
8"							900.00	
10"							1,200.00	700.00
12"			1,400.00	1,600.00	1,200.00			
14"	2,200.00	1,400.00	1,600.00	1,700.00	1,400.00	6,200.00		800.00
16"	2,500.00	1,600.00	1,900.00	2,000.00		7,000.00		
18"	2,800.00	1,800.00	2,200.00			8,000.00		
20"	3,000.00	2,000.00				8,500.00		1,000.00
22"	3,500.00	2,400.00				9,000.00		
24"	3,800.00	2,800.00						1,500.00
28"								2,200.00

Note: Add an additional $500.00 for Toddler body

Shirley Temple

16" Composition Shirley Temple "Baby Take a Bow." *Photo courtesy of McMasters Doll Auction.*

The Christmas season of 1994 marked the 60th anniversary of Ideal's introduction of its composition Shirley Temple Doll. In the midst of the Great Depression, when people needed an escape from the worries of their everyday lives, a darling child danced and sang her way into the hearts of the nation. Ideal's founder, Morris Michtom, once wrote while negotiating the rights to the name Shirley Temple: "This nation needs a beautiful doll to cure this depression." The charming Shirley Temple Doll was created by master doll artist Bernard Lipfert to the specifications of Ideal, Michtom, and Shirley's mother, Mrs. Gertrude Temple. Mrs. Temple's approval was obtained only after more than twenty-eight molds were rejected.

The five-piece composition body, jointed at the neck, shoulders and hips, was unusually well-formed and life-like with a rounded tummy, well-proportioned limbs, stocky legs with defined calves, and even dimples on the derriere. The flesh colored composition may be either light pink or with a sallow cast. Two distinctly different finishes were applied to the composition. The first was a flat, dull matte-like finish, the other a shiny high gloss. A soft blush kissed the knees, elbows, and backs of the hands. The second and third fingers were molded together. Beautifully styled mohair wigs, ranging in shades from pale yellow to rich golden-coppery blond, had large sausage curls placed vertically around the head. The dolls had hazel, brown, or green eyes with either real or painted eyelashes and single-stroke eyebrows. Shirley's open mouth with six upper teeth had lips which were a soft shade of red with orangish tones. Dimples on either side of her smile were the finishing touch.

Four different markings have been found on the composition Shirley Temple Dolls. The first prototypes were marked "Cop./Ideal/N & T Co." on the head only. The second dolls, mostly 18 and 22 inch sizes, were marked "Shirley Temple" with the familiar "Ideal" in a diamond trademark below. The third mark is "Shirley Temple Corp. Ideal." Finally, the most commonly found Shirley Temple Dolls were marked with a size number on both the head and body. There are also genuine unmarked Shirley Temple Dolls. Some dolls were marked on both the head and body; others were marked on either the head or the body. During the process of assembling the dolls, various combinations occurred. It stands to reason that occasionally two unmarked pieces were joined together to create a genuine unmarked Shirley Temple.

Genuine Shirley Temple outfits from 1934 to 1936 were designed by Mollye Goldman. They include:

Baby Take A Bow: cotton dress of red or blue polka dots with white and red coin dot ruffled collar.

Bright Eyes: aviator costume with red belted leather jacket and matching cap; also red plaid dress with white collar and cuffs, red bow trim.

The Little Colonel: elaborate organdy dress of either pink, green, lavender, or blue with attached slip, lace trimmed tiered ruffles, lacy bloomers showing under dress, beautiful bonnet with plume and fabric flower trim.

Curly Top: black velvet bodice and yellow or green taffeta skirt, embroidered flowers and appliqué trim, white fur coat, tam, and muff.

Our Little Girl: dress of either blue and white or red and white piqué with white Scottie dog appliqué.

The Littlest Rebel: cotton dress of either red and white, green and white, or brown and white with Peter Pan collar and pinafore.

Captain January: sailor suit.

Poor Little Rich Girl: silk one-piece polka-dot pajamas of either white and red or peach and blue.

Stowaway: two-piece Oriental navy, yellow, and red costume, trimmed with brass buttons.

Wee Willie Winkie: Scottish outfit.

Heidi: Dutch outfit with wooden shoes.

The Blue Bird: dress with blue skirt, white organdy blouse, red vest, and white apron with blue appliqué birds.

Texas Ranger: cowgirl ensemble, designed to coincide with the Texas Centennial (1936), plaid shirt, leather vest and chaps, holster with small gun, tan cowgirl hat.

Dresses had two types of labels and pins. One type of dress label was blue and white rayon with the Shirley Temple name in red. The second type of label was similar but also had a blue eagle and the initials "N.R.A." Original pins were made of celluloid. The first had a happy smiling face, the second had Shirley with her finger pointing to her face. Both reading "The World's Darling Genuine Shirley Temple Doll" around the outer edge.

Ideal also released a composition Baby Shirley Temple in 1935. However, Baby Shirley Temple Dolls never realized the success of the child dolls. Baby Shirley had a chubby, stuffed cloth body with composition bent arms and lower legs, molded hair or a blond mohair wig, sleep eyes or flirty eyes, two upper and three lower teeth, and the famous Shirley Temple dimples on either side of her open smiling mouth. They were marked "Shirley Temple" on the back of the head.

Ideal's composition Shirley Temple Dolls were so well marketed that they earned more than 45 million dollars in sales from their introduction in 1934 to their departure from the scene in 1939.

Shirley Temple Dolls, ranging in sizes from 12 to 36 inches, were reissued by Ideal in 1957. These dolls have a vinyl head, hard plastic body, rooted dark blond curly synthetic hair, sleep or flirty eyes, and an open/closed smiling mouth with molded and painted teeth. They are marked "Ideal Doll/ST- #" (# = size number in inches) on the back of the head and "ST - #" on the shoulder. They also wore a gold plastic pin with "Shirley Temple" written in script.

A special issue 15" vinyl doll marked "Hong Kong" was released for Montgomery Ward's 100th Anniversary in 1972. Then, in 1973 Ideal released a new Shirley Temple with an entirely different face. This 16" vinyl doll has stationary eyes and rooted hair. Eight and twelve inch dolls were reissued in 1982. Dolls, Dreams & Love, a company owned by Henry Garfinkle, released a special issue 36" Shirley Temple doll in 1984 to commemorate the 50th anniversary of the original Shirley Temple Doll. This Shirley had rooted blond

SHIRLEY TEMPLE DOLL VALUE COMPARISONS:

Size	Ideal All Composition	Baby Shirley	Brown Shirley	1957 Vinyl	1972 Vinyl	1973 Vinyl	1982 Vinyl	1984 Vinyl	Bisque Danbury Mint
8"							50.00		
11"	1,100.00								
12"				250.00			75.00		
13"	1,000.00								
14"									300.00
15"	1,000.00			350.00	125.00				
16"	1,000.00	1,300.00				150.00		400.00	
17"	1,100.00			425.00					
18"	1,100.00	1,400.00	1,200.00						
19"				475.00					
20"		1,500.00							
21"		1,600.00							
22"	1,300.00								
23"	1,400.00	1,700.00							
25"	1,500.00	1,800.00							
27"	2,200.00								
36"				1,600.00					

synthetic hair styled in long curls, hazel sleep eyes, and an open/closed smiling mouth with molded and painted teeth. It was marked "1984/Mrs. Shirley Temple Black/Dolls, Dreams & Love" on the back of the head.

During the late 1980s the Danbury Mint began making 14" bisque dolls sculpted by Elke Hutchens. These dolls were available in several different outfits and offered by direct mail. They were marked "Danbury Mint."

Shirley Temple Dolls have captured the hearts of collectors for over sixty years. She rekindles pleasant memories of bygone days with the sweet songs and adorable antics of a beautiful and talented little girl.

Reproduction Shirley Temple Dolls are not a problem. However, copies of Shirley Temple Dolls are plentiful. Examples of copies include: Madame Alexander's Little Colonel; American Character's Sally Star; Arranbee's Nancy; Goldberger's Little Miss Charming; Horsman's Bright Star; Joy Doll's Miss World's Fairest; Regal's Kiddie Pal; and even Ideal's Ginger and Betty Jane Dolls. Because a royalty had to be paid for every genuine Shirley Temple Doll sold, it was often profitable for a company to issue copies of its own dolls. Reliable of Canada was licensed in 1934 to make the Shirley Temple Doll for the Canadian market.

It is becoming increasingly more difficult to find composition dolls in perfect condition. Collectors have come to expect fine craze lines and even tiny splits on these dolls. Another common problem is crackling of the eyes. The dolls listed are in good to very good condition. Slight signs of aging do not greatly detract from their value. Restored or repainted dolls or dolls with heavily crazed, cracked, or peeling composition or badly mussed wigs would be valued at less than half the amount listed. Vinyl, plastic, and modern bisque dolls should only be purchased when in mint or excellent condition, as there is very little forgiveness for less in a modern doll.

COMPOSITION

Ideal Shirley Temple: all composition, jointed at neck, shoulders, and hips; blond mohair wig styled with curls; hazel sleep eyes, painted lashes, single-stroke brows; rosy cheeks with dimples; open slightly smiling mouth. Original, tagged "Shirley Temple" outfit. Typically marked "Shirley Temple" and size number on back of head and/or body; "Cop./Ideal/N & T Co." (on earliest prototype dolls), "Shirley Temple Ideal" (within a diamond); and occasionally unmarked.

Baby Shirley Temple: composition head, cloth body, composition limbs; molded hair or wig; open mouth; original tagged outfit. Typically marked "Shirley Temple."

Brown Shirley Temple: represents Marama character from the movie *The Hurricane*; all brown composition, jointed at neck, shoulders, and hips; black yarn hair; painted side-glancing eyes; open/closed mouth with painted upper teeth; wearing original "grass" skirt and leis, flowers in hair. Typically marked "Shirley Temple."

VINYL AND PLASTIC

1957: vinyl head, hard plastic body; rooted blond curly synthetic hair; brown sleep eyes; open/closed smiling mouth with nicely molded and painted teeth, dimples on either side of mouth; original costume; gold plastic script pin "Shirley Temple;" marked "ST-II" on back of head.

1972: vinyl head, plastic body; made for Montgomery Ward; marked "Hong Kong."

1973: vinyl head, plastic body; rooted hair; stationary brown eyes; open/closed mouth, molded and painted teeth; marked "1971/Ideal Toy Corp./ST-14-H-213" on body.

1982: vinyl head, hard plastic body; original costume. Marked "1982" on body and "1982 Ideal Toy Corp/S.T. 8-N-8371" on head.

1984: vinyl head, plastic body. Marked "1984/Mrs. Shirley Temple Black/Dolls, Dreams & Loves" on head.

BISQUE

Bisque Display Shirley Temple: Marked "Danbury Mint."

FOREIGN SHIRLEY TEMPLE DOLLS

United States patent laws did not protect against infringements by other countries.

Canadian: Reliable Doll Company had the legal rights to manufacture Shirley Temple dolls. Marked "Celichle."

French: stuffed felt swivel head stitched at back, cotton cloth body, jointed shoulders and hips, celluloid hands; face and front of neck covered with sealing glaze and painted; blond curly mohair wig; painted brown eyes glancing slightly to side, single-stroke brows, detailed upper eyelid and lashes; open/closed smiling mouth with finely molded teeth, small dimples on either side of mouth; dressed in copy of costumes from Shirley Temple films. Unmarked (generally accepted that they were made by Edouard Raynal). Not intended for export to United States. Very rare.

German: several German manufacturers produced Shirley Temple dolls. The best known is the beautiful Armand Marseille composition mold 452 or 452H. All composition, socket head, jointed composition body; 452 wears wig, 452H has molded curly hair, glass sleep eyes, rosy cheeks with hint of dimples, smiling open mouth with teeth, appropriately dressed. Marked "Armand Marseille 452 Germany" or "AM/452H/Germany."

Japan: all composition, jointed at neck, shoulders, and hips; molded and painted blond curly hair; painted brown eyes with long, painted upper lashes; open/closed smiling mouth with white between lips to simulate teeth; original pink pleated sleeveless dress, white socks, tie shoes. Marked "S.T. Japan."

FOREIGN SHIRLEY TEMPLE DOLL VALUE COMPARISONS:				
Size	Canadian Composition	French Cloth	German Composition	Japanese Composition
10"				300.00
18"	1,400.00		1,400.00	
19"		1,500.00		
20"			1,800.00	
22"			2,200.00	

Terri Lee

The Terri Lee Company was founded in August 1946, when Mrs. Violet Gradwohl and ten other employees working in one room in Lincoln, Nebraska, ventured into the doll-making business. Mrs. Gradwohl was concerned with the quality of dolls being offered to children and wanted to manufacture a doll that could withstand all the "love" a child could inflict. Her first challenge was in finding a suitable plastic—one that was both life-like and durable. The head was molded with a closed mouth, and eyes could be painted, thus eliminating eyes that were easily be broken.

Mrs. Gradwohl also wanted a wig that could be shampooed, combed, curled, and styled. She eventually received a patent for the process used to create artificial hair wigs woven from Celanese yarn. Once construction details of the Terri Lee Doll were settled upon, the only remaining area of concern was costuming. Mrs. Gradwohl decided that Terri Lee should have a beautiful wardrobe, with all types of outfits made from the finest fabrics. The clothing was designed by Mrs. Gradwohl and her daughter, Terri Lee, for whom the dolls were named.

Every little girl needs companionship, and the Terri Lee Doll was no exception. By using the same body with a lamb's wool wig replacement, brother Jerri Lee was created. Black friends Bonnie Lu, Patty Jo, Benjie, and Nanooh, an Eskimo child, were also introduced. It is interesting to note that all these dolls used the same doll mold—the only difference being either wig types or painting. Also joining the family was 11" Baby Linda. She was closely followed by 10" Tiny Terri Lee and Tiny Jerri Lee. An entirely new doll, Connie Lynn, entered the scene. Reportedly, a birth certificate with fingerprints, footprints, and a lifetime guarantee were also issued with each doll. For a small fee (labor costs only), the company would restore "sick" or "injured" dolls.

Another innovative idea of Gradwohl's was a newsletter sent to the owner of Terri Lee dolls, keeping them informed of Terri Lee's latest fashions.

The Terri Lee Doll Company, despite its success, was plagued with misfortune. The factory in Lincoln burned to the ground, prompting its relocation to Apple Valley, California. This factory closed in 1958.

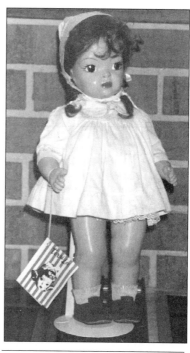

Tagged Terri Lee.

Reproduction Terri Lee dolls have been reported. They were made during the early 1950s, at the peak of Terri Lee's popularity. Reproductions may have holes in the feet. Other differences include:

Authentic Terri Lee:		Reproduction:
Measurement at waist	9¾"	9¼"
Measurement at calf	5½"	5¼"
Measurement in height	16"	15½"

Another copy is Mary Jane. This doll is often called an unmarked Terri Lee walker. This is incorrect. Mary Jane is indeed unmarked and does in fact walk; however, she is not a Terri Lee even though she looks identical to the distinctive Terri Lee.

When considering a Terri Lee Doll, check condition carefully. As with any modern collectible doll, there is little forgiveness for less than perfect dolls. Prices listed are for dolls in near mint condition.

Composition Terri Lee: all composition, jointed at neck, shoulders, and hip; wiry hair wig; painted eyes; closed mouth; appropriately dressed. Marked "Terri Lee, Pat. Pending."

Hard Plastic/Vinyl: hard plastic, jointed at neck, shoulders, and hips; good wig; painted distinctive facial features; large eyes; closed mouth; appropriately dressed. Typically marked "Terri Lee Pat. Pending" on dolls made before 1949 and "Terri Lee" on dolls produced in 1949 and later years.

Gene Autry Terri Lee: molded and painted brown hair and feathered eyebrows; decal blue eyes; open/closed mouth with painted teeth; original cowboy outfit; Gene Autry pin and Terri Lee label. Marked "Terri Lee/Pat. Pending" on back.

Mary Jane: reproduction Terri Lee; walker; sleep eyes, similar facial molding.

TERRI LEE FAMILY VALUE COMPARISONS:

Size	Terri Lee	Gene Autry Terri Lee	Jerri Lee, Lambs-Wool Wig	Patti Jo, Benji, Bonnie Lu, or Black Friends	Nanook Eskimo	Tiny Terri Lee	Tiny Jerri Lee
10"						350.00	300.00
11"							
16"	400.00	1,900.00	350.00	700.00	900.00		

Size	Connie Lynn Baby	Mary Jane Sleep Eyes Reproduction	Vinyl So-Sleepy	Vinyl Baby Linda Lee
9½"			200.00	
10"				250.00
16"		275.00		
19"	500.00			

Uneeda Doll Company

*U*needa Doll Company, founded in 1917 in New York, was also known as the Tony Toy Company of Hong Kong.

Since its inception, Uneeda has produced thousands of popularly priced dolls made from cloth, composition, hard plastic, and vinyl. The company's success in the doll industry was due to its production of good-quality dolls at competitive prices. Uneeda supplied jobbers, mail order houses, and department stores with a complete line of well-made dolls. Almost every little girl owned at least one Uneeda Doll.

By the 1930s, Uneeda was advertising over 400 different models of dolls ranging in size from 14 to 28 inches. The dolls featured molded hair or wigs and painted or sleep eyes. Uneeda's Dollikins were probably the best fully-jointed dolls ever made. Dollikins featured a unique body construction which was jointed at the neck, shoulders, upper arms, elbows, wrists, waist, hips, knees, and ankles. The joints were hidden, and allowed the doll to be gracefully posed in almost any position. Uneeda also advertised a "Magic Muscle" doll which walked by means of a weighted screw-type apparatus in its torso.

Uneeda Dolls are often found unmarked. Without their original wrist tags or boxes they are virtually impossible to identify. Markings include "Uneeda" within a diamond, "Uneeda," "U," or "UN."

This 20th century doll manufacturer is still producing play dolls. Born from the need for American-made

Bob and Original Boxed Costume.

dolls during World War I, Uneeda has proven that high quality and a fair price will be rewarded with success. Over the years, Uneeda has provided the world with many highly collectible dolls, including personality dolls, babies, toddlers, mama dolls, boy dolls, and glamorous lady dolls.

Prices listed are for dolls with no damage. Slight crazing to the composition has become acceptable to collectors as a natural occurrence and does not greatly affect the value of the doll. Expect to pay less than half the amount listed if a doll is badly crazed, cracked, or peeling, or if it has been damaged or repaired. There is little tolerance for less than perfect condition in modern dolls.

COMPOSITION

Rita Hayworth as Carmen: 14", all composition, jointed at neck, shoulders, and hips; red mohair wig; sleep eyes with exceptionally long real lashes, gray eye shadow; closed mouth; wearing original red dress with black lace overskirt and matching black lace headpiece with silk flowers decorating both dress and scarf, gold shoes. Unmarked. Gold fan-shaped wrist tag reads "The Carmen Doll/W. I. Gould & Co., Inc. Mfrd by Uneeda Doll Co./Inspired by/Rita Hayworth's/Portrayal of Carmen/in/The Loves of Carmen." **600.00**

Baby Sweetheart: 17", all composition, jointed at neck, shoulders, and hips; deeply molded hair; sleep eyes; open mouth with metal tongue and two upper teeth; appropriately dressed. Unmarked. Attached tag reads "Everybody Loves Baby Sweetheart/Produced by Uneeda Doll Co." **300.00**

HARD PLASTIC AND VINYL

Tiny Time Teens: 5", posable vinyl head, plastic body; rooted hair, painted features with real lashes. Marked "U.D. Co. Inc./1967/Hong Kong." There are several dolls in this series, including Fun Time, Beau Time, Bride Time, Winter Time, Date Time, Party Time, Vacation Time, and Prom Time **20.00**

American Gem Collection: 8¹/₂", rooted hair, painted features, nicely dressed. Marked "U.D. Co. Inc./MCMLXXI/Made in Hong Kong" on head and body. Dolls include Georgia, Carolina, Patience, Prudence, Priscilla, and Virginia. **35.00**

Little Sophisticates: 8¹/₂" mod dolls, vinyl head, plastic body, long thin vinyl arms; rooted hair; closed eyes with eye shadow. Marked "Uneeda Doll Co. Inc./1967/Made in Japan" on head and back. Dolls include Kristina, Marika, Rosanna, Penelope, and Suzana. **10.00**

Baby Sleep Amber: 11", black vinyl head, arms, and legs, cloth body; rooted black hair; sleep eyes. Marked "Tony Toy/1970/Made in Hong Kong." **12.00**

Pri-Thilla: 12", all vinyl, bent left arm; rooted hair; sleep eyes; open mouth; sucks thumb and blows up balloons. Marked "4" on head. **25.00**

Baby: 16", all vinyl; rooted hair; sleep eyes; open nurser mouth. Marked "3TD11/Uneeda." **9.00**

Magic Fairy Princess: vinyl head, hard plastic body, jointed at neck, shoulders, hips, and knees; rooted pink hair; sleep eyes; closed mouth; wearing original fairy costume of white satin top, white net tutu with glitter, plastic wings, and silver slippers. Marked "Uneeda" on head, "210" on body.

> 18" **150.00**
>
> 32" **200.00**

Dollikins: vinyl head, hard plastic body, uniquely jointed at neck, shoulders, upper arms, elbows, wrists, waist, hips, knees, and ankles; rooted hair; sleep eyes with real lashes; pierced ears; closed mouth; polished fingernails and toenails; appropriately dressed. Marked "Uneeda/25" on head.

> 8" **45.00**
>
> 12" **65.00**
>
> 19" **75.00**

Glamour Lady Bride Doll: 20", vinyl head, hard plastic body, jointed at neck, shoulders, and hips, walker body; rooted hair; sleep eyes with real lashes, tiny painted lower lashes; closed mouth; wearing original bride gown with lace veil. Marked "3" (in circle) "Uneeda." **65.00**

Country Girl: 22", vinyl head, hard plastic body, jointed at neck, shoulders, and hips, walker body; rooted hair; flirty sleep eyes with real lashes, tiny painted lower lashes; closed mouth; wearing original white and yellow polka-dot dress and matching hat. Marked "Uneeda" on head. **65.00**

Toodles: 21", vinyl head, hard plastic body, jointed at neck, shoulders, and hips, walker body; rooted hair; sleep eyes with real lashes, tiny painted lower lashes; wide open/closed mouth, molded tongue; wearing original soft cotton corduroy coat with lace trim and fabric flower corsage and matching hat. Marked "Uneeda" on head. **75.00**

Needa Toodles: 22", hard plastic head, very unusual body with composition upper arms and legs, vinyl lower arms and legs; weighted screw-type apparatus in torso causes doll to walk; saran wig; sleep eyes with real lashes; open/closed mouth with two upper teeth; hint of dimples; wearing original dress and matching bonnet. Marked "20" on head. **100.00**

50th Anniversary Antebellum Southern Belle: 25", all vinyl; rooted hair; sleep eyes, long lashes, eye shadow; closed mouth. Marked "8/Uneeda Doll Co./1967." . . **85.00**

Pollyana: rooted very blond hair; sleep eyes with lashes, eye liner; open mouth with painted teeth. Marked "Walt Disney Prod./Mfd By Uneeda/N.F."

> 11" **45.00**
>
> 17" **65.00**
>
> 31" **150.00**

Freckles: 32", vinyl head, hard plastic body, jointed at neck, shoulders, hips, and wrists; unique finger position; rooted hair; large flirty sleep eyes with lashes; freckles across nose and cheeks; open/closed mouth with four molded and painted upper teeth; wearing original nylon dress with fitted waist and sash. . . . **125.00**

Unis

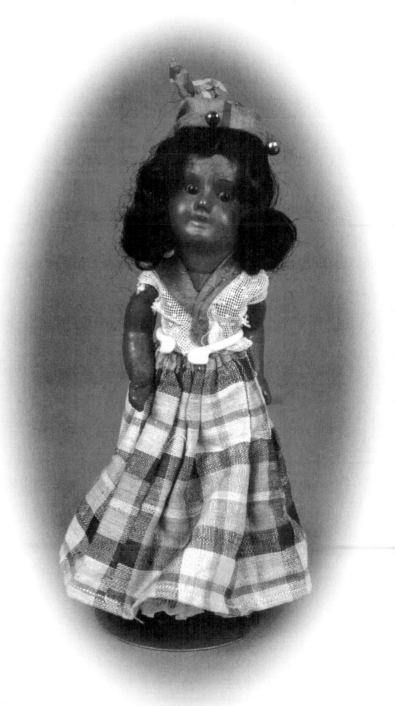

*U*nis represents a mark found on various French dolls. The Unis mark was used by Societe Française de Fabrication de Bébés & Jouets (S.F.B.J.). The letters U N I S stood for the Union National Inter Syndicale. These initials are often found in a circle or football-shaped mark and accompanied by numbers. The number to the left of the Unis mark represents the syndicate number; i.e., 71 was the number assigned to Chambre Syndicale. The number to the right of the Unis mark represents the manufacturer; i.e., 149 was the number assigned to S.F.B.J. The number beneath the Unis mark represents the mold number; i.e., 60 or 301. You will notice that these Unis dolls have a slightly lower value than the S.F.B.J. dolls with the same mold numbers. This is because the later bisque dolls were usually made from a lesser-quality bisque than the earlier S.F.B.J. dolls. Facial decoration is also usually less detailed.

The Bleuette booklet was first issued in 1916 and came out twice a year. It advertised the commercially made costumes available for the Bleuette doll. Publication continued until 1960.

Prices listed are for dolls with no damage to the bisque or composition face. Normal wear, slight damage or well-done repairs to the body do not greatly affect price. If the bisque is damaged, the composition badly crazed, or if either is repaired, expect to pay less than half the amount listed. It is perfectly acceptable to show a missing or repaired finger or joint to the body.

BISQUE

Bleuette: socket head, jointed composition body; good wig styled in long braids; blue stationary glass side-glancing eyes (not googly eyes); open mouth; appropriately dressed. Marked "71/Unis" within an oval "/149/301." Paper tag pinned to front of dress reads "Marque Deposee Bleuette 18 Rue Jacob Paris Vie."

Child: socket head, jointed composition body; good wig; glass eyes; open mouth; appropriately dressed. Typically marked "71/Unis France" within an oval "/149/301."

Princess Elizabeth: socket head, jointed composition body; blond mohair wig; glass eyes; open mouth; appropriately dressed. Marked "71/Unis France" within an oval "/149/306/Jumeau/1938/Paris."

COMPOSITION

Composition dolls used the same molds as dolly-face bisque dolls, such as mold numbers 60 and 301. They have similar features, jointed bodies, and are appropriately dressed.

8" Unis Black.

UNIS VALUE COMPARISONS:

Size	Bleuette	Child	Black Child	Princess Elizabeth	Composition Unis Doll
8"		500.00	500.00		
10"	850.00	500.00			
11"			500.00		
13"		600.00			
14"					250.00
15"		700.00	700.00	1,600.00	
16"					300.00
17"		800.00			
18"					350.00
20"				1,800.00	450.00
21"		900.00			
22"					500.00
23"		1,000.00			
24"				2,000.00	600.00
25"		1,100.00			
28"				2,600.00	
29"		1,300.00			

* Deduct $100.00 for painted eyes.

Vogue Dolls, Inc.

*V*ogue Dolls was founded by Jennie H. Graves in Somerville, Massachusetts, shortly after World War I. Graves never dreamed that her modest doll costuming business would grow to be largest doll-only manufacturer in the world.

Originally intent on supplementing the family income, Graves set out to design and make doll clothing. After convincing several department stores to purchase her merchandise, she and her neighbors started designing and sewing doll clothing. The business' sole enterprise remained the production of doll clothing until the mid-1930s. Graves then decided to buy undressed quality bisque dolls from German manufacturers such as Kämmer & Reinhardt, design clothing for them, and then sell her creations at shops across the country. Graves' specially costumed dolls often retailed for $75.00 or more—an excessive price for a doll at that time. The political climate in Europe during the late 1930s forced Graves to look to the United States for her doll supply.

In 1948, the famous Ginny-type doll was born. The original miniature doll was an instant success, proving to be one of the most enduring little dolls of all time. First introduced as a composition doll, it was known as "Toddles."

These darling little charmers were offered wearing a wide variety of well-made little girl outfits. Every year new outfits

16" Brikette.

Bent Knee Walker Ginny, Painted Lash Ginny and Straight Leg Walker Ginny.

were added, including foreign costumes and fantasy costumes. The early Toddles costumes were tied on with ribbons at the back of the garments; the later ones had hooks-and-eyes. The earliest clothing did not have attached cloth tags, while later ones did. Very rarely, a round paper label reading "VOGUE" is found attached to a garment. Various styles of shoes, including slip-on pumps and snap-closure Mary Janes, were made from several colors of leatherette.

Vogue began producing hard plastic dolls in 1948. The first hard plastic dolls had painted turquoise blue eyes looking to the left, wide-spaced upper lashes, and white highlights. In 1950, Ginny was given blue or brown sleep eyes with painted wide-spaced lashes. In 1954, Ginny learned to walk while turning her head from side to side. In 1955, the sleep eyes were given molded lashes; and in 1957 knee joints were added.

Any doll as popular as Ginny needed a family. This may not seem unusual today, living in the world of Barbie and her extended family and friend list, but the idea of companion dolls during the 1950s was a novel idea.

Ginny's family included baby Ginnette, two teenage sisters, Jill and Jan, big brother Jeff, and baby brother Jimmy. Each version had its own wardrobe and accessories.

Over the years Vogue diversified by introducing many new dolls, but production of Ginny Dolls remained constant. This perseverance may be responsible for the dramatic increase in Ginny's value. It is interesting to note that an early walker with sleep eyes and painted lashes in good condition sold for about $10.00 in 1975. Today, that same doll is valued at $350.00. Few other dolls, antique or modern, can boast of such a return.

Reproduction Vogue Dolls are not a problem. Copies of the famous Ginny Dolls are numerous. Ginny is probably one of the most often-copied doll ever produced. All Ginny Dolls were well-marked and a careful examination should ensure that you are purchasing an original.

Prices listed are for dolls with no damage. With the exception of slight crazing to the early composition dolls, there is little forgiveness for less-than-perfect, original dolls. If a Vogue doll is damaged or repaired, expect to pay about half the amount listed. Wear to the hair of the Ginny Dolls is acceptable, as this has become such a common occurrence that collectors have learned to tolerate, and quite often, correct this problem. A drop of cream conditioner smoothed over the top of the hair helps restore the shine and improve the appearance. Work the conditioner carefully into the hair. Avoid rubbing or pulling.

GINNY VALUE COMPARISONS:								
Size	#1 Ginny Painted Eyes	#2 Ginny Sleep Eyes, Painted Lashes, Straight-leg Non-walker	#2 Ginny Poodle Wig	#2 Ginny Fluffy	#2 Ginny Crib Crowder	#3 Ginny Sleep Eyes, Painted Lashes, Straight-leg Walker	#3 Ginny Black	#3 Ginny Queen
8"	350.00	350.00	400.00	1,400.00	900.00	300.00	700.00	900.00

Size	#4 Ginny Sleep Eyes, Molded Lash, Straight-leg Walker	#5 Ginny Sleep Sleep Eyes, Molded Lash, Jointed-knee Walker	#6 Ginny Vinyl Head, Rooted Hair	Modern Ginny, All-vinyl	Sassoons Ginny Painted Eyes	Sassoon Ginny Sleep Eyes	Contemporary Ginny
8"	250.00	200.00	125.00	65.00	45.00	35.00	30.00

BISQUE

Just Me: bisque head, jointed composition body; mohair wig; glass eyes; closed mouth; appropriately dressed. Typically marked "Just Me A.M.," "A.M. 310/11 Just Me," or with round paper tag on dress which reads "Vogue."

VOGUE BISQUE VALUE COMPARISONS:		
Size	Just Me	Painted Bisque Just Me
8"	1,500.00	1,000.00
9"	1,700.00	1,100.00
11"	2,000.00	1,200.00
13"	2,400.00	

COMPOSITION

Toddles: all composition, jointed at neck, shoulders, and hips; mohair wig; large, round, painted eyes; closed mouth; appropriately dressed. Typically marked "Vogue" on head, "Doll Co" or "Vogue" on back. **300.00**

Child: all composition, jointed at neck, shoulders, and hips; good wig; sleep eyes, real lashes, with or without eye shadow; open mouth; appropriately dressed. Typically unmarked or marked "13," "15," or "20" on back. Clothing tag reads "Vogue Dolls, Inc/Medford, Mass." **400.00-500.00**

HARD PLASTIC

#1 Ginny: 1948-1950, all hard plastic, jointed at neck, shoulders, and hips; molded hair under mohair wig; painted side-glancing eyes; closed mouth; appropriately dressed. Typically marked "Vogue" on head and "Vogue Doll" on back. Dress tag reads "Vogue Dolls."

#2 Ginny: 1950-1953, non-walker, all hard plastic, jointed at neck, shoulders, and hips; mohair wig with gauze strip forming cap of wig; sleep eyes, painted lashes; closed mouth; appropriately dressed. Typically marked "Vogue" on head and body. Dress tag reads "Vogue."

#2 Ginny: 1952 only, non-walker, all hard plastic, jointed at neck, shoulders, and hips; lambs wool bubble "Poodle" wool wig; sleep eyes, painted lashes; closed mouth; appropriately dressed. Typically marked "Vogue" on head and body. Dress tag reads "Vogue."

Special #2 Ginny: lambs wool wig; dressed as fluffy bunny with bunny ears.

Crib Crowd Baby: with bent-leg baby body.

#3 Ginny: 1954, straight-leg walker, all hard plastic, pin jointed; good wig; sleep eyes, painted lashes; closed mouth; appropriately dressed. Typically marked "Ginny" on head and "Vogue Dolls Inc./Pat.#2687594/Made in USA" on body. Dress tag reads "Vogue Doll."

#4 Ginny: 1955-1957, straight-leg walker, all hard plastic, pin jointed; good wig; sleep eyes, molded plastic upper lashes; closed mouth; appropriately dressed. Typically marked "Vogue" on head and "Ginny Vogue Dolls Inc./Pat. #2687594/Made in USA" on body. Dress tag reads "Vogue Dolls."

#5 Ginny: 1957-1962, jointed-knee walker, all hard plastic, pin jointed; good wig; sleep eyes, molded plastic lashes; closed mouth; appropriately dressed. Typically marked "Vogue" on head and "Ginny Vogue Dolls Inc./Pat. #2687594/Made in U.S.A." on body. Dress tag reads "Vogue Dolls Inc."

#6 Ginny: 1963, vinyl head, hard plastic body; rooted hair; sleep eyes, closed mouth; appropriately dressed. Typically marked "Ginny" on head and "Ginny Vogue Dolls Inc./Pat. No. 2687594/Made in U.S.A." on back. Dress tag reads "Vogue Dolls Inc."

Modern Ginny: early 1970s, all vinyl; rooted hair; sleep eyes; closed mouth; appropriately dressed. Typically marked "GINNY" on head and "Vogue Dolls 1972/Made in Hong Kong/8" on body. Dress tag reads "Made in Hong Kong."

Sassoon Ginny: 1978-79, thin body and limbs.
Contemporary Ginny: made by Dankin.

HARD PLASTIC & VINYL

Jill: hard plastic adult body, jointed at neck, shoulders, hips, and knees; high heel feet; saran hair; sleep eyes, molded lashes; pierced ears; closed mouth; appropriately dressed. Typically marked "Vogue" on head and "Jill/Vogue Made in U.S.A. 1957" on body. Dress tag reads "Vogue."

Li'l Imp: vinyl head, walker body jointed at neck, shoulders, hips, and knees; dimples on backs of hands; arm hook is molded as part of plastic arm and to a separate hook (gently pull arm away from body to observe); orange hair; freckles; sleep eyes; open/closed mouth; appropriately dressed. Typically marked "R & B" on head. Dress tag reads "Vogue."

Littlest Angel: vinyl head, hard plastic walker body, jointed at neck, shoulders, hips and knees; rooted hair; sleep eyes; open/closed mouth; appropriately dressed. Typically marked "R & B" on head. Dress tag reads "Vogue." Littlest Angel and Li'l Imp were produced by Arranbee, which was purchased by Vogue in 1957. Littlest Angel was marketed as such until 1961, when she became Ginny's cousin, and part of the Ginny family.

Child: all hard plastic, jointed at the neck, shoulders and hips; slender body, long legs, slightly bent arms; hands with first, second, and third fingers molded together, little finger molded separately; good wig; sleep eyes, real lashes, painted lower lashes; closed mouth; appropriately dressed. Typically marked "14" on head and "Made in U.S.A." on back. Dress tag reads "Vogue Dolls."

Jan: all vinyl, rigid body and limbs, jointed at neck, shoulders, swivel waist; high heel feet; rooted hair; sleep eyes, molded lashes; closed smiling mouth; appropriately dressed. Typically marked "Vogue" on head. Dress tag reads "Vogue Dolls."

Jeff: vinyl head and limbs, plastic body; molded and painted hair; sleep eyes, molded lashes; appropriately dressed. Typically marked "Vogue" on head. Suit tag reads "Vogue Dolls."

Littlest Angel: all vinyl, bent-limb baby body; rooted hair; sleep eyes, real lashes; smiling closed mouth; appropriately dressed. Typically marked "Vogue Doll/1963" on head and back.

Angel Baby: all vinyl, bent-limb baby body; rooted strawberry blond hair; sleep eyes with lashes; smiling closed mouth; appropriately dressed. Typically marked "Vogue Doll/1965" on head.

Miss Ginny: all vinyl, jointed at neck, shoulders and hips, teen body; rooted hair; sleep eyes; closed mouth; appropriately dressed. Typically marked "Vogue Doll/1970." Dress tag reads "Vogue Dolls Inc."

Baby Dear: vinyl head and limbs, cloth body; rooted hair; painted eyes; closed mouth; newborn baby face; appropriately dressed. Typically marked with cloth tag sewn into seam of body "Vogue Dolls, Inc." Back of left leg marked "E. Wilkins/1960."

Posie Pixie: vinyl head and gauntlet hands, cloth body; rooted hair; black side-glancing eyes; open/closed mouth; appropriately dressed. Marked "1964/Vogue/71" on head.

Ginny Baby: all vinyl; rooted hair; sleep eyes with lashes; open nurser mouth; appropriately dressed. Typically marked "Ginny Baby/10/Vogue Doll Inc."

Brickette: plastic body, ball-jointed waist, long plastic legs, vinyl arms and head, teen-type body; rooted hair; sleep/flirty eyes with lashes; smiling closed mouth; appropriately dressed. Typically unmarked. Brickette was reissued in 1980 in an 18" size.

VOGUE HARD PLASTIC & VINYL VALUE COMPARISONS:												
Size	**Jill**	**Jan**	**Jeff**	**Li'l Imp**	**Child**	**Littlest Angel**	**Angel Baby**	**Miss Ginny**	**Baby Dear**	**Posie Pixie**	**Ginny Baby**	**Brickette**
10"	175.00		125.00									
10½"				65.00								
11"						65.00						
13"		165.00				45.00		35.00	65.00			
14"					400.00		55.00					
15"								60.00				
17"									100.00	45.00		
18"												50.00
22"											100.00	100.00
25"									175.00			
27"									225.00			

W.P.A.

W.P.A. includes art dolls made in the United States during the 1930s. Under Franklin D. Roosevelt's New Deal, the Works Progress Administration (W.P.A.) allowed the United States government to become a doll manufacturer. The W.P.A. provided work for artists and seamstresses struggling during the depression. The objective of the project was to create cloth dolls representing characters from fairy tales and folk lore, and historical figures from both the United States and various foreign countries. With the exception of Japan, most countries of the world were included in the project. Japan's omission was undoubtedly due to our strained relations during that period of history. Completed dolls were loaned to major department stores for displays, and to elementary schools to be used as visual aids.

Most of the dolls were approximately 12" tall and had cotton stuffed bodies. Each torso was made from four pieces of material. Three of the seams ran the entire length of the body; the front seam stopped at the neck. The separate arms were hand sewn to the body, but the legs were typically part of the body. The soft cotton stuffing made the doll's limbs flexible, enabling it to sit. Hands were mitten-shaped and generally without stitching. The yarn wigs were individually styled according to the character. Portrait painting techniques gave the flat faces a sculptured look. The head, neck, and arms were first covered with a flesh-colored covering of oil paints. Legs and feet were not painted because they were covered with stockings and shoes. Because each doll was hand crafted, variations did occur.

Prices listed are for dolls with no damage. Normal wear or slight surface dust does not greatly affect price. If worn, dirty, stained, redressed, or torn, expect to pay less than half the amount listed. It is acceptable to have a properly mended seam or patch to the body. Again, because each doll was hand crafted, the quality of artistry and visual appeal varies, contributing significantly to its value.

Cloth W. P. A. Doll: 12", painted features; yarn hair; dressed appropriately for the character it represents. Typically marked "Michigan W.P.A. Toy Project," "W.P.A.

W.P.A. Dolls "Betsy Ross" and "W.P.A. Girl."
Photo courtesy of McMasters Doll Auction.

Museum Project Wichita," "Museum Project 1865 W.P.A.," "W.P.A. Toy Project, sponsored by Michigan State College," "W.P.A.," or "WPA Handicraft Project Milwaukee Wisconsin."

Fairy Tale Character Set: cloth; yarn hair; oil-painted features. Examples include Mary and Her Lamb, Red Riding Hood and the Wolf, and Mother and Three Little Kittens.

Nationality Doll and Famous Figures: all cloth; oil-painted features. Examples include Denmark Couple, George and Martha Washington, and Paul Revere.

Special Display Doll: 22", all cloth, painted stockinette shoulder head, jointed at shoulder and hips; oil-painted features; hands stitched with fingers and separate thumb; yarn hair.

W.P.A. DOLL VALUE COMPARISONS:

Size	Fairy Tale With One Character	Fairy Tale With 2 to 3 Characters	Fairy Tale 4 or More Characters	Nationality Dolls	Famous Characters	Special Display Dolls
12" to 18"	400.00 to 500.00	600.00 to 800.00 Set	900.00 and Up Set	200.00 to 300.00 Each Character	400.00 to 600.00 Each Character	
22" to 24"						3,500.00 to 5,000.00

Wagner & Zetzsche

The company was founded by Richard Wagner and Richard Zetzsche, both of whom worked for Naumann Fischer before starting their own business on the first day of 1875 in Ilmenau, Thürginia, Germany. Of the two partners, Zetzsche was the artist, responsible for designing and sculpting the dolls. Wagner was the practical one with the business sense. Four of the Zetzsche grandchildren—Harald, Hansi, Inge, and Barbele—were used as models for dolls.

Wagner & Zetzsche made doll bodies of cloth, leather, papier-mâché, and imitation leather. Numerous accessories, including more than 400 different designs of shoes, doll stockings, and wigs, were also made. Many of the marked Wagner & Zetzsche kid bodies are found with fine-quality bisque or china heads. Heads were supplied by Alt, Beck & Gottschalck, Buschow & Beck, Gebruder Heubach, Armand Marseille, and possibly other manufacturers of bisque doll heads.

Around 1916, Wagner & Zetzsche acquired the patent for a composition material and process called "Haralit" from P.R. Zierow, of Berlin. The material is often described as both a celluloid- and composition-like material. In truth, the material is more characteristic of composition. The character dolls of Harald, Inge, and Hansi were introduced as Haralit Art Dolls that same year. The company was in operation until at least 1938, as is evidenced by its advertisements of leather doll bodies.

Prices listed are for dolls with no damage. Normal wear, slight damage, or well-done repairs to the body do not greatly affect price. If the bisque is damaged or repaired, expect to pay less than half the amount listed. It is perfectly acceptable to show a missing or repaired finger or joint to the body.

BISQUE

Closed Mouth, Turned Shoulderhead: kid body; good wig; glass eyes with feathered brows; closed mouth; appropriately dressed. Typically marked with elaborate intertwined "W & Z," "639," "698."

20" Wagner & Zetzsche. *Photo courtesy Cobbs Doll Auction.*

Dolly-Face: jointed composition or kid body; good wig; glass eyes; open mouth; appropriately dressed. Typically marked "WuZ," "10586," and "10585."

HARALIT

Depending upon the condition, originality, and visual appeal of a Haralit doll, its value may be much higher—perhaps twice the amount given.

Harald or Hansi: character socket head, oilcloth body, jointed composition arms, several body variations exist; molded and painted hair; painted eyes; closed mouth; appropriately dressed. Marked "1/Hansi/W.Z.," "1/Harald/W.Z."

Inge: Haralit character; appropriately dressed. Marked "Inge/W.Z."

Barbele: appropriately dressed. Marked "Barbele/W.Z."

WAGNER & ZETZSCHE VALUE COMPARISON:						
Size	Turned Head, Closed Mouth, Kid Body	Dolly-Face, Open Mouth, Kid Body	Dolly-Face, Open Mouth, Composition Body	Haralit Character Harald or Hansi	Haralit Character Inge	Haralit Character Barbele
12"					1,000.00	1,700.00
12½"				700.00		
14"	1,200.00	500.00	700.00	900.00	1,200.00	1,900.00
16"		600.00	800.00			
18"		700.00	900.00			
20"		800.00	1,000.00			
22"			1,100.00			
24"	1,800.00		1,200.00			
26"	1,900.00					

Izannah Walker

*I*zannah Walker made American primitive sculpture dolls in Central Falls, Rhode Island. The dolls have heavy oil-painted features or slightly sculptured faces. They bear an uncanny resemblance to children in American folk art paintings. They are typically unmarked or marked "Patented Nov. 4th 1873."

Collectors have long agreed that Izannah Walker Dolls are wonderful, but they cannot agree on when these dolls were first made. In June of 1873, Izannah Walker applied for a patent for her "Rag Dolls." According to patent law, it was illegal for her to have made her dolls more than two years prior to her application date. Despite this, other possible dates abound. Mrs. Sheldon of the Chase Doll Company reported in *Doll Collectors of America* that the first Izannah Walker Doll was made in 1855. In *Your Dolls and Mine*, Izannah Walker's great niece, Janel Johl, variously states that the first Walker Dolls were made in 1840 (page 40); 1845 (page 39); 1848 (page 37), and 1855 (page 41). One solid bit of evidence does exist. The 1865 Census of Rhode Island lists: "Walker, Izannah F., born of American parentage in Bristol, Rhode Island, living in the village of Central Falls in the town of Smithfield with the occupation of Doll Maker." These mysteries are what makes doll collecting so fascinating. One special lady, Mrs. Monica Bessette, has devoted years to answering these questions. We wish her luck, for her sake as well as ours!

Legend tells how Izannah Walker struggled to perfect her dolls. One problem in particular was how to create a surface resistant to cracking or peeling. One night, coming out of a deep sleep, Izannah sat up in bed and heard a voice say "USE PASTE." It was after this vision that she obtained her patent for dolls. In part, her application for a patent involved layering and pressing cloth treated with glue in a heated two-part mold. The body was then sewn, stuffed, and glued around a wooden armature. Hands and feet were hand sewn. The entire doll was then hand painted in oil colors. The hair is usually painted as either corkscrew curls or short straight hair with fine brush strokes. Other characteristics of Walker Dolls are their applied ears (or on rare occasions, molded ears) carefully stitched fingers, and either

Two Izanna Walker Dolls. *Courtesy of Ellen Schroy.*

bare feet with stitched toes or feet with painted-on high-laced shoes.

The primitive beauty of Izannah Walker dolls causes them to be actively sought dolls by collectors today. Reproduction Izannah Walker dolls are not a problem. Although there are many copies of the type of cloth doll made by Izannah Walker, it is impossible to counterfeit the patina and softly aged look of an authentic Izannah Walker doll. Craft persons attempt to "age" dolls with coats of lacquer that crackle. Though charming, they do not really duplicate the aged look of the Walker dolls. If in doubt, smell the doll. Copies will have a chemical odor.

Prices listed are for dolls in fair to good condition. Normal wear with crazing and slight rubs will not affect price. If the doll is badly worn, cracked, or peeling, or has been repainted, expect to pay less than half the amount listed.

Izannah Walker: cloth doll, oil-painted covering; painted hair with soft wisps and tiny curls around face; molded facial features; large luminous eyes; applied or occasionally molded ears; closed, slightly smiling mouth; appropriately dressed. Typically marked "Patented Nov. 4th 1873" or unmarked.

IZANNAH WALKER VALUE COMPARISONS:

Size	Izannah Walker
15"	16,000.00
17"	18,000.00
18"	20,000.00
20"	22,000.00
21"	22,000.00
24"	27,000.00

Wax Dolls

Montanari Type Poured-Wax Doll. *Courtesy of Mary Jane Brummer.*

Wax-Over with Molded Hair. *Courtesy of Helen Brooke.*

There are three types of Wax Dolls: Wax-Over Dolls; Poured-Wax Dolls; and Reinforced-Wax Dolls.

New collectors often ask "How can I tell the difference between the three types of Wax Dolls?" As usual, there are very few fool-proof absolutes. However, some clues which may be of help in distinguishing the different types are:

	POURED-WAX	WAX-OVER	REINFORCED-WAX
1. Wax Color	Tinted	Clear	Tinted
2. Hair	Inserted	Wig or Molded	Wig
3. Eyelids	Molded	None	Molded
4. Degree of Realism	High	Low	High
5. Molded Hair/Hat	None Known	Often Found	None Known
6. Hollow Poured Limbs	Yes	No	No

Reproduction Wax-Over, Poured-Wax, or Reinforced-Wax Dolls are not a problem. Be aware that some dolls may have been re-waxed. A network of minute age lines on an original surface is always more desirable than a restored, newly re-waxed surface. If the surface is perfectly smooth with no cracks, dents, or scuff marks, chances are it has been re-waxed. After studying Wax Dolls you will begin to recognize the worn patina that vintage dolls acquire.

Occasionally someone will try to "fix" a Wax Doll by re-melting it with hot spoons or a curling iron or by having the head re-dipped. Although this is more often the case with Wax-Over rather than Poured-Wax Dolls, these procedures are undesirable. Attempts at restoration are easily detected.

Look for dirt imbedded in the wax. This is a sure sign that someone has been reworking the wax. A clear wax outer layer on a poured wax doll is another sign, as the original wax was tinted. When re-waxing a doll, clear wax is used as a top coat.

Prices listed are for dolls with undamaged heads. Normal wear (slight vein cracks), slight damage, or well-done repairs to the body do not greatly affect price. If a doll is badly cracked, warped, or damaged or if it has been repaired or re-waxed expect to pay less than half the amount listed. It is perfectly acceptable to show a missing or repaired finger or toe, as the doll's artistry is in its head.

WAX-OVER DOLLS

Wax-Over Dolls were made by various companies in England, France, and Germany during the 1800s and into the early 1900s. While many different materials were waxed over for doll heads, papier-mâché/composition is by far the most frequently found.

An article published in the February 1875 edition of *St. Nicholas* magazine describes the process as follows: "...a frightful looking object she is, with color enough for a boiled lobster. When she has received her color and got dry...she proceeds to the next operator who is the waxer. In the kettle is boiling clear white beeswax, and into it Miss Dolly has been dipped, and is being held up to drain. If she had been intended for a cheap doll, she would have received but one dip, but being destined to belong to the aristocracy of the doll world, she received several dips, each one giving her a thin coat of wax, and toning down her flaming complexion into the delicate pink you see. The reason she was painted so red...is that she may have the proper tint when the wax is on. And now comes the next process which is coloring her face. In this room is a long table with several workmen, each of whom does only one thing. The first one paints Miss Dolly lips and sets her down on the other side of him. The next one takes her up and puts on her eyebrows. The third colors her cheeks. The fourth pencils her eyelashes, and so she goes down the table, growing prettier at every step...."

It is interesting to note that this 1875 writing referred to beeswax. By the 1880's paraffin or ozocerite, a wax made from the residue of petroleum, was used. The presence of beeswax can usually be detected by its distinct odor. Although perhaps less appealing and not nearly as lifelike as the lovely Poured-Wax or even the Reinforced-Wax Dolls, the Wax-Over Dolls stood a much better chance of surviving through the years undamaged.

It is obvious that the quality of Wax-Over Dolls began to deteriorate towards the end of the 19th century. Despite this, many German examples of Wax-Over Dolls are quite charming in their simplicity and are welcome additions to any collection.

Early "English Wax": made in Germany and England; cloth body with short leather arms; round face shoulder head; hair inserted in split in top of head; glass eyes or sleep glass eyes operated by wire protruding from body midsection; sweet smiling closed mouth. Typically unmarked.

Molded Hair or Bonnet: cloth body with wood or wax-over limbs; shoulder head with molded hair and/or bonnet; glass eyes; closed mouth; appropriately dressed. Typically unmarked.

Extraordinarily Elaborate: intricately styled hair with ornamentation or elaborately styled bonnet; very rare.

Wax-Over Dolls with Wig: shoulder head, cloth body, most with wooden limbs, some with wax-over or china limbs; good wig; glass eyes; open or closed mouth; appropriately dressed. Typically unmarked. May be of standard quality or exceptional quality. Exceptional-quality dolls are heavily waxed and nicely decorated. Evaluate a wigged Wax-Over Doll carefully to assign value.

Singing Doll: wax-over shoulder head, cloth body, wax-over limbs; good wig; glass eyes; closed mouth; voice box in torso with push button mechanism.

Two-Faced Wax-Over: (one sleeping and other crying, or one sleeping and other awake and smiling); molded bonnet hides second face; cloth body, wax-over limbs. Body may be signed "Bartenstein."

WAX-OVER VALUE COMPARISONS:

Size	Early English Wax-Over	Molded Hair or Bonnet Wax-Over	Extraordinarily Elaborate Wax-Over	Wax-Over with Wig, Exceptional Quality	Wax-Over with Wig, Standard Quality	Singing Wax-Over	2-Faced Wax-Over
10"		350.00		250.00	150.00		
12"	700.00			400.00	250.00		
14"	800.00	400.00		500.00	350.00		
16"	900.00	500.00	2,500.00	600.00	400.00		1,200.00
18"	1,100.00	550.00		650.00	450.00		
20"	1,200.00	600.00	2,700.00	700.00	500.00		
22"	1,300.00	700.00		750.00	550.00	2,000.00	
24"	1,400.00	800.00	3,500.00	800.00	600.00	2,400.00	
26"	1,500.00	850.00		850.00	650.00	2,800.00	
28"	1,800.00	900.00		900.00	700.00		
30"	2,000.00	950.00		950.00	750.00	3,200.00	
32"		1,000.00		1,000.00	800.00		
34"					850.00		
36"					900.00		
38"					1,000.00		

POURED-WAX DOLLS

Although Wax Dolls were produced as early as the middle ages in Italy and other parts of Europe, collectors are primarily interested in the English Wax Dolls produced during the 19th century. Whether made in ancient times or today, some of the loveliest and most life-like dolls are made of wax. So life-like are Poured-Wax babies that many collectors shun them as being "too morbid." On the other hand, connoisseurs of fine Wax Dolls view them as having utter realism. By the mid-1800s, Wax Dolls were being produced as toys. While it is hard to believe that these exquisite creations were ever meant to be played with by children, their original price tags ensured that they could be owned by only the very privileged.

The time required to make a Poured-Wax doll was lengthy. First, a clay sculpture was crafted and a plaster of Paris mold made. This was accomplished by burying the clay head halfway in sand and then pouring plaster over the top. When the mold hardened it was removed from the sand. The same procedure was repeated for the other half of the head. The wax, originally beeswax and later paraffin wax, was prepared by placing it into a cloth bag and boiling it in water. It was then skimmed and placed in a another cloth bag. This purifying process was repeated at least four or five times. Purified carnuba was added to the paraffin because of its high melting temperature. The wax was then bleached by cutting it into strips and placing it on porcelain slabs in the sun. The wax had to be kept wet, or the porcelain slabs floated on water, in order to keep the wax from melting. This bleaching process took about a week. After bleaching, the wax was colored by boiling it with lead dyes or vermilion. The melted wax was then poured into heated molds. Molds had to be heated in order to prevent ridges from forming when the wax first touched the molds. After a few seconds, the two mold halves were fastened tightly together, and turned and rotated so that the melted wax could coat evenly over the mold's entire internal surface. The molds were removed when the wax congealed. While the wax was still warm, glass eyes were inserted and the eyelids molded. Next, the features were painted and hair inserted. Finally, the completed head was attached to a cloth body with wax limbs.

Although most Poured-Wax Dolls are unmarked, many have either a signature engraved on the back shoulder plate or a stamp on the cloth body. Some collectors believe Poured-Wax Dolls have a "pugged" look. Whether marked or unmarked, pugged or not pugged, Poured-Wax Dolls are easily identified. The method used for attaching the hair, the finely molded eyelids, the tinted wax, and the well-defined Poured-Wax arms and legs are all obvious indications.

Poured-Wax: shoulder head with well-molded shoulder plate, cloth body, hollow poured-wax molded arms and legs; human hair wig; glass stationary eyes, deeply molded eyelids; closed mouth; appropriately dressed. Typically unmarked or occasionally with name engraved on shoulder plate or body stamped "Montarari," "Pierrotti," or "Marsh."

REINFORCED-WAX DOLLS

Reinforced-Wax Head Dolls are generally accepted as having been made in Germany from about 1860 until 1890. They share many of the characteristics of the English Poured-Wax Doll. The method for making Reinforced-Wax heads begins with the Poured-Wax process. The head is then reinforced from within by means of a thin layer of plaster of Paris or with strips of cloth soaked in composition. The intention of this reinforcement is to give the head added strength. Don't confuse Reinforced-Wax with Wax-Over Dolls. An examination of the inside of the head would distinguish the two, but that is not always convenient or practical.

Reinforced-Wax: very good or fair quality; cloth body; wax-over forearms, composition legs, molded and painted boots; good wig; glass eyes, molded lids; pierced ears; closed mouth; appropriately dressed. Typically unmarked.

POURED-WAX VALUE COMPARISONS:

Size	Exceptional Quality	Standard Quality
14"	1,500.00	800.00
18"	2,000.00	1,000.00
20"	2,400.00	1,200.00
24"	3,500.00	1,400.00
26"	3,700.00	1,700.00
30"	4,200.00	

REINFORCED-WAX VALUE COMPARISONS:

Size	Very Good Quality	Fair Quality
12"		350.00
14"		400.00
16"	1,200.00	500.00
18"	1,500.00	
20"	1,700.00	600.00
24"	2,000.00	
26"		700.00

Norah Wellings

Norah Wellings was the chief designer at Chad Valley for several years until she and her brother, Leonard, started their own factory for manufacturing cloth dolls in 1926. The company was known as the Victoria Toy Works and was located in Arleston, England. Hundreds of different types of dolls were made representing both children and adults, fantasy characters, and ethnic groups. Made of excellent quality velvet, velveteen, plush, and felt, these detailed dolls ranged in size from 6 to 36 inches.

Most of Norah Wellings' dolls are marked with a cloth label sewn to the bottom of the foot. Occasionally the tag will be missing.

To help identify an unmarked Norah Wellings doll, look for these features:

1. The felt has a slightly rough feel.
2. Nicely painted side-glancing eyes with one white dot in upper left-hand corner.
3. Pale and slightly dotted small eyebrows.
4. Small heart-shaped mouth with thin red accent line.
5. Double-stitched ears.
6. Somewhat large hands with stitching indicating second and third fingers.
7. Seam on front and back of each leg.
8. No ankle seam.

Following the death of her brother in 1960, Norah closed the business and retired.

14" Norah Wellings Child. *Courtesy of Helen Brooke.*

NORAH WELLINGS VALUE COMPARISONS:

Size	Child	Island Character	Authentic Military	Novelty Souvenir
6"				100.00
8"				150.00
10"			300.00	200.00
12"	500.00	250.00	350.00	
14"	600.00	300.00	400.00	
16"	700.00	350.00	450.00	
18"	800.00	400.00	500.00	
20"	1,000.00	450.00		
22"	1,200.00	500.00		
24"	1,400.00	550.00		
26"	1,600.00	600.00		
28"	1,800.00	650.00		
30"	2,200.00			
36"		1,000.00		

Prices listed are for dolls with no damage. If soiled, stained, torn, or worn, expect to pay less than half the amount listed.

Child: stockinet mask face, cloth body jointed at shoulders and hips, felt arms and legs; mohair wig; painted eyes; closed mouth; appropriately dressed. Marked with cloth label "Made in England/by/Norah Wellings."

Island Doll or Black Ethnic: all brown velvet, stitched shoulders and hips; black mohair wig; painted brown side-glancing eyes; wide, toothy, grinning mouth; appropriately dressed. Marked with cloth label on foot reading "Made in England/by/Norah Wellings."

Military: Velvet body, sculptured face; mohair wig; painted side-glancing eyes; authentic military uniform. Marked with cloth label "Made in England/by/Norah Wellings;" may also have wrist tag reading "Force Comforts Committee an agreed percentage of the manufacturer's sales of the R.A.F. mascot doll is contributed to the Royal Air Comforts Fund."

Novelty Souvenir: stitched long thin floppy limbs and over-sized hands. Typically marked "Norah Wellings/Wellington England." Thousands of these small dolls were sold around the world. Ocean liners, steamships, and gift shops offered Canadian Mounties, Little Pieie People, and Tourist-type dolls.

Wilson Novelty Company

Group of Wilson Walkies. *Courtesy of Helen Brooke.*

The Wilson Novelty Company was founded by John Wilson in Watsontown, Pennsylvania, in 1930. The devastating effects of the depression left this small central Pennsylvania town in desperate need. The old adage "necessity is the mother of invention" was especially true in the creation of the little Wilson Walkies, also known as Watsontown Walkers. These dolls had a tremendous responsibility placed upon their sloping shoulders—to save the small town. That is exactly what they did!

The first Walkies were rather crude in design and appearance. They had cardboard cone bodies, pipe cleaner arms, and hand-painted faces on a round wooden head. They were dressed in scraps of fabric and paper, and were balanced in such a way that their wooden legs, moving inside the cone body, allowed them to walk along in a distinctive Walkie gait. Early Walkies were stamped "Made in U. S. A.," a marking that was used until 1938. Although the early Walkies were a bit short on quality, they were long on appeal. The company continued to grow and in the process refined the appearance of their walking Wilsons.

Walkies made between 1938 and 1940 were marked "Made in U. S. A. Pat. Pending." For a brief time in 1941 the mark was changed to "Made in U. S. A. Pat'd 12-18-40." By the 1940s, the Wilson Walkies could boast of nicely applied decal faces and wooden arms, while retaining their cone bodies and wooden legs. The company produced at least twenty-five different characters ranging in height from 3" animals with four legs to the rare 10" characters. Included in the Wilson Walkies roster are well-known Disney characters as well as the King

Features Syndicate's Popeye, Wimpy, and Olive Oyl. There were also clowns, soldiers, sailors, bunnies, penguins, Santas, Mammies, and many other wonderful characters. Walkies produced between 1940 and 1950 were marked "U. S. Patent Number 214027." Thanks, in part, to F. W. Woolworth's five and dime store marketing, the Wilson Novelty Company was manufacturing 13,000 Wilson Walkies a day. In 1949, just one year after the death of its founder, the Wilson Novelty Company was sold to a Canadian business. By 1951, the production of the Walkies had come to an end.

Over the years, Wilson Novelty Company introduced several other toys (such as a pop gun that shot out an American flag), but none could equal the popularity of these dear little walkers. Wilson Walkies have walked their way into the hearts of many collectors. Their happy faces and waddling gaits are hard to resist.

Reproduction Wilson Walkies can be found. Hand crafted in similar fashion to the original Walkies, reproductions have bright new paint and are marked on the foot with the initials of the craftsman.

Prices listed below are for dolls with no damage.

	WILSON NOVELTY COMPANY VALUE COMPARISONS:				
Size	**Collectible Characters**	**Disney and Cartoon Characters**	**Military and Common Characters**	**Animals Four Legged Animals**	**Character Walkies**
3"				200.00	
4"	150.00	250.00	100.00		
10"					400.00

Adolf Wislizenus

*I*n 1851, a doll and toy factory was founded by Gottlob Schafft in Waltershausen, Thur, Germany. In 1870, Adolf Wislizenus became a partner and shortly thereafter took over the company. By all accounts, Wislizenus was sole owner by 1878.

In 1894, the company again changed ownership, with William Heincke becoming the new proprietor. Records indicate that in 1909 A. Wislizenus was owned by Hans Heincke, who retained ownership until the doll factory went into bankruptcy in 1931. The bankrupt estate was acquired by König & Wernicke. A. Wislizenus was a doll factory, not a porcelain factory; therefore, it was necessary for them to purchase their bisque doll heads elsewhere. Bähr & Pröschild, Simon & Halbig, and, after 1910, Ernst Heubach all supplied bisque heads for Adolf Wislizenus dolls.

Early in Adolf Wislizenus' ownership, Wislizenus himself is reported to have brought Jumeau's ball-jointed doll body to Waltershausen to study and adapt for his own use. The Wislizenus factory specialized in developing extraordinary ball-jointed bodies. Subsequent owners continued to improve these designs. Several ingenious body types were registered; however, they are rarely found on the market today. This indicates that they were not overly popular at the time. One such doll body, DRGM 27 589, had an unusual construction, with the torso being somewhat long and thin and having a hint of a rib cage showing. The hips were joined to the body with a diagonal joint, allowing a full range of motion. Another unique composition body introduced by Wislizenus was registered DRGM 68 035. At first glance, one notices the body has a shapely torso with an indented waist and prominent rib cage. Upon closer inspection, it becomes evident that there are no ball joints showing. The elbows, although able to move in a natural manner, have the joint hidden within the upper arm. The hip joint is even more unusual, with the lower body coming down over the joints. The body construction allows a wide variety of natural and life-like movements. One wonders why this type of body was not copied by other manufacturers. An explanation may be that the body's appearance as a whole looks rather emaciated in the view of some collectors.

A particularly confusing mark is the number "110" with a superimposed "5" over the "0." This mark contains the size number. Many collectors try in vain to determine whether their doll is actually a "110" or a "115" when in fact it is both.

Prices listed are for dolls with no damage to the bisque. Normal wear, slight damage, or well-done repairs to the body do not greatly affect price. If the bisque is damaged or repaired, expect to pay less than half the amount listed. It is perfectly acceptable to show a missing or repaired finger or joint to the body.

Child Dolls: socket head, jointed composition body; good wig; glass eyes, feathered brows; open mouth with

25" A. W. Special.

unglazed porcelain teeth; appropriately dressed. Typically marked "A. W. Special/Germany," or "A. W. Heubach-Kopplesdorf Germany."

Unique Bodied Child: socket head, unusual composition body, long thin torso, concealed joints; good brown wig; glass eyes, heavy feathered brows; open mouth; appropriately dressed. Typically marked "252 dep," "B. P. 289," or "S.H./A.W."

Character Baby: socket head, bent-limb baby body. Typically marked "A. W. Germany."

110 Character Baby:

socket head, unusual composition body, diagonal hip joints; solid dome with painted hair; painted or glass eyes; open/closed mouth, two upper teeth; appropriately dressed. Marked "110. (5 superimposed over 0) Germany" on back of head, body stamped "AW/W/DR6M/421481."

Size	Child Dolly-Face	Unique Bodied Child	Character Baby	110/5 Character Painted Eyes	110/5 Character Glass Eyes
12"	300.00				
15"			500.00	1,800.00	4,800.00
16"	550.00				
18"			650.00		
20"	650.00		850.00		
22"			1,500.00		
24"	800.00	3,000.00	1,600.00		
26"			2,100.00		
28"	1,200.00				

Wooden Dolls

Wooden Dolls are probably the most common dolls ever produced. This inexpensive and readily available material has always been used for the making of dolls. In early history it was the only truly "free" material to be found—even rags had a monetary value. Anyone could pick up a stick and make a doll. Accurately documented dolls from the 1600s have been reported, although fewer than thirty of these treasures are known to exist world wide. Chances are very unlikely that you would ever come across one. The later wooden dolls of the 18th century are more plentiful, but still far from common.

Many of the early Wooden Dolls have been preserved in aristocratic family homes where they have been passed down through the years with other treasured heirlooms. One such example is the Letitia Penn Doll. This famous little Wooden Doll was brought to America from Europe by William Penn, then proprietor of Pennsylvania. His daughter, Letitia, presented it as a gift to Miss Rankin, the daughter of a Quaker friend. This doll is presumed to have resided in the United States longer than any other doll. She has stood as a silent witness to what must have been some intriguing times. Another famous doll makes her home in a museum in Salisbury, England. She is a perfectly preserved Wooden Doll which belonged to Marie Antoinette. Remarkably, this doll still has her entire ensemble—made by Marie Antoinette while she sat in prison awaiting execution in 1793.

There are many fine examples of beautifully carved Wooden Dolls from Germany and Switzerland. Generally speaking, Wooden Dolls have had a retrograde development. Over the years they have declined, rather than improved, in quality. The crude ugly peg Wooden Dolls made until quite recently give evidence to this statement.

Reproductions, or copies, are rather common with Wooden Dolls. Often, these copies are made for pleasure by

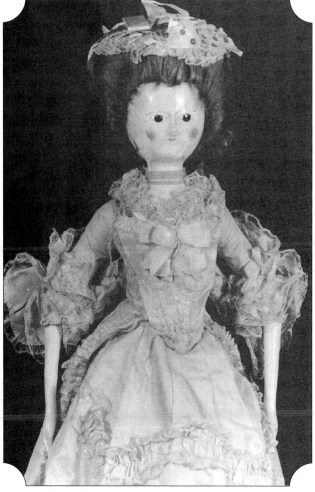

18th Century Wooden Doll. *Courtesy of Ellen Schroy.*

a craftsperson, and therefore not intended to be fraudulent. The modest price that most Wooden Dolls carry also makes the work and risk involved in reproduction rather pointless. Of course, early English William and Mary and Queen Anne-type Wooden Dolls are far from modest in price, but the patina found on authentic examples is rather difficult, if not impossible, to duplicate. This knowledge, coupled with the fact that the earliest Wooden Dolls are so very rare that only reputable antique dealers would be likely to handle them, should allow you to feel secure in the purchase of older Wooden Dolls.

Prices listed are for dolls in good condition.

ENGLISH

William and Mary: 1680-1720, carved one-piece head and torso with unique facial expression; human hair or flax nailed to head for wig; beautifully painted almond-shaped eyes with little detail, single-stroke brows extend from curve of nose and end at outer corner of eye; well-defined rosy cheeks, nose, mouth, and ears; limbs attached by various pinning and jointing methods; upper arms usually made of bound linen, carved wood lower arms and hands; separate fingers and thumbs, sometimes with detailed fingernails; upper and lower legs usually wood with well-carved toes; body covered with gesso base layer, and then delicately painted with flesh color and varnished; dressed in fashionable period costume. Unmarked.

Queen Anne: 1700-1750, more stylized, less individual appearance, great craftsmanship; one-piece head and body, linen upper arms nailed to shoulders, shaped bosom, very narrow waist, rounded fingers with fingernails, hips curved on each side to accommodate pegged tongue- and-groove joints; human hair or flax wig nailed to head; oval, almost egg-shaped head; bulbous glass or painted oval eyes; eyebrows and lashes are a series of dots; well-defined nose, ears, and closed mouth, rosy cheeks; entire body covered with gesso base layer and then painted very pale flesh color and varnished; dressed in fashionable period costume. Unmarked.

Georgian: 1750-1800, one-piece carved head and body, more rounded head; torso has rounded chest, narrow waist, squarish hips, and flat back; upper arms of linen stitched to torso through hole drilled in shoulders; lower arms and hands carved with separate flat fingers and thumbs, lower arms covered with kid with fingers exposed; legs carved to fit into carved slots of hips with pegged tongue-and-groove joints; human hair or flax wig nailed to head; well-defined nose and mouth; lozenge-shaped glass eyes inserted in head, brows and lashes indicated with painted dots; closed small mouth; entire body covered with gesso base layer and then painted very pale flesh color and varnished; dressed in fashionable period costume. Unmarked.

Early 19th Century: 1800-1840, carved one-piece head and torso, base of torso comes to a point; arms attached to body with piece of linen; legs carved to fit against either side of pointed torso, then pegged with one single peg going first through one leg, then torso, and into other leg; stitched flax or human hair wig glued to head; nicely painted facial features; painted, oversized, oval-shaped eyes, single-stroke brows; no ears; closed mouth; dark rosy cheeks; upper body and lower limbs covered with gesso layer and then painted a flesh color and varnished; typically dressed in gowns much longer than legs, often with matching bonnets. Unmarked.

	ENGLISH WOODEN DOLLS VALUE COMPARISONS:			
Size	William and Mary	Queen Anne	Georgian	Early 19th Century
14"	50,000.00	12,000.00	3,500.00	2,000.00
17"	65,000.00			
18"			5,500.00	
20"				3,200.00
24"		28,000.00	6,800.00	

GERMAN

Early to mid-19th Century: 1810-1840, carved one-piece head and torso, often carved with high waist or Empire waist; all wooden arms; tongue-and-groove joints applied to shoulders and elbows—despite the relatively unrefined workmanship, the joints are quite efficient, allowing easy mobility. Finishing techniques are less sophisticated than earlier English dolls, but faces reflect a more delicate look with carved and painted hair, at times in elaborate styles, with curls around the face and the important addition of a hair comb carved into the back of the head. Collectors often speak of "yellow tuck comb" when they are referring to this particular characteristic. The nose of these wooden dolls is most often a wedge inserted into the face and heavily painted, making it less obvious but still somewhat sharp in appearance. Earrings are found. Closed mouths. The costly gesso base layer is entirely omitted, with heavy paint being applied directly onto the wood on areas that show. Fashionably dressed in period costumes. Unmarked.

Later 19th Century: 1840-1900, carved one-piece head and torso. Very similar to the above dolls in body configuration and facial features. Artist's application of facial decoration progressively deteriorated until by the end of the century the painting was quite crude. Other noticeable changes are the elimination of the hair comb, and the hair styles tend to be less elaborate with perhaps only a bun or carved side curls. Fashionably dressed in period costumes. Unmarked.

Bohemian Wooden Doll: kid joining arms and legs to carved red-painted torso; small waist; spoon-like hands; appropriately dressed. Unmarked.

Late 19th Century: carved wooden shoulder, cloth body, wooden limbs; head with simple carved hair style; painted eyes and closed mouth; appropriately dressed. Unmarked.

Peg Wooden or Dutch Wooden: after 1900, simple construction, jointed and fastened together with wooden pegs; sharp little carved noses protruding from simple round faces; painted black hair and facial features; stick-type limbs, spoon-like hands, painted white on lower legs; black shoes, appropriately dressed. Unmarked. The pattern for peg wooden dolls varied little over the years.

Bébé Tout en Bois: (Dolls All of Wood), 1900-1914, manufactured by F.M. Schilling, its subsidiary Rudolf Schneider, and possibly others. Nicely carved head resembling dolly-faced doll; fully jointed wooden or cloth body with wooden arms and legs; good wig; glass eyes, painted brows and lashes; open mouth with teeth; appropriately dressed. Typically unmarked, or occasionally marked with the trademark "Angle," or a sticker in three languages reading "Tout Bois, Holz, All Wood."

SWISS

Early 1900s: socket head or shoulder head; beautifully carved with wonderfully expressive face; all wood or cloth body with wooden limbs; carved and painted hair often with intricate detailing; distinctive painted eyes with tiny lines going through iris to look like threading, usually with reflective white dot in middle; closed mouth; often wearing regional costumes. Typically unmarked, or possibly marked with a clothing or wrist tag.

SWISS WOODEN DOLLS VALUE COMPARISONS:

Size	Carved
10"	350.00
12"	500.00
14"	750.00
18"	1,000.00
20"	1,200.00

RUSSIAN

Matryoshka: 20th century, multiple nesting dolls, most likely from area around Bogorodskoye and Zagorsk. Dolls representing Napoleon and other military heroes were popular, as were those of various Russian folklore characters. The early Matryoshka were made by Russian peasants in their homes and have been made by the same families for generations. They are brilliantly colored, predominately in red, with flashes of yellow, orange, green, and blue. The dolls then are given a highly reflective covering that not only protects the paint, but also adds to their beauty.

RUSSIAN WOODEN DOLLS VALUE COMPARISONS:

Size	Early Matryoshka	Late Matryoshka	Modern Political
6"		300.00	
8"	1,500.00	400.00	75.00
12"	1,700.00		

GERMAN WOODEN DOLLS VALUE COMPARISONS:

Size	Early to Mid-19th Century	Later 19th Century No Comb	Bohemian, Kid Joints, Red Torso	Late 19th Century Cloth Body	Peg Wooden, Dutch Wooden	Bébé Tout en Bois
8"	1,000.00	300.00				
9"				450.00		
12"	1,600.00	500.00		500.00	75.00	
14"						600.00
16"		700.00				750.00
17"				550.00		
18"	2,200.00					900.00
20"		900.00	700.00			1,000.00
22"	2,900.00					
24"			800.00			

Manufacturer Mold Numbers

Mold numbers organized by chapter

Alexander Doll Company: none

Henri Alexandre: none

All-Bisque: 123; 124; 890; 891

Allied Imported: none

Alt, Beck & Gottschalk: 630; 639; 698; 772; 870; 882; 890; 894; 898; 911; 916; 938; 974; 978; 980; 989; 990; 996; 998; 1000; 1002; 1004; 1028; 1030; 1046; 1054; 1056; 1062; 1064; 1112; 1123; 1127; 1142; 1154; 1210; 1214; 1218; 1222; 1226; 1234; 1235; 1254; 1288; 1322; 1326; 1352; 1357; 1358; 1359; 1361; 1362; 1367

Amberg: 973; 972; 982; 983

American Character: none

Max Arnold: none

Arranbee Doll Company: 210; 341; 351

Arrow Novelty Company: none

Artist Dolls: none

Automata: 1; 2; 3; 3200

Averill Manufacturing Company: 1005; 1386; 1402; 1714; 1717; 3653

Babyland Rag: none

Bähr & Pröschild: 201; 204; 207; 209; 212; 213; 217; 219; 220; 224; 225; 226; 227; 230; 239; 244; 245; 247; 248; 251; 252; 253; 259; 260; 261; 263; 264; 265; 269; 270; 273; 275; 277; 278; 281; 283; 285; 287; 289; 292; 297; 300; 302; 305; 306; 309; 313; 320; 321; 323; 324; 325; 330; 340; 342; 343; 348; 350; 374; 375; 376; 378; 379; 380; 381; 389; 390; 393; 394; 424; 425; 441; 482; 499; 500; 520; 525; 526; 529; 531; 535; 536; 537; 539; 541; 546; 549; 554; 557; 568; 571; 581; 584; 585; 587; 600; 604; 619; 620; 624; 640; 641; 643; 644; 645; 646; 678; 707; 799

Barbie: none

E. Barrois: none

Beecher Baby: none

Belton-Type: none

C.M. Bergmann: 612; 1916

Bing Brothers: none

George Borgfeldt & Co.: 251; 326; 327; 329; 1923; 1369; 1410; 1418

Boudoir Dolls: none

Jne Bru & Cie: none

Albert Brückner: none

A. Bucherer: none

Cabbage Patch Dolls: none

Cameo Doll Company: 71 (s)

Cambpell Kids: 1910

Catterfelder Puppenfabrik: 200; 201; 207; 208; 217; 219; 220; 262; 263; 264; 270; 1100; 1200; 1357

Celluloid: none

Century Doll Company: 277; 281

Chad Valley, Ltd.: none

Martha Chase: none

China Heads: none

Cloth Dolls: none

Dewees Cochran: none

Columbian Dolls: none

Composition: none

Contemporary Collectible Porcelain Dolls: none

Dean's Rag Book Co.: none

DEP Dolls: none

Doll House Dolls: none

Door of Hope Dolls: none

Cuno & Otto Dressel: 93; 1348; 1349; 1468; 1469; 1776; 1848; 1849; 1893; 1896; 1898; 1912; 1914; 1920; 1922; 2736

Eden Bébé: none

Eegee: none

Effanbee 162; 166; 176; 172; 174

Eisenmann & Co.: none

Joel Ellis: none

J.K. Farnell & Company: none

French Bébé: none

French Fashion-Type: none

Ralph A. Freundlich, Inc.: none

Fulper Pottery Company: none

German Bisque: 50; 51; 101; 132; 136; 216; 223; 230; 806; 44611

E. Gesland: none

Godey Lady Dolls: none

William Goebel: 34; 73; 89; 120; 123; 124; 330; 350; 521

Googley-Eyed Dolls: 19; 47; 82; 83; 84; 85; 86; 87; 88; 111; 122; 131; 163; 165; 172; 173; 175; 178; 179; 180; 200; 208; 210; 217; 221; 222; 223; 240; 241; 242; 245; 247; 252; 253; 254; 255; 257; 260; 261; 262; 263; 264; 289; 310; 318; 319; 322; 323; 324; 325; 686; 950; 8589; 8606; 8729; 8995; 9056; 9081; 9085; 9141; 9513; 9572; 9578; 9594

Ludwig Greiner: none

Hamburger & Company: 1248; 1249; 5777

Heinrick Handwerck: 69; 79; 89; 99; 109; 119; 139; 189

Max Handwerck: 283; 285; 296

Carl Hartmann: none

Karl Hartmann: none

Hasbro, Inc.: none

Hertel Schwab & Company: 125; 126; 130; 132; 133; 134; 135; 136; 138; 140; 141; 142; 143; 147; 148; 149; 150; 151; 152; 157; 158; 159; 160; 161; 162; 163; 165; 166; 167; 169; 170; 172; 173; 175; 176; 179; 180; 181; 200; 208; 217; 220; 222

Hertwig & Company: 104; 150; 175; 385; 386

Ernst Heubach: 250; 251; 300; 302; 312; 320; 338; 339; 340; 342; 349; 350; 399; 414; 451; 444; 463; 452; 445; 1900; 1901; 1902; 1906; 1909

Gebrüder Heubach: 5626; 5636; 5689; 5730; 5777; 6692; 6736; 6774; 6894; 6969; 7109; 7246; 7550; 7602; 7604; 7616; 7620; 7622; 7623; 7631; 7644; 7661; 7665; 7669; 7679;

Glossary

Applied Ears — Ears that are molded separately and affixed to the head.

Appropriately Dressed — Clothing that fits the time period and doll style.

Ball Jointed Body — Doll body of wood-and-composition, jointed at shoulders, elbows, wrists, hips and knees, allowing movement.

Bébé — French dolly-faced doll.

Bent-Limb Baby Body — Five-piece baby body of composition with curved arms and legs jointed at shoulders and hips.

Bisque — Unglazed porcelain.

Blown Glass Eyes — Hollow eyes of blue, brown, or gray.

Brevete — French marking indicating a registered patent.

Bté — Patent registered.

Caracul — Lamb's skin used to make wigs.

Character Doll — Dolls molded to look life-like — may be infants, children, or adults.

Child Doll — Typical "dolly face" dolls.

China — Glazed porcelain.

Composition — A wood based material.

Crazing — Fine lines that develop on the painted surface of composition.

D.E.P. — A claim to registration.

Dolly Face — Typical child doll face.

D.R.G.M. — German marking indicating a registered design.

Feathered Brows — Eyebrows painted with many tiny strokes.

Five-Piece Body — Body composed of torso, arms, and legs.

Fixed Eyes — Eyes set in a stationary position.

Flange Neck — Doll's neck with ridge and holes at the base for sewing onto a cloth body.

Flirty Eyes — Eyes that move from side to side when head is moved.

Flocked Hair — A coating of short fibers glued to a doll's head to represent hair.

Ges (Gesch) — German marking indicating a registered design.

Googly Eyes — Large, round eyes looking to the side.

Hard Plastic — Material used after 1948. Very hard with excellent impressions and good color.

Intaglio Eyes — Sunken, rather than cut, eyes that are then painted.

Kid Body — Doll body made of leather.

Lady Doll — Doll with adult face and body proportions.

Magic Skin — A rubbery material used for dolls. They age poorly, becoming dark and deteriorating as the surface turns soft and sticky.

Mask Face — A stiff face that covers only the front of a doll's head.

Mohair Wig — Wig made from very fine goat's hair.

Mold Number — Impressed or embossed number that indicates a particular design.

Open Mouth — Lips parted with opening cut into the bisque. Teeth usually show.

Open/Closed Mouth — Molded mouth appears open, but no opening cut into the bisque.

Painted Bisque — Paint which is not baked into body. Is brighter in color but can be rubbed off.

Painted Eyes — Flat, molded, and painted eyes.

Paperweight Eyes — Blown glass eyes with an added crystal to the top resulting in a look with depth and great realism.

Papier-mâché — Material made of paper pulp and glue.

Pate — Covering for the opening in a doll head. May be made of cardboard, cork, or plaster.

Personality Doll — Dolls molded and fashioned to resemble a famous person.

Pierced Ears — Holes in a doll's ear lobes. Hole goes all the way through the lobe.

Pierced-in Ears — Hole for earring passing through doll's ear lobe and straight into doll's head.

Pouty — Closed mouth doll with a solemn or petulant expression.

Pug or Pugged Nose — Small, button, slightly turned-up nose.

Regional Costume — A traditional costume worn in specific region or country.

Reproduction — A doll produced from a mold taken from an existing doll.

Rub — A spot where the color has worn away.

S.G.D.G. — Registered, but without government guarantee.

Shoulder Head — Head and shoulder in one piece.

Shoulder Plate — Shoulder portion with socket for head.

Socket Head — Head with neck that fits into a shoulder plate or the opening of a body.

Solid-dome — Head with no crown opening. May have painted hair or wear a wig.

Stationary Eyes — Glass eyes which no do not sleep, also known as staring eyes.

Stockinette — Soft jersey fabric used for dolls.

Toddler Body — A short chubby body of a toddler, often diagonal joints at hips.

Turned Head — Shoulder head with head slightly turned.

Vinyl — Material used after 1950. Soft plastic.

Watermelon Mouth — A closed smiling mouth, usually with a single line.

Weighted Eyes — Sleep eyes that operated by means of a weight attached to a wire frame holding the eyes.

Bibliography

BOOKS

Anderton, Johana Gast. *More Twentieth Century Dolls From Bisque To Vinyl*. Volume I (A-H), Volume II (I-Z), Revised edition. Wallace-Homestead, 1979.

Anderton, Johana Gast. *The Collector's Encyclopedia of Cloth Dolls*. Wallace-Homestead, 1984.

Anderton, Johana Gast. *Twentieth Century Dolls From Bisque To Vinyl*. Wallace-Homestead, 1974.

Angione, Genevieve. *All-Bisque and Half Bisque Dolls*. Schiffer Publishing Ltd., 1969.

Angione, Genevieve and Judith Whorton. *All Dolls Are Collectibles*. Crown Publishers, 1977.

Axe, John. *Collectible Black Dolls*. Hobby House Press, 1978.

Axe, John. *Kewpies-Dolls & Art*. Hobby House Press, 1987.

Axe, John. *The Encyclopedia of Celebrity Dolls*. Hobby House Press, 1983.

Bach, Jean. *Dictionary of Doll Marks*. Sterling Publishing Co., Inc., 1990.

Bullard, Helen. *The American Doll Artist*. Volume I. The Summit Press, Ltd. 1965.

Burdick, Loraine. *Shirley Dolls and Related Delights*. Revised edition. Quest-Eridon Books, 1977.

Chisman, Evelyn Meude. *Small Dolls and Other Collectibles*. Drake Publishers, Inc., 1978.

Christian, Albert. *Spinning Wheel's Complete Book of Dolls*. Calahad Books, 1975.

Cieslik, J‚rgen and Marianne. *German Doll Encyclopedia 1800-1939*. Hobby House Press, 1985.

Cieslik, J‚rgen and Marianne. *German Doll Marks & Identification Book*. Hobby House Press, 1990.

Cochran, Dewees, *As If They Might Speak*, Paperweight Press, 1979.

Coleman, Dorothy S. *Lenci Dolls*. Hobby House Press, 1977.

Coleman, Dorothy S., Elizabeth A. Coleman, and Evelyn J. Coleman. *The Collector's Encyclopedia of Dolls*. Crown Publishers, 1968.

Coleman, Dorothy S., Elizabeth A. Coleman, and Evelyn J. Coleman. *The Collector's Encyclopedia of Dolls*. Volume II. Crown Publishers, 1986.

Corson, Carol. *Schoenhut Dolls: A Collector's Encyclopedia*. Hobby House Press, 1993.

Davis, Nina S. *The Jumeau Doll Story*. Hobby House Press, 1969.

Desmonde, Kay. *Dolls & Dolls Houses*. World Publishing Co., 1972.

DeWein, Sibyl and Joan Ashabraner. *The Collectors Encyclopedia of Barbie Dolls and Collectibles*. Collector Books, 1997, 1994 value update.

Doll Collectors of America, Inc. *American Made Dolls and Figurines*. Doll Collectors of America, 1940.

Eames, Sarah Sink. *Barbie Fashion*. Volume 1 1959-1967. Collector Books, 1990, 1995 value update.

Fellows, Paul. *Doll Auction Prices*. Wallace-Homestead, 1985.

Foulke, Jan. *Focusing on Dolls*. Hobby House Press, 1988.

Foulke, Jan. *11th Blue Book Dolls & Values*. Hobby House Press, 1993.

Foulke, Jan. *Kestner: King of Dollmakers*. Hobby House Press, 1982.

Fraser, Antonia. *Dolls, Pleasures and Treasures*. Weidenfeld and Nicolson, 1963.

Fuller, W., Jr. *Legend of the Cabbage Patch Kids*. Taylor Publishing Co., 1983.

Garrison, Susan Ann. *Raggedy Ann & Andy Family Album*. Schiffer Publishing Ltd., 1989.

Gibbs, Patikii. *Horsman Dolls, 1950-1970*. Collector Books, 1985.

Goodfellow, Caroline. *The Ultimate Doll Book*. Hobby House Press, 1993.

Hall, Patricia. *Johnny Gruelle: Creator of Raggedy Ann and Andy*. Pelican Publishing, 1993.

Heyerdahl, Virginia Ann (ed.). *The Best of Doll Reader*. Volumes I- IV. Hobby House Press, Inc., 1982, 1986, 1988, 1991.

Horine, Maude M. *Memories of Rose O'Neill Creator Of The Kewpie Doll*. 1950.

Hoyer, Mary, Virginia Ann Heyerdahl, (ed.). *Mary Hoyer And Her Dolls, Patterns To Crochet, Knit, and Sew*. Hobby House Press, 1982.

Hunter, Marsha. *Madame Alexander Cloth Dolls*.

Husfloen, Kyle D. *The Antique Trader Weekly's Book of Collectible Dolls*. Babka Publishing Co., 1976.

Izen, Judith. *A Collector's Guide To Ideal Dolls*, Collector Books, 1994.

Jacobs, Laura. *Barbie: What A Doll!*. Artabras, 1994.

Johl, Janet Pagter. *Still More About Dolls*. H.L. Lindquist Publications, 1950.

Johnson, La Vaugh C. *Open Mouth Dolls*. Elena Quinn, 1974.

Judd, Polly. *Cloth Dolls, 1920s and 1930s: Identification and Price Guide*. Hobby House Press, 1990.

Judd, Polly and Pam. *Composition Dolls: 1928-1955*. Hobby House Press, 1991.

Judd, Polly and Pam. *Compo Dolls: 1909-1928*. Volume II. Hobby House Press, 1994.

Judd, Polly and Pam. *Glamour Dolls of the 1950s and 1960s: Identification and Values*. Revised edition, Hobby House Press, 1993.

Judd, Polly and Pam. *Hard Plastic Dolls: Identification and Price Guide*. Third revised edition, Hobby House Press, 1993.

Judd, Polly and Pam. *Hard Plastic Dolls II: Identification and Price Guide*. Revised Edition, Hobby House Press, 1994.

Kelly, Cleo. *Kewpies In My Life*. Kelly Enterprises, 1973.

King, Constance Eileen. *The Collectors History of Dolls*. Bonzana Books, 1977.

Kunciov, Robert. *Mr. Godey's Ladies*. Bonanza Books, 1981.

Lavitt, Wendy. *Dolls*. Alfred A. Knopf. 1983.

Lavitt, Wendy. *The Knopf Collectors Guides to American Antiques: Dolls*. Alfred A. Knopf, 1983.

Mandeville, A. Glenn. *Alexander Dolls Collector's Price Guide*. Second edition. Hobby House Press, 1995.

Mandeville, A. Glenn. *Doll Fashion Anthology and Price Guide*. Fourth revised edition, Hobby House Press, 1993.

Manos, Paris and Susan. *Collectible Male Action Figures*. Collector Books, 1990, 1992 value update.

Manos, Paris and Susan. *The Wonder of Barbie: Dolls and Accessories 1976-1986*. Collector Books, 1987, 1993 value update.

Merill, Madeline Osborne. *The Art of Dolls 1700-1940*. Hobby House Press.

Merill, Madeline O., and Nellie W. Perkins. *The Handbook of Collectible Dolls*. Volumes 1, 2, and 3, Woodward and Miller, 1969, 1974.

Miller, Marjorie A. *Nancy Ann Storybook Dolls*. Hobby House Press, 1980.

Moody, Carol. *G. I. Joe Value Guide: 1964-1978*. Hobby House Press, 1989.

Pardella, Edward R. *Shirley Temple Dolls and Fashion: A Collector's Guide To the World's Darling*. Schiffer Publishing, 1992.

Reinelt, Sabine. *Magic of Character Dolls*. Hobby House Press, 1993.

Revi, Albert Christian. *Spinning Wheel's Complete Book of Dolls*. Galahad Books, 1975.

Richter, Lydia and Joachim F. *Bru Dolls*. Hobby House Press, 1989.

Richter, Lydia and Karin Schmelcher. *Heubach Character Dolls and Figurines*. Hobby House Press, 1992.

Richter, Lydia. *China, Parian, and Bisque German Dolls*. Hobby House Press, 1993.

Richter, Lydia. *Treasury of French Dolls*. HP Books, 1983.

Richter, Lydia. *Treasury of German Dolls*. HP Books, 1984.

Robinson, Joleen Ashman, and Kay Sellers. *Advertising Dolls: Identification and Value Guide*. Collector Books, 1980, 1994 value update.

Ruggles, Rowena Godding. *The One Rose—Mother of the Immortal Kewpies*. 2nd Edition, 1972.

Santelmo, Vincent. *G.I. Joe, Freedom Fighter*. Hobby House Press, 1991.

Smith, Patricia R. *Antique Collector's Dolls, First Series*. Volume I (1975, 1991 value update), Volume II (1976, 1991 value update). Collector Books.

Smith, Patricia R. *Collector's Encyclopedia of Madame Alexander Dolls 1965-1990*. Collector Books, 1991, 1994 value update.

Smith, Patricia R. *Madame Alexander Dolls Collector's Dolls Price Guide #20*. Collector Books, 1995.

Smith, Patricia R. *Modern Collector's Dolls*. Volumes I, II, III, IV, V, and VI. Collector Books, 1973, 1975, 1976, 1979, 1984, 1991, 1993, 1994, 1995 value updates, Series I-VI.

Smith, Patricia R. *Modern Collector's Dolls, Seventh Series*. Collector Books, 1995.

Smith, Patricia R. *Patricia Smith's Doll Values: Antique to Modern*. Eleventh Edition. Collector Books, 1995.

St. George, Eleanor. *Old Dolls*. Gramercy Publishing Co., 1960.

St. George, Eleanor. *The Dolls of Yesterday*. Charles Schribner's Sons, 1948.

Theriault, Florence. *More Dolls: The Early Years 1780-1910*. Gold Horse Publishing, 1992.

Theriault, Florence. *Theriault's Doll Registry*. Gold Horse Publishing, 1984.

Walker, Frances A. and Margaret Whitton. *Playthings By The Yard—The Story of Cloth Dolls*. Hadley Printing Co., Inc., 1973.

Westenhouser, Kitturah B. *The Story of Barbie*. Collector Books, 1994.

Westfall, Marty. *The Handbook of Doll Repair and Restoration*. Crown Publishers.

Whitton, Margaret. *The Jumeau Doll*. Dover Publications. 1980.

VIDEOTAPES

"Oh, You Beautiful Doll!," produced by author, Joe Blitman, 1994. (Barbie)

$\mathcal{I}ndex$